PRUSSIA
The Perversion of an Idea

PRUSSIA

The Perversion of an Idea

Giles MacDonogh

SINCLAIR-STEVENSON

First published in Great Britain in 1994
by Sinclair-Stevenson
an imprint of Reed Consumer Books Ltd
Michelin House, 81 Fulham Road, London SW3 6RB
and Auckland, Melbourne, Singapore and Toronto

A CIP catalogue record for this book
is available at the British Library
ISBN 1 85619 267 9

Typeset by CentraCet Limited, Cambridge
Printed and bound in Great Britain
by Mackays of Chatham PLC

Contents

List of Illustrations

Gerhard von Scharnhorst (*Bundesbildstelle*)

Helmuth Graf von Moltke (*Bundesbildstelle*)

Alfred Graf von Schlieffen (*E Bieber*)

Hans von Seeckt (*Bildarchiv Preussischer Kulturbesitz*)

Maximilian Harden (*Bildarchiv Preussischer Kulturbesitz*)

Walter Rathenau (*Bildarchiv Preussischer Kulturbesitz*)

Philippus Krementz, Bishop of East Prussian Ermland and later See of Cologne (*Bildarchiv Preussischer Kulturbesitz*)

Die Zeit's editor, Marion Gräfin Dönhoff (*Ingrid von Kruse*)

Prince Louis Ferdinand of Prussia in the 1930s (*Fritz Eschen*)

Königsberg Cathedral, past (*Bildarchiv Preussischer Kulturbesitz*) and present (*author*)

Novelists Theodor Fontane and Gustav Freytag (*Bundesbildstelle*)

Heinrich von Treitschke (*Bundesbildstelle*)

Oswald Spengler (*Bildarchiv Preussischer Kulturbesitz*)

Paul von Hindenburg und von Beneckendorff (*Bundesbildstelle*)

Hermann Göring (*H Hoffmann*)

The trooping of the colours in Tempelhof (*Bildarchiv Preussischer Kulturbesitz*)

Changing the guard on the Unter den Linden (*Bildarchiv Preussischer Kulturbesitz*)

The Garrison Church in Gaertner's painting of 1840 (*Märkisches Museum, Berlin*)

The Garrsion Church in 1959 (*Bildarchiv Preussischer Kulturbesitz*)

The Stadtschloss before its demolition in 1960 (*Kunstbibliothek Berlin*)

The canals of Potsdam (*Kunstbibliothek Berlin*)

Potsdam soon after the fall of the DDR (*author*)

Szczecin (*author*)

The homes of the Prussian poor known as *Mietskaserne* (*author*)

The Kaiserhaus in Posnan (*author*)

Wrocław barracks, 1992 (*author*)

Magdeburg Cathedral as it was (*Bildarchiv Preussischer Kulturbesitz*)

A rare survivor of fine architecture in the city centre (*author*)

Halle: grandeur (*Kunstbibliothek Berlin*), and decline (*author*)

A Note on Names

In most instances I have followed the convention of translating the names of kings and princes into English: Friedrich der Grosse has become Frederick the Great and Kaiser Wilhelm II has become Kaiser William or simply the Kaiser. In some cases, however, such translations begin to look rather forced: the Kaiser's second son, Eitel Fritz, cannot be rendered into English without making him look absurd. Similarly August Wilhelm has generally been referred to by his family name of Auwi, rather than Augustus William.

German titles I have left in the original when they are used together with the name. Thus Bismarck is Graf, later Fürst, Otto von Bismarck-Schönhausen, rather than Count, later Prince . . . To avoid confusion, the German title Fürst (plural Fürsten) or Fürstin indicates a non-royal prince or princess; a Graf (plural Grafen) or Gräfin is a count or countess; a Freiherr (plural Freiherren) or Freifrau is a baron or baroness. There were no Prussian dukes, marquesses or viscounts.

When referring to cities, towns or villages I have used the Prussian or German name for the entirety of the time that the place remained under Prussian or German rule. It is therefore Posen from 1793 until 1919 and not Poznań; it is Marienburg and not Malbork before 1460 and from 1772 to 1945; and Graudenz rather than Grudziadz between 1792 and 1919. In the cases of cities and towns where the current version of the name did not actually exist before 1945 (Gdańsk and Kaliningrad are two examples of this) I have used only the Polish or Russian version when speaking of the period after the Second World War.

In the index the present names of all former Prussian towns and cities are given in brackets after the German name.

A Prussian Chronology

1701	18 January, the Elector Frederick III crowns himself King Frederick I *in* Prussia. For the time being his royal crown extends only to his territories on the Baltic, *not* his Electorate of Brandenburg.
1713	Frederick I is succeeded by his son, the 'Soldier King' Frederick William I. Frederick William immediately cuts the massive state budget and imposes an austere regimen.
1717	universal state education introduced.
1720	the Peace of Stockholm. Brandenburg-Prussia finally achieves dominion over the central chunk of Pomerania, including the port of Stettin.
1730	the Crown Prince Frederick (later King Frederick the Great) attempts to flee to England. He is caught and imprisoned at Küstrin on the Oder. His friend and accomplice, Hans Hermann von Katte, is executed before his eyes.
1731–1732	Frederick I repopulates East Prussia, where the plague had cut a swathe through the local population. Most of the new settlers are Protestants from Salzburg.
1740	the accession of Frederick II, known as Frederick 'the Great'. Frederick invades Silesia. War breaks out with Austria. Torture is abolished in Brandenburg-Prussia. The order 'Pour le mérite' is founded. The new king proves tolerant in religious matters.
1742	the Peace of Breslau. Brandenburg-Prussia receives upper and lower Silesia and the county of Glatz from the Empress of Austria.
1744	the Second Silesian War.
1745	the Peace of Dresden. Frederick II recognises Francis I as Emperor. Austria recognises Brandenburg-Prussia's right to Silesia.

1756   the outbreak of the Seven Years War. Brandenburg-
            Prussia must defend itself against the armies of Austria,
            France, Russia, Sweden and the Empire.
1757   Frederick II wins the Battles of Rossbach and Leuthen
            against the French and the Austrians. At Leuthen the
            'Leuthen Chorale' is heard for the first time.
1760   Berlin is occupied by Austrian and Russian troops.
1762   the 'Miracle of the House of Brandenburg': the
            Empress Elisabeth of Russia dies. Peter III has no
            desire to continue the war against Prussia.
1763   the Peace of Hubertusburg. Brandenburg-Prussia's
            gains in Silesia are confirmed. Compulsory schooling is
            instituted for all five- to thirteen-year-olds.
1772   the First Partition. Poland cedes West Prussia, the
            Netze district and Ermland (in East Prussia) to
            Frederick the Great. Frederick fails to win Danzig.
1786   Frederick William II succeeds his uncle Frederick the
            Great.
1792   Brandenburg-Prussia participates in the coalition
            against revolutionary France. Frederick William II's
            armies are routed at the Battle of Valmy.
1793   Second Polish Partition. Brandenburg-Prussia receives
            Posen, Kalisch, Danzig and Thorn.
1794   the Prussian legal code introduced.
1795   the Third and final Partition of Poland. Brandenburg-
            Prussia extends its territories far into Mazovia as well as
            in the east. Warsaw becomes a Prussian city.
1797   accession of Frederick William III and his wife Louise
            of Mecklenburg-Strelitz.
1799   Brandenburg-Prussia remains neutral in the Second
            Coalition against France.
1806   war breaks out with France. Brandenburg-Prussia is
            defeated at the Battles of Jena and Auerstedt. Napoleon
            Bonaparte occupies Berlin. The court flees to
            Königsberg and later to Memel.
1807   the Peace of Tilsit. Brandenburg-Prussia becomes
            'Prussia' for the first time in official documents. Prussia
            loses around half its territory, including all its
            possessions west of the Elbe and the city of Magdeburg.
            The reform era opens under Freiherr vom Stein: the

	Prussian serfs are emancipated; municipal government is overhauled.
1808	the Prussian Army is reshaped.
1809	the beginnings of educational reform under Minister Wilhelm von Humboldt.
1810	Minister Hardenberg grants freedom of association.
1812	the Convention of Tauroggen: General von Yorck concludes a deal with the Russian Emperor behind Frederick William II's back. The Russians agree to fight until all Prussian territory is liberated from the French. The War of Liberation begins.
1813	the Battle of the Nations at Leipzig. Napoleon is defeated and driven from Germany.
1814	Prussian troops enter Paris. Napoleon abdicates on 6 April. The Congress of Vienna begins.
1815	the Battle of Waterloo or 'Belle Alliance'. The armies of Wellington and Marshal Blücher defeat Napoleon. At the Vienna Congress Prussia is granted the Rhineland; Westphalia; the northern half of Saxony; Danzig; and Great Poland, around the city of Posen.
1817	creation of a Prussian state church after the English model. Problems with the Catholic Rhineland.
1819	introduction of repressive social legislation designed to clamp down on liberalism and German nationalism.
1833	foundation of the Zollverein customs union to facilitate trade among the German states. Eighteen other states join the union.
1838–1839	the first Prussian railway line links Berlin and Potsdam.
1840	accession of Frederick William IV. Hopes of a more liberal regimen rapidly shattered.
1844	weavers' revolt in Silesia.
1847	Frederick William IV summons a united Landtag in Berlin.
1848	the March Revolution.
1849–1850	Frederick William IV grants a limited constitution which remains in force until 1918. As King of Prussia, he rejects the German crown offered to him by the Frankfurt revolutionaries. He creates instead the Union of German Princes.

1850	Prussia's attempts to unify Germany from above are checked by the Austrians at the Punctuation of Olmütz.
1851	Otto von Bismarck becomes Prussian ambassador to the German Diet in Frankfurt.
1857	Frederick William IV renounces his claims to Neuchâtel in Switzerland. He suffers a disabling stroke and is replaced by his brother Prince William, who becomes regent.
1861	accession of King William I.
1862	constitutional crisis over the military budget. Bismarck becomes Minister-President.
1864	the Prussians and the Austrians combine forces to attack Denmark. The Battles of the Düppel Trenches and Alsen. Denmark cedes the Duchies of Schleswig and Holstein.
1866	Prusso-Austrian War. Prussia vanquishes Austria and its allies at the Battle of Königgrätz. Prussia annexes all North German states which took the Austrian side.
1867	the North German Confederation is formed with Bismarck as Chancellor.
1869	foundation of the Social Democratic Party.
1870–1871	Franco-Prussian War. The combined states of Germany triumph over the French. Paris is besieged.
1871	on 18 January, King William I of Prussia is crowned Emperor William I of Germany, in the Hall of Mirrors in Versailles.
1872	Bismarck begins the *Kulturkampf* against Prussia's Catholic subjects. Education passes into state hands.
1878	Bismarck clamps down on the Socialists.
1883	Bismarck introduces radical social legislation.
1888	the Year of the Three Kaisers. William I dies and his son Frederick succeeds. Frederick dies of throat cancer. His son William II (the Kaiser) succeeds as King of Prussia and German Emperor.
1890	Bismarck dismissed as German Chancellor and Prussian Minister-President. He is replaced by General (later Graf) Leo von Caprivi.
1894	Caprivi replaced by Fürst Chlodwig von Hohenlohe.
1897	Alfred von Tirpitz begins building the German fleet.

1900	Hohenlohe replaced by Graf (later Fürst) Bernhard von Bülow.
1908	the *'Daily Telegraph* Affair'.
1909	the trial of the Kaiser's best friend, Philipp zu Eulenburg, for perjury.
1909	Theobald von Bethmann-Hollweg becomes Chancellor and Minister-President.
1912	the Socialists become the strongest party in the Reichstag. Because of the Prussian electoral system they remain under-represented in the Landtag.
1914–1918	the First World War. For the first time since the Seven Years War, parts of East Prussia are invaded by Russian troops.
1914	the Battle of Tannenberg.
1915	the Battle of the Mazurian Lakes. The Russians are driven out of East Prussia.
1916	Hindenburg and Ludendorff take over control of German High Command.
1917	Bethmann-Hollweg dismissed and replaced by Georg Michaelis. The Kaiser rejects the possibility of a negotiated peace in favour of a total or 'Hindenburg' victory.
1918	Germany loses the war. The Kaiser agrees to abdicate. The end of Hohenzollern rule in Prussia and Germany.
1919	the Weimar Constitution. Prussia is maintained as part of the new federal German state. Prussia rejects plans to continue the war in the east. The Treaty of Versailles leads to the cession of large parts of West Prussia and Silesia to the Poles, as well as the entirety of the Grand Duchy of Posen. The Memel region is given to Lithuania. Territorial adjustments in Schleswig-Holstein in favour of the Danes.
1920	Otto Braun becomes Minister-President of Prussia. Konrad Adenauer becomes President of the Prussian Staatsrat.
1925	Paul von Hindenburg becomes President of Germany.
1929	the Wall Street Crash accelerates the agricultural crisis in the Prussian east. Many of the large estates go under the hammer. Prussian landowners put pressure on the President to save the Prussian patrimony.

1932   Heinrich Brüning replaced as Chancellor by Franz von
        Papen. 30 July the 'Preussenschlag': Prussian
        government is suspended. The Minister-President
        (Braun) is replaced by a Commissioner answerable to
        Papen. Kurt von Schleicher takes over from Papen in
        December.

1933   30 January, Hitler becomes Chancellor. Hermann
        Göring is named Prussian Minister-President, the last
        to occupy the position.

1934   the remaining Prussian institutions disabled in the
        interests of a non-federal Germany. 21 March the 'Tag
        von Potsdam': Hiter reconciles the old Junker state with
        National Socialism.

1939   Germany occupies the Memel region in March. The
        Second World War breaks out on 3 September. Hitler's
        armies retake all the lost Prussian territories in Poland.

1944   20 July, Prussian officers and civilians are involved in
        the plot to kill Hitler at Rastenburg in East Prussia. In
        the ensuing purge many are executed. First Russian
        incursion into East Prussia at Nemmersdorf in October.

1945   January, Soviet troops sever communications between
        East Prussia and the Reich. Hundreds of thousands die
        in an attempt to reach the West. Many of Prussia's
        cities and towns destroyed by bombardment. At
        Potsdam in July and August the Allied leaders decide to
        move Poland westwards, thereby granting all lands east
        of the Oder and Neisse rivers to Poland and the area
        around Königsberg in East Prussia to the Soviet Union.
        The surviving inhabitants of eastern Pomerania, Silesia,
        West and East Prussia are forcibly repatriated. Many
        die.

1947   25 February, Prussia is formally abolished.
1948   The last inhabitants of Königsberg (now Kaliningrad)
        arrive in Berlin.

1990   East and West Germany reunited.
1991   17 August, Frederick the Great is reburied in Potsdam.

Preface

This is a collective portrait of Prussia in decline, when the administrative territory, as it had become as part of the German Reich, progressively lost its Prussian character and assumed an imperial one in its place. The process began even before the creation of the Reich in 1871, but it accelerated sharply under Kaiser William II and the main thrust of the argument therefore deals with the period from 1890 to 1945 – from the fall of Bismarck to the death of Hitler.

My desire has been to answer a number of questions about Prussia's role in the disastrous history of Germany in our century. How much was Prussia's military tradition responsible for the two wars which wrecked the European continent between 1914–1918 and 1939–1945? What was the personal contribution of Prussia's rulers, the Hohenzollern family? How reactionary a force were the Junkers? To what extent did Prussia breed an aggressively military stance through its schools and institutions? How did Prussia behave towards its subject peoples, specifically the Poles in the east? How civilised was Prussia? How Prussian was the Third Reich?

It has not been my aim to write a textbook, still less a comprehensive history of Prussia during this period. In political and economic matters it is often an otiose task to try to separate Prussia from the general history of the German Reich. I have used an impressionistic method, drawing on the history of Prussia in former times in order to show the healthy organism before it succumbed to disease.

Prussia has fascinated me since I was a schoolboy, but I had to wait until 1988 before I set foot in its capital (since then I think I have visited every province of Prussia with the exception of Neuchâtel in Switzerland and Gross-Friedrichsburg on the Gold Coast). This book was conceived then, in the course of a solitary walk in Berlin's Tiergarten. In the summer of 1989 I was back in Berlin, still bent on writing something on the history of Prussia. Having some free time, I went for a walk in East Berlin to look at the still pitted and partly ruinous buildings on either side of Unter den Linden. It was a warm June day and I went into the Bärenschänke pub in the Friedrichstrasse. There I met Ulrich, a contented citizen of the old DDR. He saw no need to unite the two Germanys, he told me, East Germany had all it needed. He was both fascinated by my project and alarmed that I should neglect East German sources. He took me off to see the Charité Hospital where he worked, and after a last drink he offered me a deal: he would send me cuttings on Prussia from the East German press, if I in return would send him a good German-English dictionary. We shook hands and parted company.

Soon after my return to England the first batch of clippings arrived. More were promised. I wrote back to offer the dictionary, but Ulrich told me to wait. Then events began to gather momentum in the East: there were protest marches in Dresden, Leipzig and Berlin which finally obliged the DDR to introduce a series of liberal measures. The Prussian (not Nazi) goose-step was one of the first things to go. Finally, on that fateful day in modern German history, 9 November 1989, the wall was pierced. As I might have predicted, I never heard from Ulrich again.

Ulrich was the first to lend me a hand with this book, but there have been many more since. In London my first thanks go to Inga Haag, a born Prussian who gave me considerable encouragement. Also in England, the following have given me valuable help: James Barclay, Dr Fiona Clarke, Helen Glanville, Peter Hamilton, Penny Hoare and Roger Cazalet of Sinclair-Stevenson, Hugh Lawson-Tancred, Dr Philip Mansel, Toby Mitchell, Dr David Parrott, Margaret Rand, former editor of *Opera Now*, and Dennis Sewell.

In Berlin I was fortunate to have an introduction to Professor Dr Werner Knopp of the Stiftung Preussischer Kulturbesitz who gave me the run of the institutions he controls and encouraged the project from the start. My friend Dr Clarita von Trott zu Solz introduced me to Ludwig Freiherr von Hammerstein-Equord, one of the last men living who was directly involved in a plot to kill Hitler. Professor Dr Clarita and Dr Urs Müller-Plantenberg, and their friend Professor Dr Klaus Meschkat were kind enough to take me off to the Brandenburg Lakes one weekend, so that I might experience first hand the landscape which inspired the writings of Theodor Fontane. Gottfried Graf von Bismarck provided me with help and advice, as did Professor Knud Caesar. I should also like to thank my friends from the British garrison in Berlin, in particular Major Peter 'Garbo' and Gail Garbutt, for providing me with so much welcome hospitality during my two long Berlin stints in 1991.

Elsewhere in Germany I received precise information on East Prussia from Reinhard Grunenberg in Oberursel who was alerted to my interests by an article I had written on Kaliningrad-Königsberg in the *Financial Times*. I met the Borussophil railway enthusiast, Andreas Kleber, quite by chance on Wrocław Główny Station (the former Breslau Hauptbahnhof). He was a mine of information on the old Prussian railway network. He was also kind enough to invite me to participate in a Prussian evening he held at his hotel, the Kleber Post in Saulgau in Baden-Württemberg. There I had the honour of airing my views on Prussia on the local television station together with no less a luminary than the ninety-seven-year-old writer and holder of the *Pour le mérite*, Ernst Jünger.

In Poland my friend Dr Eugene Dainov introduced me to Dr Paweł Gieorgica of the University of Warsaw. Without Paweł I should have been defeated by the Russian attempts to block my entry into their part of East Prussia. Through Paweł I met Jadwiga Karpińska, who drove me all the way to Kaliningrad in an ebullient mood, despite the fact that we had no more than three words of any language in common. My thanks too to Professor Bohdan Kacprzyński.

The entire manuscript was read by my agent, Peter Robinson,

who sustained me in the project throughout; and by Dr Christopher Clark of St Catherine's College, Cambridge. Parts of the book were read by Paul Golding, Inga Haag, Peter Hamilton and Ian Wisniewski. I am grateful for their comments but accept liability for all errors.

Finally, I should like to thank the staffs of the British Library, the German Historical Institute, the Goethe Institute and the German Embassy in London; the Staatsbibliotek, the Geheimes Staatsarchiv and the Bildarchiv Preussischer Kulturbesitz in Berlin; and the Presse und Informationsamt der Bundesregierung in Bonn.

Giles MacDonogh
London, 1994

Vergesst niemals dass Ihr auf preussischem Boden und in preussisch-deutschen Gedanken aufgewachsen und heute an der heiligsten Stätte des alten Preussentums eingesegnet seid. Es birgt eine grosse Verpflichtung in sich, die Verpflichtung zur Wahrheit, zu innerlichen und äusserlichen Disziplin, zur Pflichterfüllung bis zum Letzten. Aber man soll niemals von Preussentum sprechen, ohne darauf hinzuweisen, das es sich damit *nicht* erschöpft. Es wird so oft missverstanden. Vom wahren Preussentum ist der Begriff der Freiheit niemals zu trennen. Wahres Preussentum heisst Synthese zwischen Bindung und Freiheit, zwischen selbstverständlicher Unterordnung und richtig verstandenem Herrentum, zwischen Stolz auf das Eigene und Verständnis für Anderes, zwischen Härte und Mitleid. Ohne diese Verbindung läuft es Gefähr, zu seelenlosem Kommiss und engherziger Rechthaberei herabzusinken. Nur in der Synthese liegt die deutsche europäische Aufgabe des Preussentums, liegt der 'preussische Traum!'

Henning v. Tresckow, 11 April 1943
in the Garnisonkirche, Potsdam.
On the confirmation of his sons.

Oliver Clarke
Ein Vorbild

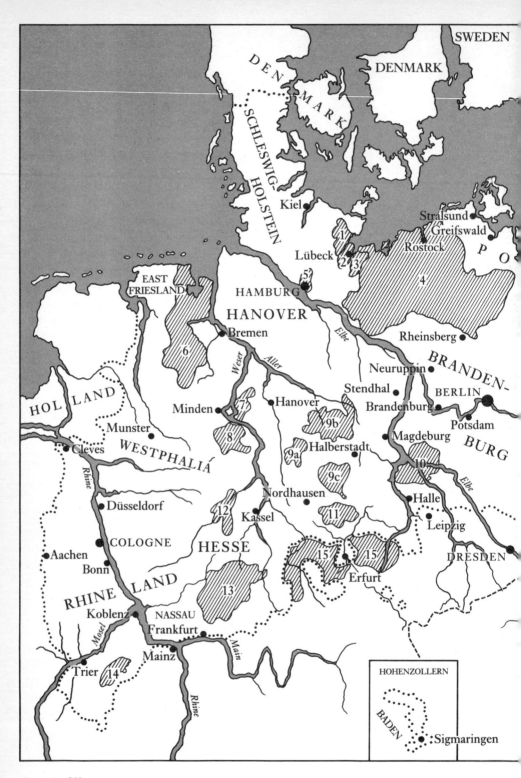

Prussia in 1866.

BALTIC SEA

Memel

Tilsit

KÖNIGSBERG

Insterburg

PRUSSIA

Stolp

Danzig

Elbing

Köslin

Marienburg

Kolberg

Allenstein

winemünde

POMERANIA

Bischofswerder

Stettin

Kulm

Bromberg

Thorn

Netze

Vistula

Landsberg

Warthe

POSEN

WARSAW

Küstrin

Posen

Frankfurt

RUSSIAN EMPIRE

Oder

Cottbus

Sagan

Oder

SILESIA

Neisse

Görlitz

BRESLAU

Ohlau

Brieg

Oppeln

Neisse

Oder

Glatz

Gleiwitz

Elbe

Ratibor

PRAGUE

AUSTRO-HUNGARIAN
EMPIRE

Enclaves, independent of Prussia

1	Oldenburg
2	Lübeck
3	Mecklenburg-Strelitz
4	Mecklenburg
5	Hamburg
6	Oldenburg
7	Lippe Schaumburg
8	Lippe Detmold
9	(a, b, c) Brunswick
10	Anhalt
11	Schwarzburg Sonderhausen
12	Waldeck
13	Ober-Hessen
14	Oldenburg
15	Sachsen Weimar

.... Prussian Border 1866

━ ━ ━ Present German/Polish Border

SCALE

0 10 20 30 40 50 miles

0   50   100 kilometres

Changes made to the Prussian border.

Introduction: Dead Bodies

Owing to . . . [the Hohenzollerns'] deeply-rooted religious fervour they all regarded themselves as being responsible to God for their actions and achievements – as the Elector Frederick I expressed it – 'As the simple bailiffs of God in the performance of His work'. This sense of personal responsibility to God automatically compelled them to keep the 'good' of the 'Whole' always before them, and to put the principle of *Suum cuique* into practice, before Frederick I had these words engraved on the Star of the Order of the Black Eagle. This *Suum cuique* could only be converted into practice by firm adherence to the following fundamental principle and basic guiding line – the creation of an 'objective State-Authority', standing above all parties and specially interested groups, and kept free from the influence of outside interests.

> William II, *My Ancestors*, London, 1929, xiv.

Zeck Trinkend zu den andern: Ick hab 'n preissischen Wahlspruch: 'suhm kwickwe', det heisst uff deitsch: jedem det Seine, mir det Mehrste.

Zeck, *drinking to the others*: I know a Prussian motto: 'suhm kwickwe', that means in German: each to his own, but the biggest whack for me.

> Carl Zuckmayer, *Der Hauptmann von Köpenick. Ein Deutsches Märchen in drei Akten*, 1931, Fischer Verlag, Frankfurt/Main, 1990, 30

Der Kurfürst:
Mein süsses Kind! Sieh! Wär ich ein Tyrann,
Dein Wort, das fühl ich lebhaft, hätte mir
Das Herz schon in der erznen Brust geschmelzt.
Dich aber frag ich selbst: Darf ich den Spruch,
Den das Gericht gefällt, wohl unterdrücken? –
Was würde wohl davon die Folge sein?
Nathalie: Für wen? Für dich?
Der Kurfürst: Für mich: nein! – Was Für mich!
Kennst du nichts Höh'res, Jungfrau, als nur mich?

The Great Elector:
My sweet child, can't you see! If I were a tyrant,
those words of yours which move me so deeply would have
already melted this heart of bronze. But please consider this:
May I cast aside what the court pleases to dictate? What
would be the consequence of such a course of action?
Nathalie: For whom? For you?
The Great Elector: For me; no! What can you mean for me!
You innocent, can you think of nothing higher than me?

Heinrich von Kleist, *Prince Friedrich von
Homburg*, Act IV, Scene I, c. 1810.

In August 1991 the German Federal Republic was suffering from
another of its traumas; once again this was occasioned by the need
to come to terms with the past of Germany. This time Frederick
the Great was rocking the boat.

Prussia's most famous ruler had been dead 205 years, but he
had yet to be laid to rest in the simple 'philosopher's grave' he
had intended for himself and his favourite dogs on the terrace of
his palace of Sanssouci in Potsdam. After his death his nephew
and successor, Frederick William II, countermanded his orders
and had him buried in the vault constructed for Frederick the
Great's stern father, the Soldier King Frederick William I, in the
Potsdam Garrison Church. In this disagreeable company Frederick the Great's mortal remains were obliged to make do until the
closing months of the Second World War.

As German victory began to look unlikely, even to leading
Nazis, Hermann Göring issued instructions to have Frederick and
his father removed from their vault. He feared what might happen
to them should they fall into the hands of the Red Army. The two
kings took off on a macabre journey, eventually coming to rest on
Burg Hohenzollern in Swabia in the south-west of Germany.

On 14 April 1945 RAF bombers destroyed much of the centre
of Potsdam, gutting the Garrison Church. A few days later
Russian tanks were to be seen among the rubble.

In 1968 the substantial ruins were bulldozed. Instead of the
great church, the rulers of East Germany had their architects plan
a vast, windy square. To replace the famous peal of bells which
had rung in the hearts of so many generations of Prussian soldiers,

a *Glockenspiel* was erected on concrete piers. The DDR had made it plain: there was no room for the bones of Frederick the Great in Socialist Potsdam.

In 1989 the DDR first tottered, then tumbled. In 1990 the two states of Germany were reunited. It was not long before the present head of the Hohenzollern family, Louis Ferdinand, began to agitate for the return of his ancestors' bodies to their *Residenz*, Potsdam. The *Garnisonkirche* was no more, but there was room for Frederick William in the pretty, Italianate *Friedenskirche* at the bottom of the hill at Sanssouci; and as for the 'Philosopher King', Frederick, was not the solution to put him in the grave he had intended for himself, on the terrace of his favourite retreat above the vineyard?

In itself, the decision to return Frederick the Great to Sanssouci would have hardly caused more than a grumble. The storm which greeted the reburial on 17 August 1990 was occasioned by the desire of the Federal Chancellor, Helmut Kohl, to attend the ceremony. Even worse, the story went round that the *Bundeswehr*, Germany's squeaky clean, politically correct army, was to present arms to the dead warlord. Was this not the cue, the liberal press asked, for a revival of Prussian militarism? Was that apparently stone-dead monster, Prussia, about to rise up from its unmarked grave?[1]

The German papers took it upon themselves to examine the legacy of Frederick the Great and Prussia. Were there no positive aspects to Frederick's forty-six-year rule? Was Prussia just an excuse for black-hearted militarism? Or was there a more positive side to its history? Were there elements of Prussia in the Federal Republic itself?

The reunification of the two states of Germany had highlighted the Prussian menace.

While the Bundesrepublik had been limited to the south and west, Prussia had been easy to forget. In 1945 the Western Allies agreed to divide occupied Germany into four zones, to be administered by the Americans, British, French and Russians. The Russian share took in Saxony, Thuringia, Mecklenburg and the core territories of Prussia: the Altmark around Magdeburg; the Brandenburg Mark; the Uckermark; and, with the exception of Stettin (which had been awarded to the Poles), Pomerania west of the Oder. Prussia's eastern provinces, those across the Oder – eastern Pomerania, Silesia, West and East Prussia – were not included in the new Germany. They were lopped off and presented to Poland. With the exception, that is, of the top half of East Prussia around the city of Königsberg. Here the Russians envisaged an ice-free port for their Baltic fleet, and snapped it up.

The inhabitants of the lands east of the Oder knew from bitter experience what it meant to live under Russian occupation. Those who could fled; they expected more humane treatment from the British, French and Americans. The arrival of ten million East Germans in the shattered towns and villages of western and southern Germany did not pass without comment from the natives of these regions. In Schleswig-Holstein, on the Danish border, émigré Prussians found a decent enough welcome in a barren, flat land not dissimilar to that they had left behind. The people of Westphalia and the Rhineland were used to Prussians, having put up with more than a century of Prussian rule. In Swabia and Bavaria, however, the local Catholic population treated the refugees with ill-concealed contempt.

For the soldiers and civilians in uniform who worked for the Allied Control Council, the bad blood between the southern Germans and the easterners was hard to understand: '*So is' es . . .*' a Catholic south German told the Englishman James Stern. 'It might well be compared, I think, with that of the French towards the Germans. And the war has greatly increased the hostility.'[2]

The Bavarians showed their dislike for the bedraggled Prussian refugees by making them as unwelcome as possible. One man from Elbing on the Baltic ran into Stern while he was looking for a bed for himself, his wife and their half-starved child. He had been turned away from the houses in the town. 'Get out, you swine from East Prussia,' he had been told, 'you can damn well bring your own beds!'[3]

In 1949 the new Bundesrepublik took over political control of the former British, French and American zones. From the beginning the new state was dominated by the Catholic south and west; only later did a Hanseatic influence from Hamburg creep in.[4] The first Chancellor was Konrad Adenauer, the former Oberbürgermeister of Cologne. Adenauer had made little secret of his 'Borussophobia' since the early days of the Weimar Republic and was determined that Berlin should never again become capital of Germany. Once the Russians had dismantled the industrial base of their own occupation zone in the east and shipped it lock, stock and barrel back to Soviet Russia, they showed some enthusiasm for a reunited Germany west of the Oder-Neisse line. This was dangled before the Western Allies in exchange for a pledge on demilitarisation, requiring a withdrawal of Allied forces from Germany.

The suggestion was aired in the 'Stalin-note' of 10 March 1952. After consultation with the Allies, Adenauer rejected the proposal. The Russian offer was kept secret from the German people till long after the Chancellor's death.

It may well have been that Adenauer believed that East Germany would fall to him as a matter of course before the decade was out, but the Cold War was to prove more persistent than that.[5] Meanwhile the Western-backed Federal Republic could wash its hands of any connection with Prussia.

Ten million refugees might well have objected to the attitude of the Chancellor in Bonn, but after everything that they had suffered in their flight, they were in little position to complain. In their stoicism they exhibited some of those famous 'Prussian virtues' which had been a hallmark of the spartan state since the time of Frederick William I: 'consciousness of duty, hard work, thrift, cleanliness and sober-mindedness'.[6]

The Bundesrepublik had a further reason to reject any Prussian heritage: the attitude of its Allies, who, despite the cessation of hostilities and the creation of the independent republic, main-

tained a military presence in their respective zones, ostensibly to
face a possible Russian enemy.

The Allies had made their attitude to Prussia abundantly clear
in the Control Council's Law No. 46 of 25 February 1947: 'The
Prussian State which from early days has been a bearer of
militarism and reaction in Germany has *de facto* ceased to exist.'
The abolition of its remaining agencies and institutions was guided
by 'the interests of preservation of peace and security of peoples
and with the desire to assure further reconstruction of the political
life of Germany on a democratic basis'.[7] It was the culmination of
a wartime foreign policy objective which in itself went back to the
First World War. During the Great War the British in particular
believed that Prussia was the chief source of conflict in Europe.
Even such unlikely warmongers as the poet Wilfred Owen thought
the war justified by the need to destroy Prussia.

But there was a more cynical attitude too: one which had very
little to do with any desire to keep the Prussian fox out of the
European chicken run. The Allies had been well aware of the
need to compensate the Poles for the loss of a third of their pre-
war territory to Soviet Russia. The Russians had sustained
tremendous losses keeping the land campaign going from 1941 to
1944 and they could hardly be expected to give up eastern Poland,
even if they had originally gained control of the land under the
aegis of the secret treaty signed by Foreign Minister Molotov and
his Nazi counterpart, Ribbentrop. Even with the entirety of
Prussian land across the Oder and Neisse Rivers, and a little bit
more around the Oder Basin, the Polish state was still not quite
as large as it had been in 1939.[8]

Much later, the Allies' laconic condemnation of nearly a
thousand years of Brandenburg-Prussian history struck the Germans as futile. One German historian described it as 'a kick from
a victorious donkey to a long dead lion'.[9] At the time, however,
the German press was slow to react. To some extent this was
because it was still heavily censored by the authorities, Russian,
American, French and British. Germany was morally, physically
and militarily defeated. The Germans' strength had gone. The

long war; the terrible events which had arrived with the occupying armies in the East; the realisation of just how brutal the Nazi regime had been, not just in the East and in the occupied countries, but also in Germany itself; the feeling of personal guilt which hit many Germans (or indeed the unrepentant emotions of any number of Nazis); and the killing winter of 1946–1947 during which many Germans perished – all contributed to the feeling of frigid resignation which ran from top to bottom of German society.

It would be wrong to say, however, that Germans failed to notice the Allied extinction of Prussia. Ruth Andreas-Friedrich commented just a few days before the publication of the order: 'Nazism began in Austria and developed in Bavaria, in Prussia it came to an end. Today we are punishing Prussia by eliminating it, the Bavarians don't wish to be remembered for their past, and the Austrians are demanding reparations. Has the world gone mad?'[10]

Another demonstration of the feeling among Prussians at the time comes from George Clare, a Viennese-born Jew who was working with the Control Council in Berlin after the war. One day he found a woman sitting in the chair on the other side of his desk, requesting permission to cross the Russian Zone to reach comparative safety in the West. She was the widow of Carl-Heinrich von Stülpnagel.

'The General von Stülpnagel who led the revolt against Hitler in France and was executed?' asked a thunderstruck Clare.

'My husband is dead,' she replied. 'I'm a German like any other German. I want no favours, nor would he have wanted any. He fought and died for Germany, not for anyone or anything else.'[11]

It was a fine demonstration of the Prussian spirit.

In the Russian Zone and later in the DDR there was an ideological need to stamp out the Prussian legacy. At first the urban proletariat and the farm workers responded warmly to the measures which drove the middle classes and the Junkers and other landowners across the border to safety in the West. But the brutality of the regime and the strain imposed by the Russians' desire to bleed the country white led to the first of the East European uprisings on 17 June 1953 when the inhabitants of Berlin and Saxon Leipzig took on the Russian army and the young workers of Magdeburg defenestrated the policemen who resisted their occupation of police headquarters.[12]

To prevent any recurrence of such incidents, the Russians and the East German leaders set great store by their policy of re-educating the young people of the Russian Zone. The German Communists who returned from Moscow after the war wrote new schoolbooks which depicted the reactionary Prussian state in all its lurid colours. Just as Hitler had been at pains to show that he descended in a direct line from Frederick the Great via Bismarck, the Marxist ideologists demonstrated that Prussianism was just Fascism by another name.[13]

Later the ideologists found it wiser not to dwell too much on Prussia in the schools. In the guidelines laid down for the teaching of history, the new leaders, Wilhelm Pieck, Walter Ulbricht, Anton Ackermann, Otto Grotewohl and Johannes R. Becher, decided that Prussia was to be shown as the force which perverted Germany and pushed the nation down the wrong path. To prevent embarrassing questions, Prussian history was to be taught only in the context of a wider, German and European picture.[14]

The leaders of the DDR had to face a problem which scarcely existed in the West: the centre of their state lay in precisely the same physical position as the centre of the old Prussian state: Berlin. They could not turn their backs on the past as easily as could the men in Bonn. Berlin had grown up under the Askanian Margraves and had become the capital of Brandenburg-Prussia under the Hohenzollern electors and kings. Unlike the Western-ers, the East Germans had to contend with the presence of emotive statues and buildings which might prove seductive to a latter generation of citizens. The answer in most cases was to destroy them.* In 1950 the free-standing walls of the gutted

---

* The desecration in the West was largely performed by the Allied armies who blew up the statue of Kaiser William I on the Deutsches Eck in Koblenz. The statue was restored in September 1993. It was perhaps understandable that the Americans should have wanted to

Berlin *Schloss* were dynamited. Despite the baroque clothing given to the huge palace by the Danzig-born architect Andreas Schluter in the last years of the seventeenth century and the first years of the eighteenth, the building boasted substantial elements which went back to the sixteenth century and beyond. Ten years later, the same alliance of explosive, bulldozer and pickaxe went to work on the ruins of the *Stadtschloss* in Potsdam. Built by the Great Elector in the seventeenth century, it had been the winter residence of Frederick the Great. A further eight years later, the remains of the *Garnisonkirche*, the sacred shrine of Prussianism, were finally removed. It was the DDR's last act of great barbarism. In the 1970s it discovered that tourism could be a valuable source of foreign currency.

Until the 1970s both the Bundesrepublik in the West and the DDR in the East maintained their attitudes towards Prussia, but there were powerful dissenters on both sides of the wire. Already by the 1950s the hearts of some West German historians had begun to melt. Men such as Gerhard Ritter, Hans-Joachim Schoeps and Walther Hubatsch used their writings to demonstrate that Prussia's legacy was far wider and more constructive than that conveyed by mere militarism; that Prussia had been characterised by the rule of law and religious toleration, ideas anathema to Nazism. In the East the first signs of the new attitude were visible in the *Volksarmee*, which was soon to adopt the goose-step invented in the time of the Soldier King by the *alte-Dessauer*, Leopold of Anhalt-Dessau. The soldiers wore acanthus-leaf shoulder flashes and sang the old hymn 'Ich bete an die Macht der Liebe' (I pray to the power of love). The highest military order of the state was named after the founder of the Prussian General Staff, Scharnhorst.[15]* Some have even gone so far as to see the DDR with its

---

destroy the shell of the Prinz-Albrechts Palais in Berlin. It had been built in 1737 and converted to royal use by Schinkel. Under the Third Reich it became the core of Gestapo headquarters.[17]
* It is tempting to believe that the same veneration for Scharnhorst has led the Russians to leave the portrait roundels of the general and his successor, Gneisenau, on the façade of one of the few remaining pre-war buildings in Kaliningrad (Königsberg); but it is almost certainly due to nothing more than negligence on their part.

authoritarian image and its adherence to the principles of command and discipline as something of a Prussian state. The hundredth birthday of Carl von Clausewitz was celebrated on both sides of the wall, but the East Germans were able to steal a march on their Western neighbours: they leaned on their friends in Poland to have the military thinker's remains transferred from Wrocław (the former Breslau) to his birthplace of Burg-bei-Magdeburg.

In 1978 in the DDR Wolf-Dieter Panse presented a television programme entitled 'The History of Prussia is a Part of our Own History'. Two years later Ingrid Mittenzwei became the first 'Ossi' to denounce the linear interpretation of German history, which saw Hitler as the product of a Prussian militarist tradition, when she wrote a reassessment of the life of Frederick the Great. Her book was the first in a stream of new books on Prussia which culminated in the Prussian exhibition at the Gropiusbau in West Berlin, running from 15 August to 15 November 1981.[16]

The trickle had turned into a stream. In the East they located the equestrian statue of Frederick the Great which had been removed for safety during the war. It was returned to its rightful place on a pedestal in Unter den Linden. From the effigy by Christian Daniel Rauch it might seem only a short step to Frederick's very bones. To bring his body back to Potsdam could be seen as an act of reconciliation between East and West. Until 1989, Potsdam, the Prussian *Residenzstadt*, remained cut off in the East while the coffins of two of Prussia's greatest kings lay, unstuck, in the West. Despite the protest from the liberal press, the gesture had a sort of symbolic beauty.

But even the return of Frederick's bones was unlikely to conjure up the singular atmosphere of the 'Prussian Versailles' in its heyday: that strangely Prussian aesthetic which sought to anchor the arts in the military. Potsdam had been the real heart of Prussia in a way that Berlin never was. It took a quintessential Prussian such as Henning von Tresckow fully to appreciate this cocktail as he found it on the streets and lakes and gardens of his favourite town: 'Military music, the parades in the Lustgarten. . . . Clouds of dust rising over marching columns . . . church on Sundays and the shimmering image of the sun on the looming tower of the *Garnisonkirche*; the lilting peal of the bells and inside the church the grey uniforms ranged on pews before dulled and tattered standards. . . . Playing the last post before the regimental head-quarters: balmy evenings, candle light, solemn music and vibrating bridges reflected in the dark waters of the canal. . . . Summer evenings by the water's edge, summer days out in the boat watching the lovely play of the landscape between the various palaces . . .'[18]

Frederick the Great might return in the company of his austere father, but where was the state they once ruled? What was left of Prussia?

I

An Empire Built on Sand

Anyone who wants to study colonisation must look at the history of the Mark Brandenburg.

Theodor Fontane 'Die Grafschaft Ruppin' in *Wanderungen durch die Mark Brandenburg*, 3rd edition, 1892. Republished by Carl Hanser Verlag, Munich & Vienna, 1991, Vol. I, 411.

It is the same old story: first an all pervading darkness only here and there illuminated by some shaft of light; then come the building of churches and monasteries; then dissolution followed by Swedes and the plague; after this there are a few big fires and a few arsonists are hanged; then the town is favoured with a garrison or some militiamen and as a rule the former monastic buildings are transformed into schools, barracks or prisons. Herein lies the history not only of the towns, but also the individual centuries, from which it is true to say that the seventeenth was always the saddest and the eighteenth always the most banal.

Ibid., 492–493.

Prussia achieved its greatest power and extent in 1866. Fewer than five years later this fully equipped and mobile world power was decanted into the new German *Reich* and its personality gradually ebbed away. Henceforth Prussian history was German history and the epithet 'Prussian' applied as a synonym for 'Spartan' or to describe an arrogant or tactless German of the old school who might have colonial ambitions towards neighbouring states.

In 1866 the independent state of Prussia lay like a thick band across the north of Germany and Poland; proceeding up the Baltic coast to well within the borders of modern Lithuania. In the west it touched France, where the Prussian Rhineland's mild climate was a boon to fruit-growers and winemakers. In the Ruhr and the Saar the state based much of its heavy industry, while on the Danish frontier the newly acquired duchies of Schleswig and Holstein added to Prussia's agricultural potential with their rich pastures. More important for the country's indefatigable military planners, Schleswig-Holstein's coastline offered excellent sites for naval bases. Westphalia had joined the Prussian bloc in the early nineteenth century, but the once proud duchy of Hanover, which had provided Great Britain with a fresh dynasty in 1714, had fallen to Prussia that very year as a result of defeat at the Battle of Langensalza. Like that of the Hessians and the Frankfurters, their attitude to their new rulers was less than cordial.

If Prussia possessed roughly as much land west of the Elbe as it had to the east, none of this was the essential Prussia. That only began at the Elbe, or at least in the Prussian 'Altmark' around the cathedral city of Magdeburg. East Elbian Prussia had a recognisable style in both landscape and people. A belt of sand stretches from the Elbe to the Mazurian Lakes, making the land notoriously unprofitable to farm. As you travelled east the estates grew progressively larger, partly as a result of historical factors, partly because more land was required to make ends meet on that exposed, weather-beaten terrain. Since the seventeenth century, Prussia had expanded at breakneck speed, but until the nineteenth century only the conquest of Silesia and the acquisition of Danzig stood out as instances of a Prussian king laying hold of a region with the expressed wish of tapping into its wealth.

Prussia's history begins neither in the east nor the west, but in that region between the Elbe and the Oder which since the end of the Second World War has formed the easternmost province of Germany. The land was not German then, but populated by Slavic tribes who had taken up residence there after the dust had settled from the great migrations which began with the decline of the Roman Empire. Some of these Slavic tribes had crossed the Elbe and their settlements stretched as far as the present German cities of Lübeck in the north, Magdeburg in the centre, and

Bamberg in northern Bavaria. The tribes were known collectively as Wends or Sorbs. On those occasions when they came into contact with the German peoples they appear to have been able to co-operate reasonably peaceably. There is even some evidence of intermarriage among the chiefs.[1]

The Wendish lands formed a buffer between the Poles across the Oder and the Germans to the west of the Elbe. Only with Charlemagne's defeat of the Saxons at the end of the eighth century did the Emperor's armies come into direct contact with the East Elbian Slavs. The result was the 'Nordmark' or 'Altmark' as it became: a border province under the control of a 'Margrave' or imperial count. At the centre of the Nordmark was the city of Magdeburg.

In 946 German Christians founded the first bishopric across the Elbe at Havelberg, at the point where the Havel River joins the Elbe. Two years later the See of Brandenburg was founded, thereby giving its name to the new Mark Brandenburg. In 968 the church in Magdeburg was elevated to an archbishopric with responsibility for the conversion of the 'underdeveloped' (or heathen) Wendish people across the river.[2]

At first the Wends successfully resisted the German colonists. The church at Brandenburg was swiftly destroyed by an uprising in 983. It was not replaced until the second wave of colonists established the present church on the cathedral island in the mid-twelfth century.[3] In general the arrival of the Germans in what was to become Brandenburg was not a violent process;[4] it was unmarked by the bloody, genocidal incidents which accompanied the settlements of Germans in Mecklenburg, Holstein or Saxony.[5] The first moves to convert the Wends were made by St Norbert's Premonstratensian Order based in Magdeburg,[6] but in the thirteenth century they were superseded by the Cistercians, who could offer the settlers a skill of considerable importance in the swamps of Brandenburg: the ability to drain marshland. Despite the ravages of the Reformation, traces of Cistercian monasticism can still be seen in the red-brick claustral ruins of Lehnin, Chorin and Zinna.

The colonists came from as far afield as the Netherlands,

Piedmont, France and England. In general, once the initial hiccups had ceased, the integration of the colonists with the Wends proceeded smoothly. The Slavs formed their own 'Kietzen' or fishing villages. In the thirteenth century their language became inadmissible before the courts, but no effort was made to stamp it out. In the eighteenth century seven Berlin regiments still issued orders in Wendish as their *Dienstsprache*[7] and in Wendish villages in the late nineteenth century, sermons were still delivered in the old Slavic language, as the novelist Theodor Fontane discovered on a visit to the Spreewald.[8]*

There were Wendish villages close to Berlin until the collapse of Germany in 1945, but for the most part the Wendish character of the Mark was a thing of the past. The largest settlements both then and now were in the Saxon Spreewald and Lausitz. Spreewald Wends still continued to play an important role in Prussian life, however: they were the chief source of wet-nurses and nannies. They were not famed for their beauty: Fontane's younger siblings were looked after by a 'gipsy-like, ugly Wend ...'[9];† although their colourful costumes were much admired by broad-minded travellers of Fontane's generation.

It was predictable that the Nazis should take a dim view of the Slavic Wends and that their language should have been discouraged under the Third Reich. At one stage the SS produced a blueprint for resettling the Wends, a project that would almost certainly have spelled extermination.[12] After the war the pendulum swung the other way, and the Russians felt considerable sympathy for this small enclave of Slavdom within the DDR. Under their pressure, the East German regime granted the Wends a measure of autonomy.

*

* Some of the old noble families of the Mark were believed to be of Wendish origin, such as the von Plothos and the Gans zu Puttlitz. The latter was thought to be the oldest family in the region until 1945. Other old families clung to Wendish first names: the 'Paridan' von Knesebecks, for example; and the 'Pritzbar' von Restorffs.[10]
† 'The wet-nurses, whose picturesque dress is so noticeable on the Berlin streets, all come from this Wendish colony [the Spreewald], which has been preserved through the many wars that have swept over this part of Germany because of the refuge afforded in the swamps and forests. . .'[11]

The Wends were finally subjugated by the first of the Askanian Margraves, Albert the Bear, in 1157. When Pribislav, the last of the Wendish princes, died, he recognised Albert as his heir.[13] With the Wends quelled, the Brandenburgers turned their attention to expansion.

From the mid-thirteenth century the Brandenburgers began to look for land on the right bank of the Oder. The Brandenburg colony in Landsberg and incursions into Silesia and Pomerania brought the Germans into contact with the Poles. In general the Christian Polish overlords welcomed the Germans, who looked set to cultivate the barren landscape. By the end of the fourteenth century the Brandenburgers had already travelled far enough to make a grab for Danzig on the Baltic, then the property of the Teutonic Knights. It is interesting that this first meeting should have proved belligerent: the Brandenburgers could not have imagined at that time that one day their destinies would be bound up with the Order's territory in East Prussia; even less that they might eventually adopt the name of the volatile heathen tribe which lived there as their own.

The Askanians died out and were succeeded by Wittelsbachs and Luxemburgs. When the last Luxemburg died, the Emperor appointed Frederick of Hohenzollern in his place. Frederick was a Swabian princeling whose family had performed the office of Burgrave of Nuremberg since the twelfth century. He was a particular favourite of the Emperor Rudolf of Habsburg, having helped secure his election to the imperial throne. For his efforts on the Emperor's behalf, Frederick was also to be given a seat on the board, as Elector of Brandenburg.[14]

It must have been a great temptation for later Hohenzollerns to exaggerate the degree of anarchy which reigned in Brandenburg at that time. The last Kaiser imagined his ancestor's arrival from the civilised west to 'a land covered with marshes and forests, a land spoilt by neglect and fallen into confusion through misrule and the innumerable ... feuds and struggles between towns and nobles; a population sunk into a hopeless state of servitude and grown savage with brutal treatment; a nobility unbridled in its egotism, inclined to the marauding habits of robber-knights, and which in culture, customs and forms of social intercourse in no way approached the South German nobility, in whose midst the Zollerns had lived for so long. In short it can be truly said, that when the Elector Frederick the First entered the Mark he found chaos.'[15]

Frederick was awarded his electorate in 1415. Notwithstanding the Kaiser's excusable tendency to overrate the importance of his ancestor, Brandenburg was indeed in turmoil. The nobles had grown overmighty through the weakness of absentee Margraves little inclined to shift their courts to the 'sandbox of the Holy Roman Empire'. Led by the Quitzow family, they put up a vigorous resistance to Frederick's attempts to bring them to heel.[16] But one by one Frederick reduced their castles and established himself as sole master in his new domaine.[17] He then retired to Swabia where he died in 1440. It took four generations of Hohenzollern electors before the family put down roots in Brandenburg.[18]

The Hohenzollerns continued to amass land in the north and east in the course of the following century, but that Brandenburg was to grow in real size in the east and west was due to the marriage of John Sigismund of Brandenburg to his cousin Mary Eleanor of Prussia in 1594. Not only did this tie reinforce Brandenburg's claims to the Hohenzollern-ruled territory of Prussia on the Baltic, it brought with it a bid to the complicated succession to the west German duchy of Jülich-Cleves. From now on Brandenburg's interests lay far to the east and far to the west.

The stumbling block to John Sigismund's claim to the western territory was his religion. Jülich-Cleves had a large Catholic population and the Elector of Brandenburg was a Lutheran. International arbitration limited him to the Protestant areas of Cleves, Mark, Ravensberg and Ravenstein. In 1613, however, John Sigismund took the unpredecented step of converting to Calvinism, thereby becoming the first German prince to discard the rule established during the religious wars, that the religion of the land should follow that of the prince. There is every reason to believe that John Sigismund's conversion was genuine, and it was certainly a bold step. Now the Elector of Brandenburg was a Calvinist ruling over a Lutheran state and one with designs on a Catholic region of west Germany. The result of this confusion was to become one of the sacred principles of the later Prussian kings: religious toleration.

An event which had taken place two years earlier was to prove even more important than John Sigismund's conversion: the enfeoffment of the duchy of Prussia. Seven years later, in 1618, the year the Thirty Years War broke out, Duke Albert of Prussia died and John Sigismund succeeded him. Brandenburg was now the neighbour of Holland in the west and Russia in the east.

II

When Brandenburg's moment came to achieve fame on the international stage it was using not its original name, but one which it had borrowed from a remote province on the Baltic: Prussia. The 'Prusai', or Prussians, were a heathen race inhabiting an area roughly the size of modern Switzerland, which lay between the Polish province of Mazovia and the Baltic Sea, between the Vistula and the Memel.

Largely left in peace by the migrating tribes of early medieval times, the Prusai were said to be of Indo-Germanic origin, like the original inhabitants of Latvia, Lithuania and Courland. Their language, now extinct, but documented by ancient grammars and vocabularies, was not Slavic.[19] Their lifestyle was not sophisticated:* their religion honoured nature; their gods were the sun, the moon and the wind. At harvest time they sacrificed a white horse as their most precious possession on the meadows before the shrine of Romowe.[21] They were generous and drunken, their only anti-social habits being a tendency to slaughter widows on

---

* '. . . without script or ability to tell the time, and with a language incomprehensible to German and Slav alike . . .'[20]

the death of their husbands and to burn slaves, dogs and falcons with a deceased warrior: 'In other words their customs were not very far from those of the ancient Germans.'[22]

The Prusai did not begin to feel the encroachments of the Poles until AD 992. Thereafter attacks continued until the mid-twelfth century, when the tribesmen decided it was time to fight back. They took to marauding the Poles who lived on their borders. These Prussian excursions must have become increasingly oner-ous to the Poles of the Vistula Basin and Mazovia, for in 1226 Prince Conrad I of Mazovia took the fateful decision to invite the Teutonic Knights to help him eject the Prusai from his land.[23]

To date, the thirty-six-year-old Order had failed to distinguish itself. Founded in 1190 as an order of knights based on the Templars, its members were also required to take monastic vows, renouncing property and eschewing contact with women. They could not display personal seals or carry coats of arms, but instead wore a uniform white mantle emblazoned with a black cross. These black and white costumes later provided the colour scheme for the Prussian and the imperial German flag.

The Teutonic Knights were originally intended for use in the Holy Land, but after the end of the Third Crusade their deployment was limited to southern Germany and Livonia. The Prussian expedition, however, was their first big opportunity to show their mettle in battle and with time Prussia became their chief *raison d'être*. At that point the Order's headquarters shifted from Venice to Marienburg on the Nogat.

Conrad of Mazovia's invitation arrived at the moment when the Knights were beginning to make a reputation for themselves. The reason for the sudden change in the Order's fortunes was the arrival as Grand Master of Hermann von Salza, the closest friend of the Emperor Frederick II. Suddenly, as the *Wahlpreusse* Hein-rich von Treitschke put it, 'Greatness entered the history of the Order.'[24]

Historians of the Treitschke school liked to see the Knights completing the chain of German settlements which had already stretched right the way up the southern coast of the Baltic, from

the Wendish lands of western Pomerania to Reval, Riga and
Dorpat in what are now Latvia and Estonia. One of the benefits
of this colonisation, thought Treitschke, was the spread of German
red-brick Gothic architecture to the lands beyond the Oder.[25]

Like the Brandenburgers, the Knights worked in tandem with
the Cistercians. The great abbey church of Oliva near Danzig was
started in 1225 and a monk from Oliva became the first Bishop to
the Prussians. Conversion was at first rapid; by 1230 the Knights
had proselytised the areas of Kulm and Löbau. Their success
changed the social basis of the Order. Originally the Knights had
not been of noble extraction, merely freemen; with time a period
of service with the Knights became a status symbol for members
of the European nobility. It was in honour of King Ottokar of
Bohemia, for example, that Königsberg was named, after Peppo
von Osterna conquered the Prussian fortress of Tuwangste,
somewhere near the site of the Russian city now called
Kaliningrad.[26]

At first the numbers of Knights were small and the Order
therefore adopted its own methods of colonisation. As soon as an
area was secured, they built a powerful stronghold or *Ordensburg*
to prevent any possible back-sliding. Originally these were constructed in wood, but eventually all the more important ones were
rebuilt in red brick. Some have even stood the test of time, despite
the destruction wreaked in the last war and the attempts of certain
Poles to rewrite the past.

Soon after the foundation of Königsberg in 1255, the Knights
began to run into difficulties. Despite their arrogant chants of
'Wir wollen alle fröhlich sein, die Heiden sind in grosser Pein!'
(Joy and gladness should fill our hearts: the heathen suffers from
our darts!), they showed themselves reluctant to convert the
Prusai. One reason for this was tactical: their numbers were small,
and the more Prussians became Christians the Knights thought,
the more their lines would be threatened by potentially volatile
Prussians. None the less, in 1260 they took the decision to destroy
the Prussian shrines. A year later the Prussians revolted.[27]

The Prussian uprising continued sporadically until 1283, when their forces, under Herkus Monte and Skomand of Sudauen, were defeated. The Knights then imposed a strict rule over the tribes.[28] They were sole proprietors of the land and began to populate it with an imported nobility from Germany. Towns were founded and German merchants encouraged to settle them. The Prussian language was actively discouraged in a way which never happened to the Wendish of the Mark Brandenburg: 'Already by the beginning of the fourteenth century,' wrote Treitschke, 'the language of the conqueror ruled, and Germans were forbidden to speak Prussian to their servants.'[29] German rule in Prussia was more draconian than in neighbouring Courland, Livonia or Estonia.

In 1308 the Poles committed their second major mistake: they invited the Teutonic Knights to help them drive the Askanian Brandenburgers out of Danzig. The port at the mouth of the Vistula had begun life as a fishing village. Its civic rights had been granted in 1236 by the Pomerenian prince Swietopelk II, who had summoned the Dominican friars from Cracow to build the church of St Nicholas. In its earliest charters the town adhered to Lübeck law. Despite persistent efforts to prove the contrary, it would seem that the town posssessed a sizeable German element from the outset. The Germans were to set the tone in Danzig and its immediate surroundings right up to 1945.[30]

It was not just the Brandenburgers who wanted control of Danzig; the Danes too were angling for possession of the key port. The Knights did their job only too well: not only did they drive the Brandenburgers away, but they rid the town of both Danes *and* Poles. From now on they could boast complete control of the Vistula Basin. This enormous advancement in the Order's fortunes was not lost on the Grand Master, Siegfried von Feuchtwangen. The following year he abandoned his headquarters in Venice and settled at Marienburg, in the stern *Ordensburg*, with its austere geometry the most uncompromising statement of the Teutons' art left in Poland.[31]

If the early fourteenth century was the glamorous period in the history of the Teutonic Knights, it was also the time when the first signs of decline began to appear. Economic problems were rife: 'The never ending wars had consumed the marrow of the territory, high customs tariffs and the behaviour of the Order embittered the townsfolk. Added to this there were unforeseen disasters: repeated poor harvests and the puzzling disappearance of the herrings from the Hanseatic fishing fields . . .'[32]

A further disaster struck when the Lithuanians began to convert to Christianity en masse as a result of the marriage of their Prince Jagiello to the heiress to the Polish throne, removing the Knights' *raison d'être* and leading to the merging of the Lithuanian and Polish crowns. With the Danes exerting pressure from the west, the Knights were now surrounded. Nemesis came at the first Battle of Tannenberg in 1410. Over the centuries, Tannenberg was to become a rallying cry for Poles, Prussians and Germans alike. In this instance a German army of 12,000 men was defeated by a Polish-Lithuanian force something like twice its size. The Peace of Thorn which was signed the following year was notably lenient towards the Knights, but they made the mistake of testing the Polish armies once again only three years later. The result was a second defeat.

The German settlers and the new nobility which had replaced the native Prusai were becoming increasingly impatient with the Order's administration. In 1440 they rebelled against the Knights and burned down the *Ordensburg* at Kulm. In 1457 the Grand Master was expelled from his castle in Marienburg by Bohemian mercenaries and forced to settle with his retinue in the castle in Königsberg. The Poles were now strong enough to dictate the second Peace of Thorn in 1460. All the Knights' land east of the Vistula and the Nogat was ceded to the Poles, including the *Ordensburgen* of Kulm, Elbing and Marienburg. The core of the Knights' land remained intact, but it was no longer a sovereign state. Under the conditions laid down in Thorn, Prussia became a fief of the King of Poland and the Grand Master had to swear an oath of fealty to the Polish monarch.

Similar disasters hit the Order in their other lands. In 1454 the Brandenburgers bought back the Neumark territory which the

Knights had controlled on the right bank of the Oder. In that same year the citizens of Danzig threw off the Order's rule and Danzig was incorporated into Poland, albeit with special status in recognition of its importance to the grain trade. Despite Polish rule, the population remained predominantly German-speaking.[33]

The need to protect the remaining lands of the Teutonic Knights may well have influenced the choice of the last Grand Masters: they were selected from increasingly important German dynasties in order to maintain powerful allies within the German Empire. In 1511 Margrave Albert of Brandenburg-Ansbach became Grand Master of the Order, thereby also becoming the first Hohenzollern to administer the Baltic region. In 1525 he dispensed with the mediaeval trappings of the Teutonic Order and transformed Prussia into a duchy under Polish sovereignty. It was a gesture typical of Albert, who exercised his renaissance humanism also in the creation of the 'Albertina', as the progressive University of Königsberg was known until its destruction in 1945.[34]

III

John Sigismund of Hohenzollern, Elector of Brandenburg and Duke of Prussia, died in 1618. It was a tremendous misfortune that his son, the Elector and Duke George William, should have to succeed him in the precise year when Germany plummeted into the Thirty Years War. History has not been kind to George William: even his own great-grandson, Frederick the Great, described his reign as 'the unhappiest of all the Princes of the House of Brandenburg ... all the scourges of the universe descended on his unfortunate electorate.'[35]

But George William was shrewd enough when it came to the Poles. In 1621 they agreed to allow him to pay homage as Duke of Prussia. This was possibly the Poles' third fatal mistake, for had they put a stop to the Brandenburgers at that moment, then Prussia would doubtless have fallen to them in the course of the

next thirty years. George William's problems began when Brandenburg was transformed into a vast battlefield by the armies of
the Empire and the Swedes. First Brandenburg city and Havelberg fell to Tilly, then Magdeburg was besieged by Wallenstein.
In Pomerania, the impending death of the heirless Duke Bogislas
aroused Brandenburg's dynastic ambitions, but George William
was too weak to take advantage. The duchy was snaffled up by the
Swedes in 1637; the Prussians only wrested the last chunk from
them in 1815.

For the Prussians, it was to be a century of nightmarish Swedish
triumphs. In 1625 the Swedes occupied the port of Pillau, near
Königsberg in Prussia. Frankfurt on the Oder was seized and four
times they marched on Berlin, bearding the Elector in his castle
in Köpenick, just a few miles to the east of the city walls. They
demanded and obtained the key Brandenburg fortresses of Spandau and Küstrin. The electoral family had no alternative but to
flee to Königsberg.

In 1631 Tilly's imperial armies finally succeeded in breaking
the resistance of the Magdeburgers. The massacre which followed
was possibly the bloodiest of the war: 'The Imperial army wreaked
on that unfortunate city every conceivable act which might be
dreamed up by the unbounded license of the soldier, when nothing
stands between him and his fury; everything that the most
ferocious cruelty inspires in man when blind hatred runs away
with his senses. With their weapons drawn, troops of soldiers ran
through the streets, indiscriminately slaughtering old people,
women and children, whether they offered resistance or not.
Houses were pillaged, the streets ran with blood, and one could
witness bodies, their hearts still palpitating, piled up in heaps, or
laid out naked, while all around there were the miserable cries of
the victims and the furious calls of their assassins . . .'[36]

The Elector George William died in 1640, leaving Brandenburg-Prussia at its lowest ebb. East Prussia was threatened by the
Swedes, anxious to control the grain ports of Königsberg, Pillau
and Memel; Jülich-Cleves was occupied by forces from Spain and

Holland; and the Swedes were still ensconced in the fortresses of Spandau and Küstrin.

George William's successor was the twenty-year-old Frederick William, who had grown up in the experience of war. He saw the importance of protecting his vulnerable portfolio of provinces, half of which had been lost since the start of the war. Prussia was particularly important for him as a source of revenue while the Swedes effectively controlled the Elbe and Oder Rivers.

To add to Frederick William's problems, nobles in the farther flung regions were deserting him for other powers; the East Prussians looked increasingly ready to throw in their lot with the Poles; some of the Baltic nobles were striving for a degree of autonomy. Frederick William reverted to strong-arm tactics. A tactical execution put paid to the secessionist tendencies of the Prussians. The next move was to provide them with jobs. Brandenburgers were fighting in just about every army in Europe. Frederick William looked at his own troops with despair: 'The scum swept to the surface by the Thirty Years War'.[37] His solution was to create a strong force of his own. The resulting 30,000-man-strong standing army was just one reason why he came to be known as 'the Great Elector'.

Another reason lay in his bold refutation of the revocation of the Edict of Nantes. In 1685, the same year in which the French King Louis XIV declared open season on his country's Protestant population, Frederick William signed the Edict of Potsdam, welcoming the persecuted Frenchmen to his own lands. Some 20,000 came over the next few years, plugging the gaps in the rather empty city of Berlin. By the beginning of the eighteenth century, one in three Berliners was a Frenchman. The French brought with them valuable crafts and trades for the backward state of Brandenburg-Prussia, and the French colony was to remain an important social element in Prussia until the end.

The Great Elector also prided himself on the independence of his judiciary. Under his reign Brandenburg-Prussia made its first move towards becoming the 'Rechtstaat' that was to be the envy of Europe at the end of the eighteenth century. In his *Kammerger-*

icht courthouse in Berlin, Frederick William had a picture depict-
ing the Persian King Cambyses skinning a judge found guilty of
an unjust settlement.[38]

The Great Elector was often thwarted in his territorial
ambitions. He dreamed of a colonial empire on the model of the
Dutch; he longed for control of the Oder basin at the port of
Stettin; but the only part of Pomerania he was to acquire was the
eastern half with the bishopric of Cammin. The Treaty of
Westphalia which brought the Thirty Years War to an end left
Frederick William in a position of equality with the other great
German dynasties, the Wittelsbachs, Wettins and Welfs, but like
these he 'wore no crown, but a good half a dozen hats: he was
Margrave of Brandenburg, Duke in Prussia, Pomerania, Magdeburg and Cleves and Count of the Rhenish Mark, Prince of
Minden and Prince of Halberstadt'.[39] Each of these disparate
territories presented him with new headaches in the form of
different characters, different laws and a crop of nobles all eager
to hang on to whatever rights they had gleaned for themselves
during the unruly years of the seventeenth century.

One problem the Great Elector did solve was that of the status
of Prussia. In 1641 he went to Warsaw to pay homage to the
Polish king as a Polish duke. Sixteen years later, with the Treaty
of Wehlau, he succeeded in scrapping Polish overlordship in
Prussia, and the sovereignty of the Teutonic Order's former
territory returned to Brandenburg. This was achieved as much by
playing off one major power against another as by force of arms.
Nor were the Prussian nobles happy to see sovereignty pass from
the Poles to the Brandenburgers: they feared a new absolutism
which would rid them of their local privileges.

In 1674 the Swedes took advantage of the Elector's absence
fighting the French in the west to march into Brandenburg.
Frederick William was obliged to lead his armies back from
Franconia to engage the enemy. He crossed the Havel at Rath-
enow where the Swedes had 'given themselves over to the charms
of the bottle'[40] to the extent that they failed to notice his approach.
The need for speed had necessitated the abandonment of his

infantry, so it was the cavalry alone which defeated the Swedish army at the Battle of Fehrbellin. Popular legend in Frederick the Great's day had it that the battle had been turned in Brandenburg-Prussia's favour by the reckless bravery of Prince Frederick of Homburg, in defiance of the Elector's explicit orders.*

Fehrbellin was not in itself a significant victory but it nonetheless 'established the fame of the Prussian army'.[41] It was the beginning also of the process of sweeping the Swedes right out of Brandenburg-Prussian territory as the Great Elector pursued them all the way to Tilsit, crossing the frozen inland sea of the Frisches Haff on a sleigh to gain an advantage over them in Prussia. The Swedes, wrote Frederick the Great in recognition of his great-grandfather's achievement, 'had entered Prussia like Romans, they left like Tartars.'[42] Once again the Elector laid siege to Stettin. The city fell in 1677 when the burghers paid homage to their new lord. For want of friends at the negotiating table in Saint Germain-en-Laye, Stettin was handed back to the Swedes in 1679.

Nor did the Great Elector have much luck in Silesia when the last of the reigning Piast dukes, George William of Liegnitz, died in 1675. By treaty obligations dating back to 1537, large parts of the chiefly German-populated duchy should have fallen to Brandenburg. The Habsburg emperors, however, decided that Silesia belonged to the Bohemian crown by default and, as the successors to the last king of Bohemia, they snaffled up the valuable territory for themselves.

The Great Elector died in 1688, only a little better off in terms of land than he had been at his accession. But if his territorial acquisitions were few, he had created the standing army and the beginnings of the bureaucracy; he had reduced the independence of the nobles and made himself master of his own house; he had also established himself at the forefront of the baroque princes of central Europe with his residence in the lakeside town of Potsdam.

* The conflict between obedience to the law and discipline on the one hand, and compassion and the recognition of inspired bravery on the other was to form the subject of Heinrich von Kleist's play *Prinz Friedrich von Homburg*, c1810.

Shortly before his death, Frederick William had a medal struck carrying the legend 'Exoriare aliquis nostris ex ossibus ultor' – 'May from my bones an avenger arise'. Revenge, however, had to skip a couple of generations, for the Great Elector's immediate successors were not greatly to alter the shape of Brandenburg-Prussia, even if his grandson, Frederick William I did finally secure Stettin by offering the Swedes the sort of cash incentive they couldn't decently refuse.

The Great Elector's son, the Elector Frederick III, is chiefly remembered for his role in raising Brandenburg-Prussia's status from that of an electorate to a kingdom outside the German Empire. The negotiations had begun under the Great Elector and were renewed soon after Frederick came to the throne. Initially there was reluctance in Vienna to seeing another Protestant kingdom emerge in Germany, but on 16 November 1700 the emperor promised to recognise Prussia. Frederick III, Elector of Brandenburg, therefore had himself crowned King *in* Prussia on 18 January 1701.

In Prussia because for the time being his kingdom lay *without* the Reich. The Elector of Saxony had become King of Poland in 1697 by the ruse of converting to Catholicism. The overwhelming bulk of his subjects remained Lutheran. The Elector of Hanover was to become King of Great Britain in 1714, yet for the time being none of the three electors was recognised as a king *inside* Germany. In the case of Prussia there were further complications in that large amounts of the former *Ordensland* lay within Poland. As far as the church was concerned the Prussian king remained the Margrave of Brandenburg until 1787.

Frederick's crown was paid for by his unstinting support for the Habsburg cause. His grandson characterised his attitude to France as one of 'blind hatred'.[43] Nor was Frederick the Great any more compassionate when it came to his general assessment of his grandfather's reign: 'He confused vain things with real grandeur. He was more attached to dazzling showiness than to simple, solid, useful things. He sacrificed thirty thousand men in various of the Emperor's and his allies' wars in order to win a crown for himself and he was only in such a hurry to have that dignity so that he might indulge his taste for pomp and justify his enormous squandering by specious pretexts . . . Vain and spendthrift [Frederick's] . . . court was one of the most luxurious in Europe; his missions to foreign courts were as magnificent as those of the Portuguese; he crushed the poor in order to line the pockets of the rich; his favourites received huge pensions, while his subjects languished in poverty; his stables and apartments resembled an oriental court more than anything in Europe.'[44]

'He was great in trivial matters and trivial in great affairs of state' was his grandson's crushing judgement, but the first Prussian monarch should not be written off so easily. The money was not merely frittered away on his court favourites. While the architects Johann Arnold Nering and Johann Friedrich von Eosander busied themselves with the new palace at Charlottenburg to the west of Berlin, Frederick had the old Berlin *Burg* converted into a superb baroque *Schloss* by the Danzig-born architect Andreas Schlüter. The dedicatee of Charlottenburg was Frederick's wife, the Welf princess Sophia Charlotte, whose passion was to converse with the Saxon Gottfried Wilhelm Leibniz, called to Berlin to found the Prussian Academy of Sciences, a sister organisation to the new Prussian Academy of the Arts. Even before he had assumed the royal title Frederick created the Fredericiana or University of Halle, whose great legal faculty was pre-eminent in the forming of Prussian civil servants until 1945.

If the Great Elector had established the Prussian 'style' with his 'Etatisme', his spendthrift son did nothing to steer the state back to the feudal, dynastic pattern of other German regimes; Brandenburg-Prussia remained colonial and military in character, the state itself its most important institution. Nor did Frederick do anything to tamper with the war machine he inherited from his father. The Brandenburgers participated in imperial campaigns throughout Europe and earned widespread recognition for their discipline. It was under Frederick I that Prince Leopold of Anhalt-Dessau, the famous '*alte-Dessauer*' and inventor of the goose-step, made his first appearance as a general in the Brandenburg-Prussian army.

IV

> Throughout my life I have been careful not to draw down the envy
> of the House of Austria on my head. This has forced me to pursue
> two passions which are really alien to me, namely unbounded
> avarice, and an exaggerated regard for tall soldiers. Only under the
> disguise of these spectacular eccentricities was I allowed to gather a
> large treasury and assemble a powerful army. Now this money and
> these troops are at the disposal of my successor, who requires no
> such mask.[45]

As part of the trappings of his new crown, Frederick I founded
the chivalric order of the Schwarzer Adler (The Black Eagle) in
1701. Its motto was *Suum cuique*, 'To each his own', and its first
recipient the Crown Prince Frederick William, later King Frederick William I.

Frederick William was the first ruler of Brandenburg-Prussia
to espouse what was to become a typically Prussian form of
statecraft which may be loosely described as spartan. He detested
show and extravagance, and for a monarch of his time took a
remarkable interest in the welfare of his subjects. His only
passions, it seems (and despite his insistence to the contrary),
were the smoky sessions of his *Tabakskollegium* and his *lange Kerls*
– the tall soldiers which made up his elite guard. The location of
a particularly tall recruit was sure to acquire favour under
Frederick William's strict regimen, and even his son, the later
Frederick the Great, was not above kidnapping a lofty Mecklenburg peasant in order to get into his father's good books.[46]

Frederick William's priorities lay with his army. On acceding to
the throne he made a complete inventory of his father's wealth
and decreed drastic economies, saving even on the feed of the
horses in the royal stables. The new court had no more need of
men like Andreas Schlüter, and the architect took himself off to
St Petersburg, where he died. When Frederick William followed
him to the grave a quarter of a century later, he left a surplus of
some eight million Thalers and an army almost twice the size of
his father's. Frederick's style was 'his own mixture of begging,

cursing, admonitions, thuggery, supplication and chicanery; that Prussian style which from making its impression would, in the fullness of time, become a trademark of the German state. From the simplicity . . . of the army uniforms (which may be correctly termed "Prussian" from 1718 onwards) and architecture, not to mention the thriftiness and – this could be seen either positively or negatively – the absolute punctiliousness in the establishment and administration of a healthy economy'.[47]

As a child Frederick William had been brought up in the same Calvinist religion which had nurtured the Brandenburg Hohenzollerns for a century. As an adult he moved closer to what was to become a typically Prussian brand of pietism which injected its character into all branches of life within the state. The medieval state was replaced by a strong bureaucracy staffed, as often as not, by commoners. The nobles went into the army. The state became the highest good.

Frederick William was only partially successful in driving foreign adventurers out of the Prussian army and replacing them with native nobles.[48] The 'cantonal' system introduced in 1733 was designed to engage the maximum number of soldiers for limited campaigning periods, allowing the peasantry to cultivate the soil when they were not needed in the colours. The peasants were drawn from individual 'cantons' thereby stamping a regional character on Prussian regiments for the first time. Those periods were few during his reign; in general Frederick William avoided direct confrontation where he could. Even without it he was finally able to wrest Vorpommern from the Swedes and establish Prussian control of Stettin and the Oder Basin in 1721.

In East Prussia Frederick William continued his father's policy of repopulating the land with farmers. A disastrous plague at the turn of the century had left 27,000 farms tenantless, but the king was able to steer half the 30,000 Protestant Salzburgers who had been expelled from their homes in the Salzkammergut towards his lands on the Baltic. By the time of his death in 1740 the Prussian population was back at its old level.

Frederick William's rigid Calvinism gave him some particularly

forthright views on the education of children. He was disappointed
by his heir, whom he found weak and effeminate. He also disliked
his interest in music, literature and the arts, pursuits encouraged
by Frederick's mother, the Welf princess Sophia Dorothea.*
The result was a childhood for the future Frederick the Great of
brutal beatings, seemingly untempered by any demonstration of
paternal love.

In 1730, when the Crown Prince was eighteen years old, he
conceived a plan to flee Brandenburg-Prussia and seek his
fortunes at the court of his Welf cousins in England. His chief
accessory in this was an officer of his father's guard, Hans
Hermann von Katte. Frederick was apprehended and both he and
Katte imprisoned.

The intervention of members of the royal family and high-
ranking courtiers was necessary before Frederick William shelved
his plan to have his eldest son executed for desertion. Katte was
not so lucky. Despite a plea for leniency from the court martial,
Frederick William returned the verdict to the tribunal with these
chilling words: 'His Royal Majesty also received a little schooling
in his youth and he learned the Latin tag: *fiat justicia et pereat
mundus!* (Let justice be done though the world should perish in
the act!) ... When the court martial has published the sentence
on Katte, let him be told that His Majesty is sorry, but that it is
better that he should die than justice be denied the world.'[50]†

The king posed as an austere Brutus but it is hard to deny that
he took a sadistic pleasure in making his son understand what he
saw as the enormity of his offence. Katte was to be executed
before the prince's eyes at the gaunt fortress in Küstrin.

* Sophia Dorothea played a double game with her husband. She encouraged Frederick on
the one hand, and played the meek wife on the other. Witness her daily letters to the king:
'Mon très cher et aymable mary, je vous aime et chésrit tendrement de tout mon coeur
mille fois plus que moi même. Je pense mon cher mary toujours à vous et ne songe qu'as
vous plaire et toute mon joy et satisfaction est quand j'ay le bonheur mon cher mary d'estre
auprès de vous ...'[49]
† The German reads: 'S.K.M seynd in Dero Jugend auch durch die Schule geloffen, und
habe das lateinische Sprüchwort gelernet: Fiat Justitia et pereat mundus! ... Wenn das
Kriegsgericht dem Katten die Sentence publicirt, soll ihm gesagt werden, dass es Sr. K.M.
leid thäte, es wäre aber besser, dass er stürbe, als dass die Justiz aus der Welt käme.'

'Mon cher Katte,' Frederick is said to have cried from his cell, 'je vous demande mille pardons.'

'Point de pardon, mon prince,' said Katte. 'Je meurs avec mille plaisirs pour vous.'

Frederick fainted as his friend's head fell to the ground.[51]

After Katte's death began Frederick's long preparation for kingship. In his prison he learned the business of administration, working with the civil servants who looked after the royal domains. When he had proved himself a good student, the king granted him his first regiment and a garrison at Neuruppin in the Mark. Here began the happiest period of his life: surrounded by friends and with the time to read and play his beloved flute, he at last had the chance to enjoy his youth.

The wild evenings in the Temple of Apollo were curtailed by the decision to foist a bride upon the unwilling Crown Prince. Elizabeth of Brunswick-Wolfenbüttel had little charm for Frederick. He married in order to retain the good will of his stern father and for the sake of the independence of his new court at his fairy-tale castle at Rheinsberg; real connubial co-operation, however, was out of the question. He was almost certainly homosexual.

By the time Frederick acceded to the throne in 1740, he had already begun to admire his father and even the terrible education he had received at his hands. The two men were perhaps more similar than many have been prepared to admit. Even before his father's death, Frederick was able to write to his idol Voltaire from Insterburg in East Prussia that he found 'something heroic in the generous and zealous way in which the king has colonised this desert and made it fertile and useful, and I feel certain you will be of my opinion . . .'[52] Later, in his *Mémoires pour servir à l'histoire de la Maison de Brandebourg* of 1767, he devoted considerable space to his father's achievements as the man who 'gave an example of austerity and frugality worthy of the first years of the Roman Republic . . .'[53]

Where he differed from his father was in his desperate desire for fame: to create an image for himself and Prussia on the international stage. His father had put the state first and himself in second position; he was 'the first servant of the state' in a way his son was not: Frederick was too motivated by his own desire for glory. It was this lust for fame which dictated his policies when he came to power.

The pretext for action was not long in coming: Maria-Theresia succeeded to the imperial throne in contravention of the Salic law which required emperors to be males. Frederick saw in this the ideal moment to seize the rich territory of Silesia. In December 1740 he told his uncle George II of England that his 'sole purpose ... [was] the maintenance of the true interests of the House of Austria'. He then commenced his 'Blitzkrieg' across the Oder.[54]

Frederick's first encounter with the enemy at Mollwitz was not a personal success. The Prussian victory that day was the work of his urbane, worldly wise general, Kurt Christoph von Schwerin. While Schwerin's troops descended on the Austrians with alarming parade-ground discipline,[55] Frederick was cowering in a flour mill having lost his nerve. His failure that day was glossed over, but he had to wait seven months to prove his own mettle at the Battle of Chotusitz. Here he deserved the laurels, and the victory secured the province of Silesia, albeit temporarily; Frederick could return to Berlin and cultural pursuits.

Berlin was to be transformed. The new opera house was built on Unter den Linden while Potsdam opened out from its medieval walls to become the loveliest of the north German *Residenzstädte*. Frederick had no desire to be remembered by later generations as just a warrior lord: 'Potsdam was no Sparta; and under Frederick II Berlin became a veritable Athens-on-the-Spree.'[56]

The war started up again in 1744. For a while it looked as if Frederick's lucky streak was at an end, but with the cavalry charge at Hohenfriedburg, he turned the tables on the Austrians. Around Frederick there grew up the myth that Prussia could produce miraculous victories out of almost certain defeats. It was a myth which appealed greatly to one Austrian, Adolf Hitler; a myth which kept him going for the last desperate months in the Berlin bunker.

Frederick had the considerable advantage of fine generals, men who were wantonly squandered in the campaigns which brought him fame. One of the greatest of these was the *alte-Dessauer* who had entered service with his grandfather. Prince Leopold's prayer for victory before the Battle of Kesseldorf is a masterpiece of Prussian compression: 'Lord God, help me, and if you don't want to, then at least don't help those rogues, our enemies, but watch over us while we fight. Amen. In Jesus' name, *march!*'[57]

The Peace of Dresden in 1745 granted Frederick a decade of peace. Now he became the Philosopher King, indulging the dream he had first had in Neuruppin and Rheinsberg. He surrounded himself with French intellectuals and imported the greatest thinker of the day – Voltaire – to join him in Potsdam. There he had his Versailles in the *Stadtschloss*, but as yet he had no Trianon. He sketched a design for an intimate little palace to crown the vineyard hill and gave the drawing to his friend, the architect Georg Wenzeslaus von Knobelsdorff, to turn into a proper plan. This was Sanssouci, a spring and summer retreat which was too small to accommodate the courtly rigmarole he despised. There was to be room only for his friends and his dogs, and no apartment for the queen.[58]

The king set great store by his coterie of French intellectuals, French painters – Watteaus and Lancrets – and Saxon musicians, but in his heart of hearts he had not been made for human company; not even that of the campaign-hardened generals who surrounded him in the field. 'He was not to be the brute his father was, but he was the coldest of cynics, a bad-tempered menace to everyone around him; loving no one and loved by none; painfully indifferent to his own appearance, unkempt, filthy, always in the same worn-out uniform; at the same time always sage, but embued with a wretched, negative spirit, inwardly profoundly unhappy, but at the same time restless in his activity, always on duty, always at his post, untiring in his detested craft; a great king to the last – but one with a shattered soul.'[59]

In peacetime he busied himself with administration. His attention to detail was phenomenal. Every minute activity was passed
to him for approval; every document covered with his scrawly
marginalia. In 1748 his first body of laws was issued as the *Codex
Fridericanus Marchicus*. While the calm lasted he built ninety
villages in Pomerania and fifty more in the newly drained Oderbruch,* ninety-six in the Electoral or Kur-Mark and forty across
the Oder in the Neumark. Frederick was justly proud of his land
reclamation in the Oderbruch to the north of Frankfurt: 'Here I
have conquered a province *in peacetime*.'[61]

In 1756 the Seven Years War broke out. It might have spelled
the end for the upstart Kingdom of Prussia, for Frederick's
enemies planned to parcel out his lands among the winners, but
Prussian victories at Pirna over the Saxons and Lobositz over the
Austrians soon put a stop to this. The defeat of Saxony laid it
open to Frederick's terrible revenge. There was something patho-
logical about Frederick's hatred of the Saxons. Not even the holy
shrines of Lutheranism in Wittenberg were spared. In his *Political
Testament* of 1752 Frederick made his ambitions towards his
neighbours – Saxony in particular – abundantly clear: 'Of all the
lands of Europe, those which come the most under consideration
are Saxony, Polish [West] Prussia and Swedish [West] Pomerania.
Saxony would be the most useful.'[62]

But for massive cash injections from Britain, Prussia fought the
combined mights of Europe alone. In Bohemia came the first
reverses: the Prussians failed to take Prague and Schwerin died a
heroic death, standard in hand, as he tried to rally the fleeing
troops. Frederick fought back and triumphed with the triple
victory of Rossbach, Leuthen and Zorndorf. At Rossbach, the
'Agincourt of the German people',[63] 20,000 Prussians defeated a
French army two and a half times their number. The king was
delighted when his cavalry rode back to the Prussian lines wearing
the Crosses of St Louis they had taken from the captured French

---

* The inhabitants of the new villages were naturally drawn from other parts of the empire.
In the Oderbruch some of the villages were settled with Slavs from Bohemia and Poland.[60]

officers.[64] In England, Frederick became overnight the hero of the people: portraits of the 'Protestant' king were hung up in drawing rooms, and pubs changed their names to 'The King of Prussia' in his honour.[65] On the battlefield of Leuthen the 'Leuthen Chorale' was heard for the first time, when from among the litter of wounded soldiers came a spontaneous melody accompanied by the words 'Nun danket alle Gott' (Now let us give thanks to God). Even the atheist king was moved to tears and the soldiers sank piously to their knees.

It was Frederick's favourite sister, the Margravine of Bayreuth, who broke the news to Voltaire: 'I can imagine your impatience to learn about things which interest you. A battle has been won and Breslau is in the hands of the King. They have seized 33,000 prisoners [including] 100 officers and fourteen generals as well as 150 cannons and 4,000 baggage carts loaded with food and ammunition, this is the news I can give you. But I haven't finished yet. . . . This battle is unique and seems fantastic: the Austrians had 80,000 men and the Prussians were only 36,000. . . . I will add another anecdote: the corps which the King commanded had travelled 42 German miles* in fifteen days, they had only one day of rest before committing themselves to this memorable battle. The King can say like Caesar: I came, I saw, I conquered.'[66]

Voltaire was probably less impressed than Wilhelmine imagined. Two years later he used his experience of Prussian warmongering to add flesh to *Candide*: 'Nothing was so lovely, so nimble, so brilliant, or so well ordered as the two armies. The trumpets, the fifes, the oboes, the drums and the cannons created a harmony that hell had never known before. First of all the cannons mowed down about six thousand men on both sides; next the musketry removed from the best of all possible worlds about nine or ten thousand rascals who were infecting the surface. The bayonnette was also good enough excuse for the death of several thousand men. The total might well have reached 30,000. Candide, who was trembling like a *philosophe*, hid as best as he could from this

---

* Over three hundred kilometres.

heroic slaughter.' Five years later his experiences allowed him some caustic jibes at Frederick the Great in the article 'War' in his *Dictionnaire philosophique*.[67]

And Frederick had not won the war. The Russians had occupied Königsberg and Frederick's forces were soundly beaten by the army of the Czarina Elizabeth at Kundersdorf near Frankfurt/Oder the following year. The situation for the Prussians was no better than after Jena forty-seven years later.[68] A miserable Frederick watching his armies flee a numerically vastly superior Russian enemy was heard to exclaim, 'Rackers! Wollt ihr denn ewig leben?' (Scoundrels! Do you want to live for ever?)

The Russians did not choose to press their advantage, and once again Frederick lived to fight another battle or two. The victories of Liegnitz and Torgau over the Austrians restored the king's fortunes and he felt strong enough to refuse any attempt to wrest territory from him at the Conference of Augsburg. The real 'miracle of the House of Brandenburg', however, was the death of the Czarina Elizabeth in January 1762 and the accession of the Duke of Holstein-Gottorp as Peter III. It was said that Peter's enthusiasm for Prussia was even greater than his interest in the throne of Russia and he brought the war to an end. He was murdered later that year, but the Stettin-born Czarina Catherine the Great had no desire to take up the cudgels against Prussia. At the Peace of Hubertusburg Frederick retained Silesia at terrible cost.

Although he had but recently turned fifty, the years of campaigning had aged the Prussian king. The brilliance of his earlier court was no more; his friends were mostly dead or gone. There had always been a strong streak of misanthropy in Frederick's character, but now it came to the fore. His regard for humanity had fallen so low that he questioned the need for enlightenment: 'Prejudice is the reason of the people.'[69] He was often alone. 'One is only happy,' he wrote, 'when one is busy. I have lost nearly all my friends and those I knew of old and I find consolation only in work and study. One must learn to be self-sufficient and to be able to dispense with society. It is a hard thing to say, but otherwise my life wouldn't be bearable.'[70]

There was no question of relaxing. Frederick wrote countless books as well as overseeing the construction of his vast Neues Palais at Sanssouci to the designs of the new court architect, Karl von Gontard. In 1764 he reorganised the Berlin garrison, removing them from their scattered billets and putting them into barracks around their own *Garnisonkirche*. The army now totalled 187,000 men, only 60 per cent of whom were Prussians. In the long wars 200,000 men and 4,000 officers had been lost, cutting a swathe through the old nobles whom Frederick loved.

Prussia was once again restocked from the cluttered west of Germany. The settlements attracted some 57,475 families, or about 300,000 people. By the time the king died in 1786, one in five Prussians had moved to the area in the previous thirty years. Frederick was once again proud of his achievement, which he described as 'the victory of diligence over ignorance and laziness'.[71] These new settlements were not the only parts of Prussia which provided scope for the western colonists: in 1772 Frederick had mooted the idea of carving up Poland between Prussia, Russia and Austria in order to prevent war breaking out between the Russians and the Turks. His own interest lay in Polish West Prussia, a tract of land which formed a corridor between Prussian Pomerania and Prussian East Prussia.

The region's population was a little over half German, with the rest made up of Poles and Cassubians.[72] Like the king's Silesian subjects, the majority of these new Prussians were Catholics. With West Prussia, Frederick also acquired a slice of Poland to the north of the Netze River, bordering on Pomerania, but he was for the time being unable to wrest either Danzig or the old *Ordensburg* of Thorn from the Poles. The fine lines of the border were not finally worked out until 1777. In the meantime Frederick had a simple, half-timbered, thatched house built at Mockrau, near that other former *Ordensburg*, Graudenz. In a style which was to become typical of the Prussians in evaluating the disorder caused by Polish rule, a report was drawn up on Frederick's new territory in West Prussia: 'The old fortified towns, called castles, lay in ruins and rubble, just like most of the smaller towns and villages. Most existing buildings seemed scarcely suitable as shelter for human beings . . .'[73]

In 1778, the sixty-six-year-old king left on his last campaign. The young Austrian emperor, Joseph II, 'in order to reduce [the people] to despotism, transformed Bavaria into a corridor to get at Alsace and Lorraine. At the same time he cut into Lombardy . . .'[74] Joseph's ambitions had been awakened by the death of the last Wittelsbach of the Bavarian line. Prussia's action in riding to the defence of Bavaria may possibly have prevented that territory from falling into Habsburg hands. In the end Joseph had to content himself with a small strip on the right bank of the river Inn, including the town of Braunau, where Hitler was born a little over a century later. As a reward, Frederick received acknowledgement of his claims to the old Hohenzollern territories of Ansbach and Bayreuth.

Frederick the Great died in 1786, 'the last of Seneca's disciples upon the Hohenzollern throne'.[75] He was succeeded by his nephew, Frederick William II. Frederick William was certainly no stoic, but history has judged his achievements less than fairly: it would be hard to argue that the decades following Frederick's death were not also part of Prussia's golden age. Not only did Frederick William's reign see a considerable flowering of the arts in Prussia, but its territory expanded beyond the wildest dreams of the colonists.

The myth of 'Fat William's' failure as a Prussian monarch dates back to Treitschke's lectures at the University of Berlin at the end of the last century. Treitschke believed firmly in Prussia's German mission, by which he meant that Prussia's primary duty was to unify Germany; it had no business expanding to the east. At the time, however, Frederick William was seen as a breath of fresh air after the last years of his misanthropic uncle's reign. Mirabeau, who was in Berlin at the time of the old king's death, reported that 'two-thirds of the Berliners are making the greatest effort today to prove that Frederick II was just an ordinary man, almost inferior to the general rule.'[76]

What with his affection for Rosicrucianism and his philandering, Frederick William certainly gave the Berliners something to gossip about. The Prussians had grown used to Frederick the Great's sexual abnegation and the stories of Frederick William's long-standing relationship with the trumpeter's daughter, Wilhelmine Enke (whom he later ennobled as Gräfin Lichtenau), were a source of constant merriment. The fact that Frederick William was not cut out to be a warlord was of greater concern: 'The profession [of arms] bores him; the details tire him, he finds the generals tedious; he goes to Potsdam, watches the parade, issues orders, lunches and leaves. On Wednesday he went to the parade ground in Berlin, he gave the order to drill the troops and left. One sees this sort of thing occur on the same field where Frederick II, great in years and glory, regularly drilled the men for two hours at a stretch, even in the depths of winter; mixing fury, criticism and praise all at once to keep the soldiers perpetually on the move. The troops were tormented, but none the less overjoyed to see the "old man" at their head, for that's what they called him.'[77]

Frederick William was more inclined towards the arts. Rather than the flute favoured by his uncle, the new king played the cello. In the spring of 1789 Mozart was invited to Potsdam and 'showered with gifts', while the king commissioned six 'Prussian' string quartets from him. Mozart completed only three of the set, but they are among the best of his late quartets. A special feature of all three is the cello part, written to give the king every opportunity to shine in performance.[78]

Nor was Frederick William any less notable for his patronage of the visual arts: it was he who brought the Silesian architect Carl Gotthard Langhans the Elder to Berlin to build the Brandenburg Gate and had it crowned with the great quadriga designed by the sculptor Johann Gottfried Schadow. A later Prussian painter was to enthuse, 'You'd have to go to Rome to see a triumphal arch to compare with it.'[79]

The *Allgemeine Preussische Landrecht* of 1794 was an even greater achievement, although it should be added that the code was commissioned by Frederick the Great and designed to his specifications. It was 'a civil code, a criminal code and a charter all in one', according to Alexis de Tocqueville,[80] containing elements of state socialism which were to form the basis of the much vaunted Prussian *Rechtstaat*. It proved durable enough: in 1945, Fabian von Schlabrendorff was able to have himself acquitted before the terrible People's Court on proving that the torture he had received at the hands of the Gestapo was contrary to the Prussian *Gesetzbuch*[81], and elements of the code are still to be found in the *Grundgesetz* which forms the foundations of the *Bundesrepublik*.[82]

It was this 'rule of law' which allowed Frederick William's Minister Graf von Hertzberg to deliver an adulatory speech before the Academy of Sciences on 1 October 1789, in which he postulated 'that the Prussian monarchy, although her excellence is chiefly the result of her power in war and her unlimited prowess, is far gentler, more lawful and moderate than most republics or constitutional monarchies.'[83]

Nor was Frederick William's foreign policy without its triumphs. In 1790 Prussia signed the Convention of Reichenbach, drawing her into an alliance with Austria which was to last half a century. In 1792 this alliance led the Prussians to war with the French, though whatever ambitions the king might have had in the west were checked when his army was routed at Valmy on 20 September 1792. Meanwhile Catherine the Great had chosen her moment to pursue Russian territorial ambitions in Poland, as a result of which Prussia received not only the coveted cities of Danzig and Thorn, but also the whole area to the south of the Netze: 2,716 square kilometres and well over a million souls. Part of the new population was of German origin, like the majority of the Danzigers, but that did not necessarily endear them to their new Prussian rulers. In Danzig the militia put up a brief fight and Anna Schopenhauer, the philosopher's mother, committed to her diary 'This morning disaster fell upon my poor town like a vampire . . .'[84]

Two years later an uprising under Kosciuszko gave the pretext for the final elimination of the Polish state. For the next twelve years Prussia's population would be 40 per cent Polish.

That same year of 1795 Prussia settled her dispute with France at the Peace of Basle. The neutrality of west Germany was to be guaranteed and Prussia withdrew from the fight against the French Republic. Two years later Frederick William died; the state was at peace and far, far larger than it had ever been. As Sebastian Haffner has written, 'Whoever marvelled at the first eight years of Frederick the Great's reign – and that takes in at one glance the entire Prussian historical establishment of the 19th and 20th centuries – can not, as these writers almost unanimously do, brand the policy of Frederick William II as a mistake, and as the beginning of the end.'[85]

V

Frederick William II lacked the warlike vigour of his uncle, but he nonetheless left a plump and healthy state to his son and successor, Frederick William III. Under this king, Prussia (as it was officially known only from 1807) was to undergo its greatest humiliation: defeat and occupation; it was shrunken in size and crippled by debts it could never hope to pay.

If Frederick William III is less of a figure of fun than his father, this is to some extent the result of the popularity of his wife, Louise of Mecklenburg-Strelitz. Queen Louise captured the imaginations of generations of Prussians and Germans and, even today, commands a public that no other female figure in the history of Prussia has ever enjoyed. Frederick William III's life was also characterised by a strong family instinct and by a fidelity to his wife which stood in strong contrast to the rather more lax behaviour of his father. Moreover, the fact that his queen died while still a young and attractive woman has added a human dimension to his reign which has distracted attention from his disastrous leadership.

Frederick William was a rather middle-class monarch, morally upright, sober-minded and thrifty.[86] One of his first decisions was to reject the vast, draughty *Stadtschloss* in favour of the rather more cosy *Kronprinzenpalais* on Unter den Linden. In his foreign policy he was keen to create a Prussian protectorate in British Hanover, something which contributed to his undoing. As far as the army was concerned he was virtually a pacifist: 'The greatest fortune of a country consists in long-lasting peace; the best policy is that which constantly bears this principle in mind and leaves our neighbours in peace. One should not get mixed up in foreign affairs ... in order to avoid being dragged into other people's quarrels. So one shuns alliances that sooner or later will develop into something of the sort.'[87]

Frederick the Great had seen Hanover as a tempting acquisition for a future Prussian state. In his first *Political Testament* of 1752 he laid plans for invading the territory at such time as the British were bound up in a conflict elsewhere.[88] But in 1803 it was not the Prussians but the French who violated Hanover and, worse, occupied the Prussian enclave of Ansbach.

In 1804 Napoleon Bonaparte crowned himself Emperor of the French, giving the Austrian sovereign, Francis II, leave to take a similar title for himself in his Habsburg lands. Frederick William was offered the chance to upgrade himself to an emperor too, but was unswayed.

Nevertheless, it was inevitable that sooner or later a conflict was going to arise with the French. In 1805 the Czar Alexander visited Frederick William in Berlin. There ensued an alliance between their two countries, sealed by a 'theatrical scene when the two swore eternal friendship'[89] over the tomb of Frederick the Great in Potsdam's *Garnisonkirche*. It was the year of Austria's crushing defeat at the Battle of Austerlitz. In the ensuing territorial shake-up, Prussia finally won control of the Electorate of Hanover. Frederick William walked straight into the trap he himself had described in his *Gedanken über die Regierungskunst*: the British promptly declared war on Prussia, confiscating its shipping on the high seas and leading Prussia into a period of economic stagnation.

Three months later, Prussia was at war with France, too, and could not look to Britain for support.

Frederick William had been duped by the wily Corsican. On 6 August 1806, he demanded that French forces be withdrawn from his frontiers and some of his Rhineland provinces returned. Napoleon refused. In Prussia itself tension mounted. Arrogant young noblemen sharpened their swords on the steps of the French Embassy in Berlin. The army was mobilised. Napoleon called for the orders to be rescinded. Frederick William refused. Prussia went into the war on its own.

On 10 October the advance units of the Prussian army were defeated at Saalfeld on the Saale and the 'Prussian Alcibiades', Prince Louis Ferdinand, was killed. Four days later came the battles of Auerstedt and Jena. At Jena the Prussian force faced a French army three times its size; at Auerstedt, slightly smaller than itself. Both were resounding defeats. The Prussians were pushed into unfavourable positions from the first; their tactics were out of date. It was a fitting revenge for Rossbach.

On 27 October, Napoleon entered Berlin. The public proved enthusiastic. While the king of Prussia fled across the Oder to Königsberg to continue the war, the emperor of the French took a day trip to Potsdam. It was his turn to visit the tomb of Frederick the Great in the *Garnisonkirche*: 'Gentlemen, if this man were still alive,' he told his entourage, 'we wouldn't be here.'[90] He then set about dismembering Prussia to the profit of her neighbours.

'The Frederican state went under with the catastrophe of 1806. What rose from Prussia's ashes after seven years of misery, foreign occupation and oppression as the new state, had little more in common with its predecessor than its name.'[91] It was the moment for reformers who had been waiting in the wings to make their strike. The two principal reformers were both *Wahlpreussen*: Freiherr Karl von und zum Stein and Karl August von Hardenberg. Both were products of the liberal, Hanoverian University of Göttingen and both had imbibed the advanced cameralist ideas of their tutor, Johann Stephan Putter or the notions of state-directed political economics fashionable in Germany in the age of Adam Smith.[92] Stein had joined the elite Prussian civil service in 1780; Hardenberg in 1791.

Stein was from Nassau, but Hardenberg was a Hanoverian, as was the military reformer, Scharnhorst. Scharnhorst's successor as Chief of the General Staff, Gneisenau, was an Austrian. Only the minor reformers who reshaped Prussia after Jena were actually Prussians: Humboldt, Schön and Boyen. In the years leading up to Waterloo, these men put through a body of reforms which reshaped the ailing state. The first steps were made to liberate the peasants from serfdom; self-administration was granted to the cities; sections of the officer corps were opened up to the middle classes; nobles and bourgeois were accorded equal rights in the ownership of land; Jews were granted rights for the first time; there was freedom of association; and the army was shaken up from top to bottom. Many of Stein's ideas were inspired by the French physiocrats and the teachings of Adam Smith. Others were of local provenance as the reformers had passed through the hands of Immanuel Kant at the University of Königsberg; their attitude to state service was steeped in the categorical imperative of duty.

Stein and Hardenberg's reforms were by no means universally popular. Many members of the old nobility reacted strongly to what they saw as an infringement of their ancient rights. The leader of the reactionaries was the voluble Friedrich Ludwig von der Marwitz, who was wont to dismiss Stein as a meddling foreigner: 'Stein has begun to revolutionize the fatherland, the have-nots are at war with the landowners, industry is against agriculture, the ambitious against those for order.'[93] Marwitz wanted a reform of the nobility to weed out those who refused to accept the responsibilities of their caste, and who embraced middle-class ideas. By 1810 Marwitz had made such a nuisance of himself that Hardenberg had him locked up. Like most of the Prussian reactionaries, however, he found his vocation three years later when he was able to lead his peasantry into war.

Money was the chief problem besetting the Prussians after the crippling 1807 Treaty of Tilsit. The French demands could not possibly be met. Even after Hardenberg had resorted to the time-honoured trick of robbing the churches of their lands he still didn't have enough. In 1810 the French demanded that Prussia hand over Silesia in compensation.

Nor was the situation any better for the king's subjects. The French bled the land white. Friedrich Leopold von Hertefeld's letters to his daughter present a catalogue of French plunder, robbery and rapine; a torture made all the worse by the fact that it continued from 1806 to 1812 without a break. Lower down the social scale, the future Pastor Carl Gottlieb Rehsener watched the slaughter of his family's livestock while the horses were rounded up for the army's use.* Nor did the French stop at robbing the natives: the memories of the atrocities committed in the east were still vivid in the minds of the East Prussians a hundred years later;[95] Bismarck liked to excuse his hard-heartedness towards the French in 1870–1871 by reminding Jules Favre, 'Our trees still bear the marks where your generals hanged our people on them.'[96]

Certain Prussians began to take the law into their own hands. In 1809, Major Ferdinand von Schill of the 2nd Brandenburg Hussars led his men out of garrison and turned them into the first ever *Freikorps* after the model of the Spanish partisans who were so successful against Napoleon in Spain. Schill was eventually tracked down and killed in Pomerania, but his example proved an encouragement to other young Prussians such as Freiherr Adolf von Lützow.[97] In Berlin, the poet Heinrich von Kleist found a new vocation in his veiled attacks on the occupying forces through the press.

The king was at his lowest ebb. A memorandum written in April 1809 shows that he had lost the confidence of his ministers and considered abdication: 'I am ready and have decided to hand

---

* The French had no apparent affection for Pomeranian cooking. Offered goose-dripping and dumplings rather than their more usual white bread and broth, they threw them out of the window. Frau Rehsener, already at a loss as to how to feed her family, was not amused: 'Oh the sin of it!'[94]

over the reins of power to whomsoever the Nation deems or recognises as more worthy ... The only thing I would keep for myself in these circumstances would be the possibility of living an independent and untroubled life as a private citizen in my own land ...'[98]

Fortunately for Frederick William, a rift emerged between the Czar and the French Emperor which altered the face of the war. Napoleon demanded that Prussia form an alliance with him to help him fight the Russians. This was signed on 24 February 1812, but Frederick William also sent Scharnhorst to negotiate with the Czar; a secret military convention was the result.

Under the terms of their alliance, Prussia had to provide the French with an army corps to fight in Russia. This force was eventually entrusted to General Johann David von Yorck, a true-blue Prussian reactionary with little time for reformers and even less for Frenchmen. In the meantime both Scharnhorst and Gneisenau had resigned from the Prussian army and together with Boyen and the young Colonel von Clausewitz had joined the Russian army in St Petersburg. A German legion was formed and plans were laid to win Yorck over to their side.

Yorck's army was stationed just to the north of the Memel at Tauroggen. At Christmas that year, he agreed to meet the German General Diebitsch who was fighting for the Russians and who had broken through to Yorck's rear. Yorck was suspicious of Diebitsch and even more so of the General's adjutant, Clausewitz. At issue was the old Prussian virtue of obedience and Yorck's suspicion was only slightly allayed when Graf Dohna, an East Prussian nobleman, brought him word from the Czar that he was prepared to fight until Prussia was restored to its position among the powers. Yorck resumed negotiations with Diebitsch, but kept the king abreast of everything. When Clausewitz drew up the Convention of Tauroggen pledging Yorck's corps to assist the Russian army, Yorck sent a Major von Seydlitz to Berlin to obtain the king's consent. Frederick's reply was ambiguous: act 'according to circumstances', he told Yorck.

Yorck wavered: 'Gentleman, I do not know what I shall say to the king about my action. Perhaps he will call it treason. Then I shall carry the consequences. I shall put my grey head willingly at the disposal of His Majesty and die gladly, knowing that I have not failed as a faithful subject and a true Prussian.'[99] As it turned out, the king got cold feet and published Yorck's recall in an official organ; Yorck, however, refused to heed the announcement: 'Up to now no general has ever received his orders via the newspapers,' he said. He was never quite sure that he had done the right thing by disobeying orders on this occasion. Later he refused an honour urged on him by a now grateful sovereign: 'I must fear, having my anxieties raised by events in the past, that on future occasions of state I may act against my own convictions, and therefore in one way or other make a mistake at the decisive moment.'[100]

Yorck's crisis of conscience is significant: it was the old Prussian conflict between obedience and duty. Both Yorck's decision to defy his king, and the Convention of Tauroggen, set important precedents which were not to be forgotten in the darkest days of the Second World War.

Prussia's German mission was beginning to emerge and increasingly the word 'Prussian' was being replaced by 'German'. This was the case with Dohna and Clausewitz's Committee for *German* Affairs. The surging tide of nationalism began to affect the king himself. Swept along by the waves he called for all citizens to take up arms against the French on 3 February 1813. On 10 March he founded the order of the Iron Cross: a starkly simple Maltese cross made in the state's iron foundries. The Iron Cross joined his great-uncle's *Pour le mérite** as the highest Prussian, and later German, military honour until Hitler and the Third Reich replaced it by a system of Byzantine complexity.

The national cause had a strong effect on the schoolboys and students of Prussia, who flocked to the colours. Joined by the Swedes and the Austrians, the Russian and Prussian armies

---

* The *Pour le mérite* had been a civil decoration, which Frederick the Great converted to military use. After 1945 it reverted to its civil vocation.

engaged the French decisively at the Battle of the Nations at Leipzig from 16 to 19 October. It was a crushing defeat for the French leader. By New Year's Day 1814, the Prussian army had crossed the Rhine. On 31 March Field Marshal Blücher entered Paris. On 6 April Napoleon abdicated.

The prestige Prussia gained in that campaign had been some-what tempered by the time the powers settled down to discuss peace terms in Vienna in October. Even France appeared to merit more respect than Prussia. Russia was angling for total control of Poland, in which case Prussia hoped for compensation in the form of Saxony. The Russians were not opposed to this, but the Austrians were. They had bitter memories of the Seven Years War and drew the line at having Prussians as their neighbours right along the Bohemian border. The issue had not been satisfactorily resolved when in March 1815 Napoleon escaped from Elba. The Hundred Days of his new empire was brought to an end by the Prusso-British victory of Waterloo, or Belle-Alliance as it is known in Germany.

With Napoleon defeated and exiled to St Helena, the confer-ence reconvened. Despite their role in the final elimination of the Corsican, neither Britain nor Prussia gained the most from the talks. Britain maintained a lofty detachment while a new role was carved out for Prussia as the guardian of its neighbouring German statelets: 'The wild horse was tamed and harnessed.'[101] To enable it to carry out its duties Prussia was granted a strip of the Rhineland consisting of 150 small territories which had formerly been the property of the princelings of the Church. The popula-tion was overwhelmingly Catholic and Cologne was Germany's metropolitan see. To pander to Prussia's ancient longings, the king was given a big piece of northern Saxony, including Luther's Wittenberg and the lower Lausitz, to round off his possessions on the Neisse. Otherwise Frederick William was compensated with the last piece of the Pomeranian jigsaw: Swedish Pomerania, to the west of the Peene, with the cities of Stralsund and Greifswald. In Poland Prussia maintained Danzig, although it lost most of the lands won through the Third Partition in 1795. In terms of purely

Polish territories Prussia now administered Great Poland, or the 'Grand Duchy of Posen', with the cities of Posen, Gnesen and Lissa.

Prussia and Austria were to keep the peace in Germany, but Prussia was very much the junior partner. On 8 June 1815 the old Holy Roman Empire was replaced by a German confederation composed of just thirty-seven independent states ruled by the most important German princes, as well as four city states.

It was a new, peaceful, *arriviste* Prussia which joined the ranks of the great nations in 1815;[102] a moral example to the other states of Germany. There were ten, later eight, provinces under the control of an *Oberpräsident*, covering a surface area of 278,000 square kilometres. Here lived 10.4 million Prussians. The provincial presidents also played their part in the *Staatsrat*, or council of state, along with the royal princes, commanding generals and thirty-four royal nominees. In 1823 regional diets were created with limited debating powers, but in their political impotence they were a long way from the idealistic conception of Hardenberg, who had envisaged a modicum of democracy creeping into the Prussian body politic. Earlier the king had merged the two Protestant churches under his own headship to form a single state church on the Anglican model. Bishops came later. It was inevitable that the institution of an official church should erode the Prussian principle of religious tolerance. Almost at once the state came down hard on the Catholic bishops in the Rhineland. In the east, in particular in Pomerania, the first half of the century saw the development of a Prussian form of religious fundamentalism: Pietism.

On the economic side the new customs union or *Zollverein* encouraged the economic development of Prussia within Germany. Society was far from free: the police poked their noses into every aspect of life, but this failed to inhibit a second flowering of the arts in Prussia, and one which was to produce its loveliest blossoms under Frederick William IV. Hegel and Schelling made their homes in Prussia and, in terms of home-grown talent, the post-Belle-Alliance period saw the emergence of La Motte Fouqué, Arnim, Brentano, Chamisso, E. T. A. Hoffmann, Schinkel, Rauch, Mendelssohn, Savigny and Ranke. Prussia's warlike persona receded: 'When in 1864 it was decided that a victory salute should be fired to celebrate the storming of the [Danish] trenches at Düppel, no one could be found who could tell them the right number of volleys to discharge in the circumstances.'[103]

Frederick William IV, who succeeded in 1840, was a monarch of rare intelligence and sensitivity. His education had been conservative and carefully planned and he had learned much from the estatist thinkers and politicians Ancillon, Haller, Bonald, de Maistre, Schelling and Schleiermacher. His political views had been further shaped by Stahl and Ernst Ludwig von Gerlach.[104] His chief passion was for art and architecture. Like Frederick the Great he dabbled in design and his sketches show him to have been a competent draughtsman. Even before his reign the architects Schinkel, Persius, Stüler and von Arnim never lacked for patronage, nor did the landscape gardener Peter Lenné. It was Frederick William IV who made Potsdam what it was before 1945. His achievement was infinitely greater than that of Ludwig II of Bavaria.

His conception of statecraft was also artistic, even to a fault. He was a romantic who desired keenly to be loved by his subjects and wanted to look after their needs, but his romanticism also inclined him towards the rather un-Prussian doctrine of divine right. His admiration for all things medieval also made him reluctant to break with the idea of Germany as a federation of princes held in check by Vienna. Although he started his reign by restoring Arndt to his chair at the University of Bonn and by lifting the police tail of the bigoted nationalist gymnast 'Turnvater' Jahn, his rule was characterised by the rigid censorship imposed by his *Kultusminister* Johann Eichhorn. In the café society of Berlin in the 1840s Eichhorn was believed to be omnipresent: hence Friedrich Engels' famous sketch of a violent argument between the Berlin intellectual côterie, *die Freien* ('the Free'), shows a squirrel* in the top

---

* Das *Eichhörn*chen in German.

left-hand corner of the picture.[105] Heinrich Heine mocked this mixture of progressiveness and reaction. In 1844 he described the king as a 'foolish blend of the extremes of his age'.

It was not always easy for Frederick William to communicate his theocratic, paternal brand of kingship, although it was a notably mild period in the administration of the Grand Duchy of Posen. In Silesia in 1844 the revolt of some Luddite weavers against their employers had to be put down with some severity. The weavers themselves became the heroes of the Prussian Socialist movement even though their protest only highlighted their pre-industrial working conditions.*

Frederick William appears to have grudgingly accepted the need to see Prussia equipped with a constitution and national assembly, even if it was to be disproportionately balanced in favour of the princes and noble estate owners. The United Diet of 1847 was composed of 237 noblemen, 182 representatives of the towns and just 124 property-owning peasants. As a further check to the democratic aspirations of the people, a *Herrenhaus*, or house of lords, crowned the edifice, with seventy princes and counts providing the members. The United Diet proved an insufficient palliative to the Prussians. This became abundantly clear in March the following year when Frederick William's theocratic state succumbed to the tide of revolutions which rolled over Europe.

The novelist Theodor Fontane was one of those who took to the streets: 'It all began to seethe after February, in Berlin too. One had had enough of the old society. Not that we had suffered, no, that wasn't it; we were ashamed of it. Seen from a political perspective everything was antiquated in our country and that made us keen to obtain ever more unrealistic things. All this was dressed up in a sort of halo and wrapped in the proviso of "wanting to serve true freedom and sound progress". Another reference to the "traditional land of wisdom and historical continuity". This ignored just one small point: in England there had

---

* In 1892 the playwright Gerhart Hauptmann had a great success with his dramatisation of the weavers' revolt: *Die Weber*. The play inspired Käthe Kollwitz's dramatic series of etchings entitled *Ein Weberaufstand*: a weavers' revolt.[106]

always been freedom, in Prussia, never; England was given form in the time of Magna Carta, Prussia in the period of full-blooded absolutism, the epoch of Louis XIV, Charles XII [of Sweden] and Peter the Great.'[107]

The March days caused Frederick William considerable grief. The pent-up frustrations of the people were unleashed on the army and its almost wholly noble officer corps. The king, who liked the idea of a united Germany in the form of a strong federation of princes, was persuaded by his minister, Heinrich von Arnim, to issue a promise of German unity. The words the king uttered on that occasion, 'Henceforth Prussia merges into Germany', were written by Arnim.[108]

This was a powerful statement as far as the men in the Frankfurt Paulskirche were concerned. They had come from all over Germany in order to draw up the blueprints for a German nation. All eyes were on Prussia, the one German state capable of welding together the sort of Germany they hoped for. Austria was not in the running as the majority of its citizens were not of German stock. When Danish troops occupied the duchy of Schleswig, the Paulskirche liberals asked the King of Prussia to intervene. Frederick William sent in his army under General von Wrangel, but Europe's major powers threatened to come in on the Danish side, and Prussia suffered a humiliating blow to its self-esteem.

In the course of these trials, Frederick William succeeded in introducing his notorious Prussian constitution with its three-band voting system, an indirect franchise based on three separate tax brackets. Each bracket chose the same number of 'electors' who in turn elected their deputies. The system was contrived to ensure that it required fewer rich landowners to elect a deputy than poor peasants. It nonetheless remained intact until the First World War. It was perhaps ironic that this strangely weighted parliament should find a home in the old Palais Hardenberg.[109]

In the Frankfurt Paulskirche, the deputies were running out of steam. Having decided the shape of Germany in March 1849, in May they offered the crown to Frederick William; but the king's concept of divine right was so ingrained that he decided that it was not theirs to grant. Without the consent of the princes he could do nothing. A majority of Germany's crowned heads were in favour; Austria, naturally, was not. Nor, with the exception of Württemberg, would the kings accept the draft constitution. New uprisings in Saxony, the Palatinate and Baden made it look as if the nightmare of revolution was about to start all over again. The rulers of all three lands asked the Prussians for help. In Baden in particular, the army suppressed these last flickerings of 1848 with memorable brutality.

But Frederick William had not lost his taste for Germany. In May his minister Joseph von Radowitz drew up the sketch for a treaty aimed to create a federal state. The princes of twenty-eight states pledged their support, but the Catholic kings of Bavaria and Württemberg held aloof. Radowitz prepared a constitution, too. The following year a parliamentary session was organised in Erfurt in Prussian Thuringia where delegations were invited to work on different aspects of the new constitution. By now things had gone quite far enough for the Austrian Minister-President, Fürst zu Schwarzenberg, who summoned a meeting of the German diet under an Austrian presidency. Twenty-two member states boycotted the Austrian call.

Schwarzenberg's action initiated a struggle for supremacy between Prussia and Austria. Prussia mobilised its army; Austria responded by demanding a dissolution of the Erfurt conference and the demobilisation of the Prussian army. Within the Prussian hierarchy both Radowitz and Prince William were in favour of pushing the Austrians to the limit, even if that meant war; but Frederick William took other advice. On 29 November 1850, Schwarzenberg and the new Prussian Minister-President, Otto von Manteuffel, signed the Olmütz Punctuation. Prussia agreed to demobilise. It was the end of their bid for supremacy. 'Austria had returned [from suppressing its own revolutions] like a wrathful Odysseus, found its German house occupied by Prussia and decided to clear the interloper out without further ado.'[110]

It was the 'Jena of 1850'.[111] Eight months later Otto von

Bismarck was appointed Prussia's Ambassador to the Federal Diet
and policy towards Austria underwent a fundamental change.

VI

Wag's um den letzten Preis zu werben
Und mit der Zeit, dem Volk zu geh'n:
König von Preussen, Du musst sterben,
Als deutscher Kaiser auferstehen.

(Boldly may he grasp the final prize
The time has come, the people roar.
A German Emperor must now arise
The King of Prussia is no more.)[112]

Franz von Dingelstedt, 1866

Frederick William IV suffered a stroke in 1857 and died three
and a half years later in January 1861. His last years were marked
by periodic bouts of insanity and in October 1858 his brother,
Prince William, took over as regent. Attempts were made under
William's grandson, William II, to have the first Hohenzollern
Kaiser dubbed 'the Great' after the model of Frederick II, but the
epithet never stuck. If anything William I was the second *Soldaten-
könig*, never out of uniform, living and dying a soldier. In his
Nüchternheit, William was every inch a Prussian, living a spartan
life which differed in virtually all things from that of his grandson
and adulator, William II.

It was his soldierly reputation which made him unpopular at
first: the Berliners dubbed him 'der Kartätschenprinz', or 'the
Prince of Bullets' after it was alleged that he had ordered shots to
be fired into the crowd in March 1848. He was in favour of
German unification from the first, and regretted his brother's
conduct at Olmütz, having been prepared to fight it out with
Austria. He believed 'whoever wants to govern Germany must
conquer it first . . .'[113]

It is not the place here to examine the constitutional crisis in
Prussia which led first to the appointment of Otto von Bismarck-

Schönhausen as Prussian Minister-President and ultimately to German unification. It is sufficient to say that the king and his *Landtag* were at loggerheads over financing army reform, for which the latter were refusing to vote funds. William threatened to abdicate in favour of his son, Crown Prince Frederick, and finally, on 17 September 1862, Bismarck was appointed to sort out the mess.

Bismarck played up the role of the Junker, the feudal knight coming to the aid of his king: he told him 'that he felt like a vassal from Electoral Brandenburg who sees his liege lord in danger and is ready as a loyal royalist to put all thoughts of his own away and to pursue the fight against the deputies "come hell or high water".'[114] Almost as soon as he had accepted office he set about making friends who would later become useful as he welded together his Prussian-led, unified Germany. A revolt had flared up in Russian Poland and Bismarck obligingly closed the frontiers to prevent the Polish revolutionaries from making their escape into Germany. Later Bismarck could count on the Czar owing him a favour.

It was not long before the Danish succession gave him an even greater chance to test his skills in foreign policy. King Frederick VII of Denmark had annexed Schleswig and imposed a new constitution on Holstein. This had brought about strong protests from the Frankfurt Diet, where the German population of the Baltic duchies had become something of a *cause célèbre*. Frederick VII died childless and he was succeeded by King Christian IX of the Glücksburg line. As King Christian's acquisition of the duchies had not been agreed at the London conference, a rival claim to the duchies was advanced by Prince Frederick of Augustenburg, one no more agreeable to Prussian interests than that posed by the Danes.

It was agreed that a joint Austrian/Prussian army should be sent to drive out the Danes. The Austrians sought to restore the idea of a 'personal union' between the duchies and the Danish crown, but Bismarck was in favour of downright acquisition and managed to bring William round to his point of view. Working in tandem with the Austrians made it unlikely that a European coalition would act against them as they had threatened to do in 1848 or indeed that the acquisitive Napoleon III would make any attempt to seize the left bank of the Rhine.

On 16 January 1864, Christian agreed to revoke the new laws. On 1 February the Austro-Prussian armies entered Schleswig. On 18 April the Prussians won a resounding victory over the Danes at Düppel in northern Schleswig and the Danish army withdrew from the disputed territory. With the Peace Treaty signed in Vienna on 30 October, the Prussians and the Austrians took joint possession of Schleswig-Holstein and the Duchy of Lauenburg. The condominium was to prove a tinderbox which would force the issue of who was in charge within the Reich. Already, in August 1863, Bismarck had prevented William from attending a meeting of the German Princes under an Austrian presidency in Frankfurt. The idea had been to underline how unification might take place under the Austrian scheme of things. With William absent the conference never took off.

After the peace with Denmark there were plenty of opportunities for the victors to fall out over Schleswig-Holstein. In negotiations the Austrians tried to win back the county of Glatz in Silesia which they had lost to Frederick the Great. In return the Prussians would be given the duchies of Schleswig and Holstein. When this solution did not appeal to the Prussians the Austrians began to agitate for the Augustenburg claim. Under the terms of the Convention of Gastein it was finally agreed that Prussia would get Schleswig and Austria Holstein.

Meantime Bismarck was squaring foreign governments in the event of a war breaking out between the two German superpowers. In 9 April 1866 he made an astonishing call in the Frankfurt Diet for a German franchise based on universal male suffrage, a demand guaranteed to win him support from the middle-class liberals. At the same time the Italians began to arm, creating a diversion which would result in their taking control of Austrian Venezia, the penultimate fragment of Italy still lying outside the unified state. Austria mobilised her armies, as ultimately did

Prussia after Bismarck had assured William that the Habsburgs were interested only in settling their claims by war.

Germany gathered into armed camps with Saxony, Württemberg and Bavaria preparing to enter the war on the Austrian side. Napoleon III, anxious to appear to be promoting Italian nationalism, demanded that Venezia be given first to him before being handed over to the Italians. The immediate spark, however, was provided by the Austrian breach of the Convention of Gastein, when they demanded that the Schleswig-Holstein issue be submitted to the Diet for arbitration. At this point General Manteuffel moved into Holstein, sweeping the Austrian armies before him. Diplomatic relations were severed on 12 June, Bismarck making it clear that every vote for Austria in the Diet would be interpreted as a declaration of war. Despite this Saxony, Hanover, Bavaria, Württemberg, Electoral Hesse, Nassau, Frankfurt and Meiningen all sided with the Austrians. Of the south German states only Baden came out for Prussia.

It was the last German *Brüderkrieg*, and as such it has left deep scars.[115] On 29 June, the Battle of Langensalza was fought near Erfurt in Thuringia. Here the ancient rivalry between the Welfs and the Hohenzollerns was ended when the Hanoverian army surrendered. The Prussians handled their defeated neighbours with scant tact: although the Hanoverian princes were able to escape to safety, the new rulers behaved in a lordly manner, going so far as to set up a war memorial in the Hanoverian *Residenzstadt* of Celle.

A skirmish at Gitschin sent the Austrian army back to positions in Königgrätz in Bohemia, where the decisive battle of the war was fought on 2 July. Each side mustered an army of 220,000 men. The Prussian soldiers carried the day at a cost of some 10,000. The Austrians lost 44,000. By 18 July, the Prussian armies were at Nikolsburg in Moravia, only nineteen kilometres from Vienna. Bismarck was aware that the Prussian communications were stretched and his armies wracked by disease. With the generals he had to fight off territorial claims which found their echo in the Prussian royal family, who envisaged the return of

Ansbach and Bayreuth as well as the cession of parts of Bohemia and the whole of the hated Kingdom of Saxony. William was particularly insistent about Saxony, and it took all the eloquence of Bismarck and the Crown Prince to prevent him from taking his full revenge on the Wettins for siding with Austria, once again.

At the Peace of Vienna in August, Germany formed into two power blocks north and south of the Main. Prussia won Schleswig-Holstein, Hanover, Electoral Hesse, Nassau and some other Hessian territories as well as the city of Frankfurt/Main. In Frankfurt Prussian soldiers behaved with particular severity, threatening to turn the city over to plunder if the war indemnity was not met at once. The mayor committed suicide as a result. A formal peace followed in Prague in February 1867 when the North German Confederation was formed. Prussia with its new territories formed a solid landmass with twenty-four million inhabitants. To this were added another twenty-two small states with a total population of just six million. One liberal deputy compared the situation to 'a dog living with its fleas'.[116] Prussia also controlled seventeen out of forty-three votes in the new Bundesrat as well as the right to make foreign policy for the *Bund*, to make and end wars, to administer the army and to appoint the federal Chancellor. For the liberals it was now time to go one step further and unite the whole of Germany behind the banner of the principle of nationality.

There is no evidence that Bismarck thought this would happen immediately. Most probably he foresaw a gradual change coming about through greater commercial links and the extension of the *Zollverein*. South Germany, however, proved poorly organised and little able to fend for itself and soon all but Bavaria were looking to Prussia to give them direction. Mutual alliances were formed and it was agreed that Prussia would lead Germany in the event of a war. Only Bavaria stayed out of this arrangement.

The pretext for this war was increasingly likely to come from France. Napoleon III's empire was tottering, and he badly needed a foreign policy success to endear him to his people. The cry in France was 'revenge for Sadowa!'* His eyes ran from the south to the north before settling on Luxembourg, a principality which was a member of the German *Bund*. Bismarck saw Napoleon's lust for German territory as a means of speeding up the unification process. The opportunity did not present itself, however, until the French chose to make an issue of the Hohenzollern candidacy for the Spanish crown.

In 1869, quite independently of any German diplomatic pressure, the Spanish Cortes decided to invite Prince Leopold of Hohenzollern-Sigmaringen to assume the Spanish throne. Leopold came from the Catholic branch of the family which had remained in Swabia while their cousins had departed to rule Brandenburg in the east. In 1852 the Sigmaringen Hohenzollerns had elected to make their small principality into a part of Prussia, but there was never any great love between the two branches, now irrevocably divided by religion. As it turned out Prince Leopold was not at all keen to desert his gothic castle in Sigmaringen for Madrid. Bismarck, however, encouraged him to accept.

Despite Spanish attempts to keep the candidacy a secret, the story became known in France. The French not unnaturally saw it as a Prussian intrigue and were considerably alarmed by the idea of Prussian encirclement. They sent their ambassador, Benedetti, to Bad Ems where William had gone for a cure, and insisted that William press Spain to withdraw the offer. William had no objection and the Sigmaringens duly complied. Next the French asked for a guarantee and, indeed, an apology at a time when the issue was believed to be settled beyond all doubt.

William's conversation with Benedetti took place on 11 July 1870. Two days later Bismarck, who had been enjoying the whole story of the Sigmaringen candidacy, received a long telegram from William at Bad Ems, relating the full exchange of conversations with Benedetti. Bismarck was at his Pomeranian estate of Varzin

* The Bohemian name for Königgrätz.

with the War Minister, Albrecht von Roon, and the Chief of Staff, Helmuth von Moltke. To them it looked ominously like a repetition of Olmütz, particularly to Moltke, who was itching to put his army to work. Bismarck then hit on the cunning ploy of editing the telegram to show the French in an even worse light and promptly despatched it to the press for publication. On 19 July France declared war.

Prussia and her allies won an overwhelming victory over the French, providing Bismarck with just what he needed to bring together the disparate elements of Germany. After the Battle of Sedan in September when the French Emperor was taken prisoner, increasing numbers of German princes began dropping in on military headquarters in Versailles to put forward their own ideas about how a future Germany should look. The idea of an empire was thought to be particularly exciting to south Germans, but the King of Prussia proved unwilling to accept the change of status.[117] Once again Bismarck was able to to make the potion work: knowing that Ludwig II of Bavaria was up to his ears in debt, he offered him money. On 3 December, Prince Luitpold of Bavaria brought William a letter from Ludwig asking him to accept the title of emperor. Initially the king was 'quite beside himself from indignation and seemed glum'. The Crown Prince, who was rather more taken with the imperial idea than his father ever was, explained to William that it meant 'glory for Prussia and enlightenment for Germany', but the king remained unconvinced and saw in 'Kaiser and Reich . . . only a cross for himself and above all for the Kingdom of Prussia.'[118]

When Geheimrat (privy counsellor) Abeker saw the king a week later for the third time to try to persuade him to accept the title, he approached with trepidation; the last time he had 'come away in the greatest disfavour . . . the king having retreated into his bedroom in great anger and excitement'.[119] On 16 January 1871 the princes had agreed to the title German Kaiser. William, who by this stage had accepted the inevitability of empire, held out for 'Kaiser of Germany', feeling that 'German Kaiser' sounded too presidential. With bad grace he gave in to the pressure: 'My son is heart and soul behind the way things have turned out. It doesn't matter an iota to me. I shall stick to Prussia.'[120]

The scene was then set for the German princes, led by the Grand Duke of Baden, to proclaim William I of Prussia the German Kaiser the next day – precisely 170 years after the Elector Frederick III had crowned himself King Frederick I in Prussia. Not even the whole galaxy of princes in uniform nor the splendour of Versailles' *galerie des glaces* was able to put William's mind wholly at rest: 'Later I shall be called what I please, and not what Bismarck decides for me.'[121] He was still sulking. The day before he had even burst into tears: 'Tomorrow is the saddest day of my life,' he wailed. 'We are carrying the Kingdom of Prussia to the grave and you, Graf Bismarck, are responsible.'[122]

II

The Last King of Prussia

Every time I walk down Unter den Linden and look at the corner window of the palace I'm reminded of the old Kaiser William. As on so many occasions when I came here from Königsberg, but mostly, however, when I arrived here from Paris in 1887, and my steps took me in this direction, I saw the old Kaiser at the window carrying out his work: he read all sorts of letters, signed them and strew sand on his wet signature. Passers-by made no fuss about all this, only a few strangers like me used to stare reverently up at the window. At noon, however, the guard was changed. From far away one heard the sound of trumpets and drum-rolls. Out surged street urchins and layabouts to the rhythm of the music and between the crowds appeared the drummer with his long, gold-inlaid beadle which he lifted to the musicians and soon they were playing in a different key before the palace. Then along came the guards with majestic bearing, wearing white breeches and blue coats, throwing their legs forward while keeping their eyes right. This way they could see their Field Commander at the window who stood there bolt upright and before whom the passing people and soldiers bowed. When the troop has passed on and the sound of the music had died down the deeply moved crowd they left in their wake broke into a phrenetic hurra directed towards the window, overjoyed to find themselves face to face with their beloved sovereign. That was the zenith of the Prussian imperial rule . . .

> Lovis Corinth, Berlin, 27 September
> 1923. In Irmgard Wirth, *Berliner Maler:*
> *Menzel, Liebermann, Slevogt, Corinth,*
> *in Briefen, Vorträgen und Notizen,*
> 2nd edition, Berlin, 1986, 256–257

Prussia's last king and Germany's last Kaiser broke in on this world on 27 January 1859. Anticipating the successful delivery of a baby boy, the old Field Marshal von Wrangel smashed a window of the royal palace and shouted out into a crowd alerted by the salvos of the guns, 'Children! It's a fine recruit!'* The guns had

---

* *'Kinder'*, German military slang. See below, p. 134.

also roused the boy's grandfather, the Prince Regent and later first Kaiser William: not even waiting for his carriage to be brought round, he jumped into a cab.[1] It must have been with some disappointment, therefore, that at first sight his grandson appeared lifeless, the charge of three earnest doctors who were trying everything possible to make him take his first breath.[2]*

The Prussian court was at pains to maintain secrecy about the difficulties surrounding the heir's birth, and the injuries which he may have sustained at the time: so much so that the first rumours appear to have surfaced in Britain, whither they were carried by the Britons attached to the suite of Princess Victoria, the baby's mother and daughter of Queen Victoria. The full story did not emerge in the German press until the days of the Weimar Republic, when the royal household could no longer suppress press treatment of the question of how William II, the future Kaiser, got his withered arm.

One suspects that the adult Kaiser, too, had his reasons. He wanted to put the blame for his deformities on to someone, and this someone was to be the surgeon, Medizinalrat, Professor Dr Eduard Martin. Martin was accused of not proceeding directly to the palace when summoned; of wounding the child in the course of delivery; and of deciding that the baby was born dead, therefore putting it to one side while he busied himself with the mother.[4]

In April 1931 Martin's son, another physician called Professor Dr August Martin, wrote to the Kaiser to put straight the record from his father's papers. Martin senior had got into his coach immediately on receiving the message and had 'driven directly to the palace'. On arriving he found two other doctors there and

---

* Compare the version of events in the Kaiser's authorised version of his own birth: '. . . the sight that met him there was not one of those coarse, red-faced, squealing infants who frown themselves sourly into this vale of tears, but a delicate, pretty baby, with an exquisite texture of skin, smooth and rosily pale, the tiny blue veins faintly visible at the wee temples, and unusually alert and wide-open sapphire-hued eyes already showing a grave underglow, as if the very beginning of life was for him an especially perilous undertaking, to be met with extreme energy . . .

'The first little cry heard by the grandfather startled him; it was a sharp, curious little cry, not of pain, but of simple self-assertion. "I am here!" it seemed to say, and the Regent shook with mirth while yet his eyes were liquid with emotion.'[3]

together they delivered the child, being particularly careful not to apply pressure to the softer parts of its body. The child did not breathe at first but by 'continuous rubbing ... cold dousing in a hot bath and short, sharp slaps on his buttocks' Dr Martin 'managed to get the child to breathe. The first cries were greeted by those present with a huge sigh of relief.'[5] The Prince Regent was visibly relieved and pumped the doctor's hand in gratitude, adding, with a reference to the slapping of the baby's buttocks, *'Aber so schlägt man nicht preussiche Prinzen!'* (But you don't hit a Prussian prince like that!)[6]

Three or four days later the new prince was found to have a slack left arm. The doctors who diagnosed the deformity were not the same team as that employed by Dr Martin, but Martin's son was convinced that the problems were incurred in the mother's womb and not in the course of the birth. The deformities affected the baby's whole left side and even, to some degree, the hearing in his left ear.

Given the extent of the damage to the child's body, it seems unlikely that a difficult delivery was responsible. It is more probable that William suffered from cerebral palsy brought on by a shortage of oxygen during his time in his mother's womb.[7]

Clearly a plucky child from the first, William overcame his disabilities wonderfully – he rode, swam, shot and played sports with distinction – but the need to compensate weighed heavily on his psyche and he was at pains till the very end of his life to hide the offending arm from the public gaze.

In his Political Testament of 1752, Frederick the Great had laid down certain precepts for the education of a Prussian prince. Above all, it fell to the boy's tutors to see to it that his head didn't grow too swollen; bad teachers, wrote Frederick, 'drum into him such a stupid opinion of his illustrious birth that he believes himself a sort of divine being whose will is law* and who must live like Epicure's gods, in an eternal state of quiet.'[8] To be fair to

---

* 'Regis voluntas – suprema lex' – see below, p. 122.

Georg Hinzpeter, the prince's tutor, every effort was made to make William aware that he was an ordinary mortal: it appears to have been the boy himself who evolved the notion of his own superiority. One departure from tradition was that William was not obliged to learn Polish. (Frederick the Great had believed that after French, Polish and Latin were the most important languages for a young Hohenzollern.[9])

William attended a Gymnasium in Kassel where he met and shared classes with ordinary, middle-class children and later he spent four semesters at the Prussian University of Bonn, flitting from subject to subject. Previous to his matriculation, there had been a project to send him to Balliol College, Oxford, where he would have been taught by T. H. Green and Arnold Toynbee and spent his time with such undergraduates as the later Lords Milner and Curzon. One of William's English biographers rightly calls this a 'fascinating possibility'.[10]

Despite the efforts of Hinzpeter, the Crown Prince and the Crown Princess, William's head continued to swell. Zedlitz-Trützschler later recorded in his diary: 'Certain principles of morality were developed in the Kaiser in his youth by the influence of his teachers, and later by the panegyrics of obsequious servants, until they fostered the arrant conviction that he was called on to play the judge over everybody and everything.'[11] It was Zedlitz's misfortune that he was the constant victim of the Kaiser's arrogance and insensitivity. A few days later he noted, 'The Emperor's desire is not to be instructed but to be admired, praised and confirmed in his resolutions. He is so penetrated by the sense of his own superiority that he looks upon all attempts to enlighten him merely as irritating and presumptuous. Any exception to this rule is an illusion, and indeed can only occur when he chances to be in the right mood, which does not happen often.'[12]

One of the means employed to make the young William get over the stigma of his deformity had been to make sure that he always won at games. Later this foolish if well-meaning indulgence was extended to military manoeuvres, so that there is little wonder that the Kaiser felt that he was invincible in the field. Zedlitz found him 'ignorant of much that ordinary mortals learn only through the constant struggle to cope with the difficulties of life. There can be no other explanation for the Emperor's profound ignorance of the world, of his utter inability to judge men aright, his arrogance, his obstinacy, his overweening vanity, his readiness to lend an ear to adroit flattery. These are the reasons why in many respects he has never grown up.'[13]

Whether or not he blamed her for his physical imperfections, William had little time for his mother, and his attitude to his increasingly sick father was also often lacking in respect. When his grandfather was dying, and therefore too ill to see to state papers, William resented the idea that these papers be shown to his father, also near to death from throat cancer. He was reported to have told his friend Graf Philipp zu Eulenburg, 'It is very questionable if a man who cannot speak has any right whatever to become King of Prussia.'[14] On the other hand he worshipped his Prussian grandfather and as late as 1940 he was referring to him as 'William the Great' – an epithet which had failed to take root among the German people.

The other grandparent he decided to idolize was his English grandmother, Queen Victoria. As an infant he had met his grandfather, the Prince Consort, and was apparently very taken with the military orders on his chest 'and kept moving his hands as if he wanted to play with them'.[15] An English court painter described him as 'the worst' of the 'little Turks' among the royal children, but Queen Victoria retained a soft spot for her Prussian grandson. Later he would repay her trust. 'What a woman!' he said in the course of her visit to his dying father's bedside in 1888. 'One could do business with her.'[16]

Queen Victoria died on 22 January 1901, five days before William's forty-second birthday, and in the middle of the celebrations to mark the bicentenary of the Prussian monarchy. On the 18th both William, by then the Kaiser, and Queen Victoria's third son, the Duke of Connaught, accompanied by a bevy of invited princes, had attended a misty celebration of the Prussian dynasty at the Opera House. As soon as the Kaiser heard the news from Osborne, he caught the train to London. Arriving in Britain with Connaught, the Kaiser announced, '*No notice* whatever is to be taken of me as Emperor . . . I come as grandson.'[17] According to his daughter, Victoria Louise, a large crowd had surrounded the station waiting for his arrival. As he got off the train an 'ordinary man walked up to my father and said, "Thank you, Kaiser." '[18]

The Queen was still conscious when the Kaiser and the Duke of Connaught arrived.[19] 'Pushing people aside with his usual impetuosity, William made his way to the sick bed and there he remained. The occasion was one which he never forgot. Asked long afterwards if it was true that he had held the Queen in his arms as she died, he replied: "Yes – she was so little – and so light." '[20] Victoria Louise tells the same story: 'The Queen of England died in the arms of the German Kaiser'.[21]

II

The Kaiser received me in such a state of indignation that I went to see the Court Physician to enquire into the state of His Majesty's health and to ask whether he should be treated with greater consideration. Niedner said yes and also mentioned that for His Majesty a weekend at Homburg was the lesser of two evils, for there was a possibility of a complete breakdown for this highly nervous man, of whom before the war we had all entertained an entirely false impression. It would have been an entirely different matter had he worked, but this he never did. This afternoon he went on a long drive through the Rhine Valley. I refused the invitation to accompany him.[22]

The Kaiser was highly strung and possibly mad. Even before the First World War had taken its toll on his nerves, courtiers such as Princess Marie Radzwiłł, diplomats and members of his own ministry were casting serious doubt on his ability to rule. He referred to Bismarck and Moltke as 'dogsbodies and pygmies'.[23] His friend Eulenburg admitted to the Kaiser's terrible temper about which he could do nothing. In 1898 there was talk of an 'alarming growth on his inner ear'[24] and a possible need to operate.

Mad or not, the Kaiser had a particular brand of loopiness which was all his own. In September 1896, for example, he wrote to his cousin the Czar: 'The development of the Far East, especially its danger to Europe and our Christian faith, is a matter which has been greatly on my mind since we made our first move together in the spring. At last my thoughts developed into a certain form and this I sketched on paper. I worked it out with an artist – a first class draughtsman – and after it was finished had it engraved for public use. It shows the powers of Europe represented by their respective genii called together by the Arch-Angel Michael – sent from Heaven – to *unite* in resisting the inroads of Buddhism, heathenism and barbarism for the defence of the Cross. Stress is especially laid on the *united* resistance of *all* European powers, which is just as necessary also against our common internal foes, anarchism, republicanism, nihilism.'[25]

Busy courting the English for a possible alliance in December 1903, the Kaiser nonetheless thought it a suitable moment to give his own interpretation of the Battle of Waterloo: 'We must not forget that the German legions and the German troops of Blücher on the day of Waterloo saved the British Army and the Duke of Wellington from annihilation.'[26] He wanted no one in his presence who might mar his rose-tinted view of the world and his position in it: 'I want no prophets of evil about me,' he said.[27]

'Incapable of learning from experience', 'Caesarism', 'folie d'empereur' ... The accusations mounted up. He told the Englishwoman Lady Mary Montagu, 'As for having to sink my ideas and feelings at the bidding of the people, that is really unheard of in Prussian history or [the] traditions of my house. What the German Emperor, King of Prussia thinks right and best for his people he does.' In Vienna a joke did the rounds according to which the Kaiser 'wanted to be the stag at every hunt, the bride at every wedding and the corpse at every funeral!' As his own Chancellor, Bülow, put it, 'His objectivity has disappeared without trace and subjectivity now rides a vicious, stamping steed.'[28]

Once the First World War began, his courtiers started to complain more openly of the Kaiser's cerebral inadequacy. Fury with England for seeking to protect Belgian neutrality made him summon the ambassador, Goschen: 'This was the thanks for Waterloo!' he told him as he handed back his insignia of Field Marshal of the British Army and Admiral of the Fleet.[29] When he heard of the death of Colonel General Helmut von Moltke, his Chief of the General Staff and the nephew of the great Moltke, 'the Kaiser was affected deeply. He complained that he would have no one now who was familiar with the language to accompany him on his Scandinavian visits.'[30]

By the time it became crystal clear in October 1918 that Germany had lost the war, the scales had fallen from the eyes of the senior commanders. As Admiral Albert Hopmann put it, 'What Germany has sinned in the past three decades it must now pay for. It was politically paralysed through its blind faith in, [and] its slavish submission to, the will of a puffed-up, vainglorious and self-estimating fool.'[31]

A number of his senior commanders must have heaved a sigh of relief when he agreed to abdicate as King of Prussia and German emperor, and to seek asylum in neutral Holland. Later the Dutch king allowed him to purchase a manor house at Doorn.

Considering that religious tolerance was one of the pillars of Prussianism in the formative years of the state, the Kaiser's prejudices are one of the ugliest sides of his unattractive nature. He had a deep dislike of Catholicism, a religion to which a good third of his Prussian subjects subscribed, including the Sigmaringen Hohenzollerns, who had remained in their original homeland of Upper Swabia. In 1895 he sacked the Badenese Freiherr Marschall von Bieberstein, on the grounds that as a Catholic he could not have any Prussian feelings.[32] The Catholic Prince Hohenzollern was treated with great suspicion and debarred from attending certain court discussions.[33] In 1907 the Kaiser spiked Prince Frederick William of Hohenzollern's marriage to Gräfin Paula Lehndorff when he wrote: 'He can marry her, but I will tolerate no morganatic marriages and he must renounce both his title and his property. W.I.R.'[34] Paula Lehndorff was a Protestant from the great East Prussian family. Poor Frederick William's next choice fell on a Catholic Hohenlohe. The Kaiser decided that this marriage was tolerable, but that the children must be brought up as Protestants. He was particularly resentful of the Jesuits, that same order which had once found a refuge in Prussia when they were banned by every other state in Europe. He believed them to have been responsible for the breakdown in the marriage of the Crown Princess of Saxony, a former Princess of Tuscany who had eloped with her children's tutor.[35]

But at least Catholics were Christians of sorts, and the Kaiser maintained that only 'a good Christian can be a good soldier'. As Zedlitz pointed out, this argument was flawed: 'he seems to have quite forgotten the Japanese, Napoleon I, Frederick the Great, Caesar, Alexander the Great.'[36] Some of these opinionated outbursts came close to anticipating the racialism of a later German warlord. While dismissing the French and the English as 'niggers' the Kaiser insisted that Jesus Christ was 'never a Jew'.[37] On 23 February 1917, he told a group of German Balts that a Russian bishop had recently ordered a pogrom of the Jews 'and that the same thing would soon happen here. Then the war profiteers would get to know their Lord God.'[38] In his search for the guilty parties who had been behind his exile in 1918, Jews, Jesuits and Freemasons came high up on his list. In December 1919 he made this choice utterance: 'The most profound and nastiest outrage that a nation has ever brought about in its history, the Germans have brought down on themselves [when the were] seduced and [mis-]led by the race of Juda they hate so much, and who were enjoyng their hospitality! That was all the thanks they got! No German must ever forget this and must not sleep until this parasite is swept from German soil and exterminated! This venomous toadstool on the German oak!'[39]

The Kaiser was naturally proud of his position at the head of the Prussian church and in this capacity he came down hard on courtiers who missed out on chapel attendance. Yet occasionally a frankly immoral tone creeps into his statements, as in the case of the two Catholic German missionaries who were murdered in

China in November 1897: 'We must make use of this splendid opportunity immediately.'[40] Nor was William as constant as some commentators have maintained. Before his marriage there is evidence to suggest that he had quite a number of love affairs. Princess Katharina Radziwiłł alludes to his numerous infidelities even after his marriage to Princess Augusta ('Dona') of Schleswig-Holstein-Sonderburg-Augustenburg in 1881.[41] Before his marriage he appears to have become embroiled in a threesome with two streetwise women called Ella Somsičs and Anna Homolatsch. The latter ran off with his cufflinks and showed them around Vienna. Later she had a daughter whom she claimed to have been the Kaiser's. These two women had to be bought off. With a French woman called Elisabeth Bérard there was an exchange of letters, which were hidden in the safe of the Persian Embassy and eventually discovered in 1956, when they were printed in the German popular magazine *Quick*. Perhaps the Kaiser felt that he had burned his fingers by getting caught on these two occasions, or else he believed that such behaviour was incompatible with his status as a king and emperor, for all evidence of his philandering peters out after 1888.[42]

Women, he told Lady Mary Montagu, 'were to marry, love their husbands, have lots of babies, bring them up well, cook nicely and make their husband's home comfy for them (sic).'[43] Clearly, this was his attitude to Dona, who, whether from want of brains or for some other reason, seems to have complied to the limits of her ability. She produced six stout sons and a daughter and, given her position, had little need to show her prowess in the kitchen or, indeed, wield a broom. The Kaiser nevertheless grew bored with his wife. Zedlitz recalls an occasion when the Kaiser had been reading to himself all evening, then suddenly turned on Dona: '"Do you mean to spend the night here?" The Empress said, "No, William, but I did not want to disturb you, as you have been so busy reading the whole evening." To which the Emperor replied: "Well, what else could I do? It is so incredibly dull here."' Part of the problem seems to have been Dona's reluctance to leave him alone.[44] His close friend, Philipp Eulenburg, expressed himself shocked by the 'extent to which the imperial bed had been raised to cult status by the Kaiserin'. The Kaiser had told him of her 'wrinkled, prematurely aged face and grey hair'. Eulenburg, who had problems of his own on that score, advised William to sleep in a separate bedroom and to keep the door locked.[45]

When Dona died at Doorn in the province of Utrecht in 1921, the ex-Kaiser decided against all odds to have her buried in Germany. His adjutant, Sigurd von Ilsemann, found there was something suspicious about the Kaiser's plan: 'Though the Kaiserin did once say that she would like to be buried in Potsdam, had she known then how things were going to turn out she would certainly have wanted to be provisionally buried in Doorn. . . . Here the Kaiser could visit her grave daily, in Potsdam possibly never.' Ilsemann probably put his finger on the root cause when he added, 'Without question the grave in Potsdam will become a sort of place of pilgrimage for many Germans.' Even Victoria Louise tried to dissuade her father, but to no avail. Dona was buried in the Antikentempel at Sanssouci on 19 April before a crowd of over 200,000 mourners.[46]

In June 1922, Princess Hermine of Schönaich-Carolath (née Princess of Reuss) paid a visit to Doorn. The Kaiser's manorhouse was festooned with red roses for the occasion and Ilsemann asked Hermine (or 'Hermo' as her family called her) how well she knew the Kaiser. She replied that she had met him only twice: once at a race-meet in Breslau and the second time, fleetingly, at a party. The widowed Kaiser was not enjoying living out his exile without female company. After three days the prescient Ilsemann noted in his diary, 'I have no doubt that the Kaiser is about to propose.'[47]

The Kaiser's nineteen-year marriage to Hermine seems to have been happy enough. The new wife was a strong-willed, ambitious woman who managed to push the Kaiser some way towards an agreement with the Nazis in the early 1930s.

Another of the Kaiser's unpleasant attributes was a rather cruel sense of humour. To compensate for the weakness of his left hand, he had developed considerable strength in his right. This he liked to demonstrate on shaking hands, turning his rings round so that they bit hard into his guest's fingers.[48]

The high-ranking officers and courtiers who came on his Baltic cruises were subjected to on-deck gymnastics and physical jerks, something which the sensitive Philipp Eulenburg described as a 'wholly repulsive spectacle'. In his merrier moods he would then chase the diplomats off to bed. During the Moroccan crisis Admiral Müller noted in his diary, 'Great silliness this morning during our exercises. His Majesty cut through Scholl's braces with a pen knife.'[49] When, in 1914, the American Ambassador, James Gerard, visited the Neues Palais in Potsdam in the company of Colonel House, the Kaiser told them they looked 'like a couple of crows' in their dress suits, adding 'that we were like two undertakers at a feast, and spoiled the picture'.[50]

One prank which rebounded badly for the vain William occurred when he crashed a party given by his son Prince Adalbert at Kiel, where he was living in rather luxurious conditions while serving in the navy. The Kaiser wore a mask, managing to pass undetected for the best part of the evening.[51] He was dressed as the Great Elector and while still disguised he got into conversation with a woman who took him for the Crown Prince, whom she knew well. 'Your Royal Highness is magnificently disguised. But what have you done to look so fat? Have you padded yourself out with a cushion?' The Kaiser was highly offended, but later got his revenge by mentioning the incident as often as he could in the woman's company: 'Naturally she knew there was no cushion there, but I think she said it on purpose. She knew perfectly well who I was.'[52]

The dividing line between humour and sadism was a thin one for William. In his early youth he 'nearly unleashed an international incident by pinching the King of Bulgaria's behind',[53] and slapping often formed a part of the treatment. Ministers were not exempt. Cross at the slow work in rebuilding the Opera House he 'tweaked von Rheinbaben [finance] by the ear, and several times hit von Breitenbach [railways] on the shoulder in a far from friendly manner.'[54] On a shoot he held a colonel down in the snow and rubbed his nose in it in front of the beaters. At the same time he referred to a Silesian count as 'you old pig'[55] and the War Minister as 'you old ass'.[56] Sometimes the Kaiser picked on one person in his entourage in particular. This was the case with the Controller of the Household, Egloffstein, who was obliged to resign because his nerves could no longer take the strain. He had made the mistake of complaining that his drink was too cold. The Kaiser took hold of Egloffstein's cup, plunged his fingers into it and took a sip. Giving it back to the Controller he said, 'Now the temperature is right.'[57]

During the war the Kaiser revelled in tales of bloodletting. On 30 August 1914 he was leaving church after Sunday service when he received a telegram from Hindenburg announcing the total defeat of the Russian Second Army in East Prussia. He decided that the battle, which had been fought at Ortelsburg-Neidenburg,* should be called Tannenberg, to reverse the Polish victory of that name five hundred years before. This was calculated to annoy the Poles, who were now vital to Germany's war effort. Worse, however, was the train journey later that day: 'the Kaiser – as he has often done recently – positively revelled in blood! "Piles of corpses six feet high . . . a sergeant killed twenty-seven Frenchmen with forty-five bullets, etc . . ." Appalling! Moltke, who was sitting beside him, was undergoing tortures.' Only four days later the Kaiser gave orders that all the cabinet chiefs were to dine with him in the evening: 'A great honour, but no great advantage. The conversation is never on a particularly lofty plane. Bloodthirsty details from the front he finds interesting, but shows little comprehension of the gravity of the whole situation . . .'[58]

The Kaiser could be tender and even charming when he wanted. He was able to see the funny side of the 'Köpernickiade',†

---

* In the Masurian Lakes region. The original Battle of Tannenberg was fought near Osterode, a considerable distance away on the other side of the administrative centre of Allenstein.
† See below, pp. 137–139.

and the diplomat Fritz von Holstein prevailed upon him to release the author, Wilhelm Voigt, from prison.[59]

To Ambassador Gerard he lamented the sinking of the *Lusitania*, adding that 'no gentleman would kill so many women and children'.[60] And despite his interest in carnage he was able to upbraid his soldiers in 1918 for not looking after injured Britons, not even helping them though they were lying right in their path: 'He had seen to it personally that they were bandaged and carried down the line.'[61]

III

> The conviction that the court camarilla which existed around the Kaiser was harmful and unhealthy for the empire was undoubtedly true. He was also not alone in subscribing to this viewpoint. Many Germans were repelled by the mixture of fawning, boastfulness and Byzantinism which had begun not only to infect the tone of the court, but also the higher echelons of the civil service. The great danger of the cabal around William II – this Harden saw clearly – lay in the fact that people who were responsible to no one, who were subject to no control, who occupied no official position, had achieved an inscrutable, uncheckable influence over the running of the state. The half constitutional, half absolutist form of German government lent them an all too fertile pasture for part private, part official conspiracy. William II had none of the statesmanlike geniality of a Frederick II [the Great]; none of the modesty of his grandfather William I; and none of the sense of his father – Frederick III's – wife. Uncertain and highly strung, by turns modernistic and addicted to the doctrine of divine right, [William] appeared to be particularly endangered by the camarilla and the camarilla appeared thereby doubly dangerous.[62]

As the foremost German journalist of his day, Maximilian Harden took on the role of Germany's censor. Of all the things which disturbed him about the Kaiser, the worst was the existence of a court cabal which would lead the ruler to dispense with the flimsy imperial constitution and rule alone. To a very large degree Harden's witch-hunt against the homosexuals in the Kaiser's entourage was based on just this; for example, Harden believed

Philipp Eulenburg to be encouraging the Kaiser to believe that his own judgement was all he needed.[63]

Harden's awareness and Fritz von Holstein's desire for revenge after his resignation in 1906 led to an unholy alliance directed at the court camarilla. Holstein had not believed that his resignation would be accepted. When it was, he thought that Eulenburg was to blame. Holstein had never agreed with the way Eulenburg had counselled the Kaiser: encouraging him to romantic notions of kingship and pushing him towards policies – such as the expansion of the navy – which put Germany on a collision course with Britain. Eulenburg came from a powerful East Prussian clan, and many of the Kaiser's intimates who gathered at Eulenburg's Schloss Liebenberg were also East Prussians: Eberhard Graf zu Dohna-Schlobitten, Richard Graf zu Dohna-Schlobitten, Emil Graf Schlitz (or von Görtz, as he was known for family reasons), August Graf zu Eulenburg and Walther Freiherr von Esebeck.[64]

'Eulenburg assumed that Holstein, as a Prussian nobleman and supporter of the Kaiser against Bismarck, was fundamentally in sympathy with traditional Prussian conceptions of royal authority.'[65] Eulenburg set out his views on kingship in a long letter to Holstein. 'The King of Prussia has the constitutional right to rule *autocratically*. Does William II do insane things? Do his methods of government go beyond *his rights*? Would the accusation of superficiality in his conduct of affairs be serious enough to charge him with impeding official activity? Have the affairs of government ever come to a standstill because of sloth or incompetence on the part of the Kaiser and King? There is no question of all this, but only that Germany and Prussia *can no longer endure* the manifestation of the Kaiser's will. It is a hard thing to say: but the creation of the German Reich, that is the transfusion of liberal south German blood into Prussia, *the combination of the* ruling statesman and the slumbering hero Kaiser, have been the ruin of the Prussian monarchy.* . . . If now the Kaiser steps forward as a

* Eulenburg is referring to Bismarck and William I. The italics are Eulenburg's throughout.

personal ruler, *he has every right to do so*, the only question is whether the consequences can be borne in the long run. *There* is above all the question: *who will win the game?* I am afraid that only a successful war will provide the necessary prestige for this [domestic] conflict.'[66]

Further on in his letter, Eulenburg's political romanticism becomes all the clearer: 'I believe in an intention of Providence in that elemental characteristic of the Kaiser to rule the kingdom himself. Whether she [Providence] wishes to ruin or help us I don't know, but it is difficult for me to conceive of the idea of the decline of the star of Prussia.'

Holstein's reply to this letter shows a far cooler form of reasoning, and indicates that Eulenburg's belief that his Prussian-ism would bring Holstein over to his side was misfounded: Holstein believed in a need to seek a compromise in Germany as distinct from Prussia. '*As for ruling with the Conservatives alone*, I had thought that we had agreed long ago that the King of Prussia could perhaps, but the German *Kaiser* could never, rule on an *exclusively Conservative* basis . . .'[67]*

This political romanticism lay at the heart of the 'Byzantinism' which had taken hold of the court; the permanent fawning of courtiers obsessed by the possibilities of a newly reborn German Empire, the heir to the heyday of its medieval predecessor.

Zedlitz writes of speeches full of '. . . Byzantine flattery and incredible self-justification'.[68] Byzantinism was even spreading to the Kaiser's entourage: 'The Emperor's autocratic manner is undoubtedly finding many imitators: the majority of the highest officers and officials are showing an increasing tendency to reactionary views. Centralisation is growing; everywhere there is supervision and personal interference. The independence of all subordinates is restricted more and more every day.'[69] The court seemed to encourage a preposterous degree of toadying on the part of old Prussian families. An example of this was Prince Dohna: 'Once he carried his servility so far that he asked the

---

* Holstein's italics.

Emperor whether his cows at Schlobitten could be graciously permitted to wear the same bells as the imperial kine in Rominten. He had to swallow His Majesty's answer: "I don't care two pence what bells your silly beasts wear." '[70]

In a frankly camp manner, the men of the Liebenberg Circle around Eulenburg made the Kaiser into a demigod, but it would be hard to maintain that any of them, except Eulenburg, was actually a 'friend' in the accepted sense of the word. Admiral Müller thought the Kaiser's lack of friends was 'his greatest misfortune';[71] possibly, however, William mistook the obsequiousness of those around him for affection. Holstein told Hatzfeldt that the Kaiser had been 'made impervious to sober political considerations by the incense strewn by the "entourage" as for example: "Compared to Your Majesty, Frederick the Great was only a silly boy." '[72]

Frederick the Great would hardly have approved. What he termed 'la gêne d'etiquette'[73] was unavoidable when it came to William; he would have been particularly appalled by the epidemic of hand-kissing which broke out at court, apparently instituted by the former sergeant, General von Mackensen.[74] Zedlitz-Trützschler took a dim view, too, especially when a new aide de camp, Major von Neumann-Cosel, began kissing the imperial hand at every opportunity. 'He has had several hints that this way of kissing hands several times a day is not quite the proper thing and it might even be called oriental, but he replied quite naively that, as he had once begun it, he could not stop.'[75]

Byzantinism meant laughing hysterically at the Kaiser's mother-in-law jokes ('too awful to repeat' noted more sober-minded Zedlitz[76]). Diplomats knew not to report what they thought the Kaiser would not want to hear, another trait which presages Adolf Hitler a quarter of a century later. Only here it was not so much fear of the consequences of telling the truth, but a conspiracy of silence to protect the beloved master from bad news. Colonel General Moltke went so far in his adulation as to mix his historical metaphors: 'Whenever I see the court come into the White Hall [of the Berlin *Schloss*] it has a quite remarkable effect on me, the

Kaiser always something medieval about him. . . . It is as if one saw the dead come back to life in periwigs and powder (*"Zopf und Puder"*).'[77]

Moltke was not the only person to see the court through rose-tinted spectacles; the Kaiser was by far the worst offender on this score. At the time of the successful German offensive in March 1918 the Kaiser was in such high spirits that he 'declared that if an English delegation came to sue for peace it must kneel before the German standard for it was a question of the victory of the monarchy over democracy'.[78] He was not above referring to his own Reichstag as 'that monkey-house'.[79] When Bismarck leaked the terms of the secret Reinsurance Treaty with Russia in October 1896, the Kaiser went so far as to summon the officers present and order the arrest of the eighty-one-year-old former Chancellor on a charge of treason.[80] 'His actual power,' wrote Zedlitz, 'which even from the first was quite unlimited, was now developing step by step into purely personal and arbitrary rule.'[81]

Things might have been tolerable had William possessed the mental capacity to rule on his own, but it was clear that he did not. As Holstein wrote to Harden in October 1906, 'In my opinion, and after constantly repeated consideration, I cannot avoid the conclusion: the personal policy of the Kaiser is at the root of all evil. He is "a brilliant temperament" (*tant pis pour un empereur*) but is totally without political talent.'[82] In a typical utterance, the Kaiser told a fawning teacher who had informed him that he was always right, 'Well, that is so. My subjects ought to do what I tell them, but they always want to think for themselves, and that always leads to trouble.'[83] Bülow expressed the despair of many a senior minister when reproached for some aspect of policy: 'You cannot have the faintest idea what I have prevented, and how much of my time I must devote to restoring order where our All Highest master has created chaos.'[84] In wartime this intervention in policy had even more disastrous results as arguably it cost yet more lives. Müller recalled a particularly outrageous moment in May 1915 when the Kaiser held forth at dinner: '[General Hans von] Plessen congratulated the Kaiser on his great services in

building up the army and H.M. replied that he was deeply
offended that the army had simply cast to the winds his teaching
and commands in the art of attack and had attacked as foolishly as
in 1870. This accounted for the astronomical losses. [General
Freiherr Moritz von] Lyncker was beside himself at this monstrously unfair criticism.'[85]

The Kaiser's flouting of parliamentary restraint reached new
heights in October 1908 when the *Daily Telegraph* printed an
interview he had conducted with Major General Edward Stuart-
Wortley at Highcliffe Castle in Hampshire. Stuart-Wortley later
reworked the interview with the help of Harold Spender.[86]* The
Kaiser thought publishing the piece would better Anglo-German
relations. Although the article had few consequences in Britain, it
caused a storm on both the left and the right in Germany, the one
furious at the Kaiser's reluctance to submit to ministerial control,
the other outraged by his alleged pro-British stance in the Boer
War. In a moment of uncharacteristic self-doubt, the Kaiser even
considered standing down. He was under considerable strain,
largely as a result of the press campaign against his friend Philipp
Eulenburg. He would have pleased no one so much as Maximilian
Harden who confessed to being 'completely overwhelmed by the
unprecedented monstrosity of the *Daily Telegraph* article . . . I will
demand *crûment*, immediate abdication. Calmly and constantly.'[87]

IV

The Emperor [seems] . . . to have no inkling how gravely he sins
against the spirit of Stein.[88]

After the frugal demands of the old Kaiser William I, the
extravagance of his grandson was not lost on the Berliners. Ever
quick to exercise their big-city wit, they were particularly amused
by the young ruler's taste for travel in his spanking new train. '*Der*

* The father of the poet Stephen Spender. He was actually on the staff of the *Daily News*.

greise Kaiser, der weise Kaiser und der reise Kaiser, they called the three emperors of 1888 – the old Kaiser, the wise Kaiser and the peripatetic Kaiser. Another suggestion was that the old Imperial Anthem '*Heil Dir im Siegerkranz*' (Hail to thee in the victor's crown)* should be changed to '*Heil Dir im Sonderzug*' (Hail to thee in the special train). From the very first it was apparent that William was going to live like an emperor.[89]

Ever fond of treats and the chance to dress up, the Kaiser made his birthday an excuse for lavish festivities. As Ambassador Gerard noted, 'The Emperor's birthday . . . is a day of great celebration. At 9.30 in the morning the Ambassadors, Ministers, and all the dignitaries of the Court attend divine service in the chapel of the Palace. On this day, in 1914, the Queen of Greece and many of the reigning Princes of the German States were present. In the evening there was a gala performance at the Opera House, the entire house being occupied by members of the Court.'[90] This was the second such celebration in Berlin in January: on the 17th the court honoured the coronation not only of the first king of Prussia, but also of the first Hohenzollern emperor. It was a rather stiff occasion, when the ladies of the court were required to stay on their toes for a considerable length of time. There was rather more *Gemütlichkeit* about the Kaiser's birthday with its ritual of present-giving.[91]

The first Hohenzollern Kaiser, whom William was seeking to canonise as 'William the Great', had been so modest in his spending that he, much like the kings Frederick William I and Frederick II before him, had left the crown in the black; in this case to the tune of twenty-two million Reichsmarks. Five months after William II's succession, the Kaiser asked for a further six million a year. At its height, William's annual income amounted to twenty-two million per annum, with the back-up of a personal fortune of some 140 million. He possessed 119,826 hectares of land estimated at a further seventy million Reichsmarks. In addition he had fifty-three *Schlösser*, three in Berlin and thirteen

---

* Incidentally, sung to the tune of 'God Save the Queen'.

more in the Potsdam area. Of all the reigning houses of Europe
William's civil list was the most generous, although the personal
fortune of the Emperor of Austria-Hungary was larger. Nor was
William entirely satisfied with his little lot: he shelled out a further
600,000 Reichsmarks to acquire a villa in Corfu where he might
indulge his passion for archaeology.[92] To furnish the new villa,
the Kaiser had three of his palaces stripped, including Frederick
the Great's fairy-tale castle at Rheinsberg. He overspent to such a
degree on 'Achilléon' that he was obliged to borrow while he
looked around for a means to yet further increase the size of his
civil list.

The Kaiser particularly admired the lavish furnishings of the
New Hotel Adlon which opened in 1907. After inspecting its
premises he told Adlon he wanted similar luxuries for his own
palace: 'Adlon . . . tell Trützschler where you got them from. I
want something of the same. . . . If these things were left in the
hands of my Court Marschal (Zedlitz-Trützschler) then I wouldn't
ever get so much as a new chair or carpet and I would still be
living in the furnishings of the Great Elector.'[93]

The Kaiser was indifferent to the dictates of *Sparsamkeit* or
thrift; not for him the marked bottle of champagne recorked after
a simple supper. He was one of the first monarchs to enjoy the
pleasure of motoring. When one of his cars broke down he told
his Master of the House that he was to 'disregard expense' and
buy more cars. 'What anything I want costs is a matter of supreme
indifference. All I ask is that everything should go smoothly and
you are responsible.'[94]

Even when he abdicated, he required the trappings of wealth to
surround him in his modest lodgings in Doorn. The decision to
grant him a portion of the Hohenzollern lands was made after a
protracted legal battle. The Kaiser had been offered Schloss
Homburg for life, but he turned it down, feeling that he would be
insecure there.[95]

In 1926 the matter was finally settled. The state took over the
following: the *Schloss*, Charlottenburg and Grunewald in Berlin;
the *Schlösser* in Potsdam, with the exception of the Cecilienhof,

Oranienburg, Königsberg, Oliva near Danzig, the *Ordensburg* at Marienburg, the Leineschloss in Hamburg, Wilhelmshohe 'the German Versailles' in Kassel, and Schloss Homburg. In addition they appropriated all the royal theatres and opera houses as well as the Schackgallerie in Munich. The total value of the property assumed by the state and 250,000 *Morgen* of land (a Prussian *Morgen* was about a quarter of a hectare) amounted to fifteen million Reichsmarks.[96]

That left a considerable amount of property and land in the hands of the Hohenzollerns. In Berlin they had the palace of King William I, the Niederländische Palais (both in Unter den Linden), Schloss Monbijou and the Prinz Albrecht Palais (later Gestapo headquarters). Each of the sons was given a villa in Potsdam and the Crown Prince the Cecilienhof, which had been built for him. In East Prussia they retained the hunting lodge at Rominten as well as Cadinen; in Kiel, Schloss Hammelseck; in the west, Burg Rheinstein, the wine estate of Schloss Reinhartshausen and a half share of Burg Hohenzollern in Swabia. The Crown Prince was given Schloss Oels in Silesia and his eldest son, Prince William, Schloss Schildberg in Brandenburg with 22,000 *Morgen*.[97] Even in 1939, despite projected Nazi land reform, the Hohenzollerns were still the greatest landowners in Germany with 97,000 hectares.[98]

The sale of some of the Kaiser's effects in 1920, including his two yachts, yielded a cheque for 69,063,535 Reichsmarks which was used to buy Doorn and convert it to the Kaiser's use. In September 1919 the furnishings for the new house had arrived from the former royal palaces: twenty-three railway wagons and twenty-five furniture wagons; twenty-seven wagons full of packages of all sorts; a wagon bearing a car; finally came five wagons carrying a kit for a hospital building complete with equipment which William donated to the people of Amerongen (where he had lived until the purchase of Doorn) and a wagon containing the imperial motorboat, to be used for cruises on the Dutch waterways.[99]

With such enormous reserves to draw on, it should come as no surprise that William was keen on both receiving and giving presents. Men were won over by gifts and rewards, another policy with an oriental feel to it, and another which was to prove an inspiration for Hitler when he came to power.[100] The Kaiser took a special pride even in buying Dona's hats, something which his daughter's Engish governess, Miss Topham, found remarkably brave. On the royal domains the local pastors were required to furnish a complete list of those living on the land together with the ages of the children, so that the Empress might give them some useful present. A favourite was soap and Miss Topham recounts how the peasant women took pride in showing Her Majesty how well they had preserved the soap from one Christmas to the next. So much for the virtue of Prussian cleanliness.[101]

As far as taste was concerned, the Kaiser favoured anything which glorified his dynasty. Despite the outrage that Kleist's *Prinz von Homburg* had caused at its first performance, the Kaiser praised it, because it showed the stern virtue of his ancestor, the Great Elector.[102] He was almost certainly better served by the severe poetry of Heinrich von Kleist than he was by the toadying efforts of the Rhinelander Josef (von) Lauff, who wrote the centre piece for the 200th anniversary of the Prussian monarchy. Two and a half years later, in Wiesbaden, Zedlitz noted, 'Three short pieces were given at the theatre, two of which were by the poet Lauff. The boastfulness, the pomposity and adulation, which were expressed in these pieces was almost unbelievable.' The Kaiser, predictably loved them, and the court (equally predictably) followed suit.[103] Similar marks of approval were not granted to progressive drama: the playwright Gerhart Hauptmann had to look elsewhere for patronage, and his realistic study of the weavers' revolt, *Die Weber*, was heartily despised by the court.[104]

The Kaiser was not unmusical, but his tastes were conservative. Wagner he dismissed as 'a quite ordinary conductor'.[105] Strauss appalled him, largely, one supposes, because *Salomé* offended against his morals: 'That's a nice snake I've reared in my bosom.' His favourite composers were Lortzing and Meyerbeer. He said as much to the conductor Erich Kleiber at Doorn, although he seems to have changed his mind about Wagner by then, or just to have been exercising his elusive tact towards a notable exponent of the German romantic tradition.[106]

The Kaiser also dabbled in the visual arts, in sculpture and architecture in particular. He was behind the pompous monuments of Berlin's Siegesallee which Lovis Corinth called 'a disgrace to German art'[107] and he was happy to add his contribution to designs for government buildings, hotels, post offices, stations and barracks. It can truly be said that the Wilhelmine style sprang from source.

V

> ... the offer made to him [Hitler] enabled him within a few months to use his position in *Prussia* as a decisive factor in the Reich as a whole! He is no statesman, and what lies behind this is the pressure of the *extremists* in his entourage; he has missed his moment. In the face of these fly-by-night demagogues our family must present a solid, united front, which for the outside world must be clearly and unmistakably documented; to this the possibly uncertain or uncounselled from all walks of life can rally. Anyway, I'm glad that on this issue your views and mine are more than in agreement.*[108]
>
> The ex-Kaiser to the ex-Crown Prince,
> 17 September 1932.

The war was fought, the war was lost; rightly or wrongly large sections of the public and even the armed forces blamed the Kaiser. As early as September 1918, the Socialist councils which were springing up within the ranks were demanding the abdication of the Kaiser and insisting that the future 'regent' (*Reichsverweser*) be no prince and no nobleman.[109] General von der Schulenburg allegedly informed the Kaiser that he had a choice as King of Prussia: he could seek death at the head of his troops or he could ride back to Berlin and put down the revolution. The Kaiser did neither; he sought asylum in neutral Holland and made a nest for himself at Doorn.[110]

* The Kaiser's italics throughout.

For the Hohenzollerns the boot was on the other foot. They
were treated as they had treated the Welfs and the Landgraves of
Hessen; an *Einreiseverbot* prevented the Kaiser from entering
Germany on any business and the Crown Prince, having also
renounced his claims to the throne, was banished to the island of
Wieringen in the Zuider Zee. Here he whiled away the time
working with the village smith, miserably lonely and bored, until
the autumn of 1923, when the politician Gustave Stresemann
finally managed to obtain permission for his return to
Germany.*[111]

The Kaiser continued to observe events in Germany with
considerable interest, ever alert to the chance of a restoration. In
November 1922 he had already seen the growing Fascist movement as a possible means of getting back his throne. After the
Beer Hall Putsch, however, he lost interest – '*Na, Gott sei Dank*,
then at least this ludicrous story has come to an end.'[112] He was
also concerned lest the Nazis should want to restore the Wittles-
bachs rather than the Hohenzollerns to the vacant imperial seat.
In Bavaria there would have been little enthusiasm for the Prussian
royal family.

All this changed when the Nazis began to look like a viable
party for government after their successes in the elections of 1930.
Already Doorn was beginning to buzz with intrigue. The ex-
Kaiser's small court divided itself between the Nationalists
(DNVP) and those who could see a future in Hitler's party. One
of the latter was Hermo, the Kaiser's second wife. Others were
Colonel Leopold von Kleist, Admiral Magnus von Levetzow and
Alexander Freiherr von Senerclans-Grancy.[113]

It was Kleist who arranged for Hermann Göring to visit Doorn.
Some care was taken to avoid any leak to the press of Göring's
arrival and the ex-air ace was announced as 'Dr Döhring', the
court preacher.[114] Ilsemann watched the Kaiserin carefully: 'Her
Majesty seems very excited about Göring's visit. She intends
paying great court to this possible kingmaker.'[115] Göring arrived

* Wieringen was reclaimed in 1926.

in the company of his first wife, Karin, who was already suffering from the illness which would kill her before the year was out. Hermo expressed great concern at Karin's health and pressed on her a wad of banknotes to pay for a cure at Altheide in Silesia.[116]

Both Göring and the Kaiser seem to have understood that the visit was not just social. Both evenings the two men stayed up late talking politics, and tea-time discussions re-covered the ground with occasional forays into archaeology. Göring was trying to win the Kaiser over to his side by playing the convinced monarchist, although he took care to limit a future restoration to the Hohenzollerns, while the Kaiser 'argued vigorously for his princely colleagues . . .'[117]

Accounts vary as to the success of Göring's trip. Karin didn't believe it had gone well. She wrote to a friend later that 'they flew at one another at once. . . . Both are excitable and so like each other in many ways. The Kaiser has probably never heard anybody voice an opinion other than his own, and it was a bit too much for him sometimes.' The Kaiser did manage a grudging toast to 'the coming Reich' to which the Nazi rejoindered 'the coming king'. 'He was careful not to tag a specific name, given there were several contenders.'[118]

The Kaiser was rather cool after Göring's departure. One evening Hermo asked him if Göring would receive some high office after the restoration. 'He would certainly get the air force,' was the Kaiser's lukewarm reply. He was beginning to lose faith in Göring's desire to intervene on his behalf and was cross with Kleist for pursuing the Nazi in an undignified way.[119]

By the time of Göring's second and last visit to Doorn in May 1932, it was beginning to be clear that it was simply not enough to have a good war record and the *Pour le mérite* to woo the Kaiser.[120] Göring was bragging, spouting propaganda and vast self-confidence on the basis of the party's recent performance in the polls. The household was addressed 'like a public meeting'.[121] Moreover Göring's 'highly spontaneous manners . . . collided with court etiquette'.[122] On one occasion 'Göring appeared at luncheon wearing plus-fours, this would not be permitted in any other guest at Doorn, but he had quickly understood that he was all licensed.'[123] The licence came naturally from Hermine, who wasted no time in having her 'demigod' placed on her immediate right at meals. Göring felt so welcome that he thought himself entitled to take over the Crown Prince's quarters, but his request was turned down by the Court Marshal.[124]

The Kaiser had already lost whatever faith he might have had in the Nazis. He told Göring that the only person who could rule Germany was 'an educated monarch'.[125] In general the Kaiser's small court had taken a dim view of the flirtation with Göring; there was little enthusiasm for the party: 'When I saw all four of them together,' wrote Ilsemann, 'Kaiser, wife, [Leopold von] Kleist and Göring. I was convinced that it was foolish for these four people to put their money on the Nazis; self-declared enemies of the German National Party (DNVP), while all the gentlemen who serve at Doorn are members of the German National Party.'[126] Kleist and Hermine were undeterred, however, and the Kaiser's wife went so far as to claim that she would be able to get Hitler down next.[127]

Hitler had already been in contact with the Hohenzollerns. In 1926 he had paid a call on the Crown Prince in the Cecilienhof. Crown Prince William was keeping his promise to Stresemann to stay out of politics, which had been to some extent a condition of his return to Germany, and evidently did not believe that Hitler was an important suitor: 'Yes, it sounds appropriate that I should be Kaiser one day . . . but for the time being I'm just a private person and I have obligations to my family alone.' The Crown Prince then capped this comment with a splendid *non sequitur* – 'As you can see I'm wearing a tweed coat and plus fours.'[128]

The Crown Prince had longed for power all his adult life. During the war he had become embroiled in the conspiracy to oust Bethmann-Hollweg. He had recently been involved in some right-wing political discussions in Breslau and he told the opera singer Geraldine Farrar, '(My father) . . . has had his chance; and I have never been given the opportunity to prove myself. What makes this situation all the more unpleasant is that I have to suffer the consequences of *his* mistakes. You will perhaps find it heartless of me to say so, but in the past twenty years I have simply had too much to swallow.'[129]

The Crown Prince had shown some early inclinations towards Italian Fascism which did not prevent him from admiring Brüning – 'the cleverest man in Germany'.[130] At heart, however, he was an opportunist. When Göring was elected to the Reichstag in 1928 the Crown Prince was quick to send his congratulations, covering his back by saying that the former flyer had served under his command in the war.[131] Stresemann's death in October 1929 released him from his pledge not to enter politics and he joined the old soldiers' league – the Stahlhelm – along with his brothers Eitel Fritz and Oskar. That much the Kaiser approved, but not his next step. Taking a cue from Louis Napoleon, the Crown Prince thought he might achieve a restoration by being elected President of the Weimar Republic.[132]

The Crown Prince had set his heart on the April elections of 1932 when he thought he might beat Hindenburg in the polls and revive the monarchy. He told Göring this.[133] For the moment he cast aside his father's opposition. Much more important was the dawning realisation that he was falling into a trap laid for him by Hitler and that his indiscretion to Göring had further reduced his hopes. Hitler was delighted for the Crown Prince to stand, for he believed, possibly correctly, that this would split the vote destined for Hindenburg, thereby allowing him, Hitler, to triumph. Hitler's superior cunning was brought home to the hapless Crown Prince in the course of a dinner party at General von Schleicher's house.[134]

Naturally Hermine was equally furious at the idea that she might not become Kaiserin because the Kaiser's son would take the throne for himself. Hermine worked hard on her husband to turn him against Prince William and his wife. In the case of the latter, Hermine knew her husband's antipathy towards the Princess: '. . . a Russo-Danish woman. . . . Her goal is just the crown. . . .'[135] What made matters worse at Doorn is that for a while it looked as if the Crown Prince might be successful. On 13 April 1932, the Kaiser learned that his son had been a guest of

Göring and that he had later been ushered in to see Hitler. When the Crown Prince appeared at Doorn in July, the Kaiser had strong words for him: 'It is an impossibility that a Hohenzollern should successfully strive for power via the red, republican, Ebertian presidential chair.'[136]

The Crown Prince withdrew from the elections and in April told reporters that his first choice would be Hindenburg, his second Adolf Hitler. The Hohenzollerns were in disarray: officially neither the Kaiser nor the Crown Prince had the right to demand the throne, as both had renounced the succession. The playboy Crown Prince was unpopular in more than one circle and many Germans had not forgiven the Kaiser. The search was on for an acceptable Hohenzollern. Eyes fell on Prince Oskar, the Kaiser's fifth son.[137] It has been alleged that he was the second of the Kaiser's children, after Auwi, to join the Nazi Party,[138] but this is vigorously denied by the present generation of Hohenzollerns.[139] Oskar nonetheless had his moments of doubt. In 1930 he wrote to his sister, 'One cannot describe the Nazis in a few words, they have a lot in their favour, [but] the programme they have adopted up till now is in need of revision.'[140]

In September 1932 Ilsemann noted the popularity of Prince Oskar, who had also had to renounce the succession as a result of his marriage to Ina von Bassewitz, who was not of royal blood. 'Many people are saying that Prince Oskar should be given the throne. As [General Graf von der] Schulenburg told me: the monarchists are making unquestionable progress but are foundering for lack of a candidate ...'[141]

With the growing political turmoil in Germany caused by the inability of any party to achieve a majority of seats in the Reichstag, Hindenburg dismissed Brüning and appointed the Westphalian Franz von Papen and his 'cabinet of barons' in his stead. Papen offered the vice-chancellorship and minister-presidency of Prussia to Hitler, then the leader of the largest party in the Reichstag. Hitler thought it politic to refuse and hold out for the chancellorship. On 17 September, the Kaiser and the Crown Prince put down their cudgels and exchanged letters, the Kaiser reporting on the discussions Hitler had had with President Hindenburg on 13 August: *'Peccatur intra et extra muros!** . . . the Field Marshal made the unbelievable mistake of telling him "He couldn't square it with his *conscience* to grant total power to the Nazis!" To which came the answer: "Your Excellency's *conscience* permitted you to hand over total power, to give free rein for years at a time, to tolerate enemies of both the Reich and the Hohenzollerns in the form of reds [*roten Socis*], radicals, Jews and Bolsheviks allied to the *Centre* Party; your conscience has allowed these criminals to wreck the country from top to bottom while every nationalist movement has been fought off or suffocated. Henceforth your conscience had better pay more attention to the nationalist movement." '[142]

'It fills me with deep sadness and concern,' resumes the Kaiser to his eldest son, 'to see what a groundless lack of *conscience* the demagogic Nazi leaders possess; that they should mindlessly squander the collected resources of national energy in their nationalist movement!' The Kaiser believed that the Nazis were inhibiting the success of other right-wing movements more out-wardly sympathetic to the restoration of the Hohenzollerns: 'As a result of this it is necessary to use all means to *support* the nationalist *movement*. The Nazi Party disposes of strong *nationalist forces*, even today a few leaders and speakers must be pulled away from the irresponsible demagogic machinery and attached to a nationalist administration. Hitler's refusal was a frightful howler and a great disappointment to the nationalist-minded elements in the nation. He doesn't have the slightest political "flaire" or any knowledge of history, else he should have known: "He who controls Prussia, controls the Reich!"† First make Prussia clean and lawful; provide order, enforce obedience and discipline and ensure her defences and the rest of the Reich will follow!'[143]

The Kaiser believed that the way to defuse the Nazi movement was to pull a few of the more acceptable elements out of it and place them in a nationalist coalition. Schleicher had a similar idea

* A sinner both inside and outside the walls. We must assume the Kaiser's italics throughout.
† Unbelievable though it may seem, the Kaiser appears to quote from the Socialist leader August Bebel! See Otto Braun, *Von Weimar zu Hitler*, 40.

of using Gregor Strasser to break the power of the Nazis and isolate Hitler.[144] Hitler, however, proved cleverer than the Kaiser gave him credit for. Ironically, this letter setting down the Kaiser's low opinion of Hitler and his followers was leaked to the Nazi hierarchy by a sympathiser on the staff at the Cecilienhof. The Kaiser was furious and tried to pin down the culprit. At one stage the Crown Princess was the chief suspect, but he later decided it must have been Kleist, and dismissed him from his staff on the grounds that he was too sympathetic towards the Nazis. He was not wrong there: Kleist went on to become a National Socialist member of the emasculated Reichstag of the Third Reich.[145]

The Kaiser's anti-Nazi witch-hunt also proved the undoing of Admiral Levetzow in December when he too decided to stand as a Nazi candidate for the Reichstag.* Levetzow's sacking came as a shock to him and he wrote the Kaiser's secretary, General von Dommes, a long letter of self-justification. This letter was minuted by the Kaiser, thereby affording some significant glimpses of the Kaiser's distrust of the Nazi Party. It is clear that the Kaiser had changed his mind. When Levetzow had first broached the subject of standing the Kaiser had said, 'Why not?' and in the course of Levetzow's three visits in 1932 there had been no inkling of any change in his attitude. Levetzow alluded to Kleist, and the Kaiser added in the margin that membership of any political party was prohibited to members of his staff. Here he was not being completely honest, as we know from Ilsemann that the majority of his team belonged to the DNVP.[146]

The Kaiser was not interested in Levetzow's attempts to sell Nazism to him. To the suggestion that a Nazi victory might lead to a greater Hohenzollern influence on German public life, he minutes cryptically that 'this hasn't worked'. The admiral then becomes quite lyrical in his picture of the coming Germany: 'In the fresh young soil of the National Socialist movement there is a field in which the seed kernels of monarchist thinking, legitimate monarchist *thinking* [the Kaiser has underscored this word and

* He was later Berlin Chief of Police.

written in the margin 'Sadly no, a screen'], which has been scattered for our nation; from this seed will one day spring the best of Germans who will become the supporters of the imperial throne [here the Kaiser has minuted 'Hitler and Göring?'] and they will make it happen, if not the imperial throne will never return [The Kaiser: 'Wait and see!'].'[147]

Levetzow brings his letter to a close: 'I have based my attitude on the confidence I have in the personality of Hitler and the trusted aides who stand close to him . . .' [The Kaiser: 'Goebbels?'] When Levetzow suggests that he wishes to throw in his lot with the best man in Germany, the Kaiser contributes a double exclamation mark. He did not reply in person, and left it to Dommes to tell the admiral that the Kaiser's original encouragement was only given because it was believed that Levetzow had already left the household and that he had financial problems which would be remedied by a Reichstag deputy's salary.[148]

Meanwhile the Crown Prince had written to Hitler to reproach him for not having accepted the post offered by Papen. 'You know how much esteem I have for you personally. My official declaration in the course of the presidential elections is proof of this.' The prince lavishes praise on Hitler's 'wonderful movement', but his aim is an alliance of the right: NSDAP, DNVP and the Stahlhelm, and he is careful to protect the latter from the ruffians of Hitler's own praetorian guard in the SA and the SS: 'The SA, the SS and the Stahlhelm are the bearers of the military ethos and as such you should divert your attentions to the Reichsbanner and the Rotmord.'*[149]

Hitler's reply was predictable enough: the same old story about his humble past and adolescence with the same romantic embellishments he supplied for *Mein Kampf*: without so much as a 'stipend', working his fingers to the bone on a Viennese building site. No mention was made of the shadier side of his 'Bummlerjahre', when he lived the life of a tramp.[150]

---

* Socialist and communist paramilitary organisations. 'Rotmord' is a perjorative designation for the communist militia.

The royal household continued to put out feelers to the Nazis until 27 April 1934, and despite some claims to the contrary, it is clear that these were not carried out behind the Kaiser's back.[151] Probably Hermine was still the loudest voice for Hitler in Doorn, especially after the departure of the leading pro-Nazi courtiers. She had spoken of Hitler with 'unbridled admiration'[152] ever since the days of the abortive Munich Putsch. In 1929 she had attended her first Nuremberg rally.[153] The Kaiser was far from being unaware of this and it is a testament to his tenderness towards his second wife that he tolerated her interference to such an uncharacteristic degree. As he told Ilsemann on 29 May 1933, 'As far as my wife is concerned the barometer reads "storm". She is in an intolerable frame of mind! Politically she means well, things can't move quickly enough to get me back onto the throne, but we won't get there by her methods. She runs after the Nazis and everything she is able to do here or in Berlin she puts down in writing, which will sooner or later do us harm if it comes to light ... Yes, it is really sad that H.M. is making my life so difficult here. As if I didn't have enough worries.'[154]

Hermine was still singing the praises of the Nazis after the Night of the Long Knives when they slaughtered a hundred or so opponents, including two Prussian generals, Schleicher and Bredow. 'She argues wildly for Hitler and [General Werner von] Blomberg and with a little less passion for Göring. She doesn't want to know too much about Goebbels and she is angry with Papen because he paid no attention to her warnings that his entourage was worthless and now it was too late.* On the one hand she thinks that not nearly enough people were shot on June 30 and on the other she says there were too many innocent people slaughtered.'[156] Hermine only lost her affection for Göring when he stood her up for lunch in Berlin in March 1936.[157]

Nor did the royal family wholly lose hope after the *Machtergreifung* of 30 January 1933. The Crown Prince attended the so-

---

* Edgar Jung and Herbert von Bose, conservative opponents of the Nazis and the inspiration behind Papen's Marburg University speech of 17 June. Both were shot on the 30th.[155]

called wedding of Prussianism and Nazism in the *Tag von Potsdam* of 21 March and remained in the Stahlhelm after it was merged with the SA. Now he served in a motorised division commanded by his cousin the Duke of Coburg. One day while wearing his *Kraftfahrerkorps* uniform he was photographed as a 'Nazi' along with his sons Hubert and Frederick. The picture, showing the prince wearing Nazi insignia, was noticed abroad and led to questions about the nature of his politics. It was also noted by a triumphant Hermine. 'Two years ago,' she told the Kaiser, 'your son was still saying that all the Nazis should be hanged, and now he's one himself!' The Kaiser was not amused and commented that his son looked like a policeman in his uniform.[158]

The Kaiser was still holding out for a sign from Berlin when on 24 March 1933 Hitler gave a speech on unemployment in which he spoke of the impossibility of a restoration. On 9 May, the Chancellor held a meeting in Königsberg with Hindenburg, with Blomberg and the Kaiser's House Minister Friedrich von Berg-Markienen in attendance. As Schleicher had told Heinrich Brüning, Hindenburg did not wish to go to his death without knowing that the restoration of the Kaiser was settled;[159] he considered his office as a simple trust, preserving Germany for the return of its emperor.[160] Possibly to please the victor of Tannenberg, Hitler claimed to be sympathetic and told the group that he saw the restoration 'as the conclusion of his work' and by this he 'meant to designate the Hohenzollerns alone', but 'the moment was not yet right. . . .'[161]

Hitler elaborated: 'The monarchical idea would prove a thankless task from which he would disentangle himself with difficulty.' It would 'run counter to [the precepts of] a National Socialist state'. It would also 'lead to difficulties with foreign governments'. Following the meeting, Blomberg told Dommes that Hitler saw himself first and foremost as a soldier: 'as such he believed it was impossible for the monarchy to return through a plebiscite or anything of that sort; only after a victorious war could the army restore the Kaiser to his throne.'[162] Hitler must have believed that the stain of defeat in 1918 could only be removed by a victory over Germany's traditional enemies.

Dommes provided the Kaiser with his own interpretation of the discussions which had taken place in Königsberg. He rebelled at the idea that the monarchy should become some sort of emblem for Germany: 'It would be a fundamental error to believe that the monarchy could be reduced to a mere decorative feature.' To the accusation that monarchy ran counter to the tenets of National Socialism, Dommes wrote: 'A far-sighted statesman has to tell himself that for the purposes of continuity in statecraft there must be a crown. Also the unbridled, all-powerful dictator must endeavour to guarantee the continuity of his work after his death and prevent it from being eroded.' Dommes was almost certainly right to suggest that no foreign government would interfere if the Germans decided to restore the monarchy. Finally he rose to the question of war: 'To talk of a victorious war in this case and make the restoration conditional on its outcome is to adjourn decisions for the foreseeable future. Clearly there is no positive desire to solve this problem.'[163]

The news from Germany was upsetting all round. The royal palaces had been festooned with swastikas including Frederick the Great's retreat at Rheinsberg. Worse by far was a speech by Hitler's agriculture specialist, Walther Darré,* delivered on 27 May in which the minister alleged that the Kaiser had betrayed the German peasantry: 'The November days [of 1918] presented him with a choice: do you want to live and die for your people? Or do you desire a nice, trouble-free life with every imaginable comfort? William II then opted for the pleasant life and the *Schloss*.'[164]

This accusation of cowardice still rankled that autumn. On 10 September Dommes wrote to complain to the head of Hitler's chancellery staff, Dr Lammers, and request an audience. He reminded Lammers of Hitler's own words that the restoration was

* *Ricardo* Walther Darré was the most international of the Nazi leaders. He was born in Buenos Aires and educated at an English public school, King's Wimbledon.

the 'crowning glory of his work'. 'His Majesty,' wrote Dommes, 'and the entire Royal Household greet the creation of a national government with the greatest of joy. As a result of this, and to stay in tune with the government, the Royal Household has ceased issuing any propaganda in its favour, thereby believing itself to be in keeping with the broad lines of NSDAP policy . . .'[165]

Dommes then goes on to mention a whole host of complaints against the Nazi-controlled press and their reports on the royal family. In several of these the Kaiser had been branded a 'freemason and a Jew-lover', while pro-monarchist demonstrations and speeches had not been reported. 'People say that a signal from above would be sufficient to tighten up on the press and render this sort of thing impossible.'[166] There had been numerous abuses of Hohenzollern property and in one case actual confiscation.

Lammers invited Dommes to a meeting at the Chancellery on 26 September in the course of which he endeavoured to convince the general that there was no government campaign behind the attacks and that they were mere 'flashes in the pan', the product of troubled times. Lammers was very keen to take Dommes up on his offer to cease propaganda on behalf of the Hohenzollerns: 'That sort of thing is way beneath its dignity.'[167] Dommes wondered whether it would not be possible to find some role for the royal princes; he suggested that they might participate in government in some way. 'Schade nichts,' was Lammers' laconic reply – 'Sorry, there is nothing.' In retrospect the Hohenzollerns must have been grateful for Lammers' intransigence.

Lammers then spoke some more about the Führer's monarchism. Hitler had pointed out that there was no clear pretender. The Kaiser and the Crown Prince had both renounced their claims to the throne, as had the Crown Prince's eldest son, Prince William, who had married a member of the minor nobility against his father's will and in contravention of the household law. Dommes, however, was explicit in his reply: 'In our eyes the head of the household is the king.'[168] He naturally did not agree that the time was not yet ripe for the restoration of the Hohenzollerns.

Despite being counselled to fly swastikas from Hohenzollern property, Dommes must have felt he was making progress and therefore asked Lammers whether it might not be possible to have an interview with Hitler himself. Lammers agreed and the meeting was fixed for 24 October. A training at the Kaiser's court came in useful, and on the appointed day Dommes started out by showering the Führer with flattery, reminding him of the small role played by the royal princes in the national revival. It was not long, however, before he turned the wrong corner by bringing up the issue of Hitler's succession: 'When his work stabilises; when he has imbued [the people] with the *Führerprinzip* which he has so often called sacrosanct; above all when he looks beyond his death and tries to prevent the power struggles which will ensue, then he must certainly look to the crown.'[169]

Hitler said modestly that he had no desire to aspire to the position of Reichs President and would remain Chancellor: 'Naturally he was aware that no one man could operate the whole system and that it should be founded on a house. He had no family; he had brought his own name into German history; in a few years it would be firmly anchored there. He had no ambitions beyond the accomplishment of the tasks he had set himself: above all the salvation of Germany from Bolshevism and the liberation of Germany from Jewish domination. That would be quite sufficient. But these tasks had not yet been achieved. Communism had certainly been crushed, but not annihilated; possibly there were still bloody battles ahead. He thought it questionable that the monarchy was tough enough to take them on . . .

'Few people understand the Jewish question.' At this point Dommes records that Hitler became passionate once again. 'He could not alter his position on this: the Jews were Germany's misfortune; they had created the revolution. . . .' Dommes noted in his report to the Kaiser, 'I had the impression that Hitler was launching an indirect attack on Your Majesty; accusing you of being a Jew-lover. I interrupted him and recounted the words Your Majesty used in 1911 after lunching with Admiral Hollmann: "It is the duty of the sovereign to make use of all the available forces in a nation. If we close the army and the civil service to the Jews, then we must give them an outlet through which they may use their intelligence and wealth for the benefit of the people, and this is science, art and charity." '

Clearly the Kaiser's wisdom made little impression on Hitler. He picked up the thread of his monologue: 'His tasks were the destruction of Communism and Judaism and he had to dedicate himself to them. He didn't know how much time was left to him. He might have passionate supporters but he possessed also fanatical enemies. He was not safe at any meeting. . . .'[170]

Dommes suggested that the monarchy was also able to deal with these problems and asked Hitler if he did not think this was so: 'He didn't answer my question, but returned to the issue of the Jews. Then he suddenly brought the interview to a close.'[171]

Hitler had left the channel open, allowing Dommes access to himself, or failing that, his deputy Rudolf Hess.[172] By 2 February 1934, Dommes had found another pretext to reopen negotiations with the Führer. Once again Darré was the cause. The Kaiser was upset by the accusation of having betrayed the German peasantry. Dommes even hints at a duel: 'As an old soldier I deplore the fact that I may not take up arms for the honour of my slighted lord.'[173]

The second audience was arranged for 27 April 1934. Dommes was still smarting from Darré's remarks. He complained of the 'not far short of libellous tendency to attack the idea of monarchy by launching into the last holder of the throne and his family. I am convinced that Hitler condemns this sort of attack as much as I do,' said Dommes, 'and I hope that just one word from him will be sufficient to suppress this underhand behaviour.'[174]

Hitler had prepared his answer in advance: he said that he had not made the November Revolution, but that one thing had to be said for it and that was it had defeated the princes. He had nothing against the concept of monarchy but had discovered the bitter truth that 'the bourgeoisie, the intelligentsia and the princes had brought little understanding to bear on his struggle; occasionally princes had abused him, the Crown Prince of Bavaria, for example, who had characterised the movement as "childish rabble". The princes tried to deny the fact that a little man together with little men could rescue Germany.'[175]

'He had his job to do. It would take between twelve and fifteen years and he wanted no one, not even the princes, to disturb him. He had nothing against the Kaiser. He had certainly made mistakes, but who hadn't?'[176] This was a heavily veiled allusion to Hitler's real thinking on the last Hohenzollern ruler whom he had never forgiven for leading Germany to defeat in 1918. In May 1942 he was to tell his table companions, 'The example of William II shows how one bad monarch can destroy a dynasty.'[177]

Once again the Führer became carried away by his own oratory: 'He would never marry, would never have children. He aspired to nothing in the way of a throne. . . .' One thing he wished to make clear: 'If Germany were ever again to become a monarchy, then this . . . must have its roots in the nation – it must be born in the Party, which is the nation. And Germany would never again be a federal state. He counted it among his greatest achievements that he had fulfilled the quest for a united state' by sweeping aside the old divisions which had preserved the character of Saxony, Bavaria or Prussia. Dommes had had his answer. All hope of a Hohenzollern restoration through the Third Reich could be cast aside.[178]

VI

The news that Prince August Wilhelm had been clouted by a policeman with a rubber truncheon on Königsberg Railway Station following a speech, aroused the greatest indignation at Doorn. The Kaiser told me, 'I put the House Ministry onto the matter at once, so that they would go round and see Hindenburg and express my outrage that the former chief of my armies cannot prevent my son from being publicly beaten by the republican police! It's a scandal! The Königsberg Police President must sack the officers responsible immediately, but of course this will never happen! My son, however, may become a martyr! And thousands of people will go over to the National Socialists and Mssrs Severing and Braun will be furious! I congratulated Auwi immediately.'[179]

The Kaiser's attitude to the Nazis was entirely opportunistic: he wanted his throne back and was prepared to do virtually anything to get it. One Hohenzollern however, felt a genuine commitment to the Nazi Party, and he was the 'brains' of the family, Prince August Wilhelm, or 'Auwi'. Auwi had always been an arty, bookish prince and, perhaps for this reason, not the Kaiser's favourite child. From Bonn University he had continued his studies in Strasbourg, which the Germans had made some effort to transform into a representative university of the new Reich. He graduated Dr Rer. Pol. and entered the civil service. While his brothers did their duty by representing the monarchy on parades and at sporting events, Auwi attended lectures and theatrical performances.[180]

Like his great-great-uncle, Frederick William IV, he was artistic and collected antiques and porcelain. He also excelled as a *raconteur*, making up fairy stories 'all by himself'. Besides the plastic arts he had a special feeling for music. He also loved nature and had a fondness for gardening. 'One of my loveliest childhood memories,' wrote Victoria Louise, 'was a trip to Venice with August Wilhelm. He explained everything wonderfully and illustrated the history of the lagoon city with a sight-seeing tour of palaces, churches and galleries.'[181]

During the Weimar Republic, Auwi lived in Wannsee, surrounded by his circle of intellectuals and artists, some of whom, we are told, were Jews. He brought the royal family into contact with the glittering cultural life of Berlin at that time, helping Max Reinhardt to stage Lessing's *Minna von Barnhelm* at Schloss Bellevue. Auwi's decision to join the SA in 1928 and the Nazi Party proper in 1930 therefore came as something of a surprise to his family, who saw the aesthete prince 'putting up with the often rather crude manners of his comrades. Politics became his passion and comradeship as expressed by the collective will of a *Kampfverband* a new part of his life.'[182]

If the Kaiser was already dismayed at having a civilian son, he was even less happy about the break-up of Auwi's marriage to Alexandra-Victoria of Schleswig-Holstein. Something of his attitude is apparent from an entry in Ilsemann's diary, recording one of Auwi's visits to Doorn in October 1924: 'At around 10 p.m. Prince August Wilhelm arrived. Dommes had gone to pick him up from the station. This was the first time he had visited his father in two and a half years. There was the usual greeting: a kiss on the hand, both cheeks, then on the hand again. We were very anxious, wondering how [the meeting] would go once the Kaiser and his son were alone together. The Kaiser, however, showed an enthusiastic desire for the General to come into dinner too, so that his *tête à tête* did not take place.' Later the Kaiser changed his schedule to avoid having to take his morning walk with Auwi.[183]

It was bad enough being rejected by his father, but Auwi suffered the same hostility from his stepmother, who made matters worse by encouraging the Kaiser in his opposition to the sensitive prince. In February 1930, Auwi told Ilsemann that 'he knew that Hermo hated him, especially since Nuremberg, where this summer she had come as Hitler's invitee. [Hermine] had asked Hitler if he didn't intend to bring her and the Kaiser back to Germany, but he had said no.'[184]

The Kaiser tolerated his wife's leanings, but at the beginning, at least, he was cross about his son's membership of the party. When, on 14 September 1930, the Nazis took 107 seats to the Socialists' 143, the Kaiser's attitude underwent a change. He began to see the Nazis as a possible means of regaining his throne and Auwi as his best link to the coming men: 'After the election results the Kaiser believed that he would become king again. Prince Auwi must be very proud "that he has backed the right horse".'[185] The Kaiser was now fascinated by the Nazis and longed for news. He was cross to learn a few days later that Hitler might have written him a letter which Auwi had failed to pass on.[186]

The bad mood passed. Auwi was cementing contacts after all. The next time he appeared at Doorn, the Kaiser greeted him with a cheery 'Ah! Guten Tag, Herr Volksredner!' (Good morning, Mr Orator!) He was nonetheless slightly worried by the thought of his son making platform speeches and had a message delivered to

Hitler asking that Auwi be exempted from this duty. Hitler replied that 'as in war, the Kaiser's sons belong in the front line.'[187] This was ironic, given his order to remove all Germany's princes from fighting units after the demonstrations of sympathy for the monarchy which accompanied the funeral of the Crown Prince's eldest son, killed in France in 1940.

The Kaiser's concern was not misplaced. In March 1931 Auwi was mixed up in a brawl in Königsberg and coshed by an overzealous police officer. As a result of the blow he lost his hearing in his left ear.[188] The wound stood him in good stead with the Nazis. As the only royal *alte Kämpfer*, he was promoted Gruppenführer or Lieutenant-General in the SA on 1 September 1933. By this time the Kaiser had had his flirtation with the Nazis and was aware that there was little to be gained from chasing them any further. He wanted Auwi's activities to cease.[189] Auwi, however, was now the toast of the party. When the family gathered for the Kaiser's birthday in January 1934 Auwi was full of praise for Hitler. 'There is no doubt that the Prince stands on excellent terms with the Führer. Hitler himself is convinced that one day he will fall victim to an assassination attempt. It is very good news for the Hohenzollerns that he [Hitler] can't bear Crown Prince Rupprecht of Bavaria.'[190]

Not even the Night of the Long Knives was able to chasten Auwi's enthusiasm for Nazism, a fact which became all the more perverse when it is known that the bloodbath very nearly claimed him as a victim. The Kaiser himself was deeply shocked, especially when he learned that General Schleicher's wife had been gunned down together with her husband: 'We have ceased to live under the rule of law and everyone must be prepared for the possibility that the Nazis will push their way in and put them up against the wall.'[191]

Auwi had been campaigning right up to the night. The *Osnabrücker Tageblatt* reported that Auwi's speech had rounded off with a 'triple *Sieg Heil* to our splendid Führer. Enraptured, the crowd sang the hymn to our immortal Horst Wessel.'[192] As an important SA leader and a friend of the murdered Gruppenführer Ernst,

Auwi was a prime target. He owed his salvation to Göring, who telephoned him in Cologne to summon him to Berlin. 'If the SS had discovered me that night I would have been shot,' Auwi told Ilsemann later, though he still had it in his heart to extol the virtues of Hitler, Göring and Himmler. He had less time for Goebbels, Darré and some others.[193] The Crown Prince thought he had gone mad.[194]

The only thing which appears to have bothered Auwi was that he now received a rather less prestigious membership number as one of the now-discredited SA. His continued membership had the power to put his father in a rage, and it is not hard to imagine that this was one of its attractions. In May 1935 the Kaiser complained that his son was signing off his letters with *Heil Hitler* or 'with the German greeting'. 'Whenever I read such things I have a premonition that Germany will soon be as good as dead!' As for Auwi: 'His fanaticism is almost insane. And what thanks did he get? What did he achieve? Absolutely nothing!'[195]

The Kaiser had forbidden Auwi to do any more work for the party, but his son paid little attention to the ban. When the pressure became too much he fled abroad for a while and then returned to his party work. Only six months after the show-down at the Kaiser's birthday party, he was helping the portly Göring to celebrate his forty-three years. The *Kristallnacht* on the night of 10–11 November 1938 brought the family conflict to the fore. The Kaiser was shaken, and forebore from one of his attacks on the Jews. 'What is going on at home is certainly a scandal. It is now high time that the army showed its hand; they have let a lot of things happen . . . all the older officers and all decent Germans must protest.'[196]

Auwi was unmoved. The days of his multi-racial Wannsee circle were long past. The Kaiser told Ilsemann, 'I have just made my views clear to Auwi in the presence of his brothers. He had the nerve to say that he agreed with the [anti-] Jewish progroms at home and understood why they had come about. When I told him that any decent man would describe these actions as gangsterism, he appeared totally indifferent. He is completely lost to our family, he simply does not belong to us any more.'[197] Auwi had the party to turn to but the party was increasingly uninterested in him and Goebbels for one agreed with the Kaiser that the prince's public-speaking days should come to an end.*

The *Kristallnacht* disturbed the old Kaiser. He wanted no more to do with the Nazis and their increasingly lawless state. This attitude did not change until 1940 when the Germans invaded Holland, arriving at Doorn on 14 May. The soldiers were led by a member of the very oldest Prussian nobility, Lieutenant Colonel von Zitzewitz of the General Staff, who informed the Kaiser he was now under the protection of the German army. After war broke out with Holland, the Kaiser had been officially under house arrest.

Hitler was looking for a sign from the Kaiser, some acknowledgement of his success, that 'the fetters of Versailles had finally been smashed'.[198] It is believed that it was either Dommes or Hermine who encouraged him to write a telegram of congratulations to Hitler on 17 June 1940, when the *Wehrmacht* entered Paris. The precise circumstances are still of some importance to the Hohenzollerns, as the post-war confiscation of Doorn and its contents happened in retaliation for the former Kaiser's apparent condonement of Hitler's war.[199]

The telegram† was far from gloating and can be construed at the very most as a grudging tribute to the skill of the army: 'In my profound emotion following the defeat of France may I offer my best wishes both to you and to the entire German army with the words of Kaiser William the Great: "What things have come about through God's bounty". In all German hearts sounds the Leuthen Chorale sung by the victorious troops of the Great King at Leuthen: *Nun danket alle Gott!*'[200] Hitler replied: 'I thank Your Majesty for your best wishes, expressed to me personally and to

---

* Auwi was bought off with a gold party badge and the rank of Obergruppenführer in the SA. The war years brought him little continued glory. In September 1942 he felt sufficiently relaxed to criticise Goebbels and Ley in the house of an Alsatian winemaker named Gillet. He was denounced and had to submit to interrogation in Berlin. He died, broken by his experiences of captivity at the hands of the Americans, in 1949.
† The Crown Prince also sent a telegram.

the German army after the fall of France. I hope that this victory will soon be crowned by our ensuring that all the forces of the German Nation blossom in the Greater German Reich.'[201]

Zitzewitz's assurances meant little. The Kaiser very soon became a prisoner of the SS in Doorn and even General von Falkenhausen, the military Governor of Belgium and Northern France, was unable to visit him. He collapsed on 1 March 1941. His ordeal ended three months later when he died on 4 June. Hitler did not attend his funeral.

III

Prussian Virtues and Vices

April 25 1757: There is a story doing the rounds ... such outrageous nonsense that no one would have believed it before now. A privy counsellor by the name of Behrens got it into his head that he was going to die on the 23rd. He had a coffin made and wrapped himself up in his shroud; then, clutching a lemon in his hand, he lay down in the coffin to wait for death. He had food brought to him there, and while he was there he wrote his will. His niece had to dress in mourning. The story caused considerable alarm when two people, who were quite oblivious of what was going on, all but died of fright when, walking into the house, the corpse – which was laid out in the hallway – suddenly began to speak. Finally the parish preacher came to try to convince him to leave [his coffin] but this was to no avail until Herr Kircheysen with two police officials arrived on the scene and pulled him out by force. His coffin has now been taken away from him and he is screaming pitifully that he is quite certain that he is going to die and that he has never been happier than he was in his coffin. Had this episode occurred in Roman times, people would have spoken of him as a great philosopher, yet Herr Behrens is seen as a lunatic, and rightfully so.

> *Aus den Tagebüchern des Grafen Lehndorff.* Herausgegeben und eingeleitet von Haug von Kuenheim.

Il n'y a point de rang ici, point d'etiquette, point d'ambassadeurs. Par cela même nous sommes à l'abri des disputes de préséances et de toutes ces chicanes de l'orgeuil des rois qui, dans d'autres cours, demandent des attentions sérieuses et qui dérobent un temps qu'on peut employer plus utilement au bien public.*

> Frederick the Great, Testament politique. In Gaxotte, *Frédéric II*, 305.

---

* There is no rank here and no etiquette or ambassadors. In this way we protect ourselves from quarrels over precedence and all that chicanery dictated by the vanity of kings which, in other lands, requires serious time to be devoted to it which could be better employed for the common good.

Borussophiliacs have made a good deal of the so-called 'Prussian virtues' though to this day an authoritative list is hard to come by.[1] Core virtues would begin with *Nüchternheit*: that blend of simplicity and sobriety which has no direct translation in English; *Nüchternheit* would also encompass a degree of spartanism and a horror of outward pretension or show. Also typical of the Prussian virtues are the readiness to serve, mostly in the military sense, but not unreservedly, and *Pflichterfüllung*, or doing one's duty. Modesty, thrift, discipline and *Opferbereitschaft* – the willingness to accept sacrifice – would also come up. They might be called the cardinal virtues. To most Prussians, however, a number of other virtues were also important. These would include hard work, self-denial, self-control, selflessness, decency, honesty, cleanliness, respect for the law, acceptance of responsibility, tolerance and punctuality.

'Üb' immer treu and Redlichkeit bis an dein kühles Grab'[2] (Show loyalty and honesty until your dying day) chimed the old glockenspiel in Potsdam's *Garnisonkirche*, and generations of Prussian recruits had that drilled into their heads on the dusty parade ground between the church and the *Stadtschloss*. Not for nothing was the garrison church one of the finest and most representative buildings set up during the reign of the Soldier King Frederick William I; for his stoicism embodied the Prussian virtues and provided an example for future generations. But if Frederick William was the first wholly virtuous Prussian, the origin of the Prussian code goes back much further, to the time of the Teutonic Knights and their austere, warrior-monasticism.

Throughout Germany east of the Elbe and the German-occupied areas to the east of the Oder, the colonial *Schwert* or *Dienstadel*, or military nobility, evolved a unique style in the need to perform their duties as knights at the same time as they tilled the newly conquered soil.[3] Not for them the gentler pursuits which developed with the waning of the Middle Ages: 'Knightly tournaments were replaced by border and family feuds. The pursuit of big game in virgin forests . . . was no courtly exercise with the noble ladies riding alongside; this required the whole man.'⁴

The martial origins of the Prussian nobility and the vast, sparse East Elbian landscape still contrived to lend a certain character to Prussian noblemen born in the last decades of the nineteenth century. 'All loyalty belonged to the king: he represented the peak of the state whom one served without reservation; his dynasty remained the symbol of life-fulfilling value. In its eastern provinces Prussia was still anchored in faith and duty. Duty called for work and service; faith meant responsibility to God and his Commandments. This gave direction to one's existence and upheld the inviolability of the law to which every man was subject. Although the world was severe and stark at the same time, it did not exclude pretensions to service. Prussia's intentions lay not just in the pursuit of power and land; in the lead-up to becoming a grown-up state in the mid-nineteenth century, it had always expended a great deal of its energy in forming and raising the level of its inner life. Above all, however, stood the ethos of public service, which was to be striven for no matter what your personal interests were. The best virtues were dedication and honesty, self-denial and modesty. More than any outward possession, counted honour and awareness of duty.'⁵

There was always a risk that, taken at face value, the virtues could become vices; that the call for obedience would lead to a particularly Prussian form of blind obedience called *Kadavergehorsam* (literally 'corpse obedience'), that consciousness of duty or the feeling of responsibility could turn into servility. These inherent dangers were not lost on the founders of the Bundesrepublik, who saw that, looked at from one angle, they could become the foundation of a welfare state, and, from the other, they could clear the way to the creation of one operated by the police.⁶

II

In 1870 the Silesian-born historian and novelist Gustav Freytag accompanied the Crown Prince Frederick (later briefly Kaiser Frederick I) on his campaigns during the first battles of the Franco-Prussian War. Freytag noted with foreboding the Crown Prince's ever-growing enthusiasm for the idea of a Prussian-led German Empire and the elaborate trappings that would inevitably come with it. In particular Freytag thought the imperial idea would corrupt the Hohenzollerns: 'What distinguishes the Hohenzollerns who, considered as men, have by no means always been greater and stronger than their fellow princes, from other kings, whose hereditary position is secure like theirs? Surely, above all, the circumstance that they have been compelled in self-preservation and in order to increase their power, to maintain the superiority of the German nation against the private interests of other illustrious families. Every great advance has been gained by them at times when this necessity ruled their lives and their actions. The dangers of their exalted position, the seclusion from the people, the empty pageantry, the persistence in a comparatively restricted sphere of views, the filling up of their days with graceful inanities, all this has had little danger for them in these two centuries of keen work. A certain Spartan simplicity and rigour has maintained discipline in the civil service, the army and the people. The new imperial dignity will soon change that . . .'[7]

Freytag painted a remarkably accurate picture of the court which would come into existence not under the Crown Prince, but under his son, the future Kaiser William II: 'All the splendour of majesty, the pomp attendant on the visits of princely personages, the court offices, the business of making costumes and decorations will increase, and, once introduced, will claim greater and greater importance. The simple blue coat of the Hohenzollerns will at last be brought out only as an antiquarian relic. The self-esteem of all the princes will be enhanced, but also the self-esteem of the nobility, and all the superannuated trash of old claims, no longer in harmony with the time, will rapidly increase.'[8]

Nor would the rot affect merely the monarchy. Freytag continues: 'The number of high-born gentlemen who receive high positions in the army, not on account of proved capacity, but on account of their birth, is already quite large enough. . . . [It is] already very difficult to maintain the old discipline and simplicity in the officers' messes; it will be possible in the future only if our princes themselves incessantly set a good example of simplicity and give the regiments no opportunity of spending money in the company of aristocratic comrades. . . . [In the civil service] a courtliness and servility will creep in which did not belong to our old Prussian loyalty.'[9]

Freytag's 'simplicity' was the old virtue of *Nüchternheit*. At its most extreme, *Nüchternheit* was little more than conscious or unconscious spartanism; the sort of thing which led Prussian holidaymakers on the Baltic coast to plunge into the sea at the tail end of the season, even though the water was only nine degrees.[10] Frederick William I provided a model for conservative 'old Prussians'. At his father's death he threw all pomp overboard and dressed alternatively as a *bourgeois* or a soldier. He worked nonstop and allowed only the simplest decoration in his building. He drank beer and avoided fancy food. He slept in a hard bed and washed outside in cold springwater.[11]

He had little time for affection. What he bestowed, he bestowed on the army and he was particularly hard on his civil servants. Functionaries who tried to quit the service were imprisoned, while those accused of lavish expenditure were dismissed in droves.[12] When in 1714 three Königsberg civil servants refused to transfer to Tilsit Frederick William wrote to the President of the Königsberg court, Graf Alexander von Dohna: 'When I order an officer to march under the command of Field Marshal Prince of Anhalt and this officer says: "I have a house and garden, a wife and child; the Prince is too nasty, I can and will not submit to his orders and I shall not march" – I say: "*Monsier* [sic], you are an old soldier and you know all too well: an officer who comes up with this sort of argument will come up before a court martial and before that he'll have his hands and feet bound in irons. And what is some scum of a writer compared to an officer!'[13]

Something of Frederick William's simple, soldierly demeanour reappeared with the first Hohenzollern Kaiser, William I. During the Siege of Paris when the German armies took over Louis XIV's palace of Versailles as their campaign headquarters, William preferred to stay in the rather more homely *préfecture* nearby. He rose at seven from an iron camp bed with little or nothing in the way of a mattress and the most rudimentary of coverings. Over his coffee he read his papers and the prepared extracts from the newspapers. Courtiers were not admitted before nine, just before the reports of the civil cabinet and the generals. At eleven he ate 'a snack', at four something more substantial was served up in his mess kit. After this he went back to work.[14]

William's simplicity was genuine enough. He liked soldiers and distrusted professional courtiers. When his ex-Minister of War and one of the three architects of German unification, Graf Albrecht von Roon, lay dying in February 1879, the Kaiser left word that he should be informed when the last hours approached. Roon was in the Hotel de Rome in Unter den Linden. As Roon's pulse slackened, the Kaiser was told that the moment had come. The Kaiser left the *Schloss* alone and on foot. 'Approaching the deathbed he said, "Roon, thank you for what you did for the army and me. Set up camp for me. Greet the old comrades. You'll find a lot of them up there." Scarcely had the Kaiser left than Roon lost consciousness and died.'[15]

The old Prussian contempt for flashiness or 'side' extended to a rather négligé approach to clothing. The distinguished East Prussian author and journalist Marion Gräfin Dönhoff remembers another old Prussian chiding her father about the shabbiness of his clothes: 'Tell me, who is it who wears your suits when they're new?'[16] Ursula von Kardorff, a descendant of an old Mecklenburg family which established itself in Prussia in the nineteenth century, was close to many of the leading opponents to Hitler among the Prussian nobility. Meeting Claus Stauffenberg for the first time she was struck by his 'south German polish'. Combined with his 'very masculine' appearance this made a mixture 'not often found in Prussia'.[17] Fritz-Dietlof von der Schulenburg, on the other hand, carried *insouciance* in sartorial matters to a degree which Ursula von Kardorff found remarkable: 'The trousers of his very shabby blue suit were crumpled and spotted with cement. "I look like a country parson, don't I?" '[18] His army uniform was 'patched' and he wore a 'ridiculous eyeglass' at all times, yet 'even if he came dressed in an old sack he would still look like a gentleman'.[19]

Bismarck used to claim that he always wore a military uniform as opposed to civilian clothes because it saved on wear and tear.[20] Kaiser William II was also rarely out of uniform. When he appeared in mufti, according to his daughter's English governess, Miss Topham, he lost a good deal of his bearing. She compared him unfavourably to British men who somehow managed to look comfortable in their clothes: 'He's really not himself when he's not wearing an army or navy uniform.'[21]

Much of Kaiser William II's character must have had its origins in his complex psyche and the physical deformities he tried so hard to conceal. Unlike his grandfather, the *Reichsgründer* William I, the last Kaiser was not a simple, *nüchtern* character. His obsession with luxury contrasted ill with the unpretentious lifestyle of the old Prussian nobility who lived mostly on the land, combining a patronal role with the pressures imposed on them by the soil, pressures which marked them out but little from the peasants. The unfortunate Schach von Wuthenow, in Theodor Fontane's novel of that name, imagines his life as it will become once his social indiscretion forces him to leave the army: 'I can see exactly how it will turn out: I'll take over Wuthenow; I'll farm, make improvements, grow rape or beet and go out of my way to offer a picture of marital devotion. What a life, what a future! A sermon *every other* Sunday, on the following a reading from the Evangelists or the Epistles and in between whist *à trois*, always in the company of the same pastor. Then one day a prince arrives in the neighbouring town, possibly Prince Louis himself, and I make an appearance while he changes his horses, waiting for him at the town gate or the inn. And he scrutinizes me in my old-fashioned coat and asks me: "How are things?" While everybody can see what he thinks: "Oh my God, what three years can do to a man!" Three years, it could be thirty.'[22]

Not all Prussian gentlemen were so immune to the charms of the simple life of the *Gutshaus* or manor: 'The great winter pig-killing session, the autumn hunts, the great swarms of bees, the milch cows and herds of sheep, they made sure we didn't go hungry. I don't recall meeting coal till much later in life, but there was always lots of wood to hand. An old man with a gammy leg chopped it into small pieces. There wasn't much money about, and luxuries were available only in tiny doses in those days.'[23]

That was East Prussia, the remote top right-hand corner of the Prussian kingdom. True to form the Kaiser also had his East Prussian estates at Cadinen and Rominten, but the rural idyll so cherished by Magnus von Braun was not enough. He decided to 'improve' Cadinen: new cow sheds were built and a vast garage for his cars with lodgings above for his grooms and chauffeurs. The old hovels where peasants, pigs and chickens had lived together in a picturesque jumble were cleared away and replaced by cottages taken from an English copybook.[24] The last refuge of Prussian spartanism was to be Rominten, up by the Russian border. In this hunting lodge the Emperor played at being a Prussian of the old school. 'It is high time you came to live here,' he told Miss Topham, 'to teach you how to forgo cushions. Here we live a hard life.'[25]

The charm of Prussian villages with their clutter of brick and half-timbered buildings around a modest church and the village pond, was lost on casual pre-war visitors; often enough it took a *Märker* such as Udo von Alvensleben to recognise the beauty and absence of baroque flummery behind their *Nüchternheit*. On one of his many journeys across Germany on the eve of the war, Alvensleben also compared Prussian towns favourably to those in neighbouring Saxony: 'Those of the Mark have a rough charm. The Medieval dominates, where in Saxony it is renaissance and baroque. They enjoyed rich times when Brandenburg was poor and unproductive. In the one there is *joie de vivre*, in the other "duty".'[26]

Here and there, in Brandenburg, Poland or the Kaliningrad province of Russia, one still comes across the occasional perfectly preserved Prussian village, but very few survived the war and escaped the vengeful blows of later generations of East German socialists, Poles or Russians. Only in the rarest instances has the manor remained standing; and only then when this relic of oppressive *Junkertum* could be put to some suitable new use, as a recreation home for members of the party or the secret police.

Before the Red Army put them to the flames, Prussian country houses were generally modest affairs. It is said that Napoleon Bonaparte was distinctly under-impressed by the princely piles which became his quarters as he charted his course through Prussia. Only when he saw Schloss Finckenstein, where he was to pass his idyll with the Polish Countess Walewska, did he mutter some restrained words of approval: '*Enfin un château.*'[27] Steinort, the chief seat of the Lehndorff family, lies to the north of the Mazurian Lakes.* When Alvensleben visited the house in August 1930, the head of the family was Graf Carol Lehndorff, an eccentric old man with only the vaguest idea of who was actually staying under his roof. Guests were put up in a suite of improvised dormitories: 'As there are no corridors, one must always walk through a series of rooms thereby disturbing someone. Everywhere there are the remnants of splendid decoration, but no comfort whatsoever.'[28] Alvensleben recalled a particular Steinort smell of 'leather, dogs, hunting and horses'.[29] Marion Dönhoff, who used to stay there with her cousins as a child, remembers the danger of opening a window at Steinort: the sashes were so rotten that there was a risk that the window would fall into the courtyard, frame and all.[30]

Nor was the Dönhoff seat, that other great East Prussian residence, Friedrichstein, 'The East Prussian Versailles', any more comfortable. Downstairs were the great rooms dating back to the

---

* Steinort is a rare survivor. It is now a Polish children's home.

time of the Soldier King. Upstairs in the bedroom the atmosphere was perfectly spartan. The rooms were equipped with bed, cupboard and wash-table, ewer and basin – 'There was no running water.'[31] Gräfin Dönhoff remembers the pangs of envy she felt on seeing a simple decorative feature in the room of one of her sisters: a porcelain rabbit with red eyes, built into a clock.

The later Generalleutnant Emil von Lessel discovered that outside the hallowed world of great houses, East Prussian life could be simpler still: '. . . no question of so-called champagne billets [*Sektquartieren*]. In the manor houses they praise the simpler sort of life. . . . The men receive a bed only in exceptional circumstances, in general they have to spend the night on straw. Also for officers was a straw sack the rule. None the less the houses were clean . . .'[32]

As a soldier Lessel could put up with a good deal of discomfort. He himself tells the story of how his chief, Graf Hülsen-Haeseler, occupied the former Welf palace in Hanover. 'The conference room was unheated as the count shunned anything which might create dust, the only things finding favour in his eyes being Godly nature. For members of the general staff assembled for the briefing it was not exactly pleasant to find no source of warmth, even in winter. When one day, however, the teeth of the *Intendan-turrat*,* an elderly officer of the former Hanoverian army, began to chatter audibly. At our next briefing he surprised us by having a crackling fire burning in the oven. The effect was merely suggestive, however, for once the scanty portion of logs had burned out it was as cold as ever. No one had ever sat on the sofa: it served as a place for stowing documents while the greater part of the floor was plastered with General Staff maps and when the count wanted to look at something on them, he lay down on the ground.'[33]

---

* A quartermaster in the British Army. Note it is the Hanoverian's teeth which chatter, not the Prussians'.

III

A Prussian courtier observes one of the Kaiser's lavish picnics: '"Ah! How times have changed!" he said sadly. "My father told me about the simple way in which old Kaiser William lived. He never went out with more than one aide de camp and never a great crowd like this! (as he said these words he designated with his hand the ranks of noblemen whose eyes were fixed on the Kaiser busy making up a strawberry punch from his own recipe). He never used more than one carriage, or two at the very most. Just look at that great procession!" And his gaze followed the long line of carriages parked in the shade not far off. . . . He shivered and shook his head, muttering words of blame and prophesying disaster.'[34]

Prussians were spartan, but not always sober. Naturally the officers' mess often hummed with drunken revels which gave the lie to the famous *Nüchternheit* of the nobility.[35] In former times the endless 'toping and brawling'[36] had led to brutal beatings during which close relatives were despatched on such slim pretexts as a missing hen or a misappropriated meadow. The East Prussians were believed to be the leaders in the field of heavy drinking; already halfway to Russia they were thought to possess hollow legs. After serving in East Prussia, however, the Silesian Lessel thought their bad reputation wildly exaggerated: 'The officer corps is made up predominantly of East Prussians while the men are to a large degree culled from Mazuria, Evangelical "Poles" from the southern half of the province, and mostly reliable, sober (*nüchterne*) people. I cannot vouch for the reputation for drunkenness which clings to our countrymen to the north and south of the Pregel.* In the Reich one occasionally hears the East and West Prussians described as "half-Russians", if this is the case then the latter must be excellent people.'[37]

In Memel on the Russian frontier, Pastor Rehsener had a far less generous view of the local population whom he found excessively given to drinking. This led him to try his hand at one or two very modern cures: 'Whenever marital problems were

---

* The river which bisects the north of East Prussia. Now called the Pregolya.

caused by drinking – which was generally the case – then [the drinker] had to swear that he would go without schnapps from that moment onwards. He had to visit me twice a day, morning and evening and I questioned him and admonished him. A wholly frank confession was an inviolable condition and at the same time it was agreed that the wife should come to me once a week and offer her own testimonial. If the man could remain true to his word in this way for a whole week it was a proof that he could leave off schnapps and that he was no longer in desperate straits.'[38]

Drunkenness was not a monopoly of the East Prussians by any means: Bismarck's Falstaffian son Herbert caused considerable worries. Fritz von Holstein, the Foreign Minstery's *éminence grise*, had this to say about the drinking habits of the Iron Chancellor's eldest boy: 'In the evenings Herbert is in a state of alcoholic excitement, in the mornings before lunch he has more or less of a hangover; after lunch he likes to take a refreshing nap with a newspaper over his knees.' One day he and a colleague decided to try out a new rifle by shooting it through the window of a civil servant by the name of Brauer. Later they came into Brauer's office to examine the effect. They made no apology for smashing Brauer's window or the expensive ventilating machine the latter had had installed. Brauer was incensed, pointing out that a clerk might well have been hit bringing in despatches. 'Yes,' replied Herbert Bismarck, 'and what silly faces the chaps would have made when the bullets went singing about their heads.'[39]

Herbert Bismarck had been one of the boon companions of Kaiser William II's youth, but the latter was by contrast an abstemious man. At his receptions white and red wine and champagne were served to the guests but neither the Kaiser nor the Kaiserin partook, contenting themselves with fruit juice. 'William is an avowed enemy of alcohol and preaches from his own example.'[40] He had contempt for English drinking habits and reserved particular scorn for whisky: 'I tasted whisky once,' he told Miss Topham, 'it's liquid fire . . .'[41]

The Kaiser's drug was not drink but power and magnificence. His father was not as different in this as some have supposed and

Gustav Freytag made the astute observation that Frederick's reign might have been 'unpleasantly surprising' had he not arrived on the imperial throne already wracked with throat cancer. Even before the Empire had become a reality Frederick had ordered new crowns for himself and his bride, Queen Victoria's eldest daughter, Victoria. 'The Crown Prince ... adhered to the view that the new imperial dignity received its due consecration only when it was regarded as the continuation of the old Roman Imperial sovereignty, and it was he who, at the beginning of the first German Reichstag in 1871, astonished the deputies by introducing the ancient chair of the Saxon Emperors into the modern inaugural ceremony.'[42] At one time Frederick even considered adopting the title of Frederick IV, as he was the first German Kaiser of that name since the father of Maximilian I, the Holy Roman Emperor Frederick III, who died in 1493.

All this seemed too great a departure from tradition for the old Prussians. Writing in 1871, Freytag had delivered his first warning on this score: 'Yes, we are decidedly averse to seeing reminiscences of the old imperial state of the Holy Roman Empire furbished up again in the House of the Hohenzollerns. We in the north have, without any great enthusiasm, submitted to the imperial title, so far as it is an instrument of political power, helping to unite our nation, and so far as it renders their hard work easier for our princes. But our Hohenzollerns are to wear the imperial mantle only as an officer's overcoat which they put on ... when on duty, and then put off again; we wouldn't for the world that they should dress themselves up with it and stride along under the crown as the old emperors did.'[43]

Frederick's son, the Kaiser William II, was decidedly more interested in being the German Emperor than he was in the humble traditions associated with the Crown of Prussia. In the days following the 1918 revolution, the East Prussian painter Lovis Corinth compiled a list of the Kaiser's follies beginning with the 'Sic volo, sic jubeo'* he inscribed in the golden book of

---

* You do what I want.

the Munich *Rathaus* at the beginning of his reign. The others were: 'Regis voluntas – suprema lex'*; shoot your parents and brothers for your Kaiser; Bismarck as William's dogsbody; the Social Democrats are fellows without a fatherland; William I called 'the Great'; that lying telegram to Ohm Krüger during the Boer War; and the secret telegrams to England.†[44]

It was a style of kingship which was bound to stretch the loyalties of those brought up in the Prussian tradition. All previous Prussian rulers from Frederick William III's time had been fundamentally pious. The Kaiser, however, had only a confused notion of what truth was: his personal will was enough. He was going to do what *he* wanted even if that meant a complete break with the Prussian tradition of *Nüchternheit*. The saddest thing about the Kaiser is that he was able to dupe himself into believing that he was carrying on the traditions of Frederick the Great as he swanned around his palaces in the presence of his favourite princes and Silesian magnates. For the bicentenary of the Prussian monarchy in January 1901 he indulged in an orgy of make-believe only to be briefly brought down from the clouds by the death of his grandmother, Queen Victoria, at Windsor. Programmes preserved from the time show the Kaiser revelling in flattery to an indecent degree as he sits through a performance of *Der Adlerflug* (The Flight of the Eagle) by Josef Lauff‡ and *Das Testament des Grossen Kurfürst* (The Testament of the Great Elector) by Gustav zu Putlik.[45]

More than anyone else, it was Kaiser William II who compromised the spirit of Prussianism and contributed the most to its demise. That *Nüchternheit* had all but disappeared by the time of the Second World War and Prussian generals reconciled it with their consciences to accept large bribes from Adolf Hitler. Witness the oldest Field Marshal in the army, Mackensen, whose sympathies were acquired in 1935 by means of a gift of 5,000

* The king's will is the last word.
† The Kaiser claimed during the *Daily Telegraph* interview (see above, p. 82) that he had sent telegrams of encouragement to the British during the Boer war.
‡ Ennobled, one assumes for toadying, in 1913.

Reichsmarks and an estate.[46] Or Kluge who, receiving a present of 250,000 Reichsmarks on his sixtieth birthday, openly referred to it as 'a tip' from the *Führer*.[47] Or Brauchitsch, who sought Hitler's assistance in getting him through a tricky divorce.[48] Or Blomberg, whose lack of self-control led him to place his trust in high-up Nazis who were keen to ruin him and remove him from his post.[49] And Manstein who, having refused to join the opposition, was nonetheless sacked by Hitler and spent his retirement travelling round Pomerania looking for the estate he had always dreamed of, 'despite the fact that everyone who had given the matter some thought, knew that Pomerania would be given to the Poles once we had lost the war'.[50]

IV

We led a simple life in the officer corps. The officers of the regiment were nearly all without private means; only a few had a monthly allowance of more than 10 Talers and a significant number had none whatsoever. The monthly wage of a second lieutenant amounted to around 20 Talers; there was a supplement for Magdeburg of five Talers and an allowance of two or three Talers for food making some 28 Talers a month from which we had to pay our mess-bills and stoppage of 5 Talers for clothing. What was left over hardly even covered the necessities of life and despite our simple life many brother officers got deeply into debt with tradesmen. At table we drank water or beer and only occasionally a bottle of wine. On feast-days there was a frightful punch made from bitter oranges which wouldn't have measured up to the most ordinary light white wines of today. There was lively companionship and whoever could muster the means could shine in balls and the best society. Most [however] were limited to the entertainments laid on by the two married subalterns. There there was roast meat and a dessert and red wine with it. Only on the occasion of the King's birthday and the regimental founder's days did they really splash out and we had French champagne; German fizzy wine was not at all known at the time. It is a sign of how simple our lives were that there were older officers who had never been to Berlin and these interesting gentlemen would declare that they had never tried an oyster and thought the idea of drinking sparkling wine other than on the [regimental] feast days was reprehensible.[51]

The pre-imperial Prussians were thrifty and modest in their expectations. Frederick the Great had spent his years of peace making economies which would allow him to mount another campaign.[52] He was not impressed by courtiers who felt their appointments insufficient to their needs and in a letter to one Baron von Blanckart he made himself crystal clear: 'If you lack the means to live without a salary I am happy to grant you permission to take up some post abroad.'[53] It will be recalled that 'travailler pour le roi de Prusse' meant working for little or no pay.

Thrift ruled even in households which were not short of money.[54] Henning von Tresckow's family estate in the Altmark near Magdeburg was not very profitable, so Henning's mother practised a fierce financial regime in her household accounts: 'The pleasures they allowed themselves were modest ones. When Frau von Tresckow had Christmas presents to buy for the village she travelled up to Berlin on the train third class. While she was in the city she also avoided unnecessary expenses; most of the time she stayed the night in the cheapest hospice.'[55]

Tresckow's mother was actually a daughter of Graf Robert von Zedlitz-Trützschler, a member of a Silesian magnate family for whom a rather more lavish existence had generally been the rule. The frugal life tended to affect the core provinces of Brandenburg-Prussia. In 1803, for example, *Gut* Trieglaff in Pomerania (not yet owned by the Thaddens, who later made the name famous) possessed no silver, no porcelain and only a very few pictures. 'Bismarck recalled seeing thatched-roofed, half-timbered Pomeranian manor houses in his youth, where the floor was strewn with sand for cleanliness sake.'[56] Field Marshal Freiherr von der Goltz was brought up on an extremely modest estate in Preussisch-Eylau in East Prussia, where 'the rectangular farmyard was [a jumble] of half-timbered buildings, white-washed and picked out with black [and at the centre] the low built, thatched-roofed manor house. [There was a] shallow pond and the little, overgrown orchard – all of which was not just redolent of a certain modesty but also a hopeless backwardness. The family was too impecunious to maintain Fabiansfelde [the name of the estate] and they grew so poor that Colmar von der Goltz' mother considered having her son learn the trade of coopering.'[57]

The very remoteness of the eastern provinces of Prussia bred in its nobles a fierce spirit of independence and, despite what was sometimes extreme poverty, they were little kings on their own land 'with fur cap, stick and potato as crown, sceptre and orb'.[58]

Even a *Märkisch* nobleman such as Fontane's Dubslav von Stechlin was most reluctant to put on the airs of a Western European nobleman and positively revelled in the simplicity of his lifestyle. Any poor soul who innocently referred to the family house as a *Schloss* was likely to get short shrift from the master: 'For you it's a "*Schloss*", but in reality it's no more than an old barracks.' Dubslav, we are told, also took pride in writing 'Haus Stechlin' at the head of his letters, in lieu of the more correct Schloss Stechlin.[59] Nor were the aristocratic lodgings of Fontane's Berlin-based nobles any more lavish. In *Irrungen, Wirrungen*, Baron Botho von Rienäcker occupies a ground-floor apartment in the Bellevuestrasse off the Potsdamerplatz, composed of just study, dining room and bedroom. He nonetheless furnished his rooms in a somewhat extravagant style with pictures by fashionable painters and a Rubens copy.[60]

Nor must one imagine the comfortable rectories of English Anglican priests: Prussian Lutheran pastors lived lives as simple as their flocks. In Memel, Pastor Rehsener had been a well paid 'candidate' employed in the house of one of the richer local merchants to teach the children. As soon as he qualified as a preacher his salary dropped from nine hundred Talers to just sixty-nine Talers and twenty *Silbergrosschen*, plus various legacies in the form of cash, firewood and oxen fodder. Even when he had added to his income by teaching six hours a week he could only bring his earnings up to three hundred Talers, a third of what he had received as a tutor.[61]

With the beginning of the Empire and even more so with the accession of William II, a new taste for luxury began to creep in. In 1890 attempts were made to limit the extravagance of officers by fixing their allowances at a fifth of their average expenditure.[62]

Here it was the Kaiser who set a bad example, and it was increasingly difficult to tell noble-born officers to lead a simple, Prussian life when their king and emperor was squandering money in such unheard of quantities. Opposition newspapers were not above saying as much. Once William II had settled into the job, he spent no more than half the year in his principal residences in Berlin and Potsdam. In March he cruised in the Mediterranean. The early part of the year was set aside for visits to Alsace, Wiesbaden and East Prussia; then in June there was Kiel Week, a conscious attempt to bring the splendour of Cowes Week to Schleswig-Holstein. In July the Kaiser set sail for Scandinavia; in August he was either in Cowes or at the Hessian Palace of Wilhelmshohe near Kassel. In October he was back in East Prussia to shoot; in November there was shooting on the estates of his favourite courtiers or Silesian magnates: Liebenberg, Letzlingen, or with the Fürstenbergs at Donaueschingen.[63]

During her time as governess to Princess Victoria Louise, Miss Topham visited thirty of the Kaiser's palaces and stayed in nine of them. The only one which gave the impression of being 'home' was the Neues Palais in Potsdam; the others reminded her of hotels.[64] It had been difficult to upgrade a number of the royal residences to give them the standard of comfort necessary to please the imperial family. The Neues Palais had been ripped apart to install the necessary bathrooms.[65] Even the royal train had been decked out with every imaginable convenience, including a bathroom.[66] For William I it had been enough to have a bathtub brought over to his Berlin *Schloss* from the Hotel de Russie once a week. Even in the last year of the First World War his grandson was worrying about the lack of a purpose-built bathroom on his special campaign train and commissioned one from some coppersmiths in Brussels.[67]

There was undoubtedly something obsessive about the Kaiser's desire to see himself surrounded by magnificence and to turn Prussia's court and capital into a rival to St Petersburg, Paris, Madrid, Vienna or London. It is wholly in keeping with his character and that of the empire that the cathedral opposite the Berlin Schloss should have been deemed too lacking in splendour to remain in the simple costume Karl Friedrich Schinkel had designed for it. To please the Kaiser the building was 'embellished', with marble, gold and silver, stuck in profusion to every conceivable surface within and without. Count Robert Zedlitz-Trützschler observed this signal decline in Prussian virtue: 'One day, one of the guides [to the building] pointed out to some visitors who were going over the Cathedral that a certain mosaic had not been approved by the Emperor. Somebody asked quite naturally: "What are you going to do about it?" "We shall remove it and make another." "What will that cost?" "About ten thousand pounds but that doesn't matter, because the chief thing is that the Kaiser shall like it." '[68]

By November 1903, Zedlitz-Trützschler was recording massive overspending on the Kaiser's new palace in Posen. The *Kaiserhaus* had been conceived as a naive affirmation of the Prussian presence in the Grand Duchy and one presumes it excited much disgust amid the very large Polish minority in the city. The cause of the increased cost turned out to be the Kaiser's insistence on separate apartments for the Crown Prince and Princess and the provision of a *cour d'honneur*. The final cost was five or six million Reichsmarks.[69] During the Second World War, Udo von Alvensleben was to point out that Hitler's flashy new Chancellery cost precisely double the amount of this last great *folie de grandeur*.[70]

The *Kaiserhaus* in Posen was a project typically lacking in tact, and hardly necessary when one thinks of the seventy-five other castles the Emperor had at his disposal, with their retinue of five hundred servants and forty cooks.[71] At Kiel Week Zedlitz-Trützschler watched with disgust as the Kaiser greeted a visit from his cousin King Edward of Great Britain by laying on dinner for 180 and tea for 220 people. Worse still was that the Kaiser chose the occasion for a tactless ramble on the inadequacy of the British political system. Zedlitz-Trützschler found the Kaiser's 'moral arrogance'. . . 'dangerously like the unctuousness of the Pharisee'.[72]

Byzantinism, a term coined to describe toadying at court, stands in stark opposition to all traditional Prussian virtues. With time even the stoutest and most martial of the Junkers could be transformed into fawning courtiers.

V

Hindenburg: I have now done my duty for seven years and I'm longing for retirement.
Otto Braun: There I can sympathise. I have been in office for nearly fourteen years, even if I am a lot younger than you. Duty, however, requires us to stand by our posts in these difficult times for as long as we enjoy the trust of the nation.
Hindenburg: *Na ja*, that is also true. For ages now I've detested all these parties and parliamentary squabbles. As a soldier I was always accustomed either to command or to obey. All this coming and going with parties suits me not a jot.
Otto Braun: I don't like it either. Sometimes I should also like just to command, that is more pleasant than negotiating, but in a democratic state you have first to convince people before you can order them about.[73]

Old Prussia was a highly stratified society with a distinctly military profile. The division between nobles and peasants was highlighted by the fact that noblemen retained their hold on the choicer parts of the officer corps right up until the First World War: the nobles commanded, the peasants obeyed. Intellectuals and professionals were generally exempted from service, thereby occupying a sort of limbo between the two as *Federfuchser* or pen-pushers. The better born among the civil servants and lawyers would have also served in one of the regiments, if only as officers of the reserve, and therefore enjoyed the right to wear uniform when it suited them. At the head of the political edifice stood the king, more often in uniform than out of it.

Field Marshal Paul von Beneckendorff und von Hindenburg was a bizarre choice for *Reichspräsident* of the Weimar Republic: an unabashed monarchist who represented the most uncompromising Prussian tradition of the *Nur-Soldat*, the soldier who refuses to concern himself with anything other than the business of obeying his superior officer and commanding his juniors. As he himself expressed it, 'the duty to serve your king and with that the right ... to be able to set an example to others through one's death.'[74]

The extremity of this tradition of service among the old *Dienstadel* made it difficult for them to shake the scales from their eyes when confronted by an inadequate monarch. When the monarchy disappeared for good in 1918, there were those who refused to serve the new Weimar Constitution, but officers and nobles such as Colonel General Hans von Seeckt decided to swallow their personal distaste for the new brooms because they recognised the legitimacy of the new regime. Similarly, many generals, whatever their political views, refused to countenance the idea of assassinating Hitler: 'Prussian field marshals do not mutiny,' Manstein told Rudolf-Christoph von Gersdorff, conveniently forgetting the example of Yorck von Wartenburg.* Asked whether he would lead the armed forces after a successful putsch, Manstein replied, 'I will always put myself loyally at the disposition of the legitimate government.'[75]

The debate will long continue as to whether Manstein's sense of *Gerechtigkeit*, or submission to the law, was appropriate in the circumstances. For Frederick the Great service had been a two-way process: he was merely the first servant of the state, and could in no way neglect his duty. The Byzantinism of the court of William II led to a complete distortion of this primitive, stoical idea: the generals stood by and allowed the Kaiser to cheat at manoeuvres. When the Kaiser's 'lessons in how not to do it'[76] stretched Waldersee's endurance to the limit, Waldersee saw to it that the Kaiser lost; Waldersee was promptly sacked.[77] As Zedlitz remarked, 'Not a soul (not even Schlieffen [Waldersee's successor as Chief of the General Staff]) ventures to whisper a critical objection, but there are not wanting men in very high, even in the highest positions, who seize every opportunity of assuring His Majesty that everything has been interesting, instructive and magnificent.'[78] Zedlitz was also appalled when General, later Field Marshal, von Mackensen 'went so far as to give us a good imitation of tears'[79] when the Kaiser paid him a visit in Marien-

---

* Yorck was not a field marshal at the time of his 'mutiny' (see above, pp. 48–49). Possibly this altered Manstein's view of his behaviour at Tauroggen.

burg. August von Mackensen was by no means a hereditary member of the Prussian *Dienstadel*: he had fought in the Franco-Prussian War as a sergeant and been ennobled only in 1899.

A well-placed sense of duty was a positive thing for many Prussians. Hindenburg may have detested the republic over which he presided, but it was not until the very end, when governments ruled only by decree, that he could ever be said to have betrayed it. As he told Otto Braun, the Socialist Minister-President of Prussia, 'You know I've never made any bones about it, I'm a monarchist and I shall remain one. [But] I have sworn an oath on the constitution and duty requires me to remain true to it.'[80]

Hindenburg also expresses a sense of discipline, carrying out a duty no matter how personally disagreeable it may be. Once again the virtue had its origin in the remote, unyielding estates of the Prussian *Landjunker* and in the training young Prussian noblemen received when they joined their regiments. As an 'Einjährige', Magnus von Braun had to serve a year with his regiment in order to be commissioned as a reserve officer. A university graduate, he had not looked forward to spending six weeks sharing a dormitory with the men. The experience was not as unpleasant as he had been led to believe. Despite the concentration on parade drill, Braun did not get the impression that that was the message behind the teaching; rather it was 'self discipline'.[81] Disorder and lack of discipline were always distasteful to Prussians. The Westphalian Heinrich Brüning recalled arriving at his ministry during the Kapp Putsch of 1920 to hear the porter complain, 'A terrible time. Even when the king has gone peace and order must reign in Prussia. These revolutionaries simply do not know discipline any more.'[82]

Like duty, obedience was a two-way process. That early defender of 'the other Prussia', Professor Hans Joachim Schoeps, used to remind his students at the University of Erlangen of the dictum of the Kurfürst Frederick III (King Frederick I), that 'kings are there for the sake of their subjects and not *vice versa*, and that it was only possible to rule well on this basis ...'[83] Frederick's grandson, Frederick the Great, told the young Duke of Württemberg in 1744, 'Don't imagine that the state of Württemberg was created for you; understand rather that providence brought you into the world to make the nation happy.'[84]*

Frederick the Great had a nasty streak. His hatred of Saxony and its rulers is well known. The plundering of Schloss Charlottenburg near Berlin had not been forgotten when in 1760 he issued orders to his soldiers to sack Schloss Hubertusburg. As an incentive to the troops he gave them leave to carry off whatever they wanted from the castle. Colonel Johann Friedrich Adolf von der Marwitz of the elite Gensdarmes regiment received the order, but, in response, simply shook his head. A few days later, at table, the king asked Marwitz if his orders had been carried out. Marwitz said no. Another few days passed and Frederick asked the question again 'whereupon the same laconic reply was heard'. 'Why not?' asked the king. 'Because in such cases one might use a mercenary officer, but not the commander of His Majesty's Gensdarmes.' The king gave the job to a French officer, a certain Guichard, who went by the name of Quintus Icilius.[86] Marwitz looked for an opportunity to renounce his command. At first Frederick refused. When Marwitz fell ill he had to accept his resignation, but once he had recovered, Frederick offered him the command of another regiment. Marwitz refused, saying that he had done his bit and now wished only for retirement. Marwitz died in 1781, five years before his king. He had the following words inscribed on his gravestone: '*Wählte Ungnade, wo Gehorsam nicht Ehre brachte*' (Chose disfavour where obedience brought no honour).[87]

In Frederick the Great's time such examples were not infrequent. The real victor of Rossbach and Zorndorf, Friedrich Wilhelm von Seydlitz, also decided to ignore one of Frederick's orders, adding, 'Tell His Majesty, after the battle I place my head

---

* 'Une femme vint présenter une requête à un roi d'Épire [actually Philip of Macedon], qui la brusqua en lui disant qu'elle devait le laisser en repos. Et pourquoi es-tu donc roi, repartit-elle, si ce n'est pas pour me rendre justice? Belle sentence dont les princes devraient se souvenir sans cesse.'[85]

Trans: A woman presented herself to the King of Epirus (actually Philip of Macedon) with a request, but he dismissed her saying that she should leave him in peace. And why are you the king, she replied, when you cannot give me justice? It is a good response and princes should bear it contantly in mind.

at his disposition, during the battle I hope still to use it in His Majesty's service.'[88]

In the mid-nineteenth century, the Marwitz family still clung to their fierce independence *vis à vis* the crown. When the future king and Kaiser William I referred to the *Landrat** of Lebus, Bernhard von der Marwitz of Friedersdorf, as 'unavoidable', Marwitz took it ill: 'If your Royal Highness believes that I am here for my own pleasure he is making a mistake! Work brings me here [*Ich bin im Dienst*]. The next time your Royal Highness comes I shall naturally stay away!'[89]

Such stories are often invoked to show that Prussian obedience was not unthinking *Kadavergehorsam*. In more recent times, shortly before Prussia's final eclipse, an officer enlisting in the 9th Infantry Regiment in Potsdam, which had inherited – among others – the traditions of the Garde-Infanterie zu Fuss, remembers a sadistic session of parade-ground drill before the old *Stadtschloss*: 'The *Grenadiere* were ordered to march right up the the Havel and then wheeled round. Then the sergeant ordered three of the men in full kit to march into the lake. This they promptly did, all but drowning in their heavy kit. They were spotted, however, by some passing officers who put the sergeants in the guardroom for three days for giving a stupid command. The three men were given three days' leave. "That was Prussian,"' says the former officer.[90]

It was also Prussian to cover for a junior officer who chose to disobey a foolish order. The same source, as an example of a wholly un-Prussian spirit, cites Manstein's refusal to cover for General Graf Sponeck, who performed a tactical retreat against Hitler's orders in the Crimea in 1941. Sponeck's action exposed 160 heavily wounded German soldiers to atrocious Soviet treatment. All of them perished. Göring came down hard on Sponeck, putting pressure on the court martial to sentence the general to death. In this instance even Hitler thought Göring had gone too

* The head of the administration in a rural *Landkreis*, or county.

far, and had the sentence commuted to fortress imprisonment. Later, after the 20 July plot, Sponeck was shot.[91]

Another instance is given by the still-controversial figure of General Walter von Seydlitz-Kurzbach who was perhaps following family tradition when he defied orders by advising Field Marshal Paulus to withdraw from Stalingrad before escape became impossible: 'The complete annihilation of 200,000 fighting men and their entire equipment is at stake, there is no other choice.' Paulus refused to listen.[92] Later, from Moscow, Seydlitz organised the Freies Deutschland committee which encouraged German soldiers to lay down their arms and desert to the Russians. Colonel General Ludwig Beck, the former Chief of the General Staff who had served in the Prussian artillery, did not disapprove of Seydlitz's actions, though he thought the Freies Deutschland committee 'politically a mistake'.[93] It was Beck, after all, who had encouraged all German senior commanders to resign their commissions at the time of the Sudeten crisis in July 1938: '[Military leaders'] obedience has a limit where their knowledge, their conscience and their sense of responsibility forbid the execution of a command. If their warnings and counsel receive no hearing in such a situation, then they have the right and the duty to resign from their offices.'[94]

One German historian has gone so far as to suggest that the 20th July 1944 was the last utterance in the long history of Prussian 'reflective' obedience.[95]

Even in the last hours of the war, in Pomerania, Christian Graf Krockow's stepfather, Jesko Freiherr von Puttkamer, was able to send a Nazi Party official packing by reminding him of the admonition given to a major on the field of Königgrätz who had sought to justify himself by saying that he had been carrying out his orders: 'Sir, that's why the king of Prussia made you a field officer in the first place, so that you would know when *not* to carry out an order!'[96]

Sadly, there are as many instances of the purest *Kadavergehorsam*. In a famous speech delivered on 23 November 1891, William II told his guards in Potsdam: 'You have sworn loyalty to me, children* of my guard, and that means you are now my soldiers, you have given yourselves to me, body and soul. The only enemy you have now is my enemy. With the present subversive activities of the socialists it could come about that I order you to shoot down your own relations, brothers, even your parents. God forbid that this should happen, but in the event you must obey my orders without a word.'[97] The Hauptmann von Köpenick's 'I'm only carrying out orders'[98] is echoed in the reply Heinrich Brüning received from the soldiers who occupied Berlin during the Kapp Putsch: 'We don't know [why we're here]; we're carrying out our officer's orders.'[99]

At his trial, the south German Colonel General Alfred Jodl practically defined *Kadavergehorsam* when he testified, 'I have been an obedient [*gehorsame*] soldier and I saw it as honourable to maintain the obedience which I valued ... These five years I worked and held my tongue [*gearbeitet und geschweigen*], even if sometimes I was of another opinion and the ridiculous things I was told to do often seemed to me impossible.'[100]

What Jodl ignored was *Gerechtigkeit*, that other Prussian virtue which means submission to the law. In Zuckmayer's *Der Hauptmann von Köpenick*, Wilhelm Voigt's brother-in-law expresses the point simply and succinctly when he tells the larcenous cobbler, 'Justice is the law, Willem. It's got nothing to do with what we'd like, it's there for all of us. That's it, Willem.'[101] Like Voigt, Göring had only the dimmest notion of *Gerechtigkeit*: 'I'm proud to say that I don't know what justice is,'[102] he told State Secretary von Bismarck. 'Such language had never been heard before from a Prussian-Minister President.'[103]

The soldier Henning von Tresckow was quintessentially Prussian. As a troop commander in Potsdam he discovered that his men had pillaged a plum tree. Reprimanding the soldiers he said, 'The property owner is not there for us, but we are here for him.' With that he insisted on buying the pilfered plums.

During the war he proved rigid when it came to not carrying out what he considered to be criminal orders. Tresckow's com-

* In German *Kinder* is the term used when referring to junior officers and men.

manding officer in Army Group C was Field Marshal Fedor von Bock, who, as it turned out, was Tresckow's uncle. When, on 13 May 1941, Hitler issued his order that all snipers and partisans should be shot without mercy, Tresckow was incensed, seeing that such brutality would stain German honour for generations to come. Tresckow went to Bock:* 'You must fly to Hitler again today. You must go together with Field Marshal von Leeb and Field Marshal von Rundstedt. I have told both gentlemen that you are coming to see them for a talk and I've had your aircraft prepared. You must show Hitler that it is a matter of trust and collectively declare that you have promised us that the troops will not be sullied by criminal commands . . .'

Bock was impressed by his nephew's mettle; he nonetheless replied, 'He'd fling me out!' Tresckow retorted, 'Then at least you will have left the stage of history on a good note.' 'Come off it, he'll despatch Himmler to deal with you.' 'We'll be ready for him' was Tresckow's reply.[104]

The final element in the Prussian military-cum-noble code was the sense of duty. The high-born Ermyntrud in *Der Stechlin* sums it up when she tells her husband: 'What binds us is not really love of life, or even love, but simply duty.'[105] Duty was at the core of General von Seeckt's rigid conception of *Preussentum*, an idea which he traced back to Kant's categorical imperative. Writing to his mother at the time of the Kaiser's abdication, Seeckt produced a predictably stoical interpretation of his responsibility to the new republic: '. . . I am, however, an officer on active duty and like any other I must hold myself in readiness to serve wherever I'm told to go. . . . I'd like to set out my position to you as well, that we are all duty bound to do and give our best, thereby maintaining order so that the Fatherland suffers no greater hardships. I can also face up to this duty, even if at times I hold aloof. One's own feelings and views must be wholly eliminated when it comes to the common good. As regards that which we, like so many others, have had to go through, we have no need to voice our feelings . . .'[106]

---

* Tresckow was Bock's Chief of Staff. He uses the familiar 'Du'.

The notion of duty would dominate Seeckt's thought all through his life, but never more so, perhaps, than when he was penning his essay on the great *Wahlpreusse*, Helmuth von Moltke. Prussia, he wrote, '. . . is wholly built on duty, just as much on the citizen's duty to the state as the state's duty towards its citizens. This conception of the state carries in its breast the higher responsibilities of both and thereby each and every one of us. This *Preussentum* is the very image of freedom. In the English liberal state the individual becomes the slave of the common good, the sole measure of his station is money. In the Marxist state the individual disappears before the mass and becomes the slave of a bloodless idea; in Machiavelli's princely state the subject becomes the tool of his lord . . . Voluntary participation is at the heart of the Prussian concept of the state, that means free assembly within a structure which is a necessary component of every individual. *L'état c'est moi* is the motto of every Prussian.'[107]

The Kaiser's son,
Prince August Wilhelm of Prussia,
in SA uniform in 1932.

His stepmother, the Kaiser's second wife
Hermine (née von Reuss). She died
in Russian captivity in 1947.

Kurt Daluege, Chief of the 'Ordnungspolizei' or 'Orpos' and the 'butcher of
Lidice'. He was hanged by the Czechs.

Erich von dem Bach-Zelewski at the time
of the Warsaw uprising. He died
in 1972 awaiting trial for war crimes.

The monument to Tresckow and his wife Erika at the Bornstedt cemetery near Sanssouci. Her father, the former Prussian Minister of War and Chief of the General Staff, Erich von Falkenhayn, is buried alongside.

Generalmajor
Henning von Tresckow.

Fritz-Dietlof von der Schulenburg before the People's Court in 1944. He was condemned to death for his part in the July Plot.

Carl Goerdeler as Mayor of Königsberg. He suffered the same fate.

The remains of Prussia's most exclusive public
school, the Ritterakademie in Brandenburg in 1992.
'Der Januschauer' was expelled from the school.

Elard von Oldenburg-Januschau.

Fürst Philipp zu Eulenburg,
the Kaiser's best friend.

Kurt von Schleicher, the last German Chancellor before Adolf Hitler.
He was murdered by orders of his successor in the Night of
the Long Knives, 30 June 1934.

The courthouse in Moabit in 1991, where Eulenburg was tried for perjury in 1908.

The town hall in Köpenick near Berlin: the scene of the 'Köpenickiade'.

The Memel-born cobbler Wilhelm Voigt, who made a laughing stock of the Prussian army. Better known as Hauptmann von Köpenick, Voigt convinced the mayor of Köpenick he was a Prussian captain in order to relieve him of the petty cash. He is shown in his prison photographs.

King William I of Prussia
who became German Kaiser in 1871.

William II, the last
German Kaiser and King of Prussia.

'Little Willie', the Crown Prince William (1882–1951),
as seen by the artist Edward Tennyson Reed.

Unter den Linden, Prussia's grandest street, by Eduard Gaertner 1853. To the right is the equestrian statue of Frederick the Great and the Opera House; on the left is the Humboldt University. The Berlin Schloss is in the distance.

The Berlin Schloss at the turn of the century. It was wrecked in the war, but restoration of the main rooms had begun by 1950 when the SED decided to dynamite it as a relic of the Prussian past.

Adopted Prussians: Scharnhorst, the Hanoverian former NCO who created the institution. Moltke, the Mecklenburger whose strategy created a united Germany under Prussian hegemony in 1871.

Prussians: Graf Schlieffen, the author of the famous plan. Seeckt, the man who created Germany's post-Versailles army, photographed at the model army's first manoeuvres in 1925.

The journalist Maximilian Harden,
whose campaign in *Die Zukunft*
destroyed the Kaiser's friend,
Philipp Eulenburg.

Walter Rathenau, the industrialist
and politician who was murdered by
right-wing thugs in 1922.

Philippus Krementz who, as Bishop of
East Prussian Ermland, bore the brunt of
Bismarck's anti-Catholic *Kulturkampf*. He
was later elevated to the See of Cologne.

IV

The Parade Ground

Be more than you seem.

> Field Marshal Graf Helmuth von
> Moltke. Quoted in Walter Görlitz, *The
> German General Staff, Its History and
> Structure, 1657–1945*, with a preface by
> Cyril Falls, London, 1953, 97.

Great achievement, small display: more reality than appearance.

> Field Marshal Graf Alfred von
> Schlieffen. Quoted in General Heinz
> Guderian, *Panzer Leader*, foreword by
> Captain B. H. Liddell Hart, translated
> from the German by Constantine
> Fitzgibbon, tenth edition, London,
> 1970, 454.

War is the eternal form of superior human existence and states are
there for war's sake; they are an expression of readiness for war.

> Oswald Spengler, *Preussentum und
> Sozialismus*, Munich, 1920, 53.

On 16 October 1906 ten soldiers* from the 4th Regiment of
Guards were returning to barracks from the military swimming
pool in Plötzensee in the north-west of Berlin, when they were
stopped by a captain from the 1st Guards' Regiment. The officer
ordered the men to follow him and together they caught a train at
the Putlitzstrasse U-Bahn station and travelled to Köpenick in the
south-east corner of the city. There was naturally no need to pay
on the Underground – the soldiers' uniforms amounted to the
equivalent of a travel pass – but the officer treated the men to
beer and sausages in Köpenick Station before commanding them

---

* Four fusiliers and six grenadiers.

to fix bayonets and advance on the Town Hall. Here, their orders were to arrest the *Burgermeister*, Langerhans, and the town treasurer, Rosencrantz, and transfer them to the Neue Wache guardhouse on Unter den Linden.[1]

The captain was not what he seemed. A Memel-born cobbler by the name of Wilhelm Voigt, he had spent a large proportion of his fifty-five years in and out of prison. In many ways Voigt was a copy-book Prussian: his grandfather had fought in the War of Liberation, his father had helped put down the revolution in Baden and as a child Wilhelm had taken pleasure in marching alongside the soldiers of the garrison.[2] Unfortunately he also had a habit of falling in with petty crooks and committing very minor crimes.

He was literate and had, to all accounts, the ability to pursue his trade as a cobbler; but his criminal record meant that it was impossible for him to obtain a passport. The result was that he was unable to qualify for a residence permit which would allow him to set up shop. Reduced to desperate straits, he struck upon the idea of dressing up as an officer and stealing a passport from the town hall. To play safe, the town hall had to be at some distance from a garrison, so that Voigt's credentials could not be checked out. For that reason his eyes fell on the working-class satellite town of Köpenick.[3]

The beauty of Voigt's plan was the use of the uniform. Much later the cobbler had the chance to talk to the corporal in charge of the guardsmen, and ask him if he had not been at all suspicious: 'He told me that he had thought he would lose his stripes and get three days in the guardhouse because he had tried not to notice me, in order to avoid having to stand to attention with his men.'[4] In Köpenick he found the police chief asleep, and was able to admonish him for laziness: 'I asked him whether the good town of Köpenick paid him to sit there and snooze.'[5] The mayor went so far as to ask for proof of his identity. Voigt pointed to the soldiers, adding, 'Now, I think that makes me legitimate enough as far as you're concerned.' The mayor was a reserve lieutenant, and Voigt consoled him by saying that he thought they bore no ill will towards him in Berlin, else they would not have sent a captain to arrest him.[6]

What rendered the 'Köpernickiade' so bitter sweet was that Voigt had come to the wrong place: the Town Hall had no right to issue passports, and he should have gone to the office of the *Landrat*.

The cobbler consoled himself with the 1,200 RMs he found in the cash register and the 4,000 in the petty cash. He made Langerhans give his word of honour not to abscond and sent him off with the soldiers. Later he changed into mufti and observed the comedy at the Neue Wache from a café across the road. A few days later he was shopped by an old companion in crime. The 4,000 RMs were recovered from his room.[7]

Voigt was released from Tegel Prison less than two years after the hijack at Köpenick and enjoyed considerable fame and a small fortune until his death in Luxembourg in 1922.[8] The left and the outside world revelled in the case, which showed the Prussian state up as a society where the army could do no wrong. The socialist paper *Vorwärts* reported, 'The world is laughing at the expense of the Prussian Junker-State.' The story naturally lent itself perfectly to theatre. By the end of the year Hans von Lavarenz had already written *Hauptmann von Köpenick*, and it was followed by pieces by Fritz Fischer-Schlotthauer, Adolf Schlegel and A. Adolpus. The only version which has remained in the repertory is that written by the Rhinelander Carl Zuckmayer in 1931; this has been filmed twice.[9]

These writers knew only too well that the figure of the Prussian reserve lieutenant had become something of a joke in Wilhelmine society. Anyone who had the right (and at least one who hadn't) donned service uniform. Feted all round after the victories of the Wars of Unification, the army's heads had been turned by the adulation, transforming the reserve officer into the 'unbearable prig of the Wilhelmine era'.[10] Civil servants, too, had to show they were all part of the great martial nation, as Zuckmayer's tailor tells the Mayor of Köpenick: 'A doctorate is a visiting-card, but reserve rank opens doors . . .'[11]

The reserve uniform was not limited to parvenus. Bismarck

upset the officer corps from Moltke downwards by parading around in a reserve uniform during the Franco-Prussian War,[12] but his king was nonetheless aware that in Prussia Bismarck needed high military rank to command authority in a world populated by so many generals. At the foundation of the German Empire, William I decided it was time to promote Bismarck to Lieutenant-General, but as the princes assembled for the ceremony in the *galerie des glaces*, the king and newly elected emperor 'looked . . . Bismarck up and down and noted that he was improperly dressed: he should not have been wearing a blue tunic, but the white uniform coat of the Magdeburg Cuirassiers.'[13]*

The army was popular. Marching to war through Silesia in 1866, Lessel remarked that the 'troops couldn't put a foot wrong'.[14] Military parades brought the inhabitants of Prussian towns and cities to their windows, if not out on to the street; and a Prussian man or woman would be expected to recognise the trim of the different regiments from the Guards to the Uhlans, or the civic regiments based in the main towns. Only those in uniform stood a good chance of being ushered into the royal presence, and this extended also to important ministers. Under William II only the War Minister had direct access to the emperor, the others having to present petitions through the Chief of the Civil Cabinet, who saw the Kaiser twice a week. The Chancellor had only one such meeting and that was occasionally cancelled. More reliable were the weekly interviews granted to Chiefs of the General Staff and the Admiralty. The Chief of the Military Cabinet was the most favoured of them all: he had three audiences a week.[15]

The army's influence seeped into every burrow. It has been shown to be untrue that Frederick the Great's village schools were staffed entirely by out-of-work NCOs, but the tenor of life in the classroom rang out with the discipline of a military society.[16]

---

* In Anton von Werner's famous painting of the scene, the Chancellor's mistake has been corrected.

Prisoners in maximum security gaols such as Plötzensee in Berlin ('die Plötze') and Sonnenburg on the right bank of the Oder ('die Sonne') were drilled in their exercise yards. Members of the civil professions were given menial ranks beside their military counterparts: an archivist ranked as a *Fähnrich*,* a librarian, only a sergeant. Until the Second World War, a professor ranked no higher than a junior lieutenant and civil servants merited only the lowest equivalence to their brethren in the services. Many of the major and minor figures of public life were old soldiers: a general was invariably president of the provincial administration, while foresters, postmasters, chamber presidents and *Landräte* were mostly retired, noble officers.[17]

The infection of public life by military manners had considerable drawbacks: 'A loud-mouthed barking tone from subordinate counter-clerks, and an arrogant and conceited manner among senior civil servants was no rarity in Wilhelmine times.'[18] While it was hardly new that the army should be seen as the path to promotion in Prussia, the increasingly offensive attitude of the army towards the civilian population was. The army was a law unto itself. The so-called Zabern (or Saverne) Affair which broke out in September 1913 was caused by the overlordly attitude of some subalterns stationed in northern Alsace.† The local inhabitants, by no means all overjoyed with their new, German, masters, demonstrated. The soldiers responded by dispersing the crowd in a brutal manner and by arresting the ringleaders (who included the president of the local court). This abuse of power by the army led to a storm of protest from the left in the Reichstag and resulted in a successful vote of no-confidence against Chancellor Bethmann-Hollweg.[19] The Chancellor survived only through the Kaiser's support for him and the army.

In almost every Prussian town or city the garrison was the centre of social life. Even today in east Germany and the formerly

---

* A potential officer with equivalent rank to a sergeant-major.
† The affair was exacerbated by the officers' use of the Allemanic word 'Wackes' to refer to the locals, calling their intelligence severely into question.

Prussian parts of Poland and Russia,* the extent of the barracks quarters is an impressive testimony to the sheer number of soldiers billeted there. The huge marine barracks of Königsberg survived the war to serve a similar function for the Russian military in Kaliningrad; the planes which ripped the heart out of Stettin failed to locate the red brick barracks buildings which fill up the area behind the main railway station (now in Polish Szczecin); Silesia was mostly out of the range of the bombers, but the Russian shelling of Breslau (now Wrocław) failed to destroy the majestic neo-classical and romanesque examples in the city centre. The neat little villas constructed for married officers are still the best houses in Olsztyn and Malbork (the former Allenstein and Marienburg); and if the garrison feeling was intentionally removed from many East German towns after the war there are still traces in places such as Frankfurt/Oder with its Halbe Stadt villas, Greifswald and, above all, Potsdam.

At the centre of this army world were the garrison churches. Those of Berlin and Potsdam were surgically removed after the war, but examples may still be seen in Poland, where they have been turned over to Catholic congregations. That in Olsztyn (Allenstein) is impressive from its commanding position above the remains of the medieval town. The most famous of all Prussia's garrison churches was Potsdam with its collections of standards captured over three centuries of war.[20] For many, the Potsdam *Garnisonkirche* was the 'holy shrine' of Prussianism, and the destruction of the substantial ruins of the church in 1968 must be seen in this light.[21]

The all-pervading influence of the army in Prussian public life had been advanced rather than diminished by the progressive infiltration of the officer corps by the middle class. Despite all his determination to keep the corps noble, the process had begun under Frederick the Great, whose wars had decimated the old noble families. During the reforms following Jena there was a

---

* Or, indeed France. In Colmar there is a seemingly endless boulevard of barracks buildings built by the Germans after 1871.

powerful incentive to open up the ranks of the officer corps with the reforming minister Freiherr Karl von und zum Stein levelling at the Junkers as an inadequate source of recruits: 'What can we expect from the inhabitants of these sandy steppes,' wrote the Rhinelander, 'these artful, heartless, wooden, half-educated men – who are really only capable of becoming corporals or book-keepers?'[22] The Chief of Staff, Scharnhorst's, insistence on opening up the profession to the middle class was probably born more of practical necessity than prejudice: there simply were not enough Junkers to do the job.

In 1861 a royal order insisted that officers should reach certain levels at *Gymnasium* or *Realschule* before they could qualify for a commission. For some of the reactionary elements, this was the beginning of the end. Junker domination of the better regiments and the higher ranks of the army proved more resilient than they imagined but by 1913 seventy per cent of the officer corps and seventy-five per cent of the lieutenants were commoners with the percentage of noble generals and colonels down to around fifty.[23]

When the first world war began all the commanding field marshals and generals were noblemen with three-quarters of them coming from the old nobility. Nor did the changes effected by the Treaty of Versailles necessarily make the 100,000-man army a more democratic institution, simply more selective. In 1913 twenty-two per cent of the officer corps was of noble birth, in 1923, twenty-three per cent.[24] Much was changed by the need to swell the officer corps after 1935, but yet again this affected the lower ranking officers far more than it did the generals, and the majority of Hitler's field marshals were relics of the old Prussian *Schwertadel*.

There were regiments and regiments. The more generations that a family had given to the army the better chance a potential officer had of joining one of the elite units. Hans von Seeckt was only a third-generation soldier, even if his father had been severely wounded at the particularly gruesome Battle of Saint Privat in the Franco-Prussian War. Seeckt chose the Regiment Alexander, a Guards regiment the name of which was changed to celebrate the

Russo-Prussian co-operation in the War of Liberation. The *Alexandriner* 'was a man of the world, a lord . . .'[25] More important to a serious-minded young officer such as Seeckt was the relationship between the regiment and the crown, 'a famous institution' where the most important features were 'loyalty, *camaraderie*, tradition, exclusivity; bearing witness to its links to history, the ruling house and the state'.[26]

Some of Prussia's most famous fighting units, such as the Gensdarmes, had gone down with the defeat at Jena and the subsequent reorganisation of the army. Others, like the great regiments of the Garde du Korps, lasted till the creation of the 100,000-man army at Versailles in 1919. Possibly the most famous of the guards regiments was the *Erster Garde-Regiment zu Fuss*, the 1st Foot Guards, or 'the First Regiment of Christendom' as it was known. The 1st Foot Guards had evolved out of the Soldier King's bodyguard, the famous *lange Kerls*. The regiment was made up of twelve companies of which the first, or *Leibkompagnie*, retained the functions of a royal bodyguard. *Leibkompagnie* soldiers had to measure 1.86 metres (6 feet 1½ inches). One former officer maintained, somewhat unconvincingly, that soldiers this tall had difficulties on parade, as their hearts had trouble pumping blood to such great heights.[27] All the regular officers and most of the reservists in the 1st Foot Guards were noblemen, originally from old Prussian families, but after 1870 there was an influx of South Germans. The exclusivity of the regiment made it a natural choice for the royal boys, who were attached to the 1st Foot Guards from the age of ten.[28]

The royal connection governed the regimental commanders, in peace-time at least. When Magnus von Braun did his reserve training in the regiment, his battalion commander was Prince William of Hohenzollern-Sigmaringen and the Commander in Chief Duke Ernest of Sachsen-Altenburg. The last commander before the regiment was scrapped was Colonel Graf Siegfried zu Eulenburg-Wicken, the leader of the East Prussian Stahlhelm after the war.[29]

It was Infanterie Regiment 9, or 'IR 9', which inherited the traditions of the 1st Foot Guards in the 100,000-man army, along with two regiments of the Brandenburg 3rd Army Corps, the Metz Infantry Regiment, the Teachers' Regiment, the Prussian Flying Troops and the German-East Africa Defence Troops.[30] With such a confusing array of constituent parts, it was perhaps surprising that the IR 9 was so quick to establish itself as the most Prussian and most aristocratic unit in the Weimar army. As much as fifty per cent of the subalterns were from the middle classes, but the majority of the battalion commanders were noblemen as were five out of seven commanders in chief. Whether noble or non-noble, the officers were royalists to a man.[31]

IR 9 was not, however, iredeemably reactionary; not even in 1st Company, which assumed the traditions of the 1st Foot Guards. From their barracks in Potsdam the officers were near enough to Berlin to be able to follow events and indulge in lively discussions on political and social issues. While they were well aware of the timeless Prussian tradition, they shunned 'snobbish imitation' of 'stale forms' and adopted the progressive slogan of the Alexander Regiment 'to do away with all service routine and to remain always open to new ideas'.[32]

The Weimar Republic injected a fresher, more analytical tone into the officers' messes. In IR 9, Henning von Tresckow and his brother officers spent some time dissecting the past and coming to grips with defeat. While mud was slung at Chancellor Beth-mann-Hollweg, the Chiefs of the General Staff were equally criticised, as indeed was the Kaiser for failing to co-ordinate the civil and military sides of operations.[33] In Wilhelmine times the atmosphere in the mess was far more lethargic and the intellectual pretensions of IR 9 would have been looked upon with suspicion. In a smart cavalry regiment such as the Erste Gardedragoner (1st Dragoon Guards), 'on average the company consisted of two junior lieutenants and one ensign. It was quite a rare exception for one or two first lieutenants to appear at dinner. One hour after the meal even those had vanished and gone to look after their own affairs or find amusement in the town.'[34]

What most Prussian officers had in common was their contempt for politics and politicians. The Reichstag was an 'Idiotenhaus',[35] its members (above all, those on the left) beneath contempt. This position was exacerbated by war: civilians had no right to meddle in the affairs of soldiers. Typical of this attitude was Elard von Oldenburg-Januschau, a West Prussian Junker and sometime Reichstag deputy who was to become one of the most unabashed *frondeurs* of the Weimar years. Oldenburg was called up to the colours in the First World War at the age of fifty-nine and promoted major on his sixtieth birthday! As a member of his friend Hindenburg's staff, he was at the heart of the military conspiracy to unseat Bethmann-Hollweg in July 1917. Oldenburg referred to him as a '*Federfuchser*' or pen-pusher[36]: 'This whole shambles is the natural result of our spineless, lily-livered political leadership which bows down to calls from our federal colleagues [*Bundesgenossen*] and Social Democrats.'[37]

Oldenburg's instinct, both then and later, at the end of the Weimar Republic, was to form a dictatorship. His hero Hindenburg once again found it difficult to reconcile his conscience to innovation: 'There's no chance of a *levée-en-masse*,' he told Oldenburg as the critical days of November 1918 set in, 'and as for a dictatorship, I can't propose that to the Kaiser. These are political matters and I'm only a soldier.' Oldenburg knew that Hindenburg was protesting too much. 'You're not merely that, you're more. All eyes are on you now. If the Reichstag is not dissolved come two weeks, there'll be no monarchy left.' 'You're exaggerating,' said Hindenburg, adding, 'The damned Reichstag . . .' With these words he began to pummel the table with his fists.[38]

Most senior officers believed that the army should be a law unto itself and could justify this, like Moltke, by alluding to the subtleties of strategy – something which would be lost on politicians unversed in the training meted out to members of the General Staff.[39] Bad memories of the behaviour of the Berlin revolutionaries in 1848 led them all too often to see civilians as potential enemies. In the 1860s, General Manteuffel had been worried about a senior officer who was known to consort with civilians, but was assured by an aide that he could be trusted. 'Very well,' said Manteuffel, 'then we can count on him if the shooting begins.'[40]

It is hard to imagine that the traditional elements of the army didn't take some pleasure in putting down the revolution which was sparked off by the armistice and abdication of the Kaiser in November 1918. The Socialist newspaper *Vorwärts* must have been a particular bugbear to the right-wing elements of the army, and we know from his biographer that young Henning von Tresckow was involved in the siege of the paper's offices on the Belle-Allianceplatz in Berlin on 11 January 1919. According to this source, Tresckow helped to arrest those people found in the building and transfer them to captivity in Moabit. By all accounts the soldiers, commanded by Major von Stephani, behaved well; the brunt of the action, however, was borne by Colonel Reinhard's *Freikorps*, who slaughtered a number of their captives and would have put as many as three hundred more to death had it not been for the intervention of the regular soldiers.[41]

Weimar would spend many of its days trying to manoeuvre itself around its small but technically efficient army. In several instances the army tried to get the better of the republic, not least through the machinations of General Kurt von Schleicher. Politicians needed to evolve a special language to control the overmighty generals and bring them to heel. Veteran Socialists such as President Ebert and Minister-President Otto Braun referred to the sons they had sacrificed on the front. Others, such as Heinrich Brüning, appealed to the army's sense of honour: 'Herr von Schleicher, we are both old soldiers, please allow me to say a few frank and honest words. I know better than anyone that for the last two years you have been trying to pursue your policies behind my back. You are the power behind the throne. That is the most nefarious thing which can exist in a state, whatever the form of government. The person who believes himself capable, or who is able to get something done, must openly take on the responsibility.'[42]

Brüning was brought down by the conspiracies generated by

Schleicher and Schleicher's access to old President Hindenburg through the the President's son, his regimental comrade, Oskar. The Papen cabinet which succeeded Brüning's might be said to have been more agreeable to the army; as Magnus von Braun pointed out, it was 'very homogenous' on one score: 'Papen, [Freiherr von] Gayl, [Graf von] Eltz, and I belong to Potsdam guards regiments. Schleicher was a regimental comrade of Hindenburg, both father and son, [Franz] Gürtner was in the Bavarian artillery, [Freiherr von] Neurath in the Württemberg . . . dragoons and [Graf Schwerin]-Krosigk the Pomeranian Uhlans.'[43]

II

The state is no academy of the arts, still less a stock exchange; it is power, and therefore it contradicts its own nature if it neglects the army.[44]

The reputation of the Frederician army was shattered by the twin defeats of Jena and Auerstedt. Reforms enacted by Scharnhorst and Gneisenau were able to weld together the remnants into a fighting force strong enough to clear Prussia and Germany of the French, but they couldn't perform this task on their own. They needed the help of their allies in Russia, Austria, Britain and the other German states. After 1815 the Prussian army went back to sleep, and it was only fully to redeem its reputation with the Wars of German Unification, more than a century after the first campaigns of the Seven Years War.

The victories of Düppel, Langensalza and Königgrätz changed all that. The world sat up and noticed that the Prussian war machine was back on the rails. Within Prussia, at least, the blunders of the other German armies in the Franco-Prussian War served to confirm a view of their own superiority. When, for example, the Crown Prince learned that he was to command the south German forces it filled him with little joy. He considered the soldiers 'quite untrained in our school', and his sense of gloom was not helped by the news that Bavarian soldiers had been discovered looting a shop.[45] Later, Bavarian units got lost and fired on their own men at Froeschwiller, and when the Bavarians actually suffered defeat at Coulmiers, the Prussians 'could not conceal their satisfaction'.[46*]

Squabbles between the German armies fighting in France would have been largely lost on the outside world. Not so the extraordinary superiority of the Prusso-German forces to the French. The Prussians had learned the importance of the railways. Moltke had shown them how quickly you could concentrate troops brought in by rail and what good condition soldiers would be in, if spared the rigours of a long march.[48] With their breech-loading rifles and Krupp cannons, the Prussians had a further superiority, especially in the accuracy of the latter. The Prussian artillery also learned to use all their guns as quickly as possible, while the French clung to an outmoded Napoleonic technique of keeping a good part of their artillery in reserve. The French were to learn this to their chagrin at Sedan: 'Never before had gunfire been used in war with such precision.'[49]

French inadequacy was not limited to equipment. Gustav Freytag pointed the finger at the lack of basic training. This been encouraged by the system which allowed richer Frenchmen to pay others to do their military service as stand-ins, a system which caused Freytag to fulminate in language which might seem odd to our ears: 'In truth our victories will bring civilisation to the French; and one of the purposes for which providence has chosen the noble German blood that is flowing on the battlefields of France, is to smite the souls of our enemies, not only with respect for our military superiority, but also with the conviction that universal military service is necessary for France. With the introduction of this highest and noblest form of military service, the possibility of insolent wars of conquest and the madness of military vainglory, that disgusting disease of the French, cease of

---

* On the other hand the Saxon army fought with distinction. Freytag, who had been for annexation in 1866, was impressed: 'such experiences make one modest,' he wrote.'[47]

their own accord. As soon as the material of the French army becomes as valuable as ours, as soon as the son of a senator and banker of Paris stands beside the workman of St Antoine in the ranks, the impudent riff-raff that now excite the public opinion of France will lose power, and the family feelings of the respectable people will have a word to say in politics. Universal military service makes a nation not only strong in war, but also peaceable in peace.'[50]

The final nail in the French coffin in 1870 was the lack of an effective General Staff. As Sir Michael Howard has written, 'As generals they were perhaps no worse than the average commanders of the Prussian corps, and if they had had, like the Prussians, the guidance of staff officers trained by a Moltke and had not been commanded by such successive incompetents as Napoleon and Bazaine they might have shown themselves incomparably better.'[51]

The pride and legends of the Second German Empire were founded on the fields of St Privat and Mars-la-Tour, far more than on the resounding victory of Sedan. Von Bredow's 'Death Ride' was to become as powerful a tug on youthful imaginations in Germany as the Charge of the Light Brigade in Britain. The day-to-day life of a soldier, however, had not changed much, and soldiers were still reduced to scavenging for food. In 1866, Emil von Lessel's unit appointed a member of the Witzleben family to look out for provisions as they made their way to Königgrätz. Witzleben returned with a small cask of Hungarian wine and a cow 'which was immediately slaughtered and divided up. It proved so tough, that one wit voiced the opinion that it had been past its best before the time of Wallenstein.'[52]

More scavenging brought them sausages and a few bottles of red wine from Assmannshausen. They even caught a goose. 'This was a capital offence, for in those days of warlike innocence hunger was permitted but plunder forbidden. We comrades turned a blind eye and we had boiled goose and fried potatoes.'[53] On another occasion in Bohemia, Lessel and his brothers earned their meal when they protected a local from 'a gang of malefactors

... who had broken into the cellar of our billet.... A pretty Jewish woman called out to the officers for help. We cleared up and as thanks we were treated to a nice kosher dinner.'[54]

With the Franco-Prussian War came the accusation that Prussian troops had committed numerous atrocities in enemy territory. In the main they were perpetrated as rough justice against snipers and irregular units operating behind the lines. Moltke himself seems to have hit on the formula of destroying a village to discourage the harbouring of snipers. The more German soldiers were killed by snipers, the more brutal became the reprisals.

In Krentzlin in the Grafschaft Ruppin, Fontane found a monument to a twenty-one-year-old volunteer who had been killed in Olivet, near Orléans. The gravestone said no more, but Fontane enquired of the villagers and the story came out. The volunteer had been shot in the process of taking the local mayor into captivity in an attempt to curb sniper activity in his sector. As his small squad had come under heavy fire, they had left his body behind and made for camp. The captain commanding had responded by sending in a patrol of a hundred hussars who had found the body stripped and plundered and, a few minutes later, the partisans fleeing though the woods. Some were killed there and then. The ringleader was found with the soldier's possessions on him and was shot next to the dead Brandenburger. 'Whether the other prisoners survived the day, I never learned,' wrote Fontane, adding that he wondered how many gravestones concealed a similar story.[55]

Lessel found the stories of atrocity and theft wildly exaggerated: 'It would be foolish to want to deny that every now and then a German soldier had made off with some stranger's property, for when one talks of hundreds of thousands there will always be a number of doubtful people; but as far as the great mass was concerned, there reigned scrupulous honesty. Men who, for example, had lost their mess spoons, and as every old soldier knows, in the field that is a very sensitive and disagreeable thing to lose, rejected silver ones without a moment's hesitation and did what they could until a valueless replacement could be found.

This is exactly what my batman did, an honest Altmärker called Kannenberg, even though his family had hated the French with a loathing for generations on end. Looking back on the atrocities committed by the Gauls in our country in the years from 1806 to 1812, it is hard to suppress a certain uneasiness that during our invasion they came off lightly. In the bottom of their hearts the French believe this was a weakness on our part and cover up for it with a filthy foam of slanderous allegation.'[56]

The Prussian army was hero-worshipped by young German boys growing up after 1870. One writer has gone so far as to suggest (not very convincingly) that even the young Heinrich Himmler was imbued with Prussian ideas in his adolescence, despite his then rigorous devotion to the Catholic church and his *Schwärmerei* for the Wittelsbach monarchy.[57] Bavaria was probably the exception to this rule; there the detested '*Preissen*' were generally the butt of music-hall jokes, and one historian recounts the story of a student looking for a room in Munich. The youth placed a small ad in a local shop: 'Great grandfather fought against the Prussians at Kissingen.'[58] The Reichs constitution of 1871 allowed the Bavarians a considerable measure of autonomy: their own ministry of war, general staff and the ability to manage their own affairs until the outbreak of war, when control passed to the Prussians. The kings of Saxony and Württemberg also retained their regiments, but overall control was in the hands of the Prussians, and their staff officers were trained in Berlin.

Non-Prussians had always served in Prussian regiments, just as non-Prussians had often been tempted by the chance to serve in the administration.[59] The flooding of traditional Prussian regiments with young noblemen from other parts of Germany caused less concern among the Prussian 'Tories' than the new style of the regiments. As Captain von Czako tells his friend the Assessor* von Rex in Fontane's novel *Der Stechlin*, 'Have a look at the old service lists one day, I mean the really old ones, from the last

* Graduate civil servant.

century and then up to 1806. There you'll find in the Gensdarmes or Garde du Corps regiments our good old names: Marwitz, Wakenitz, Kracht, Löschebrand, Bredow, Rochow, at the most the occasional lofty titled Silesian has wandered in by accident. Naturally there were also princes in those days, but the [Prussian] nobles set the tone and the few princes had to count their luck if they didn't disturb them. Now, since we've had the Kaiser and Reich all of this is over. Of course I'm not talking of the provinces, but of the guards, of the regiments under the eyes of His Majesty.'[60]

After the scandal of the Eulenburg case (see Chapter VI), the reputation of the Prussian guards regiments took a tumble. The Social Democrats even went so far as to suggest that the guards could not be trusted with the royal princes. Once again it was the old fox, Oldenburg-Januschau, who rose to defend the honour of the guards before the Reichstag. The Prussian Guards, he reminded them, had displayed exemplary self-sacrifice at the Battle of St Privat, where 315 Junkers belonging to the elite regiments had perished on the field of honour.[61]

As the inevitability of defeat became clear to all but the thickest skulls among the *Generalität* in the autumn of 1918, south German officers and politicians were not slow to detach themselves from the Prussians who, they believed, had brought about the defeat. From a political point of view they were almost certainly correct. In the general staff at least, chief among the anti-Prussian elements was Wilhelm Groener the same General who had told the Kaiser to pack his bags and make for Doorn. Blomberg believed the Württemberger Groener 'was deep down on the side of the revolution. *Preussentum*, which even after defeat remained the backbone of the Reich, was incomprehensible to him and probably hateful to boot.'[62] Others have found this appraisal 'vastly overrated', noting at the same time that Groener had been quite unabashed when he described himself as a 'south German democrat'.[63]

The Versailles settlement was bound to hit Prussia the hardest.

Prussia was seen to be behind the war and once the French bid for the west bank of the Rhine had failed, all territorial compensations were likely to occur in the east. Alsace-Lorraine had been administered by the whole of Germany, but linguistically and culturally it had far more in common with Baden and Swabian Württemberg than with any other German states. Of as much importance to the Prussian ruling classes was the army, and just how much they would retain after the conference. The British wanted to impose a volunteer army on Germany, adding that a similar system should be enforced throughout the Continent. The French and Foch bitterly opposed this. They favoured a militia with a six-month to one-year service period. The final compromise was the 100,000-man army, based on seven infantry and three cavalry divisions. The officer corps was to be reduced to 4,000 men and the dreaded General Staff abolished altogether.[64]

Generalmajor Seeckt was present in Versailles, although quite powerless to influence the outcome. In an act of pettiness he had been forbidden to wear his uniform, and he made a lame stab at insisting that this rule should be applied for Foch and the other French officers. The later General Köstring observed that Seeckt could be a 'frightful fathead for such a great man'.[65] Needless to say his complaint had no effect on the French plenipotentiaries.

The treaty was ready on 7 May 1919, and Seeckt was given two weeks to raise objections. His own particular desire was to retain the Great General Staff. After discussions with Hindenburg the Germans sought to double the number of soldiers allowed to them under the conditions of the settlement. The Allies showed no disposition to budge, although they extended the deadline until 23 June; the Germans were to come back with a simple yes or no to the treaty. For the Socialist government, Philipp Scheidemann was in favour of rejecting the treaty outright, but was worried that this would lead to attacks on West Prussia and Upper Silesia by the Poles, who were anxious to annex these regions for the new Polish state. Plans were laid for a *levée-en-masse* to defend Prussian territory, plans which might have stood a chance of success given that the infant Polish army was fully occupied in clearing the Russians away from the gates of Warsaw.[66]

Scheidemann summoned his Prussian War Minister General Walther Reinhardt, a Württemberger like Groener, but unlike Groener, one who 'completely identified with Prussian thinking'.[67] Reinhardt put forth a plan to fight, sacrificing western Germany and clinging to the areas across the Elbe. In this project, Reinhardt was supported by the Generals von Below and von Lossberg.[68] Groener despaired at Reinhardt's proposition. For him the important thing was to maintain the unity of the Reich. He saw in the project dreams 'of the glorious days of 1813'[69] and the arch-Prussian Seeckt evidently agreed with him.[70] Groener advised Field Marshal Hindenburg, who was quite naturally tempted by a scheme which would have redeemed Prussian honour if no other. On 17 June Hindenburg wrote from HQ in Kolberg in Pomerania, 'Were we to take up hostilities again we would be in a military position to reconquer Posen and maintain our borders. In the west we can hardly reckon with success in the face of a serious attack and the need to protect our two fronts, given the numerical superiority of the Entente. A favourable outcome of the operation in general is therefore highly questionable, but as a soldier I must prefer an honourable defeat to an ignominious peace.'[71]

The field marshal's report was discussed in Weimar that same day. Once again Reinhardt was for saving the eastern provinces: 'the cradle of Prussia'. [72] Groener reminded him that it was not Prussia they had to think about but 'the unity of the Reich'. Reinhardt then asked Groener if, in the case of the assembly accepting the treaty, the High Command would accept the lead in an insurrection in the east.[73] Groener uttered a 'categorical refusal'.[74] Later he said as much to Noske, making it clear that High Command would obey the law, as represented by the assembly.

On 19 June the Prussian Council of War met in Weimar. For the first time ever, the King of Prussia was absent. The majority of the generals were in favour of Reinhardt's proposal to fight on alone. 'For them the kings of Prussia had taken the wrong path in

courting the succession to the German emperors, the future of
Prussia was not in Bavaria or on the Rhine, but on the banks of
the Baltic, in Königsberg and Riga* . . . Prussia would remain
intact and put up a fierce resistance to Allied demands . . .'[75]
Noske asked them to think carefully on this matter, as he was
convinced that it would mean the loss of south and west Germany,
possibly even Hanover. Groener argued forcibly for the constitution and swayed the generals who took a 'sort of oath of fidelity to
Noske'.[76] Reinhardt fought back, backed by Below and Lossberg.
Groener could only say that if the Prussian deputies to the
Reichstag and the Prussian Landtag wanted it that way, then that
would provide a justification. The generals put their faith in Noske
finding a political solution to the problem.

Prussia's possible declaration of independence from a defeated
Germany was blocked by polls from the regions themselves. The
news was bad from south Germany, where Saxony, Baden and
Württemberg were all in favour of signing the treaty. Only Prussia
and the Hanseatic cities were against. From Upper Silesia came
the news that the people were tired of war, while the Danzigers
had told officials that a *levée-en-masse* was an impossibility.[77]
Colonel Joachim von Stülpnagel reported, 'Seeckt and I . . . met
and expressed the view that the projected, and as far as I was
concerned, deeply to be desired, struggle, remained pointless if
the representatives of the civilian population rejected it so to
completely.'[78] Scheidemann still couldn't find it in his heart to
sign the treaty, and resigned. A new cabinet under the chancellorship of the East Prussian Gustav Bauer had the onerous job of
signing all but the 'moral clauses'† of the treaty. Among the
generals only Groener was in favour. For his part, the Social
Democrat Noske had completed his shift over to the side of the
generals; as he told one of them, 'I have also had enough of this
shambles.'[79]

*

---

* A German army was still in Latvia. In all three Baltic states there were substantial
numbers of German settlers.
† i.e. those which laid the blame for the war entirely on the Germans.

The June days of 1919 were the last time a serious attempt was made to recreate a Prussian state by detaching it from the south and west of Germany. By rejecting the call to fight on alone, Prussia threw in its lot with Germany – for good or for bad. How much goodwill the rest of Germany bore towards Prussia was to be amply demonstrated in the coming months when Prussia had to deal not only with the furious attempts of the Poles to seize as much of the disputed territory as possible but also with the withdrawal from the Baltic of German forces whose role had been, in part at least, to safeguard the interests of the German-speaking minority who had settled these lands in the Middle Ages. Bavaria refused all part in the new deployments. 'Saxony tore up the Military Convention of 1867. Württemberg obstructed the enactment of laws voted at Weimar. In 1919 the *Discordia germania* first diagnosed by Tacitus showed itself as the German Republic struggled between life and death . . .'[80]

Seeckt had replaced Hindenburg as Chief of the General Staff for as long as the General Staff continued to exist. Hindenburg had not found it in his conscience to speak to the new rulers in Germany and had communicated entirely through the democrat Groener. It fell to Seeckt, therefore, to reorganise the army within the framework dictated by the Allies. Seeckt believed that the army should be a work of art, Prussia's greatest creation[81]: 'It was one of the most powerful indications of the strength of *Preussentum*,' wrote Seeckt in 1931, 'that after the terrible *dénouement* of the German army in the middle of a Germany which was just as opposed to Prussia as it was to the military, that it was able to form a German military power which, as small as it is, covers the whole of Germany while keeping its Prussian character.'[82]

With his model army (in the miniature sense) Seeckt was happy to evade Versailles as much as he decently could. His highly selective force was carefully planned. In the event of a need to expand the force, the soldiers could be bumped up into the positions of NCOs, the NCOs subalterns and the officers would then move into positions of higher command. The General Staff,

which Versailles had banned, was parcelled up and hidden –
partially, it would seem, in the Ministry of Pensions.[83]

The Verein Graf Schlieffen 'was also suspected of performing
staff services'.[84] Essentially an association of former General Staff
officers, the Schlieffenverein was necessarily a hot-bed of *frondeurs*
gathered around the person of Field Marshal Mackensen. Ludendorff was in regular attendance. Seeckt wisely made his excuses
and stayed away.[85] Turning his back on the grumblers was not
going to make the problem go away, however, and further unrest
started when the Treaty of Versailles came into effect on 10
January 1920. On that day 100,000 men were obliged to leave the
colours. Two days later there was a shoot-out on the steps of the
Reichstag building. General Walther Freiherr von Lüttwitz
refused to implement the reductions, thereby sparking off the
Kapp Putsch which brought Berlin to a standstill.

The Kapp Putsch was a particularly Prussian revolt. Wolfgang
Kapp was an East Prussian land-owner, with wide-ranging contacts with the reactionary officers of the Ludendorff circle. But
the workers who carried out the general strike which defeated the
Kapp Putsch were also Prussians, and their reward for having
helped the government out with their support was to be the
sacking of Noske, a man who had been profoundly unpopular with
the far left since his suppression of the revolutions of 1918. What
the Kapp Putsch demonstrated, was that the heavily Prussian
officer corps would rather hedge their bets in such circumstances
than come to the aid of the republic. Of the soldiers summoned
to advise Noske on whether it was feasible to proceed against the
rebels with force, only Reinhardt and Major von Gilsa were in
favour. It was Seeckt who summed up the feelings of the
Reichswehr on that occasion: 'There can be no question of our
allowing units of the Reichswehr to fight against their comrades.
Soldiers don't shoot soldiers. Were you thinking of something like
a battle before the Brandenburg Gate,' he told the impotent
Noske, 'between troops who eighteen months before had stood
shoulder to shoulder fighting the enemy? If the Reichswehr mows
down the Reichswehr, then all *esprit de corps* in the officer corps is

over. Despite my loyalty to the government and my opposition to attempts at rebellion, I cannot take responsibility for any such battle.'[86]

Seeckt promptly fell ill and didn't recover until the danger had passed. Blomberg thought the malady was fortuitous. Others have suggested he was waiting to see what the outcome would be.[87] On 18 March Seeckt was named head of the armed forces.

If Seeckt was waiting to see if he was to have a new master in Kapp, as Commander of the Reichswehr he was quick to expel the main reactionary elements and replace them with officers who were loyal to the state. Out went Generals Maercker, von Estorff and von Lettow-Vorbeck, and a General von Bergmann from Stuttgart was called in to take over Berlin garrison command. All in all sixty officers were cashiered in the aftermath of the Putsch, while orders were sent out to imprison Lüttwitz (who had fled to Hungary), Graf von der Goltz and the same Admiral von Levetzow who later left the Kaiser's court at Doorn to become a Nazi deputy in the Reichstag. The Freikorps leader Ehrhardt escaped to Austria on a forged passport and Ludendorff thought things might be more comfortable in Bavaria. While he was there he was to make the acquaintance of Adolf Hitler and become embroiled in another mismanaged *coup d'état* in 1923. Kapp flew to Sweden but later returned to Berlin to face trial. He died of cancer in police custody.[88] One officer who had shown his loyalty to the republic was Colonel Kurt von Hammerstein-Equord, who had refused to follow his father-in-law, General Lüttwitz, and had been briefly imprisoned by the *Putschisten*.[89] Hammerstein backed the right horse in 1920, a move that was to help him rise first to the headship of the *Truppenamt* and finally in 1930 to the position of Chief of Army Command.

It is to Seeckt's credit that the army remained a stabilising influence throughout the Weimer Republic. The wilder elements in Hitler's entourage were bound to want to change all this after he came to power. In the spring of 1933, the Thorn-born Danzig Nazi Hermann Rauschning had a long talk with the 'Scharnhorst of the

new age', Ernst Röhm. Röhm was unhappy that Hitler had failed
to make him a minister. They lunched at Kempinski and Röhm
'drank a few glasses of wine in quick succession. "Adolf is a swine,"
he swore. "He'll give us all away. He only associates with reactionaries now. His old friends aren't good enough for him. Getting
matey with the East Prussian generals. They're his cronies now."

'He was jealous and hurt. "Adolf is turning into a gentleman.
He's got himself a tail-coat now!" he mocked. He drank a glass of
water and grew calmer. "Adolf knows exactly what I want. I've
told him often enough. Not a second edition of the old imperial
army. Are we revolutionaries or aren't we? *Allons, enfants de la
patrie!* If we are, then something new must arise out of our *élan*,
like the mass armies of the French Revolution. If we're not, we'll
go to the dogs. We've got to produce something new, don't you
see? A new discipline. A new principle of organisation. The
generals are a lot of old fogeys. They never have a new idea.

'"Adolf has learned from me. Everything he knows about
military matters, I've taught him. War is something more than
armed clashes. You won't make a revolutionary army out of the
old Prussian NCOs. But Adolf is and remains a civilian, an 'artist',
an idler. Don't bother me, that's all he thinks. What he wants is to
sit on the hilltop and pretend he's God. And the rest of us, who
are itching to do something, have got to sit around doing nothing."

'He filled his glass, with wine this time, and went on: "They
expect me to hang about with a lot of old pensioners, a herd of
sheep. I'm the nucleus of the new army, don't you see that? Don't
you understand that what's coming must be new, fresh and
unused? The basis must be revolutionary . . . He wants to inherit
an army all ready and complete. He's going to let the 'experts' file
away at it. When I hear that word I'm ready to explode. Afterwards
he'll make National Socialists of them, he says. But first he leaves
them to the Prussian generals. I don't know where he's going to
get his revolutionary spirit from. They're the same old clods, and
they'll certainly lose the next war . . ."

'He was full of abuse of the Prussian officers. Too scared to
put their noses outside the door. Coddled cadets, that had never

seen anything but the military academy and the war office. But *he* was a revolutionary, a rebel! He nearly burst into tears. The restaurant was nearly empty by this time. The adjutant took him away.'[90]

Hitler saw fit to murder Röhm on 1 July 1934, but the day before he had had two Prussian generals gunned down in the same purge. Hitler may have had second thoughts about Röhm's revolutionary army, but he was not going to rebuild the Prussian army either. Nor did the figures add up to a revival of the traditional officer corps. In 1933 there were 4,000 officers in the army, of whom some 450 were medical or veterinary. Of the remainder about five hundred were transferred in 1934 to Göring's new Luftwaffe. About a thousand officers were found within the police, but that still left only 4,000. In a few years another 25,000 would be found. Few of these would have had much of an inkling of the traditions of the Prussian officer corps: they were young men who had grown up in the depression, men who looked on Hitler as their salvation.[91]

The occasion which led so many outside observers to assume that a revival of 'Prussianism' was taking place under the new National Socialist state was the so-called Potsdam Day of 21 March 1933. It will be recalled that the Reichstag building had been destroyed by fire on 27 February and the emasculated body, representing only the right-wing parties, now had no permanent home. Hitler and his propaganda chief Joseph Goebbels hit upon the brilliant idea of holding sessions of the parliament in the Garrison Church in Potsdam and making 21 March into 'The Day of the German People'. Coming less than two months after their accession to power, it was also the moment to show how much 'the Corporal' (Hitler) and 'the Field Marshal' (Hindenburg) were united in their desire to see the revival of nationalist Germany. Two former rivals for the presidential seat were to be reconciled, the rumours of Hindenburg's distrust and dislike of the 'Bohemian Corporal' banished for all time. On 21 March the old, traditional Germany, embodied in Hindenburg, Potsdam and

Prussia, was to be wedded to the new Germany of Hitler and National Socialism.[92]

The Prussian message was to be plugged, too. From the newsreels, the Prussian people and their *Schwärmer*, deprived of their *Landtag* since July of the previous year, could watch the great moment of reconciliation take place in Prussia's holiest shrine. Some, like the susceptible Mackensen, were taken in by the performance: 'We German officers used to be called representatives of reaction, whereas we were really bearers of tradition.'[93] Others, like Schleicher, were not. He wrote a mocking message to Groener at the end of the year claiming he could find no trace of the Potsdam spirit. The French Ambassador, André François-Poncet, was not impressed either. He noted that the Reichstag had reopened in Potsdam at a time when the régime was in the process of robbing parliament of both rights and functions. 'On March 21 a half-Bavarian [sic], half-Austrian man, who has put himself out as the apostle of the new Germany, with great pomp took his place under the patronage of the King of Old Prussia.'[94]

François-Poncet saw an augury for the revival of militarism, but even the presence of the Crown Prince did not fool him into believing that the Hohenzollerns were soon to return. 'It is a new baptism, it means to announce the redemption of Germany through the Brownshirts.'[95] The French Ambassador gave a further interpretation of the meaning of the Potsdam Day: Potsdam was to be the antidote to Weimar. Instead of the peaceable town of culture, of Goethe and Schiller, the new régime intended to promote a new idol in Frederick the Great. 'Herr Göring made it absolutely clear that it would have been difficult to find such an easily understandable and emotive symbol as Potsdam, in order to give the impression that the Hitler movement had brought a painful episode in German history to a close and a new chapter begun.'[96]

Few people in Britain, it seems, saw things as clearly as François-Poncet. G. K. Chesterton, who liked to oppose the Prussian spirit of 'heathenry and heresy' with the benign influence of Catholic Austria, saw the Potsdam Day as the writing on the wall. Learning that Hitler had repudiated Germany's war guilt over the bones of Frederick the Great, he wrote, 'Some of us are but little reassured by a man abjuring piracy over the bones of Captain Kidd or perjury upon the holy relics of Titus Oates.'[97] The British, long used to seeing 'Prussianism' as the real threat from Central Europe, put two and two together and arrived at a figure greatly in excess of four.

The German army should have had fewer illusions. Hindenburg had always maintained that he would not appoint Hitler. When his trusted Papen had suggested Hitler as Vice-Chancellor a few months before, Hindenburg admitted that he had not considered giving the 'Bohemian Corporal' any position higher than Minister of the Post Office.[98] Even on 29 January Hindenburg maintained that he would not appoint Hitler either Chancellor or Minister of War. He was brought round by Papen's assurances that Hitler could be controlled, as long as Blomberg were given the position of Minister of War. A rumour spread through Berlin that Schleicher's friend Hammerstein had ordered the Potsdam garrison to march on the city and arrest Hindenburg if need be, in order to prevent Hitler from achieving power. That any such order was given is vigorously denied.[99] Hammerstein had merely pointed out that it would be hard for a democratic army to serve Hindenburg's original idea for a coalition: an alliance between nationalist elements controlled by Papen and Alfred Hugenberg. In hindsight, perhaps Hammerstein was wrong to rule out such a move, but at the time there was a genuine feeling that any interference by the army would provoke a general strike and a communist uprising; for good reason Hammerstein had not forgotten the Kapp Putsch.* Hammerstein let the moment pass, to the great misfortune of the Prusso-German army. As Gordon Craig has written: 'In the course of the next twelve years of office, Adolf Hitler was to impose upon the army a control more rigid than any in its long existence, and to compel the obedience of its officers

---

* He never did. On his death bed in 1943 he said, 'Only don't make a Kapp Putsch, the German people must drink the chalice down to the dregs, only then will they learn to pray again and not seek protection from false gods.'

even to commands which violated their historical traditions, their political and military judgement, and their code of honour.'[100]

Blomberg was seen as the chief traitor at the time. His acceptance of the War Ministry before consulting Hammerstein deviated from accepted practice.[101] Of all the generals Papen might have suggested to play the role of keeping Hitler in check, Blomberg was one of the oddest, given his sympathy for National Socialism. Blomberg saw his role as dismantling the power of Hitler's praetorians in the SA. In return for Hitler's support in this, he compromised the army's dignity and independence, first by allowing Nazi insignia to be incorporated into army uniforms and then by permitting National Socialist propaganda to be taught as a part of basic training.[102] Blomberg saw his doubtful reward in the Night of the Long Knives of 30 June 1934. True, the SA leadership was wiped out, but a number of right-wing opponents were killed too, setting a very bad precedent. Blomberg was not the only one to utter premature approval: Hitler received a telegram of congratulation from the ailing President Hindenburg. 'You have saved the German people from a great danger,'[103] he wrote, without mentioning the shooting of his old friend Schleicher.

Hindenburg lasted only till 1 August. The next day Hitler merged the offices of Chancellor and President of the Reich and made the army swear an oath of loyalty, not to the state, but to himself personally. The oath is a puzzle, as an adequate formula had been written and sworn as recently as 1 December 1933. One explanation is that Blomberg introduced the new oath in order to get Hitler to agree to a reciprocal pledge.[104]

Once again Blomberg seems to bear a heavy responsibility for what was to become the tragedy of the Prussian tradition in the German officer corps during the Third Reich. He appears to have had little regard for the views of his brother generals. His personal interests were quirky; he was much taken with Rudolf Steiner's concept of theosophy, which made him suspicious of more blinkered career officers such as Gerd von Rundstedt. Rundstedt later said 'nobody liked him'[105] and his 'posturing as a democrat'[106] went down badly during the Weimar years.

He was to receive his come-uppance. Promoted Field Marshal on Hitler's birthday in 1936, Blomberg could be excused from thinking that he was at the top of his tree. He became careless, dressing up in mufti and going on midnight prowls in search of 'amorous adventures'.[107] On one of these he met Eva Gruhn, apparently little more than a prostitute with a lengthy criminal record. The ageing field marshal fell completely under her spell. Blomberg made the mistake of telling Göring about his love, a particularly foolish thing to do given that Göring was angling for Blomberg's job. He said he wanted to marry Eva. Both Göring and Hitler agreed to be witnesses at the wedding, Blomberg apparently believing that this would stop them from using Eva's previous life against him. Not long afterwards, however, Graf Wolf-Heinrich von Helldorf, the Berlin Police President, discovered Eva's record. When Göring heard this he put his own research department on to the matter. Eva was proved to have posed for pornographic photographs. Blomberg was ruined.

In a final monstrous gesture, he may have encouraged Hitler to take personal command of the Wehrmacht in the light of another scandal, that concerning Colonel General Werner von Fritsch. The scandal in this instance concerned homosexuality. Fritsch was a bachelor, and a story had come to Göring's attention concerning a homosexual prostitute called Schmidt who claimed to have had sex with a 'General Fritsch'. As Göring was seeking to clear a path to his own appointment to the headship of the armed forces, he found this story particularly juicy. The Prussian general was faced with his accuser, brought out of concentration camp especially to identify him. Fritsch was forced to resign and a court of honour appointed to try the case. Not long afterwards another key witness – a certain Weingärtner – contradicted Schmidt. It was revealed that the officer in question was not Fritsch, but a Colonel Achim von *Frisch*.

Despite the clear evidence of mistaken identity, Hitler did not go back on his decision and did indeed take over the overall command of the Wehrmacht.[108]

All Fritsch was able to win back was the honorary colonelcy of his regiment and, as such, he went to war in Poland in 1939. There, before Warsaw, he seems to have sought death in battle. Udo von Alvensleben noted in his diary at the time that the 'Fritsch case was the biggest scandal that had ever stained the honour of the army. It would be impossible to atone for this suicide.'[109]

With Blomberg and Fritsch out of the way and the new Commander in Chief, Walter von Brauchitsch, yet another pawn manipulated by his shady private life, Hitler was free to play the supreme warlord. His old friend Röhm had underestimated 'the idler' Hitler – he wanted to play God *and* lead the army. From now on he would surround himself with technicians such as Heinz Guderian. At the time Guderian played ball: his only criterion of assessing the quality of a commanding officer was his openness to new technical advances. Later he had the grace to record some of the drawbacks of working for Hitler: the photographic memory – 'six weeks ago you said something quite different'; a lack of determination in carrying through his projects – he did not understand Moltke's dictum 'First weigh the considerations, then take the risks'; he 'lacked the wisdom and moderation of his great examples, Frederick the Great and Bismarck'.[110]

And Hitler launched the war that neither of his idols would have risked: he attacked Russia. 'There is no necessity to take the war to Russia from material considerations,' sighed Alvensleben. 'The Russian government has sought to avoid this war at any price.'[111]

III

Land animals like us are not accustomed to live among whales, dolphins, turbot and codfish.[112]

Prussian interests finished where the land came to an end. There were areas it coveted and areas which aroused not the slightest interest from successive electors and kings. It is possibly strange that Prussia never made an attempt to create a Baltic empire, once Sweden's power began to wane, but neither Frederick William I nor his son Frederick the Great showed any inclination in that direction. For the father there was a desire to round off Prussia's borders, for the son the thrust was to the south (Saxony and Silesia), the east (West Prussia and the Netze) and the west (Hanover). Frederick the Great had an instinctive dislike of navies: 'Sea battles,' he wrote in 1776, 'are rarely decisive, from which I conclude that it is better to have the best army in Europe, than the worst fleet among the maritime powers.'[113]

Frederick's great-grandfather did have a brief flirtation with a commercial empire on Dutch lines, but the colony of Gross-Friedrichsburg in present-day Ghana was short-lived.* The first great call for the creation of a navy, significantly enough, came from the Paulskirche, during the 1848 revolution. Nor was it for a Prussian navy, but for a German one; a symbol of national unity bound to appeal to the 'middle class, nationalist . . . commercial delegates who met there. The enemy was Britain, who stood in the way of German commercial expansion.'[114] Nothing came of the project until the foundation of the Reich twenty-three years later. At the time Germany was short on national institutions: there was no national oath of allegiance, no national anthem, no national holiday, merely 'associated governments'.[115] The navy would be national and centralised in a way that nothing else was. The idea was even popular with the Polish deputies in the

---

* The ruins of the fort still exist, apparently something of a tourist attraction.

Reichstag, because it was believed that a strong navy could be used against the Russians.[116]

Among Prussian traditionalists the idea aroused little enthusiasm: the old notions remained and their views probably differed little from those adumbrated by Frederick the Great. The very idea of the Reich was far less attractive to them than it was to the liberals; the term 'Kaiser' was sheer romantic nonsense. The Hohenzollerns were kings of Prussia and words like 'Reich', 'Nation' and 'Deutschland' were as distasteful as they were radical.[117]

The navy was also middle class. Its greatest champion was a judge's son from Prussian Küstrin on the Oder, Alfred Tirpitz, but his family was far removed from the Junkers and imbued with the political liberalism of the early imperial days. That other early naval personality, Georg Müller, was the son of a Saxon chemistry professor. Both Tirpitz and Müller were ennobled when they reached the rank of captain.[118] It was certainly not impossible for a middle-class man to become an officer in the army (as some have suggested), but it was often hard to advance beyond the rank of captain. High flyers like Mackensen and Ludendorff must be seen as exceptional. In the navy, however, from the very beginning there was an opening for the middle-class candidate, and the absence of tradition meant that there would be little in the way of discouraging snobbery on board ship.[119] Its apparent liberalism made the navy particularly popular in the senior common rooms of German universities.[120]

The navy was unlikely to have found a real champion in William I, who was far too Prussian in his inclinations to give much time to such questions. Indeed, all the early naval leaders were actually soldiers, seconded from the army. The first Hohenzollern to take up the cause was William II, who was naturally attracted to the navy as a result of his rivalry with his British cousins. As Zedlitz-Trützschler said, 'It is hardly an exaggeration to call him the creator of the German Navy.'[121] The Kaiser's passion for all things nautical had begun in boyhood, when he had sailed a model of a British frigate on one of the Potsdam lakes.[122] He was immensely proud of his uniform as a British admiral,* believing that it gave him the right to dictate policy to the British navy. He even sent a long memorandum to Lord Salisbury on the subject of reforming certain practices, which led the British Prime Minister to doubt his sanity.[123]

The Kaiser was quite genuinely intrigued by naval design and actually put pen to paper to create the ideal battleship. A drawing shows a truly revolutionary concept rigged out with tall structures reminiscent of minarets and a symmetrical arrangement of gun turrets positioned along a central axis.[124] The enthusiasm which greeted the creation of the Flottenverein (Naval League) was a manifestation of the knowledge in many German circles that the country had reached the pinnacle of its power in Europe, yet remained extremely weak outside. The German Naval Law of 1898 tilted directly at Britain,[125] but either the Kaiser didn't know this or didn't care to look at the consequences of his actions and Tirpitz' plans. 'The "danger zone"... lengthened with each individual battleship.'[126] Tirpitz may have had some excuse for believing, however, that Britain would see in Germany a natural ally rather than the traditional enemies of France and Russia.

As Jonathan Steinberg has written, 'British and American historians have usually been too obsessed by the "Prussian Menace" to notice that the navy was neither Prussian nor conservative.... If the belligerence of German naval expansion was a product of the liberal tradition in Germany, perhaps the "good" Germans so beloved of historical mythology are not so good after all, and the "bad Germans", the Junker militarists and reactionaries, not so bad.'[127] Certainly, less than a generation after the Battle of Jutland, the national German navy was to prove the readiest of the three services to embrace National Socialism and in admirals such as Raeder and Dönitz (Hitler's successor) the Führer's trust was amply rewarded.

* Although it was more likely to have been a German uniform he wore to a performance of Wagner's *The Flying Dutchman*.

V

Carmine Stripes

Gryczinski was a member of the General Staff and like all of his sort he believed implicitly that there were in this world no such fundamentally different colours as the universal-Prussian-military-red and the red of the General Staff.

Theodor Fontane, *L'Adultera*, in
Fontanes Werke in fünf Bänden. Berlin &
Weimar, 1986, II, 163.

In 1912 a Prussian cavalry general by the name of Friedrich von Bernhardi caused a sensation in Europe with the publication of his book *Deutschland und der nächste Krieg* (Germany and the Next War); the shock was particularly felt in Britain, where a translation of the complete text appeared within a few months of the original German edition. The book purported to show how Germany would behave in the coming year. The author seems to have been provoked to write the book by the Moroccan Crisis of 1911 and the growth of pacifism he saw at work in the Hague Peace Conference which ended in 1907, laying down the laws of war.

Bernhardi was particularly sickened by peace and by a dangerous lack of aggression in his own people.[1] Pacifism, he said, was an illusion, 'war is the father of all things'.[2] 'In nature the struggle for existence is at the same time the foundation for all possible development.'[3] War, says Bernhardi, is a 'biological necessity', above all for the Germans who are 'shackled and hemmed in'[4] by their borders. Germany needs to achieve world power or it will soon be destroyed by its neighbours.[5]

Bernhardi's other message concerned the nature of the Germans themselves. 'Standard-bearers of free thought,' he called them.[6] 'There is no other nation which thinks as the Germans do, which knows how to combine spiritual freedom with practical life as it walks the path to free, natural development.'[7]

There was nothing particularly new about Bernhardi's thinking; much of it was rehashed from the general's gods, Treitschke, Darwin and Nietzsche. Treitschke was the son of a Saxon general. A political liberal, he became increasingly attracted to Prussia the more he saw in it the hope of German unification. He taught history and politics at the universities of Freiburg in Baden, Kiel, Heidelberg and finally, from 1874, in Berlin. During that period his views moved increasingly to the right. Germany was to be a 'greater Prussia', with the destinies of all the component parts rolled together behind the Prussian 'wave'.[8] Prussia's principal means of expression was its army. 'The Prussian army,' wrote Treitschke, 'is undoubtedly the most real and effective bond of national unity; most certainly not, as was formerly hoped, the German Reichstag. The latter has rather contributed to make Germans begin to hate and calumniate one another. But the army has educated us to political unity.'[9]

In Britain at least, on the eve of the First World War, Treitschke and Bernhardi represented the essence of aggressive Prussian militarism. When the Armistice was finally signed after four years of bloody war, those names remained, as did the concept of 'Prussianism' as war for war's sake, preferably coupled with wide-ranging annexations and crippling indemnities.[10] Prussia was permanently preparing for war, as Treitschke himself put it: 'It is not the nature of the army that it should always be fighting; the silent work of preparation goes on during peace. The world was able to perceive for the first time what the reign of Frederick William I meant for Prussia, in the days of Frederick the Great when all at once huge power that had been accumulated issued forth. The same is true of the year 1866.'[11]

That 'silent work of preparation' had, by 1866, become the work of the General Staff. It should come as no surprise that Bernhardi was a *Generalstabler*, as officers of the élite Prussian General Staff were known. Distinguishable from lesser mortals by the carmine stripes on their uniform trousers, General Staff officers spent their hours planning aggressive war, and Bernhardi's book was an eruption of General Staff thinking couched in some rather exaggerated, hot-headed language. By all reports Bernhardi was a disagreeable man, controversial, even among his brother officers; Schlieffen sacked him from the General Staff. Seeckt had no time for Bernhardis either – he wanted men in his General Staff so discreet they were as good as nameless.[12]

The creators of Prussia's General Staff were all *Wahlpreussen*, *Gastarbeiter*[13] like Treitschke. The Hanoverian Scharnhorst and the Austrian Gneisenau are well known; less so is the real founder, Colonel Christian von Massenbach, a Swabian from Heilbron, whose family had originally come from Memel less than a century before.[14] Massenbach had written to Frederick the Great to apply to join the Prussian army and was examined by the king himself. He fought in Holland in 1787, losing three fingers on his left hand, and was promoted captain. In 1791 he was a major and transferred to the quartermaster's staff, the cradle of the General Staff.[15] It was there that Massenbach's real career began. Two memos dated 1802 set out the functions of the reformed General Staff. Massenbach pleaded for an institution which would continue its work through peace and war in order to function as a centre for future planning. The office would map out 'every conceivable eventuality' concerning Austria, Russia and France.[16]

Massenbach's inspiration had come from France in the first place. In Napoleon's armies the General Staff had come into existence as an extra pair of eyes for the general, who was unable to see everything that was going on from his position on the battlefield.[17] It is thought that this admiration for the Corsican led to Massenbach's fatal mistake and later oblivion: in the event he failed to make any contingency plans for war with France – 'The thought of a war with the France he so much admired does not seem to have entered his mind.'[18] Massenbach also laid down that journeys should be made in peacetime to reconnoitre 'the terrain of possible scenes of operation'.[19] In theory this was not limited to Germany: staff officers should also have travelled abroad. Lastly, the staff was to have unrestricted access to the warlord. The king recognised Massenbach's creation in 1808 when he implemented the entire body of ideas he had drawn up.[20]

As Massenbach himself put it, 'Since 1797 three things have occupied my undivided attention: the consideration of what use might be made of the [lessons of] the French Revolution for the ruler of the nation; observations on the consequences of this Revolution for the German constitution; and finally, reflections on the necessity of consolidating a power which more from intellectual strength than force, maintains the balance between north and south and which could help us to examine both the moral and the intellectual culture of Europe.'[21] From 1806 Berlin possessed a centre for the study of the history of war, learning from past battles being the essence of the work of the General Staff.[22] The seed was there, it only required the brilliance of a Scharnhorst or a Gneisenau* to make it work to the advantage of the Prussian army. As for Massenbach, his later history is rather sad: he appears to have lost his wits on the battlefield of Jena when he was acting as staff officer to Fürst Hohenlohe. Much later he petitioned to rejoin the General Staff. It is not known whether his suit was successful.[24]

Massenbach had laid the foundations. The work continued after the double defeat of Jena and Auerstädt by the Committee for Military Reorganisation. Privileges of nobility were abolished, military service was introduced and certain cruel punishments were also scrapped. A four-section general staff was set up to handle strategy and tactics, internal administration, reinforcements, and artillery and munitions. The military service idea was enshrined in the *Krümper* system, whereby a brief period with the colours was followed by service in the reserve. The old *Ober-Kriegs Kollegium* was abolished and replaced by a proper War Ministry with departments of General War and Military Economy, the former run by Captain Carl von Clausewitz.[25]

---

* Blücher was aware of Gneisenau's worth in the field. On being awarded a doctorate at Oxford after Waterloo, Blücher expressed the view that if he was to be made a doctor, Gneisenau should be an apothecary, 'because Gneisenau mixed the potions which Blücher administered'.[23]

Scharnhorst transformed French staff thinking. He was to have some sway over his commander-in-chief's decisions where Berthier had none.[26] He was also to innovate General Staff advice to politicians by advising Hardenberg on the possibilities to be gained from the Russian alliance in 1805. 'Never stand in concentration, always do battle in concentration'[27] was one of his more important maxims. He was certainly no Bernhardi: 'Taciturn, deliberate, selfless, brave, unassuming, incorruptible and unselfish'[28] – almost a model Prussian! 'He was par excellence the man who stands in the background, advises, warns and guides.'[29]

Bernhardi would have agreed, however, that war was the father of the Prussian General Staff. After Scharnhorst's death, the task was taken over by Gneisenau, a man with a similar quota of guts and brains: 'Scharnhorst's St Peter'.[30] But this was not just the period of these two brilliant tacticians, it was also the period in which Clausewitz was to gain the experience of war and staff work which would provide him with the material for the greatest ever study of war – his *Vom Kriege* (On War) of 1832.

When Clausewitz was born in 1780, Frederick the Great's army was at the height of its fame, which may go some way towards explaining why the boy from Burg-bei-Magdeburg joined the Prussian army at the age of twelve. By 1818 he was the Director of the Berlin *Kriegsakademie* or Staff College. He died of cholera in Breslau in 1831, while acting as Chief of the General Staff to Gneisenau, another victim of the epidemic.

Clausewitz taught us that war was a fundamentally *political* act as far as civilised nations were concerned[31]; to use his immortal phrase, it was 'simply the continuation of diplomacy by other means'.[32] War 'does not belong in the realm of the arts or sciences, rather in the social world. It is the conflict between important interests which are bloodily resolved. . . .'[33] War is necessarily violent, the mustering of great forces to crush the enemy and enforce one's own will to whatever end. The aim is to render the enemy defenceless so that he may not strike back at you.[34] Clausewitz's observations were based on his knowledge of recent wars, not just the Napoleonic period, in which he played a significant role at the Convention of Tauroggen, but also the period of the Seven Years War. His influence was to be decisive when it came to later Prussian chiefs of staff – Moltke above all, but also Schlieffen and Beck.[35]

Clausewitz's thinking was a long way distant from the 'war for war's sake' arguments of Bernhardi. In the Great War these were expounded above all by General Erich Ludendorff, who did not see war as a political tool, but politics as an extension of war. To do Ludendorff justice he never claimed to be a disciple of the author of *Vom Kriege*, 'All Clausewitz's theories are redundant,' he said; war was 'the highest expression of a nation's will to live'.[36] Hitler, on the other hand, claimed to have read Clausewitz's long treatise and to express his own ideas within the framework of the Prussian's thinking. As he told his circle, 'You have not read Clausewitz, or if you have, you haven't understood how to apply it in practice.'[37]

It was an extraordinary assertion. Hitler owed far more to the Bernhardi–Ludendorff school of thought than he did to the reflective Prussian officer of the Wars of Liberation. There is no mention of racial conflict in the pages of Clausewitz; no *Lebensphilosphie*; no question of the struggle for existence based on biological theory. War is 'a passing evil'.[38] Clausewitz is careful to add that war, although violent by its inherent nature, should not lead to unnecessary cruelty: 'Civilised nations do not kill prisoners. They do not destroy cities or countries, because our intelligence plays a greater part in the conduct of war and has taught us more effective means of using force than these crude expressions of instinct.'[39]

Helmuth von Moltke joined the Prussian General Staff in 1822. Like the other General Staff pioneers, Moltke was not a Prussian. He came from Mecklenburg, the duchy to the north of Prussia which was in some ways a caricature of its more famous neighbour. Seeckt made out that Moltke had Wendish blood, adding that 'the mixture of different bloods has never been either so pronounced or so fruitful as it was in Prussia'.[40] According to Seeckt there have never been such good Prussians as those *Wahlpreussen* like Moltke.[41]

Moltke was born in 1800 in Parchin into an old noble family with branches all over the East Elbian region of Germany. His father had fought in the Prussian army before joining the Danish; his mother was from the Hanseatic city of Lübeck. Helmuth was educated in the Danish cadet corps, and didn't join the Prussian army until he was twenty-one.[42] Moltke's education was far from bookish; as he later said, as soon as he was taken away from his mother his lessons consisted of nothing more than beatings.[43] From the first, however, Moltke recognised the need to travel to broaden his mind and books to plug the gaps left by his inadequate schooling. Moltke 'himself used to recount that as a young General Staff officer he carried Montaigne and Byron in his saddle pockets'.[44] Later in life he exchanged these for the Bible, the *Iliad*, Clausewitz, Schiller, Goethe, Shakespeare, Walter Scott, Ranke, Treitschke and Carlyle.[45] Nor did his literary interests limit themselves to reading – he was commissioned to translate Gibbon into German and at one stage tried his hand at fiction. He also showed an early talent for drawing which he channelled into topography.[46]

Moltke believed in German unification from early on in his career, but thought that it could only be successfully achieved 'by the sword'.[47] He watched the development of the railway engine with fascination: here was a means of widening the area of operations for an army, which could have a profound effect on the future of Prussia. Within the General Staff itself, Moltke encouraged his subordinates to think for themselves. This was highly important: there was to be no *Kadavergehorsam*. Under the influence of Moltke, the General Staff became a little cocoon padded with the great man's thinking. This had the advantage of giving junior officers 'a high standard of morals and a great simplicity of life',[48] but the disadvantage, too, of making them feel like a caste detached from the intellectual life of the nation.

Princess Katherina Radziwiłł found the old Moltke rather cold: 'a man untouched by emotion; even his kindness is mechanical.

Herr von Moltke has the nature of a mathematician,' she said. 'He's a loner who lives shut up in himself and hates being disturbed in his moments of repose; by nature cold, unmovable, incapable of doing anyone good; never having had in the course of his long life the need to oblige anyone, much less beg a favour.'[49] This judgement none the less smacks of superficial acquaintance (it is hard to imagine Moltke cutting much of a dash in the Berlin world of Princess Radziwiłł). We know that Moltke had an insatiable appetite for literature and that he was quite able to seize on the qualities of good architecture and landscape design. For an old soldier he could also be surprisingly lacking in bellicosity. Asked by Bismarck after the Franco-Prussian War, 'After such successes what now can bring pleasure to our lives?' Moltke replied simply, '*Einen Baum wachsen zu sehen*' (Watching a tree grow).[50]

For Moltke, the General Staff was conceived like a school; a permanent education for as long as you wore the carmine stripes. 'Moltke evolved out of the General Staff, and through him the General Staff went on to evolve further,' wrote General Seeckt. The chief property of the General Staff 'school' was that the higher you rose, the more the responsibilities you had to learn: 'Every promotion brought with it a new selection.'[51] Under Moltke's influence the General Staff began to extend its educational role to the army proper. This was particularly true after the Wars of Unification, when Moltke was finally able to impress on the more dyed-in-the-wool generals that there was an incontrovertible need for forward planning.

Moltke's greatest achievements were the victorious wars of 1864, 1866 and 1870–1871. Before the conflict over Schleswig-Holstein or, indeed, the Battle of Königgrätz, many of the senior generals had little knowledge of, or respect for, the workings of the General Staff. One old Prussian general is said to have exclaimed at Königgrätz, 'Who is this General Moltke?' There was still a residual distrust of Moltke among the generals of the Franco-Prussian War who, as often as not, refused to carry out general staff directives to the letter. The war against France highlighted the intellectualism behind Moltke's methods: the

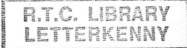

constant preparation of march tables which allowed him to work out every eventuality in the field; the use of French newspapers to gauge the way the enemy generals' minds were working; the attachment of trusted staff officers to the more wilful commanding generals.[52] This last was of particular importance. From the very beginning of the campaign Moltke's strategy was altered by the generals, either as a result of their belief that they knew better, or simply because they were too stupid to carry out orders.[53] In some instances these variations might well have led to serious setbacks, had French planning not been quite so hopeless.

The generals might have had a point: Moltke's plans were occasionally unworkable; at times demanding far too much of the troops. Moltke made mistakes: he lost touch with the main concentration of French forces on the Loire; he overextended his supply lines.[54] Above all he allowed the French to win a propaganda victory. When the war started the main neutral powers believed right to be on the Prussian side – France had very clearly brought the war upon itself. By the end of the war the Germans were seen in a different light: the atrocity stories had been accepted and the bombardment of Paris came as a shock to the civilised world. Moltke was lukewarm about shelling the city, and was pressed into doing so by Bismarck and by the force of public opinion at home.* Bismarck wanted to get the war over and done with before it either began to cause political problems at home or excited a neutral power to come in on the French side. In the end the bombing did far less damage than the fury of the revolutionary French *communards*.

Moltke was not entirely without ambitions in the foreign policy line either. He opposed the negotiated peace desired so strongly by Bismarck and planned, after the fall of Paris, to prosecute the war in the south. On 8 January 1871 he told the Crown Prince, 'We must fight this nation of liars to the very end! Then we can dictate whatever peace we like.' When the Crown Prince expressed

---

* *'Deutschland will das: Bumm! Bumm! Bumm!'* (Germany wants some boom, boom, boom) wrote one paper at the time.[55]

his dismay at this attitude, Moltke claimed, disingenuously, 'I am concerned only with military matters.'[56] It was to some degree Moltke who insisted on the cession of Alsace and large tracts of Lorraine, together with the city of Metz. Bismarck was once again opposed to such drastic surgery. As Michael Howard has written, 'It had been Bismarck's armistice, but it was to be Moltke's peace.'[57]

After the war Moltke's peace created a new problem for the General Staff: would the new Germany be obliged to fight a future war on two fronts? If so, how would the army go about dealing with both a numerically superior army and to the need to divide German forces in order to deal with attacks in the east and the west? Moltke's solution formed the grain of the later Schlieffen Plan: 'Make the smallest possible front on one side, then conduct the most powerful and most rapid war possible on the other.' When this war was won, you took the troops back to the first front and reconquered any territory you might have lost.[58]

Moltke lived on into the era of the last Kaiser. In 1882 he asked to be allowed to retire, but his request was refused. It was William II who finally permitted the old field marshal and count (since 1871) to retire to the estate which a grateful nation had granted him after the Franco-Prussian War: Kreisau in Silesia, a name which was to become rather better known as a result of the activities of his great-nephew, Helmuth James, in organising a cell of anti-Nazi resistance during the Second World War. Moltke died at the age of ninety in 1891.

The next Chief of the General Staff to leave an impression on the German public was Graf Schlieffen. William II naturally had his own views on what a Chief of the General Staff was meant to be like and decided that what he wanted was 'a sort of amanuensis'.[59] Waldersee, whom he sacked, as we have seen, for allowing him to lose at manoeuvres, noted with rare foresight, 'He wants to be his own Chief of Staff. God help our country!'[60] On his deathbed in 1904 he was still obsessed with the dangers he saw behind the Kaiser's reckless military policy. 'I pray God,' he said, 'that I may not live to witness what I see coming.'[61]

Schlieffen was not given to such Cassandra-like utterances. He was a pure technician from Prussian Pomerania, the son of a guards major, and deeply steeped in the pietistic tradition. He joined the Second Regiment of Uhlans in 1854 and was posted to the General Staff just before the Austro-Prussian War. In 1889 he became Waldersee's deputy and Chief of Staff the following year. To those who knew him well, he seemed to be the very caricature of a Prussian officer. 'The embodiment of efficiency, sense of duty and self denial, he possessed an enormous capacity for work.'[62] His obsession was with provision for the army of the future war and how 'to deploy them, align them and feed them'.[63] His problem was that first isolated by Moltke: how an inferior number could beat 'a superior number of enemies'.[64]

Schlieffen was quite impervious to anything which lay outside his domain. He expected hard work and had no sympathy for juniors who might have wished for occasional moments of normality in their lives. One later general recalled that he used to send him problems on Christmas Eve, requesting an answer the next day. On another occasion after a night spent travelling from Königsberg to Insterburg in East Prussia, an officer drew his attention to the beauty of the sunrise over the Pregel Valley. Schlieffen 'looked at the scene, remarked, "An unimportant obstacle" and relapsed into silence.'[65]

As a former head of the historical section, Schlieffen plunged himself into the history of the Seven Years War in his search for a solution to the war on two fronts. Under his guidance new army corps were created and new equipment introduced. He was perturbed by the strength of the French defences being constructed in Lorraine and saw the need to march round them and attack from the rear, thereby forcing the enemy to fight with its front reversed – as the Prussians had done at Jena. To this end he had a choice between moving his army across Swiss or Belgian soil. The former appeared too easily defended. Luxembourg had too few roads. Another possibility was the Ardennes, but here the quality of the roads made troop movement difficult. In the end it had to be Belgium.

The General Staff carried on planning aggressive war and the violation of neutral territory without anyone calling them to order. Until 1900 Belgium's defences had been turned towards France, which had exhibited a recurrent desire to annex the young monarchy throughout the nineteenth century. Suddenly alarmed by reports of German war plans, the Belgians strengthened their borders with Germany, constructing the great fortresses of Liège and Namur. This troubled Schlieffen not a little, but the more he wrestled with the problem the more he saw that there was simply no other solution. By 1905 the Schlieffen Plan had been drawn up, 'a gigantic wheeling movement through Belgium on the pivot Diedenhofen–Metz'. To cover the Russians, Schlieffen planned to leave a weak force in East Prussia and use the Austrians to create a diversion in Galicia. But there were few proper staff talks with the Austrians, and none with Germany's other allies, the Italians.[66]

Under Schlieffen the General Staff adopted an apolitical stance: he appears never to have questioned the need for the war, or to have taken seriously the necessary infringement of international law in Belgium. He continued to miss the wood for the trees, endlessly debating whether the Battles of Leuthen or Ulm provided the perfect examples of encirclement. Finally he opted for Cannae, although 'Cannae was the perfect illustration of the truth that a battle does not win a war'.[67]

Soon after finishing the 'Schlieffen Plan', the general was kicked by a companion's horse and he was forced into retirement. He died in 1913, only a year later, his meticulous staff work yet to be put into action. His last words were, 'See you make the right wing strong.'[68]

Schlieffen was replaced by another Helmuth von Moltke, the nephew of the former Chief of the General Staff, a general who had neither his uncle's brilliance nor Schlieffen's attention to detail. One of his first acts was to *weaken* the right wing. His major achievement lay in allowing the Kaiser to play at being his own Chief of Staff.

It has been suggested that Germany would have been better off if it had been Ludendorff and not Moltke who replaced Schlieffen in 1906; but where Schlieffen could conceive of no world beyond the narrow purlieus of his office, Ludendorff had rather too grandiose a view of the General Staff as an instrument of policy. He had strong links with the aggressively nationalist Pan Germans and later became embroiled not only with the hapless Wolfgang Kapp, but also with Adolf Hitler. Some have maintained that it was Ludendorff's unpopularity as well as his quarrel with the liberal Groener which led to his being posted to command a regiment in Düsseldorf on the eve of the Great War, but General Dommes thought this was not the case. 'It was a healthy principle of the Royal Prussian Army that as a precondition for translation into a high command, General Staff training had to be combined with performance in front line duties especially the important role of regimental commander.'[69]

Ludendorff was clearly a talented troop commander. Right at the beginning of the war he demonstrated the excellence of his own General Staff strategy when he captured the fortress of Liège. His success in the West resulted in his return to a staff attachment with Hindenburg in East Prussia, the scene of a successful Russian attack in the first months of the war, and now partially occupied. Hindenburg and Ludendorff were the team which brought Germany the Battle of 'Tannenberg'. The use of the emotive name of Poland's victory over the Teutonic Knights was first suggested by Ludendorff and eagerly adopted by the Kaiser.[70]

It is clear that the small amount of real talent among Germany's Great War generals lay with this duo; and more with the rebarbative Ludendorff than with the Junker Hindenburg. In the main Germany's generals were as hopeless as those on the allied side, unable to grasp military technique and obsessed with troop service.[71] Guderian suggested that had it not been for Ludendorff and Hindenburg, Germany would have lost the war in 1916: theirs was a 'superhuman and utterly thankless task'.[72] The need to muster all Germany's resources in a desperate bid to win the war led them to attempt to emasculate the already largely impotent Reichstag and drive any politician who stood in the way of their ruthless war policy from power. This was the case of Bethmann-Hollweg, sacked in July 1917. He was succeeded by complete nonentities who could be trusted not to interfere with what was fast becoming a miltary dictatorship.[73]

Ludendorff's unlikely bedfellow of November 1923, the former Corporal Adolf Hitler, had little time for the creation of Scharnhorst and Moltke. If Blomberg sold the army's soul to rid it of the spectre of Röhm and the SA, it was not long to retain Prussia's greatest contribution to the history of warfare. Until 1938, the Chiefs of Staff not only had direct access to the supreme warlord, they also shared responsibility for the actions of the commanding generals. This was scrapped by Hitler in the interests of his hallowed '*Führerprinzip*'. Now the commanding officer was alone responsible: a move which was to institute a repulsive degree of *Kadavergehorsam* in the Second World War.[74]

Guderian maintains that the General Staff ceased to exist altogether with the sacking of General Brauchitsch in December 1941. This was perhaps a means of taking some of the blame off himself when he later came to pen his memoirs after a spell in an allied prison. Guderian was Chief of the General Staff from 20 July 1944 to 28 March 1945. He was a return to the school of Schlieffen; a *nur-Soldat* who shunned any political involvement and judged every issue on the basis of its openness to technical progress. As Basil Liddell Hart wrote of him, he was more in favour of Hitler than most – possibly all – of the other Prussian generals of the Second World War, because Hitler was disposed to back technical innovation: 'Hitler manifested a liking for new military ideas and for the tank in particular, so Guderian was inclined to like him. Hitler showed an inclination to back the revolutionary idea, so Guderian was inclined to back him.'[75]

Liddell Hart is generous to Guderian. His attitude was 'similar to those of most soldiers of any country at any time'.[76] Liddell Hart ignores the intellectual tradition of the Prussian and later German General Staff to which Guderian ostensibly belonged. Tilting, one suspects, at the meditative and virtuous general Ludwig Beck, Liddell Hart writes, 'Soldiers are not trained to explore the truth behind international disputes, and if they try to wrestle with the resulting questions they are likely to be incapable of performing their task. There is a place, and a need, for the military philosopher in the study and guidance of war, but a profoundly reflective mind does not fit easily in the service itself.'[77] Of course it could be true that Liddell Hart was merely flattered by the degree to which Guderian acknowledged his debt to the writings of the British captain.[78]

Guderian's background, from his West Prussian childhood to his cadet school education and entry into the regiment his father commanded, holds no surprises. He was a typical product of the Prussian warrior caste. His real life began in 1922 when Major Joachim von Stülpnagel of the Truppenamt told him to report to Munich in order to take charge of the Motorised Transport Department. It was a staff job; Guderian was to make plans for a mobile war. He turned to the British and French theories: General Fuller, Liddell Hart and the Frenchman Martel. Everything he knew came from books – he was later to claim that he had never seen the inside of a tank.[79]

The first German experiments with mobile warfare had their comic side, even if the joke was lost on the earnest Guderian. Canvas dummies formed the first tanks, pushed around by men on foot. Later these were replaced by full-sized models made from sheet metal. From these humble beginnings the 'Panzer division' was born. The Prussian tories took a dim view: Otto von Stülpnagel thought the idea 'utopian'.[80] Guderian also quotes Hindenburg in this light: 'In war only what is simple can succeed. I visited the Staff at the Cavalry Corps. What I saw there was not simple.'[81]

Guderian was pleased about Hitler's appointment as Chancellor as he was with Blomberg's assumption of the post of Minister of War. Once again it was their interest in motorised warfare which appealed to him. The army Chief of Staff, Ludwig Beck, was not such good news. For Guderian, Beck was a disciple of Moltke, a Clausewitzian with 'no understanding of modern technical matters who . . . erected . . . a barrier of reaction at the very centre of the army.'[82] Guderian thought Beck unable to adapt to the changing nature of war,[83] a procrastinator in both military and political matters: 'He was a paralysing element wherever he appeared.'[84] Guderian was struck by a sharp remark of Beck's: 'Haven't you ever read Schlieffen?' he had asked. An ironic question, seeing how Guderian shared Schlieffen's blinkered attitude to non-military issues. Guderian's hatred of Beck reveals something far sadder, however: the complete moral destitution of Germany's greatest Panzer commander of the Second World War. Beck was indeed a procrastinator, but he nonetheless died with honour in the debacle in the Bendlerstrasse on 20 July 1944.

II

Only in practice does real ability based on knowledge reveal itself. A long period of peace will always run the risk of making the General Staff too theoretical because there has been no opportunity through war to correct and expand.[85]

The Prussian and later German General Staff was the intellectual elite of the army, a sort of military think tank revered within Germany and feared without. Cyril Falls observed that a study of the German General Staff would need to have a 'faint smell of burning' about it, as it attempted to chart the development of the office where highly competent officers sat around 'planning aggressive war'.[86]

Because the General Staff was looking for superior intellectual gifts, from the beginning it was more open to middle-class applicants than any other prestigious unit in the Prussian army. This was true even in the pre-Massenbach–Scharnhorst days: 'It was looked upon as beneath the Junker's dignity to busy himself with coloured pencils and dividers.'[87] By the time the Reich was created in 1871, the General Staff was fifty per cent middle class, containing men often imbued with strong liberal and nationalist ideas which led them to sympathise with the Pan Germans and the *Flottenverein*. The commercial classes were clamouring for protection on the high seas and found their hero in Tirpitz.

In 1870 Moltke's Staff was less than a dozen strong; by 1905 the figure had risen to nearly ten times that number.[88] Just under half of these were of bourgeois origin, trained at Germany's *Gymnasiums* or grammar schools, rather than in the *Kadettenanstalten* or cadet schools. Where it was hard for a non-noble to rise above the rank of captain in any of the prestigious units of the army, in the General Staff important departments were already commanded by bourgeois like Ludendorff, at the *Aufmarschamt* in charge of deployment, and Groener, who looked after railway transport. For Kurt von Schleicher, who came from a freshly ennobled family, the Staff must have been a relief after the snobbish put-downs he had borne from the *Uradel* or old nobles at Plön and among his brother officers in the Third Foot.[89]

Entry into this increasingly privileged elite was through the Academy of War. Already in 1804 there was an Akademie für junge Offiziere (Academy for Young Officers) in Berlin; six years later Scharnhorst transformed this into the Allgemeine Kriegsakademie, or General Academy of War. In the course of nine months officers received a training in which mathematics tended to outweigh all other disciplines, even strategy and tactics. Pupils did not, however, completely neglect gentlemanly subjects like French or horsemanship.[90]

In 1859 the training was reformed. The school shortened its name to the 'Kriegsakademie' and the course was lengthened to three years. New subjects such as military law were introduced and the amount of maths was drastically reduced. Algebra became an option along with foreign languages like French, English or Russian, and in the second or third year students could even study Japanese. In the new school tactics and the history of war assumed a far greater importance.[91] Emil von Lessel studied at the school just after the Franco-Prussian War when young officers had every opportunity to use their recent experiences to good effect. 'The school was admirably directed, teachers and students having far-reaching experience of war and there reigned a lively motivation.

Besides military science, history, languages and mathematics were catered for. I heard the lectures of Privy Counsellor Duncke on the French Revolution which were extraordinarily gripping.'[92]

After the French defeat in the Franco-Prussian War, they too were interested in the secrets of the Prussian General Staff. A study made by a French staff officer in 1871 looked hard at German education to find a reason for defeat. The Frenchman found even the education of troop commanders vastly superior to those in France, because they insisted on the *Abitur* or school-leaver's certificate, or success in an exam set by the army itself. Failing that equivalence was only granted if the candidate had done a year of university or had distinguished himself in combat.[93]

The clear advantage was that the German officer was always 'an educated man'. This was, of course, particularly true of the staff who passed through the Kriegsakademie; fifty or sixty of them a year had sat the exam. In the French General Staff students were chosen either at the officer school at Saint Cyr, or at the Ecole polytechnique, which trained military engineers. The result was that French officers had no practical knowledge of troop movement. They were kept apart from the soldiers; simple theorists, whereas every Prussian *Generalstabler* had served three years as a troop commander.[94] 'What does the General Staff do for the French army?' the report asks. 'Pretty well nothing. What should it do? Just about everything.'[95]

Guderian arrived at the school in 1913 when 'the teachers for tactics and military history were General Staff officers who replaced the troop commanders who taught the remaining military disciplines; for the general-scientific subjects lecturers from Berlin University were brought in.'[96]

From 1871 the Berlin Kriegsakademie trained all Germany's staff officers with the exception of the Bavarians, who possessed their own school in Munich. To attend the Berlin Kriegsakademie, an officer needed to obtain permission from his commanding officer. Exams were taken anonymously, so that there was no possible prejudice on the part of examiners. This helped turn the staff into the middle-class institution it was on the eve of the

Great War. About eight hundred candidates sat the exam. Of these about a fifth passed.[97]

During the First World War the Berlin Kriegsakademie was closed and a shortened course was taught at Sedan.[98] The allied terror at the ability of the Prusso-German General Staff was such that its abolition became one of the clauses of the Treaty of Versailles. It was also the first of the treaty's demands that the Germans were to break, Seeckt never having had any intention of carrying out such an act. The abolition was represented by simple semantics. The *Generalstabsoffizier* became a *Führerstabsoffizier* or Command Staff officer. General Staff training became 'training for assistants to the commanders'. On 6 July 1919 Seeckt made it abundantly clear: 'The form changes but the spirit remains the same. It is the spirit of silent, selfless fulfilment of duty in the service of the army. General Staff officers have no names.'[99]

Seeckt's conception of the staff officer's role was enormous: these officers were not only to be the backbone of the army, they were to become the pillars of the new state: 'I expect all General Staff officers to make the maximum effort to reach the highest level of military ability through consistent work. By constant care for the soldiers, by living together with them you will achieve this aim, not just becoming a reliable support for the state but also creating a school for tutors and commanders. From the ranks of the army we will sow the seed of manly thought and even when we no longer wear the uniform we will still feel closely bound with the life, work and duties of the General Staff . . .'[100]

Here was a new approach to statecraft, eminently Prussian in thinking, based on the unique training of the reformed General Staff. The General Staff was the bedrock of the state: 'Everything which now brings discord and disorder to the nation must be shunned. It is really not the moment to carry differences of opinion into the public market, it is nefarious to seek out guilty who caused mischief in bygone days . . . Once again and more than ever I must demand for the sake of the commonweal, self denial and self sacrifice from General Staff officers. I want you to be the teachers and models of the nation; as such you must stand above parties; for then you will have your hands and hearts free to work for the good of the whole. The behaviour of each and every one of us must offer the enemy the bare minimum of points of attack, both from without and within.'[101]

Seeckt's bold conception was to make the army the core of Weimar, and the pip at the centre of this was the General Staff. Everything was to be conceived in miniature; therefore his army would be able to expand in the shortest possible time to become a mass army capable of fighting a major war. To this end the number of General Staff officers attached to the commands was actually increased under the Weimar Republic. The abolition of the Kriegsakademie meant that there could be no central training. Trainee staff officers were attached to the seven commands. In the past officers had chosen whether or not they wished to take the exam for the General Staff. Seeckt changed this: he wanted all the talent in the staff. All officers aged between twenty-five and thirty with five years' service were obliged to take the 'Wehrkreis-prüfung'. After training in the regional commands staff officers came to Berlin to spend a final year attached to the Reichswehr Ministry.[102]

Exams were taken in both the military and the civil domains: formal and applied tactics; weaponry and equipment; history, civil duties, social geography, foreign languages, maths, physics, chemistry and first aid. The range of historical questions set ran from the French Revolution (1922) to the meaning of British policy in the Mediterranean (1930). It was a notably tough exam. In 1922 twenty passed, but only one of these achieved a posting at the Berlin *Truppenamt*, as the General Staff was now officially known.[103]

The secret General Staff continued to function in this way until 1930, when the army felt confident enough of the unlikelihood of the Western Allies intervening to assemble all the training in Berlin. In October 1932 a new Kriegsakademie opened its doors in Berlin-Moabit, with the somewhat clumsy title of the 'Offizier-lehrgänge Berlin' or Berlin Officer Training Course. The teachers included many officers who had served in the old imperial army, including the future Field Marshals Kluge, Model, List and Paulus and the future Colonel Generals Adam, Guderian, Halder, Jodl and Reinhardt. In the new school Seeckt's anti-political leanings were corrected by the teaching of both internal and external politics. A special feature was the school excursion in October. The favoured destination was East Prussia, where students examined the fortress system as well as the battlefield of Tannenberg.[104]

Already in 1932 the carmine stripes had reappeared on the trousers of the General Staff officers, along with a special collar flash.[105] Clearly even greater things could be expected once Adolf Hitler was in power. By the autumn of 1934, the army had already expanded to 240,000 men. It was at this moment that Henning von Tresckow took up residence in Berlin to attend the school. Tresckow was one of eighty-seven captains to enrol on the two-year course. The students spent nine months attending classes, and the remaining three attached to troop commands; this process being repeated in the second year. The syllabus had been expanded to encompass some air force training with important teachers and public figures delivering frequent talks. Mobile warfare was still banned from the lecture rooms, by express command of General Beck, the head of the *Truppenamt*. Beck's teaching was still felt in that first generation of National Socialist General Staff officers. He emphasised the weakness of the German army, 'which could only be remedied by long preparation and did not allow for risks in foreign policy or the gamble of war which would end up causing the end of the Reich'.[106] Beck taught the students 'reflective obedience' (*mitdenkende Gehorsam*).[107]

Tresckow was the star pupil of his year. Top in tactics, he was dubbed 'the Saint' by his brother officers. He also excelled in military history; as the son-in-law of the former Chief of the General Staff Erich von Falkenhayn he had access to important archive sources to write his paper on the 1916 Romanian campaign. His translator's certificate in English was 'effortless'.[108] He even managed to have a talk with Colonel Guderian on the sly, to find out something about his revolutionary views on mobile war. On leaving the Moabit school, Tresckow achieved the top posting:

the Reichs War Ministry where he was in close contact with Beck, Fritsch and Manstein.[109]

While Tresckow was a student in Moabit, important changes took place in the army and the General Staff. On 16 March 1935, national service was reintroduced with the army being expanded to thirty-six divisions. In May the service period was extended to twenty-seven years, with one year of active service at eighteen, service in the reserve until thirty-five and service in the Landwehr until forty-five. On the 125th anniversary of the creation of the Kriegsakademie by Scharnhorst, the school received a new building, a converted former barracks in the Lehrterstrasse. Hitler was present at the opening ceremony on 15 October when Beck made a speech which was slightly less ambitious in its tone than Seeckt's sixteen years before: 'We need officers who can systematically act with intellectual self-discipline, taking their conclusions right through to the end, who possess the character and the nerves strong enough to do what their understanding dictates . . .'[110]

Beck was perhaps alluding to the political sense of the students. For many Seeckt's ideal of an apolitical officer was one of the weakest points about the General Staff training, especially once Hitler had begun to see the army as a tool for achieving his own colonial and racial ambitions.

It is a question whether a little more political education would have prevented staff officers from becoming so many Guderians – men devoid of moral sense. In the main, however, the figures simply do not bear the thesis out, that the General Staff responded favourably to Hitler and the Third Reich. At the beginning of the Second World War there were 824 staff officers of whom fewer than 600 served in staff positions. At the beginning of 1945, 359 of these were dead: 149 had been killed in action, seventeen had died in accidents, ten had simply died and 143 were missing. There had been sixteen suicides 'in the main in connection with 20 July 1944'; another twenty-four had been executed for their parts in the conspiracy. Sixty officers were arrested in all, i.e. one in ten were deemed suspect and the list of victims reads like a roll call of those men who had the courage to stand up to Hitler on that tragic day: Stauffenberg, General Olbricht, Colonel Merz von Quirnheim, Field Marshal von Witzleben, General Hoepner, General von Stülpnagel and many, many more. In the aftermath of the plot it was Guderian who was placed at the head of the General Staff. On 29 July he announced that all staff officers would now undergo Nazi indoctrination. It was a political education, but of the wrong sort.[111]

III

People were not wrong to call him a sphinx, with the ever-present monocle fixed in his eye he was quite rigid for most of the time and only revealed his human feelings when by chance he descended into relaxed conversation, or spoke to a beautiful woman.

Major Joachim von Stülpnagel on Hans von Seeckt.[112]

Als er einmal stillgeschwiegen,
Ganze fünf Minuten lang,
Hiess es 'Schleicher sind Sie krank?'*

Without a doubt, the two outstanding Prussian staff officers of the twilight years were Hans von Seeckt and Kurt von Schleicher. Both were noble, both became generals and both of them played a major role in German politics on the eve of the Third Reich.

They were very different characters. Seeckt was from the *Uradel*, the old nobility whose origins had been lost in the mists of time. He was born in Schleswig in 1866, where his father was serving as an army officer. Four years later the elder Seeckt was very badly wounded at St Privat. 'I grew up in a Prussian officer's family in which there still wafted the somewhat earthy smell of the Pomeranian family home of the time. My father, who climbed to the highest reaches of the military ladder, was for me the very

* Once he was reduced to silence
For five whole minutes long.
We asked, 'Schleicher, is something wrong?'
Jingle written by Kurt von Schleicher's fellow students at the Kriegsakademie.[113]

ideal of an old-style gentleman soldier, while my mother instilled in me a blend of intellectualism, a cast iron conception of duty and selfless love virtually to the end of her earthly days. I had no need to choose a profession; I became a soldier, not because I was forced to, rather because it was obvious that I would.'[114]

Schleicher was born in Brandenburg in 1882. Although his great-grandfather had been a friend of Prince Louis Ferdinand and had died at the Battle of Ligny in 1815, Schleicher counted as a member of the *Neuadel*, or recently ennobled. His father, Hermann von Schleicher, was a first lieutenant at the time of Kurt's birth. Later he commanded a battalion in the Spreewald, where he died, relatively young, in 1908. Schleicher's mother had more influence over the boy. Her father was the Danzig shipowner and President of the Chamber of Commerce, Friedrich Heye. It was in this Danzig mercantile world that Schleicher spent his childhood: 'His devotion to the bourgeois world, which later governed all his actions, stems from this time in Danzig.'[115]

Money wasn't lacking, and Schleicher was sent to the cadet school at Plön where the Kaiser's children had been educated; it has been suggested he was a little teased about the recentness of his noble patent.[116] Despite the fact that he was not seen as a 'natural soldier'[117] Schleicher proceeded to the higher cadet school of Lichterfelde at the age of fourteen. At eighteen he joined the Third Regiment of Guards, where his brother officers included not only the later Reichs President's son, Oskar von Hindenburg, but also the later Colonel General von Hammerstein-Equord and Field Marshal von Manstein.[118]

Seeckt had also joined an elite regiment – the Alexandriner. In 1893 he married Dorothee Fabian, a great-granddaughter of both the liberal Ernst Moritz Arndt and the theologian Friedrich Schleiermacher. That same year he and his bride undertook a long journey through Switzerland, England, Belgium, Italy, France, Spain, Morocco, Algeria, Egypt and India. Seeckt had learned the importance of foreign travel from his hero Moltke, who had served in Turkey for many years. The degree to which

Seeckt believed in the mind-broadening attributes of travel was seen as 'extraordinary' at the time.[119]

That same year Seeckt entered the Kriegsakademie in Berlin, where he remained until 1896. His first posting as a staff officer was to the Great General Staff in Berlin. In 1899 he was promoted captain, rather earlier than usual[120] and packed off to Danzig as second GSO (Ib) to the XVIIth army corps. It was thought fit to rotate staff officers through troop commands, and in 1902 Seeckt did a stint with a regiment in Düsseldorf. He returned to the Staff as GSO to a division in Bromberg, and in 1906 was promoted to major in the General Staff in Berlin. He spent the winter of 1907–1908 in India before becoming Ia, or Chief of Staff, to a division in Stettin. A further troop command, this time a battalion, took him to Karlsruhe before his promotion to Lieutenant Colonel and GSO to the 3rd Army Corps in Berlin.[121]

Schleicher entered the Kriegsakademie as a first lieutenant in 1910 and like Seeckt was promoted captain in the General Staff on leaving. Unlike Seeckt, he had a light-hearted, rather social nature. He enjoyed race-meetings and was often to be seen at the Berlin tracks. On joining the staff, Schleicher had been asked his chief interest and had replied 'the railways'.[122] He was then sent to Groener. His first meeting with the Württemberger was 'the milestone of his life'.[123] Groener referred to Schleicher as his 'adopted son', a term he repeated in his will. He also introduced Schleicher to politics as the head of the war department of the General Staff. Together they met the high-ranking Socialist politicians.[124]

Until May 1917, Schleicher's training had been entirely theoretical, and unlike Seeckt he had had no contact with ordinary troop commanders. His first field posting was as Ia to an infantry division at the front. From there he went to Galicia, where he distinguished himself in a brutal campaign and was decorated with the Hohenzollern Hausorden 'with swords'. His political work had put him in a difficult position with Ludendorff, especially after he had launched an attack on the war profiteers, which the First Quartermaster-General believed was directed at him. He

spent two and a half months in Galicia, then returned to headquarters at Spa.[125] A year later he was to have a front-row seat
when Groener advised the Kaiser to abdicate. It seems clear that
under Groener's influence, Schleicher thought it was expedient to
dispense with the Hohenzollerns. Seeckt would almost certainly
have disagreed with him.

Schleicher took to politics like a duck to water. With Seeckt it
was a slow process. As a young officer he had described politics
as 'an uncomfortable theme; hard to write about . . . in the end
I've heard a lot but don't understand a lot of it.'[126] Seeckt still
lacked the role model which Schleicher had found in Groener.
Instead he turned to his now dead father: 'I often ask myself what
my father would have done in such and such a position.'[127] As war
began to look like a certainty, Seeckt expressed his misgivings
about foreign policy. He was certainly no Ludendorff, no Bernhardi: 'That world peace should ultimately depend on the
emotions of a weak man like the Czar is actually rather a sad sign
of the times. I hope we are prepared – and in a certain way – up
to it. That is some sort of consolation . . .'[128]

On 14 November 1914 he wrote to his mother to express his
pride in the Prussian army he was helping to direct: 'I hope you
will be able to experience what happens when Prussia's flags are
hoisted. And I'm looking forward to the same . . .'[129] In those first
years of war, Seeckt's tone was often aggressively anti-English as
he came under the influence of the war party in the General Staff.
The war was 'a crusade, a holy war'[130] and one which the
politicians were in danger of losing with their insistence on a
negotiated peace.

Meanwhile his star continued to rise. In April 1915 he planned
a campaign against Serbia, bringing together an army of Austrian,
German and Romanian soldiers. In June 1916 he was made Chief
of Staff to the 11th Austrian army. In December of the following
year he was placed in charge of the Ottoman army. A few months
before Seeckt's Turkish posting, there was a plan in General Staff
circles to replace Bethmann-Hollweg with Falkenhayn. In this
case Seeckt was seen as a successor to Falkenhayn in the General

Staff. Seeckt wisely distanced himself from these machinations. He was not a political officer. He was, however, in sympathy with the plot. 'The man who represents Germany's political destiny should have the following qualities and attributes: inward Prussianness [*inneres Preussentum*], he must be respected and feared abroad, present a clear front to the outside world and enjoy the trust of his own people. If the Reichs Chancellor had all that then he would be the right man to conclude the peace which our arms have rendered possible. That there exists widespread doubt is the actual cause of all disquiet . . .'[131]

If the language occasionally resembles that of Ludendorff, the intentions are not the same. Seeckt might have seen the need for the government to adopt dictatorial powers, but these would have to have been legitimised by the crown. His approach was based on the need to win the war. He expressed himself in the purest Clausewitzian idiom: 'In battle we must strive to annihilate the military potential of the enemy.'[132] The idea of a negotiated peace made him see the necessity of the second war to deal with Germany's struggle for power with Britain. Increasingly his thought turned to the idea of concluding just such a peace so that Germany would enter the next war in a better position to deal with the British: 'easily defendable borders', 'a secure material future, strength in money, raw materials and people'.[133]

In 1915, Seeckt showed a brief enthusiasm for annexations. A power block based on mutual interests was to be extended from the Atlantic to Persia, 'but please, no "German Reich"', he told his friend Winterfeld. The idea of the power block was directed at Britain once again and the British policy of a war of attrition. Briefly Seeckt took up the idea of wide-ranging annexations: the mines of Longwy and Briey; a 'dependent' Belgium with neither army nor foreign policy; and the beginnings of a central African empire. As one of Seeckt's biographers has asked, 'Was Ludendorff the godfather?'[134] By 1917, however, these ideas had been shelved. Seeckt no longer believed that there would be a German victory, and he directly criticised Ludendorff for wanting to hang on to Courland and Lithuania after the war.[135]

Seeckt was also briefly tempted to subscribe to the stab-in-the-back theory. When the Reichstag called for peace in July 1918, he asked, 'Why are we still fighting? At home they have jumped on us from behind and so the war is lost.'[136]

Germany's collapse stressed the need for reform, to rid the country of those factors which had allowed defeat to take place. Seeckt may have been a Prussian conservative, but he was by no means blind to Prussia's faults. The problem went deep, back to the land and the failure to reform agriculture in the vast Prussian sandbox. Seeckt was prepared to do battle with his own class to get through the necessary reforms: 'I completely agree with you,' he wrote to his sister in November 1915, 'agrarian Prussia has shown itself to be behind the times, in every respect. To do something about this we need a man without prejudice and who is unscrupulous enough to effect the will of the whole without paying heed to class and social considerations.'[137]

Similar were his ideas on the army itself, which required thorough-going reforms. Most important of all was to democratise the army after the war. In political terms, Seeckt favoured 'enlightened absolutism', an idea inspired by Frederick the Great, and a rigorous adherence to the Prussian virtues. In Seeckt's 'modernised Fredericianism' he conceived of a democracy which would ensure the equality of all in their subordination and duty to the state; an obligation for everyone to work towards the greater good, for the community of the common will.[138] Because he believed that the army should be both classless and without politics, he thought that the state too should dispense with class and politics. At the head of this 'social empire' stood the monarch. 'I wouldn't take a single stone away from the Prussian crown ... a contemporary, polished up and enlightened absolutism is the best form of government.'[139]

Seeckt's love for Prussia went deep. Prussia was the model for other German states to follow, Germany's greatest creation. 'This much maligned, much feared and much admired Prussia is a creation all of its own; it is in its development and character *the*

German type of state, the picture of the state in itself. It was not created in imitation of foreign models, nor did it spring from a closed class community, rather it was formed and developed from the idea of a state itself, which used all its magical force of attraction to bring together the organic elements of the whole, without destroying their individual qualities; making them serve the good of the whole; binding the rich, but weak and heavily divided German cultural life with the strength of the concept of duty [Prussia is] the only German state which knew how to win over new soil to German culture [*neuen Boden dem Deutschtum zu gewinnen*], the social state in the best sense of the word which, when it mercilessly required the sacrifice of the individual for the sake of the state, where the power of the state has always been placed at the disposal of the nation. Such a state cannot always be attractive . . .'[140]

Prussia was proof against selfishness and party interests, dogmas and ideologies through its consciousness of the state, duty, loyalty, discipline and obedience. It was a love which was to move Seeckt even at the end of his life. As late as 1930 he thought the question of Prussia's continued existence within the Reich 'the most burning question concerning the constitution'.[141]

Seeckt's passion for Prussia (if we can call it that*) may lead one to suppose that he was a German version of Colonel Blimp. This was not so. He may have had little time for democratic institutions, but this was because he believed that the state would act in the best interests of the citizen without the citizen requiring such guarantees. He thought reactionaries of the Oldenburg-Januschau school 'atrocious'[143] and was critical of the Prussian royalists he encountered in Pomerania.[144] Like many old-school Prussians, Seeckt was steeped in Lutheran piety. To his wife he spoke of his dedication to St Paul: 'How can we do our duty convincingly when we serve only man? The man who does not the highest service in his position can bear no responsibility. Serving mankind is no longer what we do. The cause we serve is a holy

---

* Captain von Velsen described him as 'not a man who gives off warmth'.[142]

one, and comes from God . . .'[145] If Seeckt's religious devotion was wholly Lutheran however, he was convinced by the need for tolerance and voted with the Catholic Centre Party, much to the chagrin of his mother.[146]

It was his sense of duty which prevented him from siding with the *frondeurs* once it became certain that the old Reich would go down with German defeat to give birth to a new Germany, and one far less to his liking. His mother wrote to him at the time to show that she understood 'a feeling for duty alone can keep you going in your work'.[147] Seeckt expressed it in his own way: 'Our duty is clear to us. We must work together to maintain the unity of the Reich and to build it up anew, we must found and develop the new army. We must open our eyes wide to this unavoidable necessity which has been imposed upon us and with a firm will take the path to recovery and and a new future.'[148]

The fifty-two-year-old Generalmajor, former Chief of the Ottoman Army and *Pour le mérite* resigned himself to the Germany of the November Revolution. For the thirty-six-year-old Major von Schleicher, November was a new opportunity to show his mettle, a chance to pursue his own ambitions during that chaotic time. The story is told that the new Chancellor Ebert, in the darkest days, picked up a telephone on his desk to find himself on a direct line to the General Staff: 'Central Headquarters, Major von Schleicher,' said the voice on the other end of the line.[149] Schleicher was now the head of the Political Bureau. Ebert was not unfamiliar with him, and had noted that he had tilted at Ludendorff's profiteering friends during the war. Schleicher assured Ebert that the General Staff was ready to help stamp out Bolshevism. In return Schleicher wanted the old officer-to-man structure resurrected. Schleicher was always careful to keep on the right side of Ebert. Even after the death of Weimar's first president, Schleicher used to visit Frau Ebert, taking with him the marzipan tart which he knew she loved.[150]

Schleicher still liked the good life: the race tracks and the opera; the music of Richard Strauss; the exquisite meals he ate at

Otto Horcher's restaurant in the Lutherstrasse.[151] The contrast with Seeckt was to be noticed once the two men began to work together. At Seeckt's house reigned 'spartan simplicity', and in contrast to the sophisticated food available at Horcher's, Schleicher had to make do with 'beer and rolls'.[152]

Seeckt treated the new state of affairs with a feeling of resignation. He returned to Germany from his Turkish command on 13 November 1918 and spent the next two months without a job to occupy his mind. In January he was posted to Königsberg to oversee the return of the German army from Russia. In April he bit the bullet in agreeing to go to Versailles as the head of the German military mission. Although he behaved in a petulant manner over not being able to wear his uniform, Seeckt was a realist when it came to the peace conference; he thought the dictated peace was a case of the 'old law of war'; the Germans would, after all, have done much the same to France.[153] In June he reported back to Weimar, where he was promoted Chief of the General Staff.

This was the moment for Seeckt to show his organisational genius. In February he had written to his sister, 'Where is the army? Can we still save a part of it? That is the question which occurs to me too, I who have given 33 years of service . . .'[154] He found Ebert and his crew 'relatively honest', preferring their attitude to that of the old bourgeois politicians like the former Colonial Secretary Wilhelm Solf, whom he found false.[155] The Kapp Putsch came as a test of his loyalty. Some have suggested that he betrayed the government in those March days,[156] but much of the evidence goes the other way. He had already mentioned his reluctance to become involved in a military revolt to the Czar of Bulgaria and had warned both Noske and Reinhardt against Lüttwitz. His refusal to suppress the revolt by force has been mentioned elsewhere. But he went to see the Chancellor's Berlin representative, Dr Eugen Schiffler, while the latter was being held in custody by Kapp's men and assured him of his support for the regime. Kapp and Lüttwitz, he told him, 'had many plus-points, but in political terms they were muddled phantasts, blind adventurers and selfish dilettantes. They are capable of pulling down and destroying a good deal, but incapable of laying a solid foundation and as a result of this they have been unable to use their initial success . . . they will therefore be ultimately booed off the stage without achieving anything.'[157]

The Kapp Putsch further convinced Seeckt of the need to ban politics from the army. In his first public pronouncement after the failure of the revolt, he announced, 'The German nation is struggling for its very existence after a large-scale attempt to kidnap the red republic. . . . We will win the battle if officers and men, unswayed by political influences, stand together and maintain order. The soldier must abstain from all politics and fight only on the order of his military commander.'[158] He hoped that the failure of the Kapp Putsch would lead more of the Prussian conservatives to support the Republic, 'the only binding element' he called the constitution. 'Officers and men should not be politicised, but they must be politically enlightened, it must be made clear to them only a *peaceful, democratic development* is possible for Germany.'[159]

If the projected 'enlightenment' came to naught, the educational standard of the whole army improved beyond measure under Seeckt. With the necessity of dismissing three officers out of four, only those who had finished a secondary school education could be considered, and these underwent a four-and-a-half-year training, two of them at military school.[160] Seeckt may have personally preferred to engage aristocratic officers, but if they were nobles (which fewer than a quarter were) they were at least educated ones. Even the simple soldiers tended to be literate. With the need to transform all the rank and file into NCOs at a moment's notice, there was no room for cannon-fodder.[161]

As a Pomeranian nobleman, Seeckt was suspicious, if not downright contemptuous, of Polish national aspirations. This accounted in part for his deep-rooted feeling that Russia was Germany's natural ally in the east: Russia and Germany had, after all, a mutual interest in destroying Poland. Like many Prussians from the Convention of Tauroggen onwards, Seeckt was an easterner: 'I see an economic agreement with Greater Russia as a solid political goal for us in the future. We must try at the very least not to make Russia an enemy. I refuse to support Poland, because of the danger that Poland will be swallowed up.'[162] In 1920, Seeckt had called the very existence of the Polish state into question in his pamphlet *Deutschlands nächste politische Aufgaben* (Germany's Future Political Tasks).[163]

It was in fact the Russians themselves who made the first move towards co-operation with Germany. A trade agreement was signed in May 1921 and in September the German-born communist Karl Radek (né Sobelsohn) and Leonid Krassin managed to interest Seeckt on talks on military co-operation. Seeckt believed himself to be maintaining a purely Bismarckian policy of co-operation with Russia. From the following year German troops were sent to train in Russia and a few Soviet officers were posted to the German General Staff.[164]

This was the first instance of close co-operation between Seeckt and Schleicher. Radek thought Schleicher 'a clever man' where Seeckt was only 'a clever general'.[165] This was probably only an appreciation of the superior political abilities of the younger man. Seeckt, however, was not wholly without political ambition. After cleaning up Germany following the various *coups d'état* which came to the surface in 1923, he was increasingly flattered by the calls for him to take over power. In 1923 he conceived a plan to succeed Ebert as Reichs President, a plan which he only dropped once he realised he would have to stand against Hindenburg. The idea of Seeckt as President of the Weimar Republic is an interesting one. It is hard not to think that his presidency would have been a good deal more successful than Hindenburg's.[166] It has been suggested that he might have known better how to deal with Hitler when the time came.[167]

As it was, Seeckt was elbowed out of the way by Schleicher. The pretext was the part played by the Crown Prince's eldest son in autumn manoeuvres of 1926. The story appeared in the press, and Seeckt took the blame. Once again Schleicher played his shadowy role; it appears that he resented Seeckt for blocking his promotion and managed to convince the War Minister Otto Karl Gessler that Seeckt had allowed Prince William to take part. Schleicher also had the ear of the President, Hindenburg, the father of his friend Colonel Oskar von Hindenburg.[168] With Seeckt's departure went the last Prussian fundamentalist to lead the German army.

Schleicher was no such thing. A self-interested schemer, he had none of Seeckt's *Nüchternheit* and sense of duty. It may well be true that Schleicher was Weimar's last chance to avert a National Socialist dictatorship, but his underhand behaviour ended up by splitting the democratic parties which otherwise might have proved able to keep Hitler on the other side of the door, and his only real support came from the supposedly apolitical army.[169] He was also behind the *Preussenschlag* of 20 July 1932, when Prussia's democratic institutions were scrapped and replaced by a Reichs Commissioner, thereby further oiling the rails for Hitler's arrival in power. Schleicher paid for his intrigues on 30 June 1934, when he was gunned down at his house at Neu-Babelsberg by the SS. He was to be the Reich's last Prussian Chancellor.

Pink Prussia

These examples are quite enough to demonstrate to us that which we must be aware of: what happens when people who have grown up in the exclusivity of the officer corps and the narrow purlieus of barracks life exercise political influence.

Robert Graf von Zedlitz-Trützschler,
Zwölf Jahre am deutschen Kaiserhof,
Berlin and Leipzig, 1924, 161.

Homosexuality is a sensitive subject. Is homosexuality ever more widespread in one society than in another? Or is it that in some societies it is more tolerated; or that the structure of society provides more openings for homosexuals in some countries? It would be hard, for example, to make a convincing argument that there were more homosexuals in Wilhelmine Prussia than there were in *fin-de-siècle* France or Edwardian Britain. Yet the Eulenburg scandal achieved an importance in Prussian history that was even greater than the equivalent case – the trial of Oscar Wilde – in England. This was due to the shock caused by the revelation that the all-hallowed, militaristic education, which Prussia was handing out to Germans throughout the Reich, provided the perfect seed-bed for homosexual activity by cutting boys off from female company and stressing manliness above all else. It was possibly this, rather than a response to Prussia's military world,[1] which led to the singular flowering of Prussian homosexuality before the Great War; the fact was that homosexuals occupied some of the most influential positions at court.

Simply because homosexuality was so widespread, heterosexual Prussians reveal themselves to be fairly understanding and tolerant in their writings at the time. Police Commissioner Hans von

Tresckow was involved in investigating numerous homosexual scandals at the time and therefore took the trouble to read the important literature on the subject. It would be difficult to conceive of an Edwardian Scotland Yard inspector immersing himself in the books of Krafft-Ebing or Magnus Hirschfeld, the author of the controversial works *Sexualpathologie* and *Geschlechtskunde*. Tresckow, however, not only read their books; he visited Hirschfeld in his study. Tresckow tells us that 'as a normally constituted man' he found the subject unpleasant,[2] but his mind remained open: 'I've seen and spoken to thousands of homosexuals from all walks of life; for homosexuality is not something which, as has been falsely suggested, is restricted to the privileged classes. Not at all, it is found as often among porters as among princes. No class or sector of society is immune. That this tendency is to be found in certain professions, couturiers and hairdressers for example, is merely proof that many male homosexuals feel female and take a special interest in female-orientated careers.'[3]

Tresckow's experience led him to reject Krafft-Ebing's contention that homosexuals were 'unhappy' people. Tresckow's contacts were far from miserable, 'happily using such female weaponry as intrigue, hypocrisy and lies'.[4]

At the heart of the problem lay the Prussian and German Criminal Code. Article 175 demanded imprisonment for male (but not female) homosexuals; but for a case to succeed, the act of sex had to be proved beyond reasonable doubt. Therein lay the rub: copulation between consenting adults was unlikely to be admitted before a hostile court and therefore could only be ascertained if the men had been caught *in flagrante delicto*, or if one party was not consenting.

Commissioner Tresckow was in favour of repealing Article 175. 'I personally take the line that this paragraph is both pointless and behind the times . . . *volenti non fit injuria* . . . Obviously the feeble-minded and the under-aged must be protected.'[5] On the other hand Tresckow agreed with those, such as Maximilian Harden, who thought there was a danger in the existence of an homosexual 'camarilla' within the court and he singles out the many homosexuals in the Prussian nobility, where he believed the problem was accentuated by inbreeding: 'I know that among the Baltic Barons, who almost always marry among themselves and where fresh blood is very rare, there are a good many homosexuals.* The same applies to German princes where marriages to relatives are the rule.'[6]

The Police Commissioner was also of the view that homosexuals tended to promote one another, and often lacked loyalty to the state. As an example he cited the case of Ambassador Fürst Eulenburg's alleged liaison with the French Consul Lecomte. 'Both had homosexual tendencies, and both knew about one another. . . . When Lecomte was exposed in [Harden's] *Die Zukunft*, he was removed from Berlin and posted to the Balkans . . . where love between men is not despised as it is here, rather it is seen as a harmless recreation.'[7] Tresckow clearly thought there was a danger to state security in an ambassador, with unrestricted access to the monarch, having a sexual relationship with the French Consul, who represented Germany's most likely enemy in the event of war.

Writing in 1922, Tresckow believed that the number of male homosexuals in Berlin had grown since 1890. He estimated their number at over 100,000 with more than a hundred pubs made over 'almost exclusively' to their use. They had their own paper in *Die Freundschaft*, which had recently been before the courts for 'depraving' the general public. Well before the Weimar Republic, the Berlin police boasted its own homosexuality expert, a nobleman by the name of von Meerscheidt-Hüllessem.[8] Meerscheidt was not untypical of the Berlin police at the time in that his appallingly inadequate salary led him to work elsewhere to bring his earnings up to a reasonable level, but in certain things he took some trouble and it fell to him to draw up a comprehensive list of the homosexuals in Berlin's high society. This list was offered to

* Tresckow is referring to the Junkers of Lithuania, Latvia and Estonia; German noblemen living outside the Reich.

the Kaiser, but he waved it aside. 'Had the Kaiser had a look at the register at the time he would have been enlightened as to the nature of his entourage and the later sensational trials which put the image of the crown in such a poor light and damaged [our reputation] abroad, might have been avoided,' Tresckow wrote.[9]

The file helped unravel the spate of blackmail cases at that time which involved members of the aristocracy. Two names Tresckow found on the list were those of the brothers Graf Hohenau, who had royal blood and enjoyed the privilege of being addressed as 'Du' by the Kaiser. Fritz was attached to the Prussian embassy in Dresden, where he was being blackmailed by one Assmann. He had the sense to resign from the diplomatic corps and retire to Italy ('the promised land'[10]). His brother commanded the Garde-kurassier regiment and was an aide de camp to the Kaiser. Tresckow warned Graf Hohenau not to practise homosexuality, but the soldier ignored his advice and was later court-martialled and imprisoned.[11]

Another who ignored Tresckow's counsel was Graf Edgard Wedel, known as 'Hofwedel' or court Wedel, to differentiate him from his father, the chief equerry 'Stallwedel'. Tresckow disliked Wedel, 'an effeminate homosexual type', 'monstrously vain' and 'prissy'; 'one might have taken him for a well-preserved old spinster.'[12] Mean and treacherous, Wedel was happy to expose Eulenburg if he thought there was a chance of saving his own skin. He was ruined by an article in the *Neue Freie Presse* which revealed that he had been caught indulging in some *al fresco* sex on the banks of the Isar in Munich. After this the Kaiser refused to speak to him, telling other members of the court, 'To think that our Edgard is another of these pigs.'[13]

Another courtier, Bodo von der Knesebeck, was Vice-Master of Ceremonies and Marshal of the Diplomatic Corps. He managed to avoid a scandal when he was blackmailed by the tailor Roder, a resourceful individual who had also exploited the Grand Duke of Mecklenburg. The police were able to prosecute Roder on other charges and Knesebeck's involvement with him was covered up. The diplomat died in office. Tresckow felt justified in keeping Knesebeck's name out of the papers. He could not be proved to have committed an offence against Article 175 and swore that there was no truth in the allegation. The policeman was unconvinced: 'A man in his position and background would not otherwise have struck up this remarkable friendship with a tailor's boy.'[14]

The files also incriminated General von Kessel, the Commander of the Gardekorps, a 'proper parade ground general' who owed his position to the fact that it had been he who had cordoned off the Kaiser's father's palace to prevent Frederick's papers from being removed by his widow. Kessel had locked the dead emperor's desk and placed the key in William's hands. Tresckow was anxious to add that there *were* heterosexual courtiers but 'these were at times in a minority and they were mostly powerless against the tight ring which had been forged around the ruler.'[15]

Not all the aristocratic victims of blackmailing rent boys were authentic. One courtier showed Tresckow a letter from a Polish Count Tyskiewicz. It said that he knew that the courtier was being blackmailed by a butcher's boy, as he was too. He, Tyskiewicz, was too poor to muster all the money demanded to send the boy to America out of harm's way, but together, he wrote, they might find the funds. Tresckow investigated the case and discovered that the Polish count was living with the butcher's boy and sharing the spoils of his blackmailing operations.[16]

It being Prussia, many erotic fantasies, both hetero- and homosexual, revolved around the army with its colourful parade uniforms. The worst to suffer in this connection were the cavalry regiments 'and many a stout country boy was physically and morally abused [by homosexuals] during his time in the colours.'[17] Tresckow received a visit from the Colonel of the Gardekurassiers (the successor to Hohenau), Prince Albrecht of Schleswig-Holstein, complaining of the problem of maintaining discipline. Tresckow provided the prince with the names of Potsdam's chief homosexual pubs and they were promptly placed out of bounds. Later the police mounted an operation to seize the ringleaders in this Potsdam vice ring. In one of the pubs they found a royal chamberlain called Hedemann von Oppen, known as 'Röschen' (little rose) as a result of his feminine appearance.[18]

Similar problems confronted the Colonel of the Gardedragoner, Prince Charles of Hohenzollern. Hohenzollern complained of characters molesting his soldiers. In the main, the local police seemed able to deal with them but they were powerless when it came to the courtiers, who included an unnamed retired cavalry captain and Graf Edgard Wedel. Many of these were shown to be frequenters of Podeyn's bath-house in Berlin's Sophienstrasse. Podeyn went by the name of the 'Baronin von Schönhausen' (Baroness Schönhausen) from the time when he ran a brothel in the Schönhäuserstrasse. The police raided the Sophienstrasse bath-house and cautioned a number of prominent homosexuals, including Prince Frederick Albert of Prussia.[19]

Another homosexual furore which touched the Kaiser's intimate circle was the case of the industrialist Friedrich Alfred Krupp. The story broke in Italy, where Krupp was wont to spend his time on Capri. Here he 'had stretched the normally limitless patience of the Italians beyond endurance, going so far as to seduce very young boys.'[20] His behaviour had become so blatant that the Italian paper *Avanti* published a series of articles about him. In Germany there were rumours, but due to Krupp's close contacts with the Kaiser, the press did not dare touch the subject.

The ever-vigilant Tresckow was anxious to avoid a scandal. He knew all about Krupp from Kommerzienrat Uhl, the manager of the Bristol Hotel in Berlin. Frau Krupp never stayed in the Bristol, preferring to lodge at another hotel, but Krupp himself was in the habit of rewarding his Italian playmates by sending them up to Berlin with a recommendation to Uhl. Uhl could only comply: Krupp was a very powerful man and a customer. When Krupp came to Berlin he would enquire after his protégés; he was particularly anxious to know if they were getting a weekly bath. After a while Uhl tired of Krupp's solicitude towards these Italian waifs and was short with the industrialist. Krupp reacted in fury, taking himself off to another hotel. The idea of seeing the boys again, however, must have lured him back, for he did not sulk for long.

Tresckow decided he would see for himself and, after talking to Uhl, he went into the dining room to eat. Many of the waiters serving that evening turned out to be Italians. When Tresckow asked one how he came to be working in Berlin's smartest hotel, he replied, 'Herr Krupp recommended that I try here.'[21]

The storm finally broke when the Socialist newspaper *Vorwärts* ran a story entitled 'Krupp auf Kapri' (Krupp on Capri) to coincide with Krupp's attendance at Kiel Week as the Kaiser's guest. Krupp cut short his stay and returned to the Villa Hugel in Essen. From Essen, Krupp's secretary, Dr Korn, travelled up to Berlin to see Tresckow. Could the commissioner do anything to prevent the situation from worsening? Tresckow told Korn, 'If Krupp has a clear conscience then he should calmly pursue the matter before the courts.' The next day was Sunday, and Tresckow was dismayed to find out from his newspaper that Krupp had committed suicide. Later he learned that Krupp's death had not been deliberate. He had unwittingly taken an overdose while in a state of great anxiety.[22]

The Kaiser could not believe the stories about Krupp. Despite all the evidence 'he had a firm and unshakeable belief in Krupp's innocence.'[23] Nor was the Kaiser alone in this. Admiral von Hollmann, who knew Krupp well, believed Krupp could not have 'indulged'. 'That he had, however, a remarkable interest in male painters, waiters and young men in general had,' said the admiral, 'through the careless way in which he consorted with them, often astonished him; he had noticed that people of his type often laid their hands on your shoulder or even went so far as to stroke your hair in an over-friendly way, but would stop short of any perverse thoughts or activities.'[24]

II

You must be paraded by me as a circus poodle! That will be a 'hit' like nothing else. Just think: behind shaved [tights], in front long bangs of black and white wool, at the back under a genuine poodle tail, a marked rectal opening and, when you 'beg', in front a fig leaf. Just think how wonderful when you bark, howl to music, shoot off a pistol or do other tricks. It is simply splendid! Nobody can make a costume as well as I can, [you] can model the head yourself. In my mind's eye I can already see H. M. laughing with us – I'm counting on a *succès fou*.[25]

> Graf Georg von Hülsen to Emil Graf Görtz.

The Eulenburgs were one of the great names of the East Prussian nobility. The family had originally come from Saxony, but had settled in the lands of the Margrave of Brandenburg before the fifteenth century. The branch of Philipp Graf zu Eulenburg was a comparatively minor one, based at Schloss Liebenberg in the Uckermark, to the north-east of Berlin. Schloss Liebenberg was later to give its name to the *Liebenberger Kreis*, or Liebenberg Circle: the Kaiser's arty, Prussian noble friends.[26]

Philipp was born in 1847 and brought up in much the usual way. In 1866 he entered the Gardedukorps regiment with two other future Liebenbergers, Graf Edgard von Wedel, who was to become the homosexual 'Hofwedel', and the East Prussian Eberhard Graf zu Dohna Schlobitten. At the *Kriegsschule* he met another important friend, Kuno, Graf von Moltke, who shared his interest in music. In 1869, Eulenburg was granted leave from the army to take his *Abitur*, or school leaving certificate. The following year he left the army for good and matriculated at Leipzig University.

At Leipzig, Eulenburg met another key component of his circle: Axel Freiherr von Varnbüler. He studied law and, in the manner of German students, did not remain at Leipzig, but migrated to the newly Germanised university of Strasbourg in Alsace, and from there to Giessen in Hesse. Here he received his doctorate *magna cum laude*. He married the Swedish Countess Augusta

Sandels, who bore him no fewer than eight children, and joined the diplomatic service. After a succession of minor appointments in Germany he was sent to Paris to work under Ambassador Hohenlohe.

From Paris he was posted to Munich where he enjoyed some success composing ballads and other literary works. His future in the diplomatic service, however, was blocked by Bismarck. 'Personally I like him, he is amiable, but in political matters he lacks the ability to judge what is important and what isn't; he allows himself to make an impression through grumbling and gossip-mongering. . . .' Bismarck thought he'd make a suitable envoy for Oldenburg, Brunswick or Lippe, but he was not earmarked for higher things. In his more lucid moments, Eulenburg was prone to expounding a foreign policy favoured by East Prussian nobles aimed at preventing Catholics from getting the upper hand. To this end he sought to prevent a Catholic league being formed between Bavaria and Austria.[27]

Bismarck was wrong. In 1871, the twenty-four-year-old Eulenburg met the twelve-year-old Prince William of Prussia at a hunt. In the mid-1880s they met again at Pröckelwitz. Eulenburg sang his songs at the piano and the future Kaiser was overjoyed, and made him sing them all over again.[28] After that meeting they became firm friends. Instead of stagnating at some minor German court, Eulenburg became Ambassador to Vienna and one of the Kaiser's most trusted advisors on all branches of policy. Bismarck was far from amused. He called Eulenburg a 'Prussian Cagliostro' and thought his influence on the Kaiser extremely dangerous.[29] Careers at the Kaiser's court were now made or broken by a word from Eulenburg.

The Kaiser attended the house parties at Liebenberg where he let his hair down, relaxed with Eulenburg's friends and enjoyed the lively artistic world they represented. At the core of the group were Kuno Moltke, the Kaiser's aide de camp from 1893 to 1902; Varnbüler, Württemberg's envoy to Berlin; and the embassy secretary Karl Freiherr von Dörnberg, who died before he could be implicated in the future scandal. On a more peripheral basis the group included Eberhard Dohna Schlobitten and his brother Richard, the two East Prussian counts who had introduced Eulenburg to Prince William in 1871; Georg von Hülsen, a one-time Prussian military envoy to Bavaria who was now Intendant at the court theatre in Berlin, and his cousin Dietrich, who was Chief of the Military Cabinet from 1901 until his dramatic death in 1908. The rest were Emil Graf Schlitz or Görtz, Alfred von Bülow and Jan Freiherr von Wendelstadt. Philipp's hunting cousins Botho and August put in an appearance from time to time, as did Walther Freiherr von Esebeck and the above-mentioned General Gustav von Kessel.[30]

When game was scarce, the Liebenbergers turned to art. Philipp Eulenburg sang the *Rosenlieder*, which had brought him fame in Munich in the 1880s and 1890s; Varnbüler enjoyed some reputation as a caricaturist; Moltke composed music and played the piano; Georg Hülsen and Görtz staged plays and entertainments and Görtz was also an amateur sculptor; but 'beneath their shared artistic interests lay another, stronger bond: that was homosexuality.'[31]

Since the famous trials of 1907–1909 there has been much speculation as to whether or not these men actually practised sodomy, or whether their homosexuality was confined to a loftier form of platonic love. Perhaps the perspicacious Zedlitz-Trützschler came close when he wrote on 26 November 1907, 'The majority of people have poorly appraised the "homosexual" question. Many homosexuals ... do not practise, but in spite of this they make their presence felt in William II's circle and in politics through their effeminate and flamboyant nature. I suppose that it was also this danger which Harden recognised. Whether Prince Eulenburg ever practised will never be proved. The general practitioner, Dr Ilberg, who knew him well, was of the opinion that he would have been acquitted at the trial and that it was only weakness on his part which prevented him from seeing it through to the end.'[32]

Eulenburg could reckon with none of the incriminating evidence which excited public interest in the near-contemporary trial of

Oscar Wilde.[33] Those attempting to confirm or deny the prince's proclivities have therefore been thrown back on his letters and diaries, or the testimony of servants and fishermen, who cut far less of a dash in the Prussian courts than the rent boys in the Wilde case. Tresckow believed that Eulenburg's guilt was clinched by a letter from Richard Dohna in which he wrote, 'You are quite simply such a liar that it severely taxes my conscience to have brought such a fellow into the intimate circle of our beloved All Highest Lord, King and Kaiser.'[34] Which looks like no evidence at all.

Philipp Eulenburg fathered eight children, but it is clear that sexual intercourse with his wife was performed from a sense of duty, and 'Eulenburg's wife bored him as much as she bored his friends: "I enjoy family life little," he wrote to Varnbüler on 13 August 1877. "I gladly go my own way.... The dog which ceaselessly and pitilessly drives [me] back is an acquired sense of duty. Heaven knows it is not innate." '[35]

More convincing evidence that Eulenburg may have infringed Article 175 comes from a letter of 24 October 1912 from Varnbüler to Kuno Moltke. Philipp 'starts from the fictional standpoint that he is innocent and I believe (although I go along with the fiction but at the same time raise the objection – "Why don't you fight a struggle to bring the thing to an end, once and for all") that it would do some good if it were to put an end to all the theatrical pathos of these protestations and reproaches. This pose is his last resort and he hopes thereby to maintain the trust of his family and a few friends by using it. I don't have the energy to destroy it for him, and nor do you.'[36]

During his Viennese years, Eulenburg was closest to Kuno Moltke; theirs was clearly a romantic friendship even if there was no sexual liaison. During those days, Moltke's marriage was breaking up and Eulenburg arranged Moltke's transfer to Vienna to spare him the 'gruesome'[37] relations he was having with his wife. Gräfin Moltke was not happy with Eulenburg's interference. Once she witnessed her husband pick up a handkerchief Eulenburg had dropped and press it to his lips. Both Eulenburg and Moltke were using Varnbüler as a *confidant*, and it would seem that the Kaiser too was trying to protect the sensitive Moltke from the worst of his marriage. '*Mein Dachs!*'* wrote Varnbüler to Moltke. 'I am probably not mistaken that it is an intensification of your pain not to be able to hide all the ugliness from him [the Kaiser], from *Liebchen*.† But do not torture yourself unnecessarily on this account, he is man enough to silence harmful gossip, and he knows and loves you too well in your individuality, to let a shadow of guilt fall upon you.'[38]

Both Moltke and Varnbüler expressed themselves in a language which can only be described as camp. Philipp Eulenburg, or 'Phili', as he was known to his friends, became 'Philine' in their letters, and was often referred to as 'she' or 'her'.[39] Writing to Varnbüler at the end of March 1891, Moltke poured out his heart about Eulenburg. '*Mein alter Dachs*! I'm now about to set off for Stuttgart. I long for old Philine ... I must see her. I feel that this loss‡ brings our dear circle closer together ... On the 8th I'm going down to Munich with P. The family is coming on later.'[40]

Once Moltke's family was no more, the correspondence between Moltke and Varnbüler became even more unbridled. '*Mein Dachs*,' wrote Varnbüler to Moltke on 24 October 1898. 'And now my little rascal you are free. Now it is the time to come back to me; to my wide-open heart; banished is all mistrust, all shyness, all false shame ...'[41]

Evidence against the other Liebenbergers is not lacking. Wendelstadt was notorious in Bavarian high society and there were rumours about Eberhard Dohna.[42] Georg Hülsen had to sue the opera singer Frank after he accused him of homosexuality. At the time Hülsen made out that the accusation had been dreamed up by his enemies at court and the Kaiser stuck by his theatre Intendant. As late as July 1907 the Kaiser 'was put out by the events touching on his circle and had repeatedly asked him [Hülsen] whether the fellow [Frank] had been punished yet.'[43] The Kaiser not only valued Hülsen as a friend, he also enjoyed the

* Literally 'My badger', but closer to 'My rascal'.
† Sweetheart. A Liebenberg name for the Kaiser.
‡ An allusion to the death of Karl Dörnberg in St Petersburg.

risqué pantomimes he dreamed up for the All Highest's amusement, such as getting Graf Görtz to dress up as a poodle, in a
skimpy costume with 'a marked rectal opening', and perform tricks.

Costume performances of this sort appealed to the Kaiser, and
they continued to amuse him, even after his entourage was under
attack from the press for its louche sexual behaviour. Writing in
his diary on 8 February 1909, Zedlitz-Trützschler recorded the
tragi-comic scene at Schloss Donaueschingen, reporting the
strange death of the Chief of the Kaiser's Military Cabinet, Georg
Hülsen's cousin, Graf Dietrich Hülsen-Haeseler. The events had
occurred the previous November. There had been a fox-hunt and
in the evening the house party – including the Princesses Hohenau
and Fürstenberg – were gathered in the great hall of the castle.
'Suddenly Count Hülsen-Haeseler appeared in a ballet skirt – not
for the first time – and began to dance to the music. Everybody
found it most entertaining, for the Count danced beautifully, and
it is an unusual experience to see the Chief of the Military Cabinet
capering around in the costume of a lady of the ballet.' After
finishing a dance, however, Hülsen collapsed and died: 'What
made the whole tragedy more poignant was that the music
continued while the doctor was busy with the dead man.'[44]

Events of this nature have called the Kaiser's own sexuality into
question. Despite his interest in Viennese prostitutes, he was
clearly happiest in male company and found his wife's calls for
attention irksome. In a letter written in his curious English to
Marion Gräfin Dönhoff, he announced 'I never feel happy, really
happy at (sic) Berlin, only Potsdam that is my real "el dorado"...
where one feels free with the beautiful nature around you and
soldiers as much as you like, for I love my dear regiment very
much, those such kind, nice young men in it.'[45] Maximilian
Harden believed he had evidence that the Kaiser had actually had
sex with both Eulenburg's fisherman friend Jakob Ernst and with
his secretary, Karl Kistler, but this seems rather improbable.
More likely is that the Kaiser was 'repressed'.[46] One German
scholar has gone so far as to call him a 'closet queen'.[47]

*

The homosexual activities of the Liebenberg Circle were finally brought to the public's attention by an article in *Die Welt am Montag* entitled 'Die perverse Kamarilla'. The paper accused the Liebenbergers – rightly, as it turned out – of being responsible for the downfall of the liberal Chancellor Graf Caprivi.[48] Maximilian Harden was much more concerned with the possible security risk which underlay the friendship between Eulenburg and Raymond Lecomte.[49] *Die Welt am Montag* had merely hinted at the activities of the Liebenbergers; Harden's *Die Zukunft* went straight to the point. On 17 November 1907, he ran an article under the heading 'Praeludium' in which he mentioned Moltke and other members of the circle: 'all nice people . . .' concerned with the affairs of the mind, advised by 'an unhealthy late romantic visionary. . . . Today I point to Philipp Friedrich Karl Alexander Botho Prince zu Eulenburg und Hertefeld, Count von Sandels, as the man who with untiring zeal has whispered to Wilhelm the Second and still whispers to him that he has been called to rule alone and that, incomparably blessed as he is, he should expect and implore light only from that seat in the clouds from whose height the crown has been bestowed upon him; only to that should he feel himself responsible. The calamitous activity of this man shall not at least continue in the dark . . .'[50]

Harden had fired his first salvo, and he was to remain true to his promise. The following week there appeared a second article entitled 'Dies Irae': 'November 1907. Night. Open field in the Ucker district. The Harpist: "Have you read it?" The Sweetie: "Last Friday!" The Harpist: "Do you think there'll be more?" The Sweetie: "We have to count on that possibility; he seems to be informed and knows about the letters which mention Sweetheart . . ." The Harpist: "Inconceivable. Yet they are reprinting it everywhere. They want to get at our throats." The Sweetie: "A band of witches. Away! Away!" The Harpist: "If only he doesn't find out about it!" '*[51]

* A parody of Goethe's *Faust*. The Harpist is Eulenburg; the Sweetie, the sweet-loving Governor of Berlin, Kuno Moltke; the Sweetheart was naturally the Kaiser. The men are concerned lest he should read the articles in *Die Zukunft*.

A week later the third article appeared under the heading 'Cave Adsum'. The die was cast. Harden had told Holstein that he intended only to remove those people who were 'politically dangerous'. 'For the time being, at least only a quiet warning.' In the paper Harden made himself quite clear: 'Should it be necessary, I shall speak louder. But will be pleased if the cosy group to which I concede every private amusement will give up politics and save me (and others) a painful duty.' Eulenburg took the hint. After the appearance of the third of Harden's articles, he despatched an emissary in the shape of Baron Alfred Berger to tell the editor that he was going abroad until further notice. He then slipped across the border to Switzerland.[52]

The police must have read this attack with interest. It was no news to them, except that Tresckow noted that Kuno Moltke was 'possibly the most honourable and least dangerous of the whole clique'.[53] For the time being they failed to act to restrain Harden. They had received no orders from above. Harden for his part had every reason to believe that he had cleared Prussia of a malign influence on the crown, but he doubted the permanence of Eulenburg's resolution. He wrote to Holstein on 14 December 1906: 'The Harpist has gone to Never-Never Land; he has therefore kept his word. But for how long?'

Not long at all. Eulenburg's self-imposed exile was cut short by a meeting of the Order of the Black Eagle convened for 17 January. The prince had only been awarded the Black Eagle nine months before and did not think he would be forgiven for not attending.[54] Harden did not find his excuse convincing. He wrote to Holstein: 'Phili-Filou* has come back from Territet† for the Eagle Chapter . . .'[55] The journalist therefore believed that he had been licensed to continue the fight and was no longer bound by his conversation with Berger. On 27 April 1908 he drew attention to another homosexual scandal to reopen the attack on Eulenburg. 'Prince Frederick Henry of Prussia was forced to give up the

---

* French for cheat or liar.
† In Switzerland.

leadership of the Order of Knights of Saint John (*Johanniterorden*) because he suffers from an hereditary sexual perversion. Does a milder code apply to the Chapter of the Black Eagle? There sits at least one whose *vita sexualis* is no more healthy than that of the banned prince.'[56]

So far the Kaiser had seen nothing of this. Although the attacks on his 'best friend' had been going on for more than six months, no one had had the courage to tell him. Edited highlights of the papers were presented to him in the form of cuttings, and he had no idea what a unfavourable image the court was beginning to arouse in the public eye. No one in the immediate entourage could bring himself to break the news. Finally, the Crown Prince was saddled with the job.[57] The Kaiser was furious. He ordered that Eulenburg should be 'gereinigt oder gesteinigt' (cleared or stoned).[58]

The ball began to roll. On 6 May Privy Counsellor Friedheim of the police was summoned before the Kaiser in the presence of Generals Plessen and Hülsen. 'The Kaiser asked him if he had read the series of articles in *Die Zukunft* and what he thought of the covert but clear attacks on the homosexual tendencies of Fürst Eulenburg, Graf Hohenau and General Kuno von Moltke: "Harden is a damned bounder, but he would not have made these attacks if he had not possessed ample material to hand."'[59] The Kaiser now asked to see the police list of homosexuals which he had once so forthrightly waved aside.[60]

The following extracts from Commissioner Tresckow's diaries are as clear an indictment of the cloud-cuckooland atmosphere of the Kaiser's court as we will ever see. The following day was a Sunday, and Tresckow passed his Sabbath going through hundreds of cards in the files. Feeling that it would be unnecessary to expose so many prominent figures, he selected twenty or so and wrote observations on the characters involved. These cards went now to the Police President von Borries, who promptly removed more cards 'out of pity'. Tresckow and Borries then took the remaining cards to the Minister of the Interior, Bethmann-Hollweg, who told the policemen that 'it was the Kaiser's intention

to clear the court of this sort of element. He had himself
recognised Eulenburg, Hohenau and Moltke as homosexuals and
they were now finished as far as he was concerned.'[61]

Bethmann-Hollweg now proceeded to strike more names off
the list. He expressed some curiosity at others and seemed
surprised about 'Hofwedel', who had served with him in the 1st
Gardedragoner. Some names could not be shown to the Kaiser,
such as that of his own second son Prince Eitel Fritz. Bethmann-
Hollweg said that the prince 'had caused him great concern as
both at court and in officers' messes his interest in men, and
soldiers in particular, was openly discussed.' Tresckow was also
aware of rumours: 'But I knew nothing factual which attested to
the prince's homosexual activity.' Bethmann-Hollweg turned next
to Prince Frederick Henry. 'The poor boy moves me deeply. I
have asked General Hülsen to advise him to live abroad for as
long as possible and not to return to Berlin. . . . His inclinations
are an evil legacy of his forefathers.'[62]

At court, Zedlitz-Trützschler made light of the revelations. 'As
a matter of fact, the Emperor has never taken Prince Eulenburg
(and still less Count von Moltke) seriously in politics. Besides,
Prince Eulenburg has no political ambitions, and above all it has
been a long time since he has been in close touch with the
Emperor. Of late they have met in Rominten only once a year,
and the Emperor has gone every autumn to Liebenberg . . . The
chief talent of Prince Eulenburg was his unequalled gift for
anecdote*, by which he could entertain the Emperor from
morning till night . . . If the Emperor had really taken him
seriously we should have seen many more astonishing things in
the political world than have actually come to pass.'[63] Zedlitz's
account doesn't quite tally with what we know from Eulenburg's
letters; nonetheless, it must have been true that by 1908 Liebenberg no longer held the place in his heart it had in the 1880s and
'90s. Zedlitz thought that the stories about Eulenburg were true,

---

* Miss Topham says the same. See *Souvenirs de la Cour du Kaiser*, 235.

else he would have acted physically towards Harden and had him shot, or beaten up.[64]

On Monday 8 May Tresckow's day started with a visit from the head of his 'pederast-patrol' who brought him a report on the French Consul Raymond Lecomte. Lecomte was a regular visitor both to Liebenberg and to Berlin's homosexual pubs and dance halls. At court, if not at Liebenberg, Lecomte had earned himself the title of the 'King of Pederasts'. The next piece of news which Tresckow received was that Moltke, encouraged by the successful libel action which Hülsen had launched against Frank, threatened to take Harden to court. Moltke had prepared the way on the previous Friday by resigning his commission along with two other Prussian officers whose names had appeared in Harden's articles: Hohenau and Johannes Graf von Lynar.[65]

Homosexuality, or rather reports of it, filled the policeman's days. On Tuesday he received a visit from the Silesian magnate Graf Malzahn-Militsch, who expressed concern about his brother-in-law, Graf Günther von der Schulenburg. Tresckow knew a number of incriminating stories about Schulenburg, and these he offered to Malzahn. Later that week he went away on leave: 'What a blessing it was to have a week when I did not have to listen to details of pederasty and perversion.'[66]

The reprieve was short-lived. He returned to find that Harden had received Moltke's summons on 2 June and that the press had responded by launching a volley of articles about the homosexuals at the court. It transpired that Moltke was actually being blackmailed by one Axel Petersen, who claimed to possess details of the soldier's homosexual activities going back to the time when he was military attaché in Vienna.

On the 11th a raid on Podeyn's bath-house produced a heavy trawl of elderly homosexuals and young soldiers; at least one crowned head was among those interviewed by the police. Tresckow declined to reveal his identity. While the police responded to the mood of the time by clamping down on homosexual orgies, the press conducted its own *chasse aux pédés* through the pages of their journals. On the 15th the *Charlottenburger Stadtlaterner* published a report claiming that the Chancellor's nephew had been caught with a Pole in Munich.[67] Even the Chancellor had suffered a calumny of this sort, and had responded with a swift and decisive libel action.

At the height of this witch hunt, Edgard Wedel returned from a holiday in Italy much concerned that he might be drawn into the scandal now that the press had thrown all restraint to the winds. Like all the others, he paid a call on Commissioner Tresckow. His talk with the policeman revealed a new problem which was emerging with the scandal – anti-semitism. Harden, whose real name was Witkowsky, was the obvious target.* Wedel asked Tresckow, 'Is it this Jew then who is currently reigning in Prussia and dismissing generals and ambassadors from their posts?'[69]

There was considerable speculation about just who was supplying Harden with the information for his attacks on the courtiers. Chancellor Bülow rather disingenuously suggested that it might be an embittered Fritz von Holstein, who had not forgiven Eulenburg for his dismissal.[70] The truth was that Bülow himself had not been above giving *Die Zukunft* information, worried that Eulenburg might meddle with his desire to pursue a foreign policy distinct from that set out by the Kaiser.[71] Holstein was not much worried either. As early as 1 May 1906 he had written to Eulenburg, 'I am now free, I need exercise no restraint, and can treat you as one treats a contemptible person with your characteristics.'[72]

Harden had not needed Holstein. Eulenburg had quite enough enemies. Harden had heard first of Eulenburg's homosexuality from Bismarck, at whose feet he had sat at the end of the Iron Chancellor's life.[73] At first he had not taken Eulenburg's homosexuality seriously. It was Holstein who must have convinced him of the danger of having such men in positions of power. In an early exchange between these unlikeliest of bedfellows, we read Harden writing in May 1907, 'our position endangered by a few

* When Harden died in 1927, Goebbels wrote in *Der Angriff*, 'We regret the death of this man only in that it deprives us of settling accounts with Isidore (sic) Witkowski in our own way.'[68]

pansies. With all due respect I cannot support that opinion.'[74] Holstein seems to have won him round, but only because of the homosexuals' supposedly nefarious influence on the Kaiser, *not* because they were homosexuals. Many people acknowledged this at the time. Zedlitz-Trützschler wrote in his diary: 'Attacking with Article 175 and the question of homosexual tendencies can have only been a pretext as far as Harden was concerned. Naturally we only recognised this later . . .'[75] Apart from Bülow, there were plenty of others at court who were ready to help ditch Eulenburg and his friends. Some of these were very close to the Kaiser indeed, reflecting once again the inability of those around the All Highest to tell him the truth: his sister Princess Charlotte of Saxe-Meiningen, Graf Hülsen-Haeseler (he of the tutu) and another of the Kaiser's very closest friends, Fürst Max Egon von Fürstenberg.[76]

Meanwhile the court scandal had led to increasing paranoia in military circles, and the regimental commanders from the Berlin and Potsdam garrisons joined the queue in Tresckow's ante-chamber. 'Almost daily the commanders of the guards regiments from Potsdam and Berlin came to ask us how they might combat the habitual pederasty of the soldiers.' Tresckow was aware that the Police President had had to write to the garrison commanders to try to put a stop to male prostitution by soldiers who plied their trade in the Tiergarten by night. Was this a vestige of Frederick William I's policy of giving soldiers profitable work to do in peacetime? The commerce was largely confined to men 'who belonged to an educated milieu'. Not just sex-starved professors and civil servants, however: one day one of these moonlighting guardsmen caused particular offence when he offered his services to Minister Bethmann-Hollweg, out for an evening stroll.[77]

The enormous extent of the problem began to depress those involved in trying to uphold a more decent image for the Prussian state. The scope of the homosexual network drove Commissioner Tresckow to despair. 'In earlier times one had to be a freemason or pay court to influential women in order to carve out a career for oneself, now it is more practical to have homosexual inclinations or at least to pretend to have them.' That same day, Tresckow was introduced to the new Germany military attaché to Paris: 'The most feminine man I've ever seen. . . . It's really a scandal!'[78]

Whatever the truth of the Kaiser's own feelings about homosexuality, the scandal was inevitably going to damage his reputation in the public eye. When the same Graf von der Schulenburg who had caused Graf Malzahn's visit to Tresckow decided to sue a Munich editor for printing a story about his own leanings, it gave the court the opportunity to read out some of his letters in the course of the trial. In one of these Schulenburg had speculated on the Kaiser's sexual tastes: 'His Majesty is always surrounded by queers (*warmen Brüder*). If, however, he doesn't guess the tendencies of these people, then he is all the more taken in by them, or he is so used to them that he can no longer appreciate the truth of the matter.'[79] Schulenburg's libel action did him little good all in all. He was awarded derisory damages of 50 RMs, and his reputation was far from saved.

In the meantime Philipp Eulenburg had taken the curious step of asking the Prenzlau police to investigate his private life. Given the feudal nature of life in the rural Uckermark, this was unlikely to be particularly thorough. Still, Eulenburg took what steps he could to cover up. A pile of homosexual books he had bought in Leipzig from the specialised publisher Max Spohr were placed in a folder and Graf Edgard Wedel's name was scrawled across it. Eulenberg's attempts to incriminate 'Hofwedel' were to lose him any sympathy he might have retained with his peers when he was obliged to admit to his duplicity at his trial.[80] Tension was high in Berlin, where the examining magistrate in the Moltke case had decided that the trial was not in the public interest. Moltke had therefore launched a civil action. The trial opened on 6 June, with the judge assisted by two lay jurors, a milkman and a butcher.[81]

It was sensational theatre. 'In the morning the Moltke–Harden trial, in the evening Caruso,' wrote the *Vossische Zeitung*. 'The demand for tickets at the drama in Moabit [court house] is no less great than for the first appearance of the King of Tenors at the Berlin Opera House . . .'[82] The most important evidence came from Moltke's ex-wife, Frau Lili von Elbe, who was quite happy to write the general off as a pervert, and the sexologist, Dr Magnus Hirschfeld, who dubbed Moltke 'a feminine man' with 'abnormal sexual reactions'.[83] The case went against Moltke and the judge threw it out. It was at this point that the Prussian government decided to intervene. The judgement was revoked and a retrial called. There were obvious instructions from above to have Moltke's name cleared. This was not only of doubtful legality, but it also left Harden in the invidious position of having to prove that Moltke had contravened Article 175. In the second trial Frau von Elbe was shown to be the woman scorned, her testimony full of flaws. Eulenburg was called and said under oath that he had never committed any illegal acts. Hirschfeld felt it prudent to go back on his previous testimony.[84] The verdict in the first case was routed and on 3 January 1908, Harden was sentenced to four months' hard labour. Moltke's honour was declared 'clean and without a stain'.[85]

After the trial the Kaiser was overjoyed. He wanted to rehabilitate his friends and was only prevented from doing so by members of his entourage. The Chancellor, Bülow, was also over the moon; he had got rid of two dangerous men, Eulenburg, who was lying low while he awaited the findings of the Prenzlau police, and Harden. But Harden showed himself rather more resourceful than anyone had imagined: not only did he launch an appeal at the Supreme Court in Leipzig, he performed a stroke which was brilliance itself. He got a Munich paper, *Die Neue Freie Volkszeitung*, to accuse him of suppressing evidence against Eulenburg in return for bribes. Harden promptly sued the editor, Anton Städele, for libel. Not only was there the advantage that in Munich judge and jury would not be swayed by the Prussian authorities, but the witnesses Harden intended to call all concerned a trouble-free period of Eulenburg's life when he lived in Munich.[86]

Harden had been collecting evidence. Public-spirited Germans had been writing to him to tell of shady episodes in the former ambassador's past. One, signing himself 'A German', wrote from Starnberg on the Bavarian Starnbergersee, mentioning a fisherman who lived in nearby Feldafing.[87] His name was Jakob Ernst. Further enquiries revealed another important witness in the person of a milk dealer named Riedl. The trial opened on 21 April 1908, the Bavarian judge being assisted by a bank manager and a chemist. Riedl's testimony was quickly deemed unreliable. He had no fewer than thirty-two convictions. The 'drifter' Riedl was not going to win the case for Harden. Ernst was another matter. A humble fisherman who had been no more than seventeen or eighteen when the Prussian ambassador had come up to spend his summers on Starnberg Lake in 1883–1884,[88] Ernst had been whipped in to take the Prussian nobleman out on to the lake for romantic boating expeditions. Ernst was silent at first, but he broke down under cross-examination. 'We did dirty things!' he said.[89]

Eulenburg was appalled. He had no idea that Harden had this up his sleeve. In his diary he called Riedl and Ernst's testimony 'monstrous lies'.[90] The Bavarian court was of another opinion, and awarded for Harden. In Leipzig charges against Harden were dropped and tempers ran high in Prussia with considerable bad blood against the Bavarians. Eulenburg had apparently been unwell a good deal recently. When he heard the news from Leipzig, he took to his bed again. It was there that he was confronted by Riedl and Ernst on 7 May. Standing before his bedside in Liebenberg, the crooked milk dealer and the fisherman 'stood by their scandalous allegations'.[91] Eulenburg was arrested for perjury and brought to Berlin for trial. His probably psychosomatic ailment intensified. Everyone was against him, 'the Jews, high finance, the court and the government.'[92]

The police almost certainly knew as much about Eulenburg's activities as Harden, if not more. In the course of their investigation they gathered no fewer than 144 allegations of improper conduct against the former ambassador.[93] Tresckow had been sent to Liebenberg at the end of January to take a deposition from Eulenburg himself. Both President von Borries and Oberstaatsanwalt* Isenbiel wanted to protect their backs in two particular

---

* Similar to a British or Commonwealth QC.

instances where they thought Harden might win his case. One was Eulenburg's connection with the 'King of Pederasts' Lecomte. The other was a blackmail matter dating back to Eulenburg's period in Vienna. Eulenburg had allegedly been caught in a homosexual bath-house and over the next few months, he had been blackmailed to the tune of 60,000 crowns.[94] Perhaps even more shocking for the public as a whole was the fact that he stood accused of finding the money in the public purse. A third accusation against Eulenburg was that he had aroused the suspicions of the staff of a Berlin hotel by sharing a room with his manservant Göritz.[95]

Eulenburg knew how to be *bon prince*. Perhaps because of Tresckow's Silesian noble patent, Eulenburg told him to bring a gun, as there were boars to be had in the woods. He arrived to find sandwiches and port laid out for him in his room. Refreshed, he went down to see Eulenburg. The former ambassador parried the policeman's questions, serving up observations on the evilness of mankind.[96] When Tresckow pressed the point, Eulenburg stagily grabbed his hand and 'gave me his word of honour as a Prussian nobleman that he had never performed immoral acts with any man'. Tresckow then alluded to the weighty files in the police department. 'Sadly I have a brother who is that way inclined and I am often taken for him.'[97] It was true: Graf Fritz Eulenburg was well known. In 1898 he had been obliged to resign his commission after his wife publically denounced him as a homosexual.[98] Tresckow felt inclined to give Eulenburg the benefit of the doubt. The explanation was not improbable, and Eulenburg could explain the presence of the manservant in his room by the fact that he had been seriously ill at the time. Tresckow thought Eulenburg's whining unmanly, but in general he was inclined in his favour.[99]

All this was changed by the Munich case. On 27 June, the policeman went to see Eulenburg on trial for perjury in the gaunt new court house in Moabit. He was not in the dock as such, but laid out on a stretcher wearing 'blue spectacles to conceal himself from the glances of the judges'. No one was quite able to say whether his condition was genuine or not, but it had the advantage of preventing the charges from sticking. He was piling on the agony (something which is more than apparent in his diaries[100]). 'He looked old and emaciated and was accompanied by his wife and two of his sons,' wrote Tresckow. The policeman was impressed by the jury: 'They looked stout and worthy, these middle-class gentlemen and artisans into whose hands had been commended the fate of a prince and Knight of the Black Eagle.' More impressive still in a macabre sort of way were the witnesses for the prosecution: 'about sixty of them including a smattering of aristocrats, but chiefly fishermen and peasants from the Starnbergersee.'[101]

Almost immediately the trial opened, the gravity of it began to dawn on all concerned. Eulenburg's perjury appeared to be of the grossest sort. The judge decided that the mass attendance of fashionable Berlin at the Moltke trial was something to be avoided in this instance and from 2 July it was held *in camera*. That day Tresckow lunched at the Bristol, and was astonished to see Kuno Moltke breeze in to a dining room filled with Berlin's best society while his friend fought for his honour in a Moabit courtroom. Four days later Tresckow was in court to hear the letters of Graf Richard Dohna, but more damaging by far was the testimony of Riedl and Ernst, who maintained all they had said in Munich: 'the Prince banged his fist on the table and exclaimed, "But Ernst, you cannot say such things, it is simply untrue."'[102]

As the material in the prosecution's armoury became ever greater, Tresckow was all the more certain that Eulenburg had committed the 'immoral acts'. It was a busy time for the commissioner, working at night to complete his reports and constantly pestered by journalists anxious to glean the details of a trial conducted behind closed doors. One day he got home at 4.00 p.m. for a quick bowl of soup when a servant announced Prince B ... 'He sat down at the table at once and once I had finished took coffee with me. He had come from Paris where I had written to him to inform him of the events taking place in the trial and of the fate of his friend Edgard Wedel. He gave me all sorts of news:

that the Kaiser had requested that both young Grafen Hohenau, the General's sons,* be transferred to provincial regiments as he didn't want to have a Hohenau in the Guards from now on. Then he spoke of the bad impression the scandal was making abroad; and how much Germans were being mocked for the fact that the Kaiser felt so much at home in this *galère*; that he had chosen an awkward moment to get rid of people whom he had once held in such unabashed esteem.'[103]

In Moabit, Eulenburg's condition had deteriorated. On 17 July it was decided to transfer proceedings to the Charité Hospital. Tresckow was even more convinced of Eulenburg's guilt. 'There is an ever greater stack of incriminating material and every right-thinking man must now be certain of the accused's guilt.'[104] Eulenburg's health worsened in proportion to the evidence massed against him. As it was now determined that he could not even follow the case, the judge adjourned until such time as he could. Before losing consciousness, Eulenburg made a little speech about honour, but Tresckow had heard it before: 'For me he was just a player, acting out his last scene in the manner of all theatrical people. During my visit to Liebenberg I allowed myself to be led because, despite long experience, I did not believe that a Prussian nobleman could tell such lies.' With Eulenburg's collapse he hoped that the smutty trials which were so bad for Germany's international image would come to an end. Just before it was finally called off, he was visited by a reporter from *Le Matin*. Tresckow played down the significance of the case to the Frenchman and expressed the hope that Eulenburg would be seen as 'an exception'. With sadness he noted 'the sceptical smile' on the journalist's face, and realised that this was not to be.[105]

Eulenburg was briefly brought back to trial, but when his health collapsed a second time, the case was put off indefinitely. Harden had to pay the damages due to Moltke, but was amply compensated out of secret government funds. The Kaiser, now robbed of

---

* The children of the elder Hohenau implicated in the scandal. Prince B . . . is almost certainly the Chancellor, Bülow.

the few friends with whom he felt he could relax, was a bitter man when he wrote to Houston Stewart Chamberlain at the end of 1909. 'It has been a very difficult year which has caused me an infinite amount of acute worry. A trusted group of friends was suddenly broken up by Jewish insolence, slander and lying. To have to see the names of one's friends dragged through all the gutters of Europe without being able or entitled to help is terrible. It has upset me so much I had to have a holiday and rest.'[106] Sadder still was the damage the case did to the reputation of the once virtuous Junkers.

VII

The Junkers and the Court

In the Kurmark the nobles are voluptuous; they have neither the robust character of the Pomeranians nor the intelligence of the [East] Prussians. The Magdeburg nobility has more wisdom and it has produced some great men.

The Silesians from Lower Silesia are what one might call good fellows, a bit stupid, but this is simply the result of the poor upbringing they have received*: they are vain and are fond of luxury, spending money and titles; and they hate hard work or that stern application made necessary by military discipline; the person who one day takes on the task of reforming the education of the nobility will become the Prometheus who inspires them with celestial fire. Those from Upper Silesia have the same vanity but more intelligence, but at the same time they have less attachment to the Prussian government due to the fact that they are all Catholics and the majority of their families settled there under the Austrian crown.

Noblemen from the County of Mark and Minden have supplied some good material for the state; their upbringing is a little crude and does not give them that lustre which comes about through social usage; but they have a greater talent than that, and that is that they make themselves useful to their country.

The [noblemen] of Cleves are imbeciles, confused and sired in their fathers' cups, they have neither natural talent nor have they acquired any.

> Frederick the Great, Testament
> politique, 1752, quoted in Gaxotte,
> *Frédéric II*, 290–291.

The Junkers were the nobility. The word derives from 'Junge Herr', or young lord. In theory this was a courtesy title granted to the younger sons of the higher nobles. In practice it denoted minor nobility.[1] The Junker was no monolith. He was a creature of variety. Nor was he confined to Prussia: Junkers inhabited the

---

* Frederick is alluding to the fact that they were until very recently subjects of the Habsburg Emperors.

entirety of the 'flat land' which lay between the Elbe and the
Baltic. There were Junkers in Mecklenburg, which never fell to
Prussian rule, just as there were Junkers in Silesia, Pomerania and
in East and West Prussia, which did. There were Junkers in the
Baltic states, too, with their estates spread out across the countries
now known as Lithuania, Latvia and Estonia. Prussia did not
make the Junkers, but for better or for worse the Junkers became
the backbone of Prussia.

As the area had once been entirely populated by Slavs, the
Junkers came from other parts of Germany and Europe. Families
like the Schulenburgs or the Moltkes spread themselves thinly,
with branches in both Mecklenburg and Brandenburg. Many
families in the Mark were established before 1300: Alvensleben,
Arnim, Pfuel, Katte, Itzenplitz, Rochow, Bredow, Jagow, Quitzow
and Winterfeld.[2] At the same time names like Wedel, Goltz and
Marwitz were already to be found on the far side of the Oder, in
the Neumark.

The German *Schwertadel* was deemed to have its uses in that
thinly populated land, and Slavic princes were not indisposed to
invite them in as settlers. In Pomerania it was the bishops who
first summoned the Germans. In Vorpommern to the west of the
Oder, the chief families were the Rohr, Behr, Ramin and
Schwerin. Although the area east of the Oder was still largely
under Polish vassalage, here came the Zitzewitz, Pirch, Natzmer,
Kameke, Dewitz and Eberstein. The Puttkamers, later one of the
most distinguished Prussian families, were like the Kleists almost
certainly of Slavic origin.[3] Southern Pomerania was colonised by
Manteuffels, Podewils, Glasenapps, Massows and Lettows, all
names which were to have a resounding ring to them in later
Prussian history.[4]

Silesia did not become a part of Prussia until the mid-
eighteenth century, but that in no way inhibited the German
settlers. In 1300, Silesia paid homage to the crown of Bohemia,
but gradually the towns and cities were adopting German law.
Many of the leading families were of Polish origin; Brauchitsch
and Heydebrand were two of these which one might easily have

assumed to be Teutonic; possibly the Rothkirch, Schönaich, Seherr-Thoss and Seydlitz families were, too. In the high Middle Ages these were joined by indisputable Germans with names like Aulock, Haugwitz, Kalckreuth, Kessel, Nostitz, Prittwitz, Pückler and Schaffgotsch.[5] By the sixteenth century, the Silesian Junkers had already established a path quite distinct from the Pomeranians, or West Prussians, German nobles who lay outside the orbit of the Elector of Brandenburg. The comparative fertility of the soil and the size of the estates was one factor; another was that the Silesians had begun to focus their attentions on the Reichs capital, Vienna.

Silesian Junkers were deemed more highly cultured than their counterparts across the Oder or the Warthe: by the seventeenth century the leading families had begun to educate their sons by sending them on prolonged journeys abroad, something which only the richest families of East Prussia, Lehndorffs and Dönhoffs, could manage. To some extent Silesia was radically altered by Frederick the Great, who pursued a policy of making life difficult for nobles inclined towards the Habsburgs in the hope of driving them out. The important families who came over to Frederick's side were flattered with princedoms to keep them sweet. According to Prussians, Silesians were ever more obsessed with titles than their German-speaking neighbours.[6]

Upper Silesia presented Frederick with a problem. Here the overwhelming majority of his new subjects were Catholic and the nobles Polish. The official language, however, was Czech. The repressive policy towards the peasantry scandalised even the Prussians. Serfs were still bought and sold. In winter, they said, the peasants slept naked in the byre, in summer in the haystack. As both sexes slept together, the practice gave rise to 'unrestrained sexual promiscuity'.[7] Throughout Silesia, the huge extent of the estates made the landowners into 'magnates' with lifestyles quite distinct from their poor cousins in the other Prussian provinces. The wealth of the Silesian noble, his possible Catholicism, his reputation for being not altogether honest and his possession of

high-flown titles almost unknown in the Mark, all contributed to
a certain distrust.

There were naturally settlers in West Prussia before the Poles
recovered the land after the second Peace of Thorn. Some of
these remained true to their Germanity over three centuries of
Polish rule: families like the Unruh, Goltz, Zehnen and Blanck-
enburg are all examples of this. Others were assimilated, often
changing their names to something Polish. Lehndorffs became
Mgowski; Horns, Rogowski; Rohrs, Trczinski; Kalcksteins, Sto-
linski or Oslowski. Junkers sought advancement under the Polish
crown, like Ewald Goltz, who became Royal Treasurer in the
fifteenth century. Both members of the Puttkamer family and the
Dönhoffs were made 'woiwode' or counts.[8]

Among the most famous Junker families were the big landown-
ers from East Prussia. The Poles had not only granted East
Prussia to the Teutonic Knights, they also awarded estates in
Kulm, Ermland and Courland to the Germans, Bohemians,
Walloons and Poles who lent a hand in subduing the Prusai.
Flemish and German law was enforced from the thirteenth
century onwards, from Kulm to well within the borders of present-
day Russia.[9] Some old Prusai families were assimilated into the
new German nobility of East Prussia: Saucken, Perbrandt and
Bronsart von Schellendorf, for example; others were of purer
German descent: Dohna, Eulenburg, Kanitz, Schlieben, Dönhoff,
Egloffstein, Wallenrodt, Truchsess, Lehndorff, Kuenheim,
Kalckstein and Finckenstein.

Beyond the Prussians were the Baltic Junkers, the 'Barons':
Rosen, Ungern, Üexküll and Keyserlingk. For centuries they lived
their Germanic lives in splendid isolation. There were no German
peasants in the Baltic States, and their nearest German-speaking
neighbours were the merchants in the towns and cities: Riga,
Dorpat and Reval. There is a story that the 'Czar Liberator'
Alexander II once asked one of these German grandees from
Courland (in presentday Lithuania), 'How does it come about that
you Germans have managed to hang on to your *Deutschtum* despite
the fact that you have been part of the Russian Empire for more

than five hundred years?' 'Your Majesty will excuse the expression,' repled the Baron, 'but when a horse is born in a pigsty, no matter what happens, it will not become a pig.'[10] It was not until the beginning of the present century that there was any move to settle German farmers in the Baltic states, and many of these were slaughtered during the advance of the Red Army after 1918. When the Treaty of Versailles created the states of Lithuania, Latvia and Estonia the following year, the German estates were sequestered. The Baltic barons had nowhere to go but Germany. Some became political agitators like Hitler's friend Max von Scheubner-Richter, the most revered martyr of the 1923 Putsch.

Once Brandenburg-Prussia had achieved a status all of its own within Germany, there was a further influx of blood, some noble, some seeking ennoblement through feats of arms. The Great Elector's Field Marshal Derfflinger was one of the latter.* Important among the former were the Huguenot nobles who fled to Brandenburg after the revocation of the Edict of Nantes in 1685. Many of these names also survived until the fall of Germany in 1945: de la Motte-Fouqué, Fourcade de Biaix, de l'Homme de Courbière, de Duchat de Dorville, le Tanneux de St Paul (whose estates were in East Prussia), Verzenobre de Laurieux, Arnault de la Perière and de la Chevalerie.[11] Others were attracted by the idea of serving Prussia either as soldiers or as civil servants – *Wahlpreussen*. The family of that self-styled 'Prussian Tory' Elard von Oldenburg-Januschau was originally from the nobility of Bremen. In the Middle Ages they took the short step to Mecklenburg. It was Oldenburg-Januschau's great-grandfather who was lured into the Prussian army by the image of the Great Frederick. He married a von der Trenck and settled in East Prussia.[12]

Many Mecklenburg families found they lacked opportunities to shine in that feudal backwater. Their shift to Brandenburg-Prussia

---

* When Derfflinger died, the Elector Frederick III (later King Frederick I) had a medal struck for his field marshal. On one side was a portrait of the soldier, on the other his coat of arms borne by Hercules and Mars. The inscription ran: *His Majoribus* – by these forefathers.

was as natural as that of a talented Irishman moving to London.
Blücher and Moltke are the most famous of these migrating
Mecklenburgers; families like the Bülows, Belows, Flotows,
Bernstorffs and Levetzows only marginally less so. The Bernstorffs were a talented dynasty who lent out their services to the
Hanoverian, British and Danish governments before going over to
Prussia in the nineteenth century.[13] Albrecht von Bernstorff
became Foreign Minister and Ambassador to the Court of Saint
James; Joachim-Heinrich was Ambassador to Washington during
the Great War and a notable liberal thereafter. His nephew,
another Albrecht, of Schloss Stintenberg, also served in the
diplomatic corps. He retired to Mecklenburg once the Nazis came
to power and made his views on the new rulers more than
adequately felt. They murdered him as the Russians entered
Berlin on 23 or 24 April 1945.[14]

Titles were rare, and at the very beginning, non-existent. This
was also the case in some German regions west of the Oder,
Hesse, for example[15], but in no part of Germany was the quasi-
total ban on titles so long-lived as in the core provinces of Prussia.
Of the families which laid claim to higher nobility, possibly only
the Grafen von Lindow in the county of Ruppin and the Gans zu
Putlitz were genuine. Prussian families were even slow to adopt
the particle 'von' which is the normal badge of nobility in German-
speaking countries. In the Middle Ages the Latin words 'armiger'
and 'miles' distinguished the noble from *hoi polloi*. The *vons* crept
in from the sixteenth century onwards.
    The nobility was born in the colonial times from the knights
who helped settle the flat land. The estates they carved out were
known as *'Ritterguter'* – knights' estates, and should, strictly
speaking, have remained in noble hands. Only they didn't. Nobles
lost their money and had to sell up, and despite the impediments
placed in their way by successive Prussian electors and kings, they
were occasionally purchased – even before the nineteenth century
– by commoners. These non-noble *'Rittergutsbesitzer'* could then
aspire to nobility in the following generation, if their sons served

ten years in the army. Naturally with the army 90 per cent staffed by noblemen in the eighteenth century, it was an uphill climb to obtain a commission. These *novi homines* were called *Neuadel* or new nobles, to distinguish them from the old nobles or *Uradel*.[16]

In one of his best known outbursts, Frederick William I attacked the East Prussian Junkers' increasing drift towards self-autonomy: 'I will crush the authority of the Junkers,' he said in a curious amalgam of German and French which was all his own, 'and found my sovereignty on a rock of bronze.' His power was also underpinned by the progressive expansion of the civil service and, ironically enough, state service became an alternative profession for the Junkers after the army. Naturally a vastly expanded bureaucracy necessited the creation of a *noblesse de robe* after the French model; clever lawyers and administrators would be rewarded with noble patents. One does not, however, get the impression that Frederick William was all that keen on ennobling the *'Federfuchser'* or scribblers, as he contemptuously referred to his civil servants. A story is told about one overachieving civil servant who was to be ennobled and who presented the Soldier King with a sketch of his intended coat of arms. Frederick William took the sketch and altered it: he added two inkpots and in the place of the eagles' wings, drew a brace of goose quills. When the civil servant saw how the king had mocked his pretension, he decided he didn't wish to be a Prussian nobleman after all.[17]

The title of 'Freiherr' or baron was almost always imported from elsewhere. In East Prussia, the old office-holders of the Prussian dukes had styled themselves 'Barones ducatus prussiae' in the sixteenth century, before the Baltic duchy was merged into Brandenburg. Those Junkers who served the Polish or Swedish crowns in Courland or Pomerania were rewarded with the title of *Freiherr* or *Graf* which they took with them into the Brandenburg-Prussian service when the time came. As late as the mid-nineteenth century, a diplomat like Heinrich Alexander von Arnim suffered in his foreign postings from his lack of title compared to the ambassadors from countries more lavish with them. His use of the title Freiherr brought him into conflict with Frederick William

IV. It was ruled that the title did not exist in Brandenburg, even if the oldest Märkisch families – Arnims, Bredows, Jagows and Klitzings – had long since added it to their names. True to form, William II had none of these scruples. Under his reign a certain degree of tolerance crept in, provided the families in question exhibited the right political credentials.[18]

Titles of nobility became far easier to obtain in the Kaiser's time. In this William marched in step with a European phenomenon of the late nineteenth and early twentieth centuries. Certain military ranks, such as a naval captaincy, led to ennoblement: the case of both Müller and Tirpitz. The reasons for ennoblement were not always so worthy, and there were plenty of louche financiers and bankers who were able to grease the appropriate palms and slide into that hallowed world. Members of poor but honourable dynasties such as Hans von Tresckow were appalled at the trade in titles: 'The nobility is an old historical institution; no longer a class, for such a thing has special rights and duties and these ceased long ago.'[19]

The Kaiser was quite happy to create princes, too. In 1900 he raised four of his friends to the rank of *Fürst*, including Philipp Eulenburg. To members of former ruling houses this was an outrageous act. Prince Hohenlohe, who referred to Eulenburg as the 'arch-scoundrel', echoed the attitude of certain members of the old French nobility during the Empire, when Napoleon rewarded his supporters with ever more extravagant titles: 'So many new princes. Soon I'm just going to call myself Mr Hohenlohe!. . . It's fortunate that Axel [Varnbüler] is not Prussian; else he'd soon become a count, dirt poor but well-endowed in children. It's strange, after 66 and 70 Bismarck became a prince and Moltke, Roon and a few others were raised to counts. Since then, when we have really far less success to boast about, these elevations have increased in inverse proportion.'[20]

The simple truth was that money and showiness – *mehr Schein als Sein* – was becoming the tenor of Wilhelmine society, with the the Kaiser taking the lead with his entourage of rich Silesians and mediatised princes. In this world the Junkers simply couldn't keep up. Many, like Hans von Tresckow or Emil von Lessel (both, exceptionally, Silesians) had lost their estates years before because of the constant division of the land among cousins. The wisest created *Fideikommisse*, family trusts, permitting the nobles concerned to leave the entire estate to just one heir; similar to the English system of primogeniture. The vast majority of estates possessed nothing approximating to a *Schloss*. In 1600 in the Kurmark, for example, there were 1,600 villages and 887 noble *Ritterguter*, but only sixty-six families with *Schlösser*. On the other hand there were families like the Schulenburgs at Lieberose who owned two whole towns and thirty estates, and a splendid renaissance *Schloss* at the centre of it all.[21]

In contrast to the Kaiser and his monied coterie, the Junker's life was simple and unostentatious. Even the Dönhoffs, who bordered on magnate status within East Prussia, travelled third class on the railways.[22] The more remote the region, like eastern Pomerania or East Prussia, the more unchanging the routine, even in our own century: the morning prayers, the life revolving around the stables and studs.

The tragedy of the Junkers was that the rot had set in and set in early. Before the Napoleonic invasion there was already an agricultural crisis in Prussia. During the war the Continental Blockade exacerbated the difficulties of the landowners. There was no market for the grain they shipped from Danzig and Königsberg, and the English had responded to the situation either by increasing their own production or by buying in from elsewhere. In the Oldenburg family it was touch and go whether they would remain in East Prussia. There was a project mooted to up sticks and settle in the Crimea, where the soil was considered better suited to grain farming.[23]

Increasing numbers of Junker families went bankrupt, were forced to sell out to their neighbours or, worse, to the richer bourgeoisie of the towns, ever anxious to possess the estate which would be their first step to ennoblement. The years immediately after the Napoleonic Wars were particularly grave: in 1817 eighty-

seven estates in Pomerania were sequestered after their owners
could no longer afford to pay their bills; in 1825, 112; in 1828,
109. In 1826, 154 East Prussian estates failed, and ninety-nine in
Silesia. The situation was worst in East and West Prussia, where
two *Oberpräsidenten* of the first rank, Theodor Schön (later von
Schön) and Hans Jakob von Auersfeld, fought hard to preserve
the noble patrimony. It was Schön's father-in-law, Field Marshal
von Brünneck, who had the idea of introducing merino lambs to
East Prussia to revitalise agriculture. The efforts of the civil
servants were only partly successful: the East Prussian Hippels
lost all but one of their twelve *Ritterguter*; the Beneckendorff und
Hindenburgs lost all but Langenau and Neudeck; Graf Fincken-
stein-Gilgenburg lost a total of thirty-two estates. The crisis lasted
well into the 1830s.[24]

Although the middle years of the century provided an upturn in
the economy when many Junkers had the money to rebuild their
simple manors, it changed nothing in the nature of the soil. It has
been estimated that whereas twenty-three per cent of the soil in
Silesia was useful for agriculture, only seven to eight per cent of
Pomerania and East Prussia was of any value to the farmer
Junkers. Moreover, the growing period for corn and cereals, not
to mention the ubiquitous potato introduced by Frederick the
Great, was between thirty and fifty per cent shorter than in middle
or west Germany. Crops had to be brought in quickly at the onset
of winter, ripe or not. From the 1860s Russian cereals began to
flood the market at a price which could not be equalled by the
Junkers. As the landowners could not afford to feed armies of
workers all the year round, they were forced to rely on seasonal
labour from Poland and the Ukraine, but much of this was now
more interested in the industrialised west of Germany. By the end
of the nineteenth century one was as likely to hear Polish as
German spoken in parts of the Ruhr. This was not the only
Ostflucht or 'flight from the east'. Many of the old families thought
it easier to throw in the towel than to try to compete with the
cheap grain on the market. They too took the road to the west.[25]

The land meant a lot to the Junkers. As one wrote, 'a family stands or falls with the ownership of land and soil'.[26] Many were to fall when the crisis worsened again in the 1890s. Since the '70s cheap grain had come in from America and the right-wing parties in the Reichstag had pushed increasingly for protection for the German farmers. Already the centre and the left of the house had begun to advocate the breaking up of the large estates and the settlement of German farmers on the land. Even the idea of salvation through sheep-breeding was imperilled by cheaper wool from Australia and South America. Between 1886 and 1897 24,355 estates went under the hammer, a total of 850,514 hectares. In general the larger *Fideikommisse* fared best, but not always: between 1882 and 1895 a thousand estates of between one hundred and one thousand hectares were auctioned. The Junkers responded to the crisis by creating their own protective organisations: the *Deutsche Adelsgenossenschaft* was formed in 1874 with the idea of a 'Christian resistance to the rule of mammon'. A similar, Catholic organisation – the *Verein katholischer Edelleute* – had been formed in Silesia six years earlier.[27]

The crisis focused on East Prussia, a province with a character quite distinct from other parts of the country. In the first half of this century many Prussians saw Elard von Oldenburg-Januschau as the East Prussian archetype: forever plotting, forever conniving for the greater good of his fellow Junkers. He it was who dreamed up the expression 'a lieutenant and ten men' before the First World War to denote a particularly Prussian way of getting things done. Oldenburg told the Reichstag, 'The King of Prussia and Emperor of Germany must be in the position at any given time to tell a lieutenant: "Take ten men and close down the Reichstag."'[28]

His attitude towards the Socialist deputies in the Reichstag was bound to be provocative. When one of his political opponents rose to complain about his reactionary, undemocratic statements, Oldenburg announced, '*Na*, I'm quite aware that I'm the oak against which every pig likes to scratch itself.'[29] Udo von Alvensleben – the refined Junker from the oldest family in the Altmark – was fascinated by Oldenburg's German. 'His vocabulary stretches

from the jargon of the old school *grand seigneur* – rich in borrowings from other languages – to the reeking dung heap German [*Misthaufendeutsch*] of the landowner who gets his hands dirty.'[30]

It hadn't helped the embattled attitude of East Prussians like Oldenburg-Januschau that the province had been the one region of Germany to be invaded during the First World War. The year which preceded the Battle of the Masurian Lakes had reawakened memories of a previous Russian invasion during the Seven Years War, when the land and the towns had been wrecked by the Czarist army. Once Hindenburg and Ludendorff had sent the Russians packing, East Prussia again became the centre of reactionary thinking within the core provinces. Naturally Olden-burg-Januschau was not absent from the councils of the *Bund der Landwirte* (Union of Landowners) which included not only the virtuous *Oberpräsident*, Adolf von Batocki, but also Wolfgang Kapp, leader of the 1920 Putsch. Later the leading lights of this association – Kapp and Graf von Brünneck-Belschwitz – formed the *Heimat Bund* (Home Union) for the protection of East Prussia.[31]

Oldenburg was not ready to travel with Kapp all the way to Berlin. At the beginning of 1920, the Director of Agriculture, as Kapp was then, came to see Oldenburg on his estate and asked him for his support. Oldenburg advised Kapp against the Putsch. He told him to take over East Prussia and turn it into a self-sufficient state 'with the goal of founding a new Prussia from here'. Berlin would be conquered from East Prussia. Oldenburg also told the civil servant Kapp to take riding lessons: 'The person who gets Berlin must come through the Brandenburg Gate on horseback.'[32]

The Treaty of Versailles, which cut the Baltic territory off from the rump of the Reich, created endless problems for the East Prussians, and drove them further to the right. Already by December 1918 a number of manor-houses in the Grand Duchy of Posen had been burned to the ground and it was thought that the agitation would soon spread to West Prussia, where the Polish population was in a majority in the south and south-west. Some of the old nobles found the idea of belonging to a Socialist German state quite unacceptable, and there was even a suggestion that a neutral German state, made up of elements of Silesia, Pomerania and East and West Prussia, be created between Germany and Poland. Some of the magnate families in Upper Silesia preferred the idea of belonging to Poland to a left-wing Germany. Graf Hans von Oppersdorff-Oberglogau was one of these. Graf Ernst von Seherr-Thoss was of the other opinion: 'I'd rather be a German beggar than a Polish count.'[33]

After the plebiscites in Upper Silesia, Mazuria and West Prussia had decided which towns and villages were to remain German and which were to be awarded to the new Polish state, the Poles began a policy of confiscating German estates. A third of the German estates in these areas had been taken over by 1924, a total of more than half a million hectares. Some of these were given up voluntarily, as the owners found them increasingly difficult to run under a hostile Polish administration. In 1925 a new Polish law was passed, aiming to give over the remaining land to the peasantry. By 1939 the process was still incomplete, though another 685,667 hectares of German land had been taken over by the Second World War.[34]

There were some moves made to protect German property within Poland, especially in those areas where a considerable number of German landowners still existed. These were brought together by the German Union in Warsaw, led by Fürst Pless and a Polish politician of German origin, Senator Hassbach. Some landowners went so far as to put their sons in the Polish army in order to protect their land from sequestration.[35]

It was in this hostile world that the East Prussians found themselves cut off from the Reich, with only a railway line serving to link them with family and friends on the other side. Journeys to the 'Reich'* were a major frustration in themselves. The train

* In the summer of 1992, the author met an Upper Silesian German in Opole (Oppeln) who also referred to visiting Germany as travelling to the 'Reich'. It was something she had done only once in her sixty years: in 1991.

stopped at every tree, like a dog; and the Polish authorities searched passengers at regular intervals on the pretext that they might be smuggling goods out of Poland![36] The war had killed off a high percentage of the estate owners and their sons and much of the land was administered by widows. A particularly turbulent tour of the east in Weimar's twilight years brought home to Heinrich Brüning just how bad the situation was, and how little hope he had of bringing about a solution: 'Over and over again when I considered it in the cold light of day, I came to the conclusion that von der Marwitz was possibly right in his criticism of Stein's reform projects before the War of Liberation. Even today, 120 years later, the east was not ready for democracy, even of the most limited sort. For the first time I recognised the results of the heavy losses incurred by the eastern nobility in the World War. The widows had turned to the estate managers for advice who all belonged to the extreme right and who had been responsible for organising these desperate scenes.'[37]

Brüning's problem was how to convince the richer Germans of the south and west that they should pay to alleviate the misery of these easterners. He knew they wouldn't accept it. He also saw how low the president's stock had fallen in Prussia and Pomerania, the very areas where one might have imagined he had the greatest support. 'To my astonishment and horror it was brought home to me that the Reichs President's popularity was very low.' Hindenburg, said Brüning, relied on his advisors, members of the Neudeck Camarilla like Oldenburg-Januschau, who didn't tell him the truth. 'The Hindenburg-myth, which still thrived in the west and south, was already dead in the east.'[38]

The crisis in the east revolved around the question of settling farmers on the big estates which were now going bankrupt in their hundreds. In 1930 Minister Hans Schlange-Schöningen, himself the owner of a Pomeranian *Rittergut*, calculated that over 600,000 hectares were mortgaged at 150 per cent of their value while another 1,215,000 hectares were mortgaged at one hundred per cent.[39] The first 600,000 hectares were to be auctioned off in three months if nothing could be done. It amounted to 'three frontier provinces up for sale'.[40] Money had come from Berlin, but it was having little effect: 60 million Reichsmarks in 1927, 100 million in 1930. It fell to Schlange-Schöningen to work out the plans for settling hundreds and thousands of poor German farmers on land which had for centuries been the livelihood of the Prussian Junkers.

Schlange-Schöningen had rather less faith in Hindenburg than Brüning. He visited the old soldier at Neudeck to explain to him the workings of the scheme, and had the impression that Hindenburg couldn't follow his argument, his mind ever floating back to Königgrätz where he was first blooded in battle in 1866.[41] Brüning thought the president too honest to be swayed by his camarilla. 'If anyone succeeds in raising doubts,' he told Schlange-Schöningen, 'he will call me to give him an explanation when he returns, and in a quarter of an hour everything will be cleared up . . .'[42] Brüning had believed the old man when he told him, 'Before God I swore an oath on the constitution. You must help me never to break it.'[43]

From the right's side the arguments were also cogent. The diagnosis was the same even if the prescriptions varied. Magnus von Braun, who was soon to replace Schlange-Schöningen as the minister responsible for *Osthilfe* (East-Relief), had drawn up his own figures. He showed just how underprivileged the east was compared to the west: 40 per cent fewer roads than Westphalia, 60 per cent fewer railway lines than the Rhineland. East Prussia paid from 10–12 per cent more for goods and received 10–12 per cent less for those produced in the province. In 1932 100,000 hectares of Pomerania had not received any fertiliser because the landowners had not had the money to purchase any. In East Prussia industry was working at 30–40 per cent of capacity. Meanwhile the auctioning of the big estates was proceeding at an even faster rate than the settlement of the land.[44]

In 1927 Gut Neudeck in West Prussia was a victim of the same process. The president's sister-in-law was selling the last of the Beneckendorff und Hindenburg estates. Oldenburg-Januschau stepped into the breach. He launched an appeal in industrial and landowning circles to buy the estate and present it to the president.

In the end Neudeck was purchased for 'Oskarchen', Hindenburg's son and aide-de-camp, to allay any suspicion of bribery. Neudeck was back in Hindenburg hands and there was an added bonus: the president was now a near neighbour of Oldenburg-Januschau.[45]

Oldenburg is disarmingly frank about his motives in his memoirs, to the degree that later commentators have possibly exaggerated the role he played in the downfall of the Brüning administration. Close proximity brought about a 'lively and constant exchange of ideas'.[46] Oldenburg sought, as he had always sought, by influencing Hindenburg to 'abolish parliament and to erect a dictatorship . . .'.[47] When Brüning could no longer govern through a parliamentary majority, Oldenburg's projects appeared to be coming to fruition. The politician was obliged to ask the field marshal for permission to govern by decree. But Hindenburg's answer was always the same, to the intriguing Oldenburg, just as much as to Brüning or Schleicher: 'Be quiet, I know all that, but you forget that I swore an oath to the constitution.'[48]

Oldenburg was certainly not alone in trying to bring the president round to his way of thinking. Neudeck was visited by a large number of mainly East Prussian noblemen who wanted to whisper a word in his ear. Chief among these were Papen's Interior Minister, Freiherr von Gayl, the Director of the East Prussian Chamber of Agriculture, von Hippel, the former *Oberpräsident* von Batocki, plus a smattering of Dohnas, Eulenburgs, Mirbachs, Cramons and, last but not least, Magnus von Braun, the former *Regierungspräsident* in Gumbinnen in Prussian Lithuania. Braun had been sacked as untrustworthy after the Kapp Putsch.[49] These men made up the 'Neudeck Camarilla'.

Not all of them were anxious to lead the president astray. Marion Gräfin Dönhoff, who was in her twenties then and a member of one of East Prussia's top families, insists that Batocki had nothing to do with Brüning's downfall, nor, she says, did Graf Brünneck-Bellschwitz play any part in it. She cites a letter of Brüning's written after the war, which laid the blame on

Schleicher and State Secretary Otto Meissner* and not on the East Prussian and Silesian nobility.[50] This sounds perfectly feasible, but it does not remove from Hindenburg the interest in preventing the continuation of the colonisation policy which was the darling of the Prussian Socialists under Minister-President Otto Braun: 'From his point of view Hindenburg had not fought the battle of Tannenberg to see the whole structure of the province now dismantled and the old conservative element, who had served and died in the army for centuries, chased from their estates.'[51]

It was true that Otto Braun took a passionate interest in the settlement question. As an East Prussian from Königsberg, the idea of breaking up the large estates had amounted to an obsession since his earliest years.[52] It was not hard to convince Hindenburg that these were Socialist ideas levelled directly at the freedom of the individual to choose his own course. More important still were the findings of one of the chief *frondeurs*, Gayl, who wrote to Hindenburg on 24 May 1932 (Brüning was ousted less than a week later) to make him aware of how wide-reaching the plans were. He reported the discontent present both on the land and in the towns of the Prussian east: 'Attrition is making frightful progress in the souls of the easterners. It is having a laming effect on the fighting strength of the province which has up till now been the pillar of the national military determination faced with the Poles. This observation does not exclude the military either. In this critical time we must avoid anything which saps the will to fight . . .'[53]

Here was something to alarm the old field marshal if he wasn't alarmed enough as it was. Further, the bill giving the government the power to sequester and settle the estates made it clear that the landowners were 'robbed of all possibility of being able to retain their estates in the event of an improvement in the economic situation'.[54] The next time Schlange-Schöningen saw Hindenburg, he expressed 'strong misgivings' about the bill. When

---

* An Alsatian Vicar of Bray. Meissner (1880–1953) served as Chief of Cabinet to Ebert, Hindenburg and Hitler.

Hindenburg finally refused to grant Brüning the emergency powers necessary, the Chancellor had the impression he was reading from a series of points which a third party had 'written in large letters on a piece of paper for him'.[55] Brüning resigned on 30 May, leaving the path open for Papen, Schleicher and Hitler.

The East Prussian nobility had its tally of Hitler enthusiasts, much like every other region of Prussia and Germany. These included at least one member apiece of the Dohna and Finckenstein families. In most instances the noblemen, and women, were closer to the more socially acceptable Göring than they were to Hitler: that was true of Frau Viktoria von Dirksen or the Prince and Princess zu Wied. There was also a buccaneering element, men like Dietrich von Jagow, Udo von Woyrsch and Hans-Peter von Heydebreck. Woyrsch was in the SS and played a major role in the bloodbath of 30 June 1934, in which Heydebreck (SA) was murdered.

Gauleiter Erich Koch continued to agitate against the big landowners, even going so far as to have Walter von Hippel imprisoned for two and a half years. Most of the Junkers distanced themselves from the movement, some of them from mistrust of the more radical programme the Nazis wished to introduce. They had all heard the speeches of Goebbels and Darré, which held little appeal for these conservatives. Walter von Corswant-Cuntzow even asked Hitler if the Nazi party were not just another version of the KPD (Communist party) 'without the Jews'.[56] For some Nazism made only the shallowest incursion into their lives. For an eccentric old landowner like Carol Lehndorff, having to host the Prussian equivalent of the village fête must have been within his capacities in the Weimar years, but in 1935 the local party representatives came to inform him that this year he must say something about the 'nation' and the 'Führer'. The old count went out on to his balcony at Steinort to address the villagers, said a few words and finished up with the cry, 'Heil . . . ? Blast, what's that fellow's name again?' After a few moments of hopelessness, 'Well then, *Waidmannsheil!* (Good Hunting!)'[57]

II

> The Berlin season lasts from about January 20 for about six weeks. It is short in duration because, if the *hoffähig** people stay longer than six weeks in Berlin, they become liable to pay their local income tax in Berlin, where the rate is higher than in those parts of Germany where they have their country estates.[58]

Frederick the Great had a plan, which somehow never really took off, to transform the Wilhelmstrasse into an avenue of noble palaces on a scale even greater than the Viennese Herrengasse.† The Junkers, however, showed little inclination to forgo their country estates for Berlin and what with his wars and other preoccupations, Frederick gave up his idea of making Berlin into a city of splendour, a Vienna, Paris or Rome.[59]

Once Germany became an empire, however, there had to be a court worthy of the name, an idea which accorded ill with the martial traditions of the state. Under the first Kaiser, the stuffiness and tedium of court routine came as a cold shower for those who conceived of life among royalty as a magnificent pageant. Princess Radziwiłł is particularly scathing about Berlin life in the last years of William I's life: 'The immediate entourage of the Emperor is not to be recommended in any way. It is a gathering of valetudinarians. At the present time the court resembles the furniture in an old museum.'[60]

The Polish princess found few of the courtiers to her liking. Court ceremony was orchestrated by the Grafen Pückler and Perponcher – one of them blind, the other: 'it would be better not to say too much about the other.'[61] Even an old rake and 'mangeur de coeurs' like Graf Lehndorff had settled down with a new wife

---

* Presentable at court.

† Frederick the Great would shudder in his grave to see what has happened to the Wilhelmstrasse now. For years called Otto Grotewohlstrasse, one of the last acts of the ailing DDR was to line it with gimcrack blocks of flats in the most execrable taste. They appear so flimsily built that there must be a chance that they will fall down before too long. The entire western half of the street was blown up by the Russians to make the Berlin Wall easier to patrol. Only a few pre-war buildings remain on the eastern side.

and become quite docile. State occasions were judged by the quality of the buffet.⁶² For Princess Radziwiłł only in the company of some of the mediatised princes and Silesian magnates, the families who were to come to the fore at the court of the emperor's grandson, was one likely to find any real style. One of the former was Graf Stolberg-Wernigerode, who inhabited a huge, largely neo-gothic pile in the Harz Mountains where he lived a feudal life on one of the largest estates in Germany. Stolberg had married a Princess Reuss, from another mediatised family in Thuringia. House parties at Schloss Wernigerode were lavish affairs which brought together the royal princes, Bülows, Reusses, Albedylls and Lehndorffs.⁶³

Berlin society was a brief wintry flourish. Few but the grandest families maintained a permanent residence in the capital, because few could afford to. Most of the Junkers stayed in hotels on their rare visits. All of which gave Berlin high-life a sad, provincial air: 'Gallantry is an unknown quantity here,' wrote Princess Radziwiłł at the same time observing that 'adultery flowers like a plant in its natural habitat'.⁶⁴ This sexual licence had been noticed before, not least in the scurrilous writings of the eighteenth-century Austrian actor, Johann Friedel.⁶⁵

William II believed he could inject a high moral tone into his court and was particularly firm with adulterers, even if he was completely blind to the unbridled homosexual activities of his closest friends. One of his particular bugbears was his cousin, Prince Joachim Albrecht. Graf Robert Zedlitz-Trützschler had been Joachim Albrecht's adjutant before he was appointed Controller to the Royal Household in March 1903. In his previous incarnation he had found it quite impossible to keep the prince out of harm's way. Talking to his father, Prince Albrecht, did not help either. Zedlitz found him 'very unworldly'. He too had fallen foul of the Hohenzollern moral code by his second, morganatic marriage and had been obliged to retire to Saxon Dresden where he built the ravishing Schloss Albrechtsberg on the rising ground above the Elbe.⁶⁶ Joachim Albrecht was advised to go abroad, and preferably not to return. He did in March 1908, after a period spent in German South West Africa. When he appeared at a court ball the empress refused to give him her hand. A few days later the Kaiser banned him from wearing his uniform.[67] The Kaiser justified his – rather myopic – priggery: 'I must act sternly in matters of morals against members of my own family. I must give exemplary warnings to my sons.' Zedlitz was unimpressed with the Kaiser's reasoning: 'This system of morality which bids a man ruin others in order to safeguard the virtue of his sons does not appeal to me.'[68]

Despite its brevity, the Berlin season had its great occasions and grand balls. The court moved to Berlin from Potsdam on 1 January,[69] inaugurating the events of the season. The first great evening was the *Schleppencour*, so-called from the long trains or *Schleppen* worn by ladies of the court. The balls started promptly at 8.20 and proceeded with stultifying formality while the Kaiser, the Kaiserin and the members of the royal family endeavoured to 'make a circle', or circulate among the guests.[70] Supper was served at 10.30 and the ball came to an end an hour later. Departing guests were offered a glass of hot punch and 'a peculiar sort of local Berlin bun, in order to ward off the lurking dangers of the villainous winter climate'. The stiffness of the Kaiser's court proved too much for the high-living Edward VII of Britain: denied whisky, cards and the right to smoke a cigar '. . . the King went off to bed'.[71]

The new dances which were at this time making their entry from the United States were looked on with suspicion. The Kaiser was specific in issuing orders that no one should dance a tango or a turkey trot at any of the season's balls or 'go to the house of any person who, at any time, whether officers were present or not, had allowed any of these new dances to be danced'.[72] This, wrote Ambassador Gerard, effectually extinguished the turkey trot, the bunny hug and the tango, and maintained the waltz and the polka in their old estate.[73] Gerard thought this attempt to maintain 'spartan simplicity' was ridiculous, as was the ban on polo-playing for army officers.

At Whitsuntide came a ceremony which dated back to the time

of Frederick the Great: the *Schrippenfest*, named after the long white rolls which were handed out to the soldiers of the Potsdam garrison on that day. It was a good pretext for a review of the troops, but once the martial ceremony was over the soldiers ate, at trestle tables under garlands of fir and pine, a traditional concoction of beef, prunes and rice. After the meal the Kaiser circulated among the troops accompanied by his family, asking the soldiers if they had enjoyed their meal.[74] In the last week of June, society was expected to be present at Kiel Week, the Kaiser's attempt to imitate the Cowes Week Regatta on the Isle of Wight. One of the features of Kiel Week was a Germanic *Bierabend* or beer evening.[75] Similar was the great Christmas celebration at the New Palace in Potsdam where the Kaiser's *aides de camp* tucked into a 'monstrous carp which looked like a porpoise'.* That too was cooked in beer. The porpoise was followed by plum pudding in a sauce enriched with schnapps.[77]

William I had caused a sensation at court by giving holders of the Black Eagle precedence over the mediatised princes. Such a furore broke out that the princes refused to attend court balls. Eventually a compromise was reached 'which pleased no one'. The Knights of the Black Eagle had precedence over the members of the former ruling houses, *but not their wives*. Once this strange measure had been introduced, we are told, an 'armed peace' reigned at court between the two opposing factions.[78]

For the first Hohenzollern Kaiser it was natural to believe that the Prussian soldiers he had invested with the Black Eagle were superior to the foreign princes who flocked to the new capital of the Reich. There were precious few of them anyway. His grandson sought another solution to the problem: to make his friends among the mediatised princes members of the order and to expand its membership to include a far greater number of souls. In 1887, when William I was still at the helm, there were twenty-five

---

* Prussia's most famous carp until the winter of 1864 were the 'Mooköpfe' in the park at Charlottenburg. When they finally expired they were 150 years old and none was under four feet in length.[76]

knights; in 1899, forty-three; in 1912, fifty-five. The eagle had lost its rarity value.[79] When the younger Moltke was given the Black Eagle Holstein quipped, 'His uncle fought a victorious campaign, epigones that we are we can do just as well on three manoeuvres.'[80]

The second most important civil decoration was the Red Eagle. In 1905 Graf Görtz, the Kaiser's Liebenberger poodle and amateur sculptor, caused a storm when he was given the Red Eagle for having constructed a monument to the Kaiser's ancestor, Admiral de Coligny, the martyr of the 1572 St Bartholomew's Day Massacre in Paris. On 7 March a female courtier groused that Görtz would have been amply compensated by the 'Universal Distinction'.[81] It provided plentiful ammunition for the popular wits who marvelled at the new *Ordenslust*: 'We cannot give everybody a chicken for his pot on Sunday, but we will see to it that everyone has an order in his buttonhole.'[82] It was a long haul from the days when the Attic simplicity of the Iron Cross was all a Prussian might desire and when Heinrich Alexander von Arnim could complain after the Battle of Ligny that he had received 'more scars than medals'.[83]

There was no shortage of medals in the Kaiser's day. When Eulenburg finally saw fit to return his decorations to the Kaiser from his bed at the Charité Hospital, it made an impressive list.[84] The Kaiser was certainly not above awarding medals to himself. Precisely half way through the Great War William II was conducting his own fierce campaign against German game. Müller noted with ill-concealed distaste: 'This afternoon His Majesty bagged his second and third stag, and appeared this evening wearing his *Pour le mérite*, two Iron Crosses and the Hunter's Jubilee Badge.'[85]

The Kaiser went on dishing out medals to the end, and indeed beyond. In the middle of the November Revolution in Berlin, the owner of the city's most powerful publishing house, Hermann Ullstein, was taking refuge in the stairwell of the office building with his chief reporter, Hofrat C. M. Schmidt. Bullets were flying and it was thought safer to keep clear of the windows. Ullstein told his reporter that at all costs he must maintain close contacts with the new regime after the Kaiser's abdication. Suddenly, to their surprise, they saw a grumpy postman, soaked through from the pelting rain, wandering through the deserted offices of the building: '*Wo find' ick hier'n Hermann Ullstein?*' (Where do I find one Hermann Ullstein?) he asked. Ullstein admitted it was he and was passed a package from the royal heralds' office. On opening he discovered the War Service Cross (*Kriegsverdienstkreuz*) 2nd Class, graciously bestowed for Ullstein's work during the war.[86]

VIII

School and University

I have very little memory of it: a huge classroom with a blackboard; a suffocating atmosphere despite windows permanently open and tribes of boys in rough wool and canvas jackets; unkempt or barefoot, or wearing clogs, who struck up a frightful din.

Theodor Fontane, *Meine Kinderjahre*, in *Werke*, I, 192.

From as early as 1717, every Prussian child enjoyed the right to go to school. A little learning, however, was quite enough. The timetables which have come down to us from the reign of Frederick William I or his son Frederick the Great show the syllabus limited to hymns, Bible readings, spelling and the simplest arithmetic. Too much education was a dangerous thing: it might encourage the peasants to leave the villages, where their *raison d'être* was to provide recruits for the army, and head for the towns where conscription might easily be avoided. Reading was important, however; Frederick the Great in particular set great store by having NCOs who could read. The simplest way of guaranteeing this was to send the village children to school.[1]

Like everything else in Prussia, education went into decline at the end of the eighteenth century and during the years of the French occupation. During those years the future Pastor Rehsener attended a school in Neustettin in Pomerania. Life was hard and particularly unpleasant was the food. 'Breakfast in the *pension* was a glass of water and a piece of stale bread. Lunch was alternatively composed of gruel or cornmeal soup and potatoes cooked with goosefat or milk. We didn't have any butter or meat, that had been eaten up by the French.'[2] On the other side of Pomerania, in Swinemünde, where the eight-year-old Theodor Fontane went to live in 1827, the educational prospects were rudimentary. Having tried out the school, Fontane's mother thought it kinder to send the boy to a tutor – the inevitable 'Herr Candidatus': a young clergyman waiting for a living to fall vacant. In rich or noble households these trainee clerygman were housed under the eaves and treated as somewhere in importance between a country cousin and a member of the domestic staff.

However paltry, the Prussian *Allgemeine Schulrecht* was nonetheless pioneering legislation of European significance. In 1788 the Prussians laid the keel for another innovation of no lesser importance: the *Abitur* or *Reifeprüfung*. Here the credit goes to a Silesian nobleman called Freiherr Karl Abraham von Zedlitz und Leipe, a former pupil of the Brandenburg Ritterakademie who had risen to the top of the Royal *Oberschulkollegium*. Then as now, the *Abitur* was to be the examination for university entrance.[3] A patron and friend of Kant, Zedlitz was later manoeuvred out of his job by an intriguing Rosicrucian, and it was not until 1834 that the *Abitur* became universal.[4] In 1809, Zedlitz's *Oberschulkollegium* was swept away by the reforms, and replaced by a new 'Kultus' ministry under Wilhelm von Humboldt. The ministry was to combine the management of Prussian education with the arts, the sciences and the administration of the church. One of Humboldt's most important reforms was to create the system of *Gymnasiums*, *Realschulen* and *Volksschulen*, by which all children attended school according to their academic abilities. At the top, the *Gymnasium* concentrated on the humanities: Latin, Greek and history. Later the *Gymnasium's* training was deemed to be too narrow and the *Realgymnasium* was created to provide a more modernistic schooling. Latin and Greek continued to be taught in the 'Humanistisches' *Gymnasium*.[5]

Prussian education was generally both broad and tolerant. In the mid-nineteenth century a school such as the Joachimsthal'sche Gymnasium in Berlin, which aimed at filling posts in the higher civil service, taught conversational Polish.[6] Naturally there was a specific need for Polish-speakers, given the number of Polish subjects of His Majesty in the Grand Duchy of Posen and West

Prussia. The Poles were chiefly Catholics, but they did not make up the entirety of the Prussian Catholic population by any means. In Graudenz in West Prussia, the rich were Evangelical virtually to a man, the poor, both German and Polish, Catholic. Separate Catholic schools were slow in coming, but by 1847 the first was open for business.[7]

In 1834, in Marienwerder, also in West Prussia, German was taught to Poles 'without spiteful compulsion',[8] the same rule being applied to Prussian Lithuanians in Gumbinnen. A Pole started school at the age of six and German was introduced in the third class. No Pole, however, might proceed from the second to the first class without showing a mastery of German.[9] Bromberg in the Grand Duchy was less than half German, and ten per cent of these were lowly Catholics.[10] Here the government chose not to enact compulsory education after 1815.[11] In the private schools frequented by the upper classes, Polish was confined to religious classes and singing.[12] For the time being the spirit of *laissez faire* triumphed in the Grand Duchy.

During the Weimar Republic, ministers were conscious of the need to provide schools for the Polish minority in Mazuria, West Prussia and Upper Silesia. Even before the Treaty of Versailles redrew the German borders in the east, the *Kultusminister*, Haenisch, provided for the possibility of Polish children receiving religious instruction in their mother tongue, as well as reading and writing lessons to improve their knowledge of Polish. This rule was particularly important in towns with sizeable Polish populations such as Allenstein in Mazuria. It was also suggested that the teaching be offered in parts of Berlin, the Rhineland and the Ruhr, where the inhabitants were often Polish.[13]

In southern Ermland, the first minority schools for Poles were opened in 1929. The biggest of these, in Allenstein itself, had only twenty-seven pupils in 1937–1938. There were two others in the town. In that same year there were no pupils on the books whatsoever in one of these. Taking all the minority schools together, the average number of pupils was under nine. There had none the less been a project to open a Polish *Gymnasium* in Allenstein in 1924 and in 1937 a Polish *Realschule* opened in Marienwerder. A private *Gymnasium* near Oppeln served the needs of the Poles in German Upper Silesia. It would, however, be a mistake to see the absence of Polish schools in areas like Mazuria as a major bone of contention between the Germans and the Poles. In the referenda organised by the Allies in 1920 between 86 and 97 per cent of the local population voted to remain in Germany.[14]

The education of the elite centred on Berlin and Potsdam. By all accounts Bismarck had a miserable education, wrenched away from his Pomeranian idyll and plunged into the 'synthetic spartanism' of the Plamann Institute in Berlin.[15] The regime certainly sounds unpleasant: a 6 a.m. start; milk and bread; stale crusts as a mid-morning snack and lunch: those who couldn't finish it were obliged to contemplate it at their leisure in the garden until the entirety had been consumed.[16] Bismarck later referred to Plamann's as a 'civil cadet school',[17] and was relieved to be removed and sent first to a *Gymnasium* in the Friedrichstrasse and finally to the Graue Kloster in the Klosterstrasse.

Naturally the cadet schools remained the favoured destinations of Prussian boys, followed by the *Ritterakademien*: Brandenburg, Liegnitz in Silesia, Kolberg in Pomerania and Halle in Prussian Saxony. Also in Halle were the Francke'sche Anstalten, founded at the end of the seventeenth century by August Hermann Francke. This was an institution imbued with a strong dose of Pietism. Boys were prepared for university entrance and infected with missionary zeal. Francke's creation was protected by Frederick William I, and influenced his own cadet schools as well as the *Ritterakademie* in Brandenburg. Here Heinrich Alexander von Arnim was sent. Another favourite was Rossleben near Magdeburg, which had been nurturing noble children since the mid-sixteenth century.[18]

Girls were as often as not educated at home, as was the case of poor Effi Briest in Theodor Fontane's novel of the same name. For the grandest there were schools in Potsdam and Charlottenburg, such as the Kaiserin Augusta Stift. The advantage of the

Augusta Stift at the end of the nineteenth century was that it was from here that playmates were selected for the Kaiser's only daughter, Princess Victoria Louise.[19]

Visitors to the Cathedral Island in Brandenburg who proceed as far as the brick gothic cloister will notice two marble war memorials inscribed with what appears to be a tally of the most famous names in the history of the Brandenburg Kurmark. Particularly moving is that recording the deaths in the Second World War, as it includes not only those who died for Hitler, but also the names of one or two he had murdered for their role in opposition.[20] This is the last vestige of the old Brandenburg Ritterakademie, or noblemen's academy, which in its 240-year history mirrored the rise and fall of Prussia itself.

The Ritterakademie was founded in 1705, just four years after Frederick I crowned himself in Königsberg. The old Premonstratensian cloister of the cathedral was largely empty and the number of cathedral prebends had been dwindling year by year since the Reformation. The idea was to stump up capital from the noble families in the Kurmark surrounding Berlin, Potsdam and Brandenburg itself, so far all the *Ritterakademien* had been founded at a considerable distance from Prussia's heart at Brandenburg. The idea must have appealed to the Crown Prince, later King Frederick William I, who in true Calvinist style set considerable score by matters of education. 'Pupils,' he wrote in 1710, 'must be kept constantly busy and supervised, otherwise the human will is inclined to slackness and every form of vice.'[21]

From the very first the education was to be humanistic. A timetable from 1712 shows the standard doses of Cicero and Euclid. The course was also meant to be useful to Prussian noblemen, and therefore included lessons on heraldry, genealogy and reading newspapers.[22] In the nineteenth century the school came increasingly under attack for the narrowness of its social intake. This led the Ritterakademie to accept its first bourgeois scholars in 1845, although the school's prospectus is careful to stipulate that these should come from the *higher* bourgeoisie, who

were increasingly taking over the *Ritterguter* of nobles. The school
was still dominated by the Junkers, however, and when Frederick
William IV visited it in 1856 he greeted the pupils with a cheery,
'Good morning, Junkers!' The boys duly intoned, 'Good morning,
Your Majesty!' The royal visit was a moment of great importance
in the history of the school: the king came surrounded by generals
and ministers, including his interior minister, Karl Marx's father-
in-law, von Westphalen.[23]

A sprinkling of middle-class estate owners hardly assuaged the
clamour from the left. The Ritterakademie remained highly
exclusive. Not for nothing was 'der Januschauer', Elard von
Oldenburg-Januschau, a pupil in the early 1870s. Oldenburg's
career at the school was cut short when he was found to be the
ringleader in a minor revolt. Once a year, at the end of the
Christmas half, the Ritterakademie played host to an open day
and ball. The ball was a forerunner to the opening of the Berlin
winter season and an opportunity for debutante sisters and cousins
to show their skill on the dance floor. A feast of 'salad and fruit,
fish and meat and game – from venison to wild boar and pheasant'
was also provided, and that which was left over after the dance
was divided up among the boys. In 1873, however, it was decided
to scrap this generous custom. The Januschauer was not put off,
and mounted a raid on the store: 'I can still see one of my school
contemporaries, a man who was later to achieve fame as a cavalry
general and corps commander in the First World War, backing
off with a huge salmon under his arm.'[24] These were the humble
beginnings of Oldenburg's conspiratorial existence.

At the turn of the century the Ritterakademie received an
important new master in Dr Huldenreich Kehr, a reserve captain
who almost doubled the size of the school. In 1903, it began to
receive day boys from the city when the ancient 'Saldria' grammar
school ceased its humanistic vocation and went over to the modern
curriculum. From then on, pupils requiring teaching in the ancient
languages came to the Ritterakademie, which continued to be the
bastion of classical learning until its own teaching side was wound
up by the Nazis.[25]

Naturally given the social backgrounds of the boys – even those without the tell-tale 'von' before their names – the Weimar Republic was not popular in the Ritterakademie. The director of the school in that period, Professor Ziehen, was a former Plön schoolmaster who had taught both Princes Auwi and Oskar. Academic standards were high with a well above average success rate in the *Abitur* exam. In 1932 the school filled both Rhodes Scholarships available to Germans for study at Oxford.[26]

Weimar failed to interfere with the running of this flagrantly undemocratic institution; it was the Third Reich which was to be its undoing. Ziehen had moved from the nationalist DNVP to the Nazi NSDAP in 1929, but he remained a conscientious head-master until his departure in 1934. His successor was Georg Neuendorf, who had received instructions from the ministry to steer the Ritterakademie into National Socialist waters. The Nazi handling of the Ritterakademie is further evidence of the move-ment's contempt for the Junkers as a whole. Those who were at the school at the time when Neuendorf arrived were increasingly convinced that he had only been appointed to close the place down. The pupils were not slow to show their contempt for the new headmaster, one of them firing at his study window with an air rifle. This provided the pretext which the Nazis desired: in the new year of 1937, the Ritterakademie was closed.[27]

Although lessons ceased, the school continued to take boarders who attended classes at the Saldria. The institution therefore limped on, resisting various attempts at *Gleichschaltung* (the Nazi term for bringing institutions into line with National Socialist ideology) as well as a project to turn it into an SS 'home'. Eventually one of these SS schools was actually lodged in a vacant part of the buildings, though there was no pedagogical contact between the schoolboys and the SS boys. Total assimilation of the school into Nazi ideology did not take place until after 20 July 1944, when daily prayers were abolished and replaced by a reading more in keeping with the spirit of Nazism.[28]

As the Ritterakademie was a Prussian school, one might easily be led to believe that the atmosphere was spartan in the extreme.

To some extent this was dictated by the austere monastic buildings, a legacy of the rigorous Premonstratensian monks who had served the cathedral. Sport was naturally encouraged, physical education in Germany having the nationalist implications associated with it by its first advocate 'Turnvater' Jahn who, at the time of the Napoleonic Invasion, had encouraged gymnastics to foster military awareness. In the summer the boys swam in the lakes surrounding the Cathedral Island, often in water under 15 degrees. The favoured competitive sport was coxed fours. Stress was placed on the virtues, especially those firmly anchored in religion: loyalty, obedience, discipline, self-sacrifice, comradeship and modesty.[29]

School started early by British standards (it still does in Germany). In 1844 in summer the boys were up at five, and at six in winter. In 1938 this had become 6.25 and 6.50 respectively. Punishments, however, were a good deal less severe than those to be suffered in an equivalent British institution of the period. In 1844 there were no beatings, and discipline was generally confined to the removal of free time. Detention was the severest penalty.[30] In 1920 most punishment was in the form of extra work, writing lines and detentions. Prefects, however, enjoyed the right to box the ears of young delinquents, rap their hands with rulers if they had neglected to wash, or, *in extremis*, cane the younger boys.[31]

In other respects the Ritterakademie was similar to an English public school, although considerably smaller – rarely did the number of pupils, day boys and boarders, exceed 150. There was a head boy called the *Primus Omnium* and prefects called *Senioren*. There was also fagging, the fag being referred to as the *Leibulx*. It was the *Leibulx*'s job to keep the *Senior*'s desk in order. The Nazi school inspectors were scandalised by the continuation of fagging at the school and it was they who outlawed the practice.[32]

Despite the midnight feasts and other features of any boarding-school life, the Ritterakademie placed emphasis on self-discipline in a way that a British public school did not. Newspapers of every available colour were available in the common room and the boys took an interest in politics. During Weimar they were chiefly inclined towards the monarchy, but some support was shown for the Nazis in the early years. After 1934, the boys were increasingly 'distrustful'. One head boy successfully introduced the Hitler Jugend (Hitler Youth) into the school, but that ultimately had the advantage of limiting interference from the main HJ organisation within Brandenburg. Another head boy had to stand down in the mid '30s when it was reported that he had shouted 'Bring back the Kaiser' during a midnight feast and sung 'Heil Dir im Siegerkranz'.[33]

In nearly two and a half centuries of existence, the Brandenburg Ritterakademie produced 27 diplomats, 32 holders of court offices, 93 senior civil servants and 96 generals. The real source for officers were the *Kadettenanstalten* or cadet schools, so often seen elsewhere in Germany and the outside world as the fount of aggressive militarism and Prussian arrogance. It was the Soldier King, Frederick William I, who put this military stamp on Prussian education. The schools founded during his reign all had a military purpose, from the military academy to the engineers' academy and La Pepinière, the army medical school.[34] Martial education became a Prussian trademark with the added incentive of attracting fee-paying foreigners. At the turn of the century a General von Elpons started a military academy for foreigners who wanted to enter the German army. It attracted Chinese, Japanese and a very large number of Turks.[35]

The *Kadettenanstalten* dated back to the time of the Great Elector, who created a first military school in Kolberg in Pomerania in 1653, and another in Küstrin in 1666.[36] Frederick William I united the schools of Magdeburg and Kolberg in Berlin in 1717. By 1721 there were already 236 cadets at the institute. Frederick the Great expanded the system, creating schools at Stolp in eastern Pomerania and at Kulm in West Prussia. In 1765 he also founded the Académie des nobles, the forerunner to the Kriegsakademie. His successors installed cadet schools in Kalisch in Posen and Potsdam.[37] Kalisch and Kulm were awarded to Poland after the Treaty of Tilsit, and only Kulm was returned to Prussia in 1815. After Waterloo, however, the cadet schools were confined to Kulm, Berlin and Potsdam, until Bensberg and Wahlstatt were opened in the late 1830s.[38]

By 1840 the cadet schools were training over seven hundred pupils at any one time.[39] The provincial schools took the boys aged from ten to fifteen before passing them up to Berlin, where they remained until joining the army at eighteen. There were considerable opportunities for grants for the sons of officers and even NCOs who had distinguished themselves in action, though these were not available for the children of commanding officers and generals.[40] The generosity of these grants meant that the cadet schools became the only viable means of education for the sons of poor nobles: those whose estates had been whittled away to nothing by successive partition among brothers and cousins, and who could only keep body and soul together by serving in the army.

One of these was Emil von Lessel, who was sent to Bensberg, near Cologne, in 1859. It was a rough beginning for a boy of ten. The food was frugal enough: gruel and dry bread for breakfast; soup, vegetables and meat for lunch; soup and a snack in the evening. Those who had the means supplemented their diet with milk and 'Apfelkraut', a thick, sweet reduction of apple juice. On the king's birthday, or on the school feast day, the boys were treated to a roast and a bumper of wine. Lessel tells us that for the boys from beyond the Oder, especially the East Prussians, this was their first experience of wine.[41]

For most of the boys there was only one holiday a year, during the 'dog days' of summer. At Christmas the poorer children, especially those whose families were away in the east, remained at the foundation. The directors tried their best to allay homesickness by laying on a big feast at Christmas which was 'celebrated in a beautiful and tender way. Many a poor boy stood astonished before the great Christmas trees and the richly furnished buffet, which they had never experienced at home.'[42]

In 1863, Lessel graduated to the Hauptkadettenanstalt in the Neue Friedrichstrasse in Berlin. The four cadet companies were lodged in a quadrangular building with its back to the Spree (when the wind blew off the river 'it did not smell of roses'[43]). The dormitories were pleasant and airy. The teachers lived alongside to keep the boys in order. They ate in messes of twelve in a vast hall decorated with marble plaques telling the names of former cadets killed in action. In the hall or 'Feldmarschallsaal' there were portraits of kings and field marshals and the sword of Frederick the Great. Out in the courtyard they had re-erected six marble statues of the heroes of the Seven Years War which had previously stood in the Karlsplatz.[44]

Cadets were divided into groups of between eight and ten, each with its own dormitory and common room. At one end of the former was a huge work table, at the other the wash stands. Every boy had his own camp bed, locker and wooden stool. 'Lying on the bed during the day was strictly forbidden, it was seen as effeminate anyway.'[45] The regime was even more rigorous than that imposed on the boys at the Ritterakademie: a drum-roll woke them at 5.30 in summer and 6.00 in winter. There was half an hour to wash and dress followed by three-quarters of an hour's work and a quarter of an hour for breakfast. Lessons began at seven or eight and continued till four, six days a week. On Sunday the cadets attended the service in the Berlin Garrison Church nearby. Those who had invitations could then leave the institute. In practice this meant only those boys lucky enough to possess family in Berlin.

'The clothing was of good quality, great value was placed on keeping it clean. Servants polished our shoes and ordnance officers cleaned our shortened flintlock rifles, but otherwise cadets themselves had to keep everything in good shape and sew on any torn-off buttons.'[46] Uniforms were worn at all times on the foundation. On days off the boys had the right only to wear their own caps, shoes and belts. The idea was to make all the boys feel equal, even when there were wide differences of family wealth. If a boy's family could not provide him with these items of leisure wear, the school bought them for him. Lessel denies that there were any more cases of cruelty than at any other Prussian school.

In the Neue Friedrichstrasse the cadets did the same classes as equivalent children at a *Gymnasium*. The more successful sat the officers' exam at the end of their studies, others entered as

Degenführnriche, potential officers, and underwent further training before they took the exam. If a boy was not physically big enough to serve, he spent another year at the school in the *Oberprimaner*. There were some children at the school who did not come from military backgrounds: these were sons of civil servants and teachers, and known as *elterliche Gemäuer* – chips off the old block. Dancing lessons were given by a teacher from the royal ballet, and all the boys learned to ride. At Bensberg the boys had called one another 'Du', at the *Hauptanstalt* the formal 'Sie' was the rule; and a surname *tout court* was frowned on – it was never 'Lessel', but Kadett von Lessel.[47]

The purpose was, of course, to prepare the boys for the front and the military training was of great importance. Every day there was between half and three-quarters of an hour of drill and after the summer vacation there were exercises in Schönhausen, Pankow or Schöneberg 'which was open land in those days, for Berlin was a long way off being the metropolis'. Red-letter days were those of the great Berlin garrison parades when the cadets formed the right wing of the infantry in the march past. The smallest boys were not allowed to participate, something that caused great pain.[48] The 'gently smiling face of the old king as he rode before us and greeted the cadets will be remembered by everyone who took part to the end of their days.'[49]

'Often the sun burned hot on the field at Tempelhof* and stretched the endurance of the as yet inexperienced young warriors who stood on parade for hours on end under helmet and busby, but "to be yellow" or to back out was counted as a disgrace and many a young hero collapsed, ashen, face forward where he stood. Whoever received a wave from a father, uncle or brother in one of the regiments on parade, grew an inch in his boots and gained important kudos among his comrades.'[50] Another excitement for the noble cadets was the selection of *Leibpagen* and *Hofpagen* for the court. The former were attached in pairs to the persons of the royal princes and princesses, the latter were given

---

* To the south of Kreuzberg. Now the site of Berlin's inner-city airport.

general court duties in resplendent red and silver uniforms. During meals they stood behind the seats of the guests and were rewarded with bits of cake. Their pockets were lined with leather to make it easier for them to conceal these tips.[51]

For Lessel the great excitement came when war broke out with Denmark in 1864. When a member of the *Selektaner*, the Institute's top class, was wounded in the Battle of Düppel 'the whole corps felt itself elevated'.[52]

By the time Guderian arrived at the Hauptkadettenanstalt in the years before the First World War after attending a cadet school in Badenese Karlsruhe, it had moved from the Neue Friedrichstrasse to Lichterfelde in the south-western suburbs of Berlin. The old soldier looked back on those years with pride: 'When I remember my instructors and teachers from these formative years it is with emotions of deep gratitude and respect.' The cadet's life was one of 'austerity and simplicity', the studies based on those at the *Realgymnasium*: modern languages, maths and history. 'The standards reached by the cadets were in no way inferior to those of similar civilian institutions.'[53]

The so-called 'Prussian Eton'[54] was Plön in Schleswig-Holstein. Here the education was 'semi-military', and not administered from the Prussian treasury like the cadet schools proper. It was here that the Kaiser sent his boys, but instead of putting them through the school itself, he lodged them in a *Schloss* nearby, and selected pupils from the school were brought out to spend the day with them, attending their lessons and sharing their meals. One of the more curious ideas dreamed up by the princes' governor, General von Gontard, was to train the boys in farm work. They learned the mysteries of manure, sowing, ploughing, digging and planting, as well as how to look after cows, geese and hens.[55] Miss Topham, who was sent to Plön to give Prince Joachim extra tuition in English, was less than impressed by the work of digging up potatoes and tossing them to the geese, but she found the teachers at the school surprisingly sympathetic. As well as the agricultural duties set out by Gontard, the Kaiser wanted all his sons to learn a trade: a tradition of the Hohenzollerns. The Crown

Prince was apprenticed to a turner; Eitel Fritz proved the keenest farmer and later put what he had learned to good use in the gardens of his home, Villa Ingenheim.[56]

The high level of education required for potential officers meant that in many cases they would have been equally able to enter a university had they so desired. The army was the most prestigious choice of career, but the civil service lay not too far behind, and for a young man wishing to join the administration, university education was in most cases a must.* Law was the favoured subject, and most of the better heeled Prussians would have wanted to join a student *Korps* where they could spend their time in duelling and drinking. The smartest of these were the Borussia in Bonn, which had had Hohenzollerns among its members; the Saxo-Borussia, the Guestaphalen and the Vandalen in Heidelberg; the Canitzer in Leipzig; or the Sachsen in Göttingen.[57] The cost of living varied enormously from one university to another, which might easily influence the choice of some parents, already finding it hard to sell their timber and grain on the market. Göttingen was cheaper than Heidelberg, and Heidelberg was cheaper than Bonn.[58]

The Prussian student often preferred to study elsewhere in Germany rather than in his native land. Until the nineteenth century Prussian universities were small. In 1789 there were a little over four hundred students in all.[59] The oldest university was the Albertina in Königsberg, then the Viadrina in Frankfurt an der Oder, Halle and Duisburg. With the conquest of Silesia Frederick the Great inherited the Leopoldina in Breslau with its magnificent baroque buildings on the Oder.

The Prussian universities were rethought during the reform period, with Wilhelm von Humboldt closing down the small faculty in Frankfurt and creating the University of Berlin in the former palace of Prince Henry. Humboldt introduced what was to become the classic German brew: a mixture of teaching and

---

* The Schwerin family provide an extreme example of the preference for military over civil careers. Until 1900 they had bred 280 army officers and just six *Herr Doktors*.

research. With Prussia's new acquisitions in the Rhineland after 1815, the tiny University of Duisburg was also shut down. The French had scrapped the universities of Bonn, Cologne, Trier and Mainz during their occupation. In April 1815 Frederick William III promised his new subjects a provincial university modelled on Berlin or Breslau. In 1818 the university opened in the former prince's *Schloss* in Bonn.[60]

Besides Bonn, the grandest German universities were Heidelberg, Leipzig, Göttingen and Halle. Heidelberg was the choice of Heinrich Alexander von Arnim prior to entering the diplomatic corps in 1820.[61] The Kanitz in Leipzig was a pub where the smartest students met to discuss the burning issues of the day, which often meant sitting up all night drinking.

Bismarck was sent to Göttingen in Hanover in preference to Heidelberg because his mother feared the influence of Badenese liberalism and beer drinking on her son.[62] Instead he fought no fewer than twenty-five duels.[63] Halle was above all the university for those with their eyes fixed on entering the Prussian service. With this end in view, Joseph Freiherr von Eichendorff, like the poets Arnim, Brentano and Novalis before him, went to Halle to study law. He arrived in 1805 to find the university a 'state within a state'.[64] The enemy was the 'townee', known here as the 'philistine', 'a thousand-headed dragon' composed chiefly of local artisans. On hearing the cry of '*Burschen heraus!*' (All fellows outside), the students grabbed their swords, and without asking the reason why, fought pitched battles with the townsfolk till well into the night. A year later, after the Battle of Jena, the town took its revenge on the hated student population when Napoleon closed down the university. The students were thrown out on to the streets and what possessions they had of any worth were sequestered by their landlords.[65]

Had it not been for the fame of Immanuel Kant and Christian Jakob Kraus, the Albertina in Königsberg might languish in similar obscurity to the universities of Frankfurt an der Oder and Duisburg. Kant is best remembered today, but in terms of influence on a generation of reforming Prussian civil servants,

Kraus is the more important of the two. He was the Professor of Practical Philosophy in the university and taught his pupils the need for a total change in the relationship between the Prussian subject and the state. 'In his opinion, not just individual parts, but the whole Prussian state was rotten to the core': there was increasing despotism in the administration and an ever greater pursuit of pleasure among the rulers. Everything worthwhile was gradually being destroyed. The state was led by 'a brutal feudal clan of so-called noblemen'. Kraus's attacks on the preconceptions of the Prussian state might have had even more effect in a country not so inherently conservative as Prussia. His pupils became reforming civil servants rather than politicians: talented (and sometimes brutal) *Oberpräsidenten* such as Theodor (von) Schön and Eduard (von) Flottwell.[66]

It was possible to pass through Königsberg without absorbing the teachings of either Kraus or Kant. Carl Gottlieb Rehsener took up residence in the Collegio Albertino in around 1810. He was given a room in college which didn't appeal to him: low-ceilinged with brick walls and two tiny windows boasting a few panes, but otherwise stopped up with paper and rags. There was soot, straw, feathers and cobwebs everywhere and a fire which 'might have served to roast apples a couple of centuries before'. 'Into this hole was I to crawl, all alone in the cold with winter coming on.'[67]

Rehsener was also miserably poor, and to save money he economised on food. He went at midday to the inn where he had a bowl of hot soup and a piece of bread. In the evening it was a roll and a small glass of beer. In the morning, a piece of bread and a glass of water. Later a further economy drive forced him to forgo the soup. Things began to improve for Rehsener when he got a new room and won the right to eat commons in the college itself. The food in the college hall was nothing special, 'the soup too thin, the grey peas in the terrine scuttled around the floor as if they were trying to make for the hills; instead of fish there were bones; instead of meat, more bones . . .'[68]

The students decided to protest. They organised a procession through the city: 'A steaming terrine led the way; followed by vegetables and goat meat, as we referred to it; salvers and plates, salt and bread, and knives and forks brought up the rear; everyone carried something; the tablecloth formed a flag at the front. The procession went sedately and honourably its magnificent way.'[69] The authorities got the hint and the protest was a 'shining success'.

Rehsener had his fill of fights between the 'philistines' ('everyone is a philistine who is not a student') and the undergraduates; and took part in an action to avenge the honour of the student body after a university officer's daughter danced with an officer in preference to a student. Instead of picking on the officer, we note, the students directed their wrath at the girl herself. In all this, however, although Rehsener changed his mind several times about the course of studies he wished to pursue, we hear no mention of the world-famous philosopher who had breathed his last only six years before.

Finally Rehsener opted for theology, and it proved a wise choice. He was taken into the house of one of the richest merchants in Königsberg: 'Sparkling evenings with music and dancing. In particular I spent nice Sundays out in Juditten, [on a] pretty estate . . . with garden, park, vineyard and wood. Everything which eyes, ears and palate might have wished for, was here or in town.' Rehsener had fallen on his feet. 'I had free board, free lodging, a pleasant life and 400 Talers a year, more than I could spend. First I was the poorest, now I was easily the richest of all the students.'[70]

There was not much of the categorical imperative of duty in Rehsener's student days. Nor was there any in Hans von Tresckow's. The later police chief also attended Königsberg University for a couple of semesters: 'I was more often on the fencing salle and down at the pub than in the lecture hall.'[71] After a year he migrated to Berlin, which had been re-endowed in a bid to make it Germany's best university after the proclamation of German unity in 1871. Tresckow was assisted by a sixteenth-century bursary designed to look after the educational needs of members of the Selchow and Tresckow families.

In Berlin, Tresckow found Treitschke. He continued to drink in a largely East Prussian circle, but Treitschke's lectures 'I never missed. He knew how to captivate his audience, who filled up every seat in the great auditorium. Every time he mounted the dais, there rose up such a monstrous stamping of feet to greet him, the traditional student form of honouring a beloved professor. As for Treitschke, he couldn't hear the din at all: he was as deaf as a post, he could, however, see how much he was loved by the clouds of dust.'[72] Tresckow spent all of a semester in Berlin before going on to Strasbourg.

Tresckow was hardly an overachiever, but he was nonetheless well educated by today's standards thanks to the rigours of a Prussian education at school and university. He left Strasbourg without completing the studies necessary to take the *Referendar* exam, which was vital if he wanted to join the administration. He took the other Prussian route instead and joined the army. As a poor man, however, he found the mess expenses too onerous and he was obliged to resign his commission and join the Berlin police. Here he found many former officers whose experiences had been similar and only a smattering of 'Herr Doktors'. Most of the latter were ensconced in the ranks of that other great Prussian institution: the civil service.

IX

Civil and Political

Friedrich Harkort, a deputy to the Prussian Landtag complains of the idleness of Prussian diplomats:

'I would urgently like to recommend that Harkort be attached to the Legation here for a few months; the old windbag would very soon begin to sing in duet with Holstein the song with which Leporello opens Don Giovanni.'*

Bismarck to von Schleinitz, St Petersburg, January 1861. Quoted in Norman Rich, *Friedrich von Holstein: Politics and Diplomacy in the Era of Bismarck and William II*, Cambridge, 1965, vol. I, 17.

Like so many of Prussia's most typical institutions, the civil service took form in the time of the Soldier King Frederick William I. The huge army he assembled needed a body to administer it. This led to the creation of the *Generalkriegskommissariat*. A few years later the *General* and *Finanzdirektorium* was established with control over *Kriegs- und Domänenkammern* in the provinces. Frederick William demanded absolute precision from his civil servants, and hard work. There is a story that the king was taking an early stroll through Potsdam one morning when he saw a traveller trying vainly to wake the keeper of a post-house who had yet to open his door. When the king noticed this he broke in the bedroom window of the postmaster and laid about the man with his cane before finally chasing him from the building: 'He expected punctuality from his civil servants.'[1]

---

* Notte e giorno faticar
per chi nulla sa gradir;
piova e vento supportar,
mangiar male e mal dormir.

I work all night and all the day
For one who's never happy.
I brave the wind and pouring rain,
I sleep ill and eat badly.

Something of the stern spirit of the Solder King lived on in the Prussian civil service, right to the very end. The Kaiser's ministries had developed, however, out of those formed by the Stein-Hardenberg reforms. Following the innovations introduced by Frederick the Great and incorporated in the Prussian legal code, it became necessary for a civil servant to pass a series of exams before entering the service. In practice this meant that most civil servants had done three years of law at a university, spent a year as a *Referendar* in the courts as assistants to the judges, followed by two more *Referendar* years attached to a ministry. Providing the candidate was successful in his exams, at that point he could enter the ministry proper.[2]

It was a tough system, and one of which the Prussians were justly proud. No other country possessed such highly trained civil servants, and Treitschke wrote off the amateurish British system as nepotic.[3] In 1883 the system became even tougher, when the *Referendar* period with the courts was extended to two years and the period formerly served in the ministries was transferred to provincial *Oberpräsidiums*. The final change occurred in 1906 when the court service was once more reduced to one year and the administrative training time increased to three. This was the system which survived till the end of the Weimar Republic and beyond into Nazi times. Such a long training meant that most did not start gainful employment before they were thirty. In the meantime about a quarter of them had presented a dissertation entitling them to use the title of 'Doktor'.[4]

The service was overwhelmingly Prussian, even after 1870. Chancellor Hohenlohe thought it well nigh impossible to bring in a useful assistant who had not passed through the stations of Prussian *Landrat* (who administered the smallest territorial units in the state – the *Landkreise*) or *Regierungsrat* (the provincial civil servant in the *Oberpräsidium*). In 1890 the Badenese Freiherr Adolf Marschall von Bieberstein had considerable reservations about taking on the job of State Secretary at the Foreign Office because he thought his life would be made difficult by the

Prussians under his command.[5] Five years later Marschall von
Bieberstein was sacked because, as the Kaiser put it, 'he was
sick and tired of this man from Baden who had no Prussian
feelings . . .'[6]

Behind Marschall's dismissal was almost certainly Eulenburg,
who was then at the top of his greasy pole and had put it about
that he 'always preferred Prussians for such appointments'.[7] At
the end of the same year the Kaiser wrote to his favourite to say
that he intended to teach the Reichstag what it meant to be a
Prussian: 'Because the Prussian element must once again break
through. And the Prince [Hohenlohe] is too old, and he can no
longer handle both foreign affairs and the Ministry of State, and
the present Vice-Chancellor [Bötticher] is a cowardly wash-rag.
Bülow will be my Bismarck,' said the Kaiser, 'and as he and my
grandfather pounded Germany together externally, so we two will
clean up the filth of parliamentary and party machinery
internally!'[8]

After four years in office, Chancellor Hohenlohe still felt
defeated by the Prussians around him: 'South German liberalism
cannot stand up to the Junkers. There are too many of them, they
are too powerful and they have the kingdom and army on their
side. . . . I have to struggle to keep Prussia within the Reich, for
all these gentlemen couldn't give a damn about the Reich and
would prefer to get rid of it before too long.'[9]

The civil service was also exclusive when it came to religion.
Although Catholics comprised a third of all Prussians, few managed to make it into the higher reaches of the service. Of the fifty
or so high-ranking diplomats in the Foreign Office, only five were
Catholics, in the more menial positions. Baptised Jews could serve
in the civil service and the banker Bernhard Dernburg became
director of the Colonial Office, but they remained excluded from
the Foreign Office, where the possession of a noble patent was
almost a *sine qua non*. In 1914 the office boasted eight princes,
twenty-nine counts, twenty barons, fifty-four lower nobles and
eleven bourgeois. The only middle-class diplomats to achieve

consular rank held their posts in Peru, Venezuela, Colombia and Siam.[10]

Civil service pay was not great. On the one occasion that the *'éminence grise'* Fritz von Holstein was invited to dine with the Kaiser he was discovered to possess no evening dress.[11] Holstein was a bachelor who lived in a small flat: 'His library consisted of a handful of volumes on history and political philosophy, and the furnishings of his flat were utilitarian and frugal, unrelieved by articles of beauty or special interest.'[12] Holstein's life was simply his work: 'In almost every respect he was the model Prussian civil servant: able, hard-working, honest, frugal, simple in manner, monastically dedicated to the service of the state.'[13]

Holstein was born a Prussian nobleman. One of the advantages for those who were not was that they might achieve ennoblement through ascending to the highest offices of the service. Friedrich Karl Lucanus was born in Halberstadt in the Harz Mountains, the son of a chemist. In the service he was referred to as 'der Apotheker'. He was raised to the nobility as head of the Civil Cabinet and in 1897 he became a knight of the Kaiser's inflated Black Eagle chapter.[14]

For a qualified civil servant who possessed a landed estate, the perfect solution was to become the local *Landrat*. There is a story that in the more remote provinces such as eastern Pomerania or East Prussia the official would stick his head round the door at 11.00 a.m. to ask his clerk if there was anything to sign: '*Jawohl, Herr Graf,* two [letters].' 'Well, that is quite enough.'[15] The *Landrat* received, in addition to his salary, a large grant towards expenses to allow him to host local assemblies and take on staff. In 1891 sixty-two per cent of the *Landräte* were noblemen, a somewhat lower figure than the number of *Regierungspräsidenten* and police commissioners. Here the figure was closer to seventy-five or eighty-five per cent.[16]

Just over sixty per cent of all *Oberpräsidenten* were Junkers. Which is not to say that they were unqualified for the job. In general a Prussian *Oberpräsident* was highly capable, if, like everyone else, a little short on political education.[17] This could be a problem for the official when he was obliged to choose between two roles: was he representing the region to the central government, or central government in the region? Certainly the *Oberpräsidenten* had to please the Kaiser by their actions, for after 1870 the office was increasingly seen as a springboard to a ministry.[18] Old families had their uses in that they could represent the Kaiser at regional functions in the manner of the English Lord Lieutenant. In 1918 eleven out of twelve were noblemen, but that was soon to change under Weimar,[19] when a Noske or an August Winnig, men who had made their names in the Social Democratic Party, aspired to the office. The role of the *Oberpräsident* remained unchanged until 1932. Under the Nazis the majority of *Oberpräsidenten* were also party Gauleiters.[20]

The *Oberpräsident's* role was a perfect demonstration of the Prussian preference for administration over politics: ideally, the official was above the horse-trading of politics. His job was to be fair and wise. The continuation of this conservative, apolitical system exasperated some, such as one state secretary who cried out, 'Is it possible to have liberal government here? In the past twenty-five years there has been no *Landrat*, no *Regierungsrat*, no *Regierungspräsident*, let alone an *Oberpräsident*, no bureau chief, not even a local counsellor in the whole of the East Elbian region who was not conservative right down to his bootlaces.'[21] The government turned a blind eye to the blurred edges of the system which allowed a small number of civil servants to sit in the *Reichstag* or the Prussian *Landtag* as deputies; naturally they were on the right of the chamber.

Good behaviour, not rocking the boat, had its own rewards: medals and civil titles might come your way. The widespread use of high-sounding forms of address has disappeared from Germany since the war, and now only survives on this scale in Austria. On the eve of the First World War, however, it was something which particularly struck Ambassador Gerard, arriving in Germany from democratic America: 'One of the most successful ways of disciplining the people is by the "Rat" system. "Rat" means councillor, and is a title of honour given to anyone who has attained a certain measure of success or standing in his chosen business or profession. For instance, a businessman is made a commerce "rat", a lawyer a justice "rat", a doctor a sanitary "rat", an architect or builder a building "rat", a keeper of the archives an archive "rat" and so on.* The "rats" are created in this way: First a man becomes a plain "rat", then later on he becomes a secret "rat" or privy councillor, still later a "court secret rat", and later still a "wirklicher", or really and truly secret court rat, to which may be added the title of "excellency",† which puts a man who has attained this absolutely at the head of the "rat" ladder.'[22]

The higher grades of the civil service enjoyed considerable prestige in imperial times. If the money was poor they derived satisfaction from their shining image in society. It stands to reason that such people were not happy with the events of November 1918 and the fall of the monarchy; and that they were even less happy with the Weimar Republic which cleared the stage for the parties of the centre and left.

One of these was Wolfgang Kapp. The Kaiser had not had a great regard for Kapp, and used a rude word to describe him which prudish publishers of a previous generation have thought best to conceal from us.[23] The Kaiser may not have appreciated Kapp's ancestry: his father had been a revolutionary in 1848 who had emigrated to the United States, his mother a 'highly gifted Jewess'.[24] He had been born in America, but went to school in Berlin and then studied in Tübingen, Göttingen and Berlin. His first civil service appointments had been in Hanoverian Celle and in Prussian Minden before he entered the Ministry of Finance, where he remained until 1890. His contact with East Prussia was through his wife, the daughter of a *Rittergut* owner called Rosenow from Dulzen by Preussisch-Eylau. He married in 1884 and moved to East Prussia six years later.[25]

In 1906 Kapp became the director of the East Prussian chamber

---

* Kommerzienrat, Justizrat, Sanitätsrat, Baurat, Archivrat . . . Clearly Gerard is enjoying himself with his rats.
† Geheimrat, Wirklicher Geheimrat, Excellenz . . .

of agriculture, putting his experience to good use to help his fellow landowners. His first venture into politics didn't come until September 1917, when he founded the German Vaterlandspartei in Königsberg with the blessing of both Tirpitz and Ludendorff. Although August Winnig, who took over from Batocki as *Oberpräsident* of East Prussia, was moving steadily to the right, Winnig did not approve of Kapp and was aware that he was up to something. 'You are suspicious of me,' Kapp told Winnig, 'you think I'm preparing a Putsch. But I'm too clever for that.'[26] A similar suspicion was present in Berlin, where Kapp's name came up ever more frequently in the winter of 1919 to 1920.[27] His connections with other *frondeurs* such as Lüttwitz and Ehrhardt were too well known.

By all reports the Kapp Putsch was well received in East Prussia, for reasons which have been elaborated elsewhere: East Prussia felt isolated, cast off from the Reich and was more prepared than most parts of Prussia or Germany to accept adventurers who might bring about a radical solution to their *malaise*. In the little town of Goldap in the far east of the Mazurian Lakes, everyone 'breathed a sigh of relief'.[28] In Tilsit on the border with the new, and aggressively anti-German, state of Lithuania, everyone was happy 'with the possible exception of the Jews'.[29]

The civil servant's Putsch, however, was largely brought down by the civil service. After hedging their bets for three hours the bureaucrats in the Welfare Ministry decided against taking orders from Kapp. They contacted the Finance Ministry to put a stop to his access to cash. 'In this way the Kapp Putsch foundered on the very first day.'[30]

The civil service may have baulked at illegal acts, but they were capable of a degree of sabotage against the Weimar State when it suited them. The ministers who replaced the stately Junkers after 1918 were not always to their taste. This was clearly the case with Otto Braun, the Königsberg-born Socialist who was to be Minister President of Prussia for most of the Weimar Republic. Braun's first brush with his staff at the Ministry of Agriculture merely confirmed his worst fears. The ministry had been one of the most reactionary of the lot as a result of its tight links with the estate owners in the east.[31] Many of them were actually landowners or Junkers, and Conservative Party voters to a man.[32] The fact that Prussia was now a republic 'was such a monstrosity' that they hesitated even to use the word, and referred to it as the 'Freestate' instead.[33] That they continued to do their jobs after 1918, Braun could not attribute to any great love for the new regime; 'Much more it was the outpourings of a good Prussian sense of duty and not a little out of concern for the social lives they led.'[34]

Braun greeted his new staff together with his colleague from the Independent Socialists (USPD), Hofer. In the meeting room 'they stood shoulder to shoulder' from the ministerial directors down to the typists, 'waiting to see what was going to happen. Hatred, disapproval and mistrustful curiosity stamped all over their faces, none showed the slightest sign of joy or contentment; any sympathy for the new regime and its exponents. It was as if we, who stood before them, were their betrayers.'[35]

Braun must have derived a certain amount of satisfaction from the fact that the boot was now on the other foot. When he had been one of ten Socialist deputies in the Landtag before the war, the civil servants had been supercilious.[36] The bureaucrats resisted their new chiefs. 'Files began to pile up on my desk. An old civil servants' trick: they wanted me to drown in paperwork to put me off the pleasure of sticking my nose into things in the future. But they had not reckoned on my East Prussian toughness, my capacity for hard work; they underestimated the stamina I still possessed in those days.'[37]

The experience was seminal for Braun and later influenced his determination to break up the big estates in the east: the battle which ruined him and his government, and ended up by removing representative government in Prussia altogether at just the moment when the Hitlerians looked set to seize power.[38] Braun could have acted with more tact. Erich Koch-Weser, the Interior Minister at the beginning of the Weimar Republic, said that Braun 'made the mistakes that all parvenus make ... but he was a good man.'[39] The liberal, cosmopolitan aristocrat Graf Harry Kessler also saw both sides of the argument: 'Most of the ministers are Jewish. Südekum, the one and only representative of the *ancien régime*, with his fine, white-haired ambassadorial head; he is also, so I hear, the only one to address the others as "Herr". In general during debates the ministers use the style "comrade". . .'[40]

The year of the Kapp Putsch, 1920, also saw the publication of an important and highly influential book, which went to the heart of the old Prussian system of government and administration: Oswald Spengler's *Preussentum und Sozialismus* (Prussian Socialism). The book had originally been planned as part of Spengler's most famous work – *The Decline of the West* – published 1918–1922, but Spengler evidently believed that his examination of *Preussentum* could make its own way in the world.

The book was strongly affected by the events of the November Revolution which had caused the Brunswick-born Spengler considerable grief. 'The indescribable ugliness of the November days is quite without precedent,' wrote Spengler, 'no great moments, nothing inspiring, no great men, no memorable lines, no bold crimes; only pettiness, disgustingness, folly.'[41] Spengler's purpose in writing *Preussentum und Sozialismus* was to define a German socialism 'free of Marx', a thinker 'strong in his negative aspects but helpless when it comes to positive values'.[42]

Spengler's fundamental conviction is that Socialism is an idea elaborated by the Prussians, essentially in the time of the Soldier King. It is based on a strict opposition to capitalism. 'The German, or rather Prussian instinct was as follows: power belongs to the whole community. The individual serves the community and the community is sovereign. The king is only the first servant of the state. . . . Everyone has his place. Some command, others obey. This, since the 18th century, is authoritarian socialism, essentially illiberal and anti-democratic in as much as France and Britain are liberal and democratic. It is also clear, that the Prussian instinct is anti-revolutionary.'[43]

Spengler makes it clear that *Preussentum* is divorced from any idea of specific geographical borders within Germany. '*Preussen-tum* is a feeling for life, an instinct, an inability to take an alternative line [*ein Nichtanderskönnen*]; it is the perfect example of spiritual and intellectual thinking and because of this, in the last instance, it also possesses lovable qualities that have long been noticeable in one race, and all the more so in the best and most characteristic members of the race . . . There are genuine Prussian natures all over Germany – my mind turns to Friedrich List, Hegel and so many other engineers, organisers, discoverers, scholars, and above all in a type of German worker – and there have been since the days of Rossbach and Leuthen countless Germans who possess a piece of Prussia deep in their souls, a capacity which never fades and which suddenly reveals itself in the great moments of history.'[44]

Spengler, like Treitschke before him, wanted to see Prussia as a club open to all Germans who took pride in the history of their race, and who believed in the idea of a 'Prussian mission'. 'It does not concern itself with individuals, the individual must sacrifice himself to the whole. A man does not stand up for himself here, but everyone for everyone else with that inner freedom in the greatest sense of the word, the *libertas oboedientiae*, freedom in obedience, in which the best examples of Prussian discipline have always excelled. The Prussian Army, the Prussian civil service, Bebel's working-class movement – these are examples of this disciplinary mentality.'[45] 'Genuine *Preussentum* heeds no one; it is feared.'[46]

Prussian socialism is to be found in the simple blue uniform adopted by the Soldier King, 'the expression of . . . public service'[47]; the simple piety of certain Prussian figures – Queen Louise, William I, Bismarck, Moltke and Hindenburg – which is expressed inwardly, having no need to reveal itself to others. Outwardly, says Spengler, Prussian piety expresses itself in a sense of duty.[48] The pietism is both 'impractical and provincial'; 'a man's whole life was there to serve'. The primitive life of the Junker 'in the midst of toil and misery made sense only under the spell of a superior duty.' Such ideas were behind the Hohenzollerns and the 'heirs to the East Elbian knights'. Theirs was a deep-seated 'suspicion of simple wealth, luxury, comfort and pleasure ... All these things are worthless in the face of the imperative of knightly duty.'[49]

Spengler's enemy here is capitalism, which he blames on the English. Capitalism is simply economic Darwinism. The opposite is Prussian Socialism: 'Frederick William I was, in this sense, the first conscious Socialist and not Marx.' It required Kant, however, to work it into an effective formula: the categorical imperative. From 1700 onwards English philosophy tended to sensualism. A century later Prussia evolved its own school in idealism, when Hegel taught the 'cruel destiny of states'.[50]

Where English life pitches rich against poor, Prussia opposes command and obedience. Monetary considerations were not, says Spengler, a consideration in Prussian life: *on travaillait pour le roi de Prusse*: 'That means doing one's duty without some filthy ogling after profit. The salaries paid out to officers and civil servants since Frederick William I's time were laughable in comparison to the sums handed out even to members of the middle classes in Britain. In spite of this people were hard-working, selfless and honest. Rank was its own reward.'[51] 'Here in the strictest sense of the word, there was no such thing as a private individual. Every man worked within the system with the exactitude of a well-ordered machine. ... In this way even the management of industry could not be entrusted to private hands. ... It was an office and the politician responsible was a civil servant, the servant of the community.'[52]

In this way Spengler saw the Prussian civil servant in a very different light from Otto Braun. The model was his fellow *Wahlpreusse* Stein, not one of the self-motivated minor landowners who might have battled for the interests of their own beleaguered class. 'The Prussian civil servant type is the best in the world. They were created by the Hohenzollerns. They guarantee the possibility of socialisation through their inherited socialistic capabilities. ... The worker must be wrought in his image if he is to cease to be Marxist and to become Socialist. 'The "state of the future" is a civil service state.'[53]

Preussentum und Sozialismus was widely read and admired – not just in the universities of the Weimar Republic, but also by men as fundamentally different as Gregor Strasser and Hans von Seeckt. By 1924 65,000 copies of the book had been sold and even after the end of the Second World War, when Germany lay in ruins and Prussia had become a dirty word, copies changed hands on the black market for large sums or their equivalent in cigarettes or other commodities.[54] One of those who discovered Spengler's work as a young man was Fritz-Dietlof Graf von der Schulenburg, the son of the former Chief of Staff to the Crown Prince, General Graf Friedrich von der Schulenburg and Freda Marie, née Gräfin von Arnim.[55]

Fritz-Dietlof was born in London in 1902 while his father was Military Attaché at the embassy. He studied at Göttingen, where he was an enthusiastic member of the *Sachsen* with a passion for duelling which left his face a network of scars; a monocle permanently fixed into his left eye did nothing to render his appearance less forbidding. A friend later described him as looking like 'a lugubrious . . . robber baron'.[56] From Göttingen Schulenburg migrated to the lesser, Hessian University of Marburg, then entered the civil service as a *Regierungsreferendar*.[57]

Schulenburg read deeply in neo-conservative literature, not only Spengler but also Moeller van den Bruck and Ernst Jünger. Already in his *Referendar* years he was noted for his radicalism and eccentricity and went by the title of 'der rote Graf' or the red count.[58] Like many Germans, not just the upper classes, he thought the Versailles Treaty was a disgrace. He was, on the other hand, also openly critical of the leadership which had brought Germany to defeat, and did not exclude the army (which he might easily have preferred to the civil service as a von der Schulenburg) or the Kaiser.[59]

Schulenburg embraced an ideology anchored in the Prussian virtues and a streamlined interpretation of the statecraft of Frederick the Great.[60] Like Spengler he expressedly rejected all Western systems in favour of Prussian models. He was no democrat and believed that a wise and paternal administration precluded the necessity of representative institutions. He showed his commitment to the community when he was posted to Heiligenbeil in East Prussia and saw the local fishermen all going down with a mysterious sickness which they attributed to the water of the Haff. Schulenburg traced the ailment to the discharge of cellulose waste into the Haff and mounted a campaign against the factory owners. This led him into considerable difficulties with the administration in Königsberg, but he could not be induced to change his own position.[61]

How much Schulenburg had been influenced by Spengler was readily apparent from a paper he wrote in the early 1930s, when he described the role of the civil servant in the old Prussian state: 'On the basis of their position and functions, the civil servants were the representatives of the idea of the state, leaders of the nation. Civil servants became ministers. The king was the unquestioned ruler, the obvious representative of the state. But he also served the state like the bureaucrats; and he was in a certain sense as their supreme commander, a member of the bureaucracy. The civil servants represented the state and decided on its policy.'[62] This slightly romanticised conception of the civil service in the seventeenth and eighteenth centuries strengthened Schulenburg in his desire to erect an ideology of reformed 'Fritzism'. Stein was another hero, the classic Prussian state servant.[63]

It was also a picture which appealed to the Nazis, especially those of the 'North German school' under the brothers Strasser. The Prussian virtues and the glorious days of Frederick the Great were seen as perfect educational tools to reform the mentality of the nation in the regime which followed Weimar. For their part, most Prussians looked on this Nazi neo-Prussianism with considerable scepticism.[64] Spengler had also added to this idea of Prussia as Germany's salvation and through reading *Preussentum und Sozialismus* Gregor Strasser had been able to elaborate a form of Nazism slightly at variance with Hitler's own, but which tended to appeal more to the Germans of the north. For one thing it tended to put more emphasis on Socialism, albeit of a German or 'Prussian' sort.

Schulenburg was increasingly attracted by this line of thought. He wanted radical solutions. It was this desire which led him to join the Nazi Party on 1 February 1932; his number: 948,412. Partly it was a family decision: his brothers had all joined and his father, the old general, had left the DNVP and stood as a Nazi candidate for Mecklenburg, where the family *Schloss* was.[65] Hitler also seemed capable of enacting those 'radical solutions'. After hearing Hitler speak in Königsberg in October 1932, Fritz-Dietlof wrote to his fiancée: 'He speaks with great seriousness, everything he says comes from his own experience: the struggle and the suffering of the whole nation, he speaks from firm belief, there stands a man who believes in something, conviction stands behind his every word . . . He is a prophet, an educator, and the hope of millions.'[66]

Schulenburg's radicalism precluded any question of class loyalty, above all in East Prussia where Junker landowners were using every trick in the book to hang on to their estates. Once the Nazis came to power, Fritz-Dietlof supported the Gauleiter Erich Koch in his efforts to carry out a modified version of the policy which had brought down Braun and Brüning. In his utterances at the time, Schulenburg showed himself to have absorbed some of the thinking of the Nazi agriculture minister Walther Darré. Schulenburg thought the nobility of the future would be formed from the peasantry.[67]

It would be a mistake to say that Schulenburg was wholly taken in by the Nazis. He disliked a good many members of the movement whom he described as 'repulsive vermin'.[68] He thought it was possible that many of these would be replaced by a 'Prussian, north German element', and he set about convincing cousins and friends on the need to join the movement. His real hero was Gregor Strasser: 'He is a new type of leader; both a man of the people and a leader, with instinct and a feeling for the finer nuances, a sort which we haven't had in Germany since the

Peasant Wars. It is wonderful too, to hear the humorous way in which he dismisses the Herrenklub*. I believe in Strasser . . .'[69] The ideal solution for Germany, thought Schulenburg, was Hitler as Reichs President, i.e. occupying the honorific role, the figure-head, while Strasser would be Chancellor.[70]

Schulenburg was looking for a new form of *Preussentum*: an alliance between the Prussia of Frederick the Great and the national thinking of the younger members of the right wing in Weimar times.[71] Once the Nazis had achieved power, he advo-cated the *Gleichschaltung* of the old civil service; to bring it into line with the *Führerprinzip*, the *Landrat* would also function as the Nazi *Kreisleiter* or local party boss. Schulenburg was not alone in his enthusiasm for the new system: it should be recalled that Henning von Tresckow, a young Junker from a similar back-ground was also inspired by Nazi ideas until the inherent lawless-ness of the system was brought home to him by the Night of the Long Knives on 30 June 1934. Schulenburg also worked on his friends, the Balt, Graf Nikolaus von Üxküll and Cäsar von Hofacker, to bring them over to the Nazi viewpoint.[72] Both men, like Schulenburg himself, were to be closely bound up with 20 July 1944.

Schulenburg had been in Heiligenbeil at the time of the *Machtergreifung*. On 1 March he was transferred to Königsberg as a *Regierungsrat* and director of the political office of the NSDAP under the Gauleiter Erich Koch. In his new functions he was successful in having the *Oberpräsident*, Dr Wilhelm Kutscher, removed for not acting in the spirit of National Socialist ideology. His attack on Kutscher was so fierce that even the President, Hindenburg, complained about it. Nor was Göring, the new Prussian Minister President, so anxious to get rid of Kutscher as Schulenburg, being rather more wedded to a certain continuity than the more radical Nazis like Schulenburg.[73] Schulenburg also wielded his new power against the reactionary nobility of East

---

* Elite social club in Berlin. Many of the members were politically inclined noblemen, generally right-of-centre.

Prussia, advancing the work of the new 'Erich Koch Foundation' which brought in settlers from the west.

In his adhesion to Nazism in those years, Schulenburg was a thrusting and ambitious young bureaucrat with an all-too-genuine desire to see Germany shaken up from top to bottom. He believed that the good qualities of the Prussian past could be welded on to the body of the dynamic Nazi movement, with Strasser at the head. All his hopes, however, were dashed when, on 30 June 1934, Strasser, along with a hundred or so other people considered dangerous to the new regime, was summarily murdered by members of the SS. Schulenburg himself left with his new wife for an unspecified location in the Mazurian Lakes, his support for Strasser being well known among his Nazi colleagues. If it took him several more years to rid himself completely of the feeling that there were decent elements within the Nazi camp, his attitude was never to be the same. When he did finally throw off all affection for Nazism during the war, he was to become one of the most effective, dynamic and relentless opponents of Hitler.

II

> Germany will pay the price for the honour of having the most incapable parliament which has ever existed. . . . It is not in vain that all the vital force of the nation is concentrated in one man . . . Prince Bismarck who has paved the way for the fall and destruction of his country, in smashing everyone who might have been capable of carrying on his work.[74]

Bismarck acted in Prussia's interests when he united Germany between 1866 and 1871. It was, however, the arch-Prussian Bismarck who inflicted Prussia's mortal wound. Prussia could just about manage to subdue the liberal, parliamentary ambitions of the Rhinelanders who became its citizens in 1815, but once Prussia had to assume the political will of Hessians, Frankfurters and Hanoverians after 1867, it was clear that the cohesion of Junker interests would be progressively whittled away.

Not every Prussian desired Bismarck's Reich and quite a few abhorred his methods of bringing it into being: Bismarck found opponents even among the Pomeranian noblemen who formed his own circle of friends. The core of this group had been the pietist Adolf von Thadden-Trieglaff,* who believed that noblemen held their 'offices' from God alone.[75] It was a two-way process: the nobleman commanded the community, but he served it too. This idea was uppermost in other members of the circle around Frederick William IV: the brothers Leopold, Ludwig, Wilhelm and Otto von Gerlach, Friedrich Julius Stahl and Joseph Maria von Radowitz.

The most remarkable of these was Ludwig von Gerlach, a bold conservative thinker who played a part in virtually every major event in Prussian history in the nineteenth century: he was decorated in the Wars of Liberation; was an important influence on Frederick William in the 'pre-March' period; was a member of Frederick William's reactionary 'camarilla'; and survived to become a strong critic of Bismarck's Germany.[76] Gerlach was never much taken by the romantic nationalism which began to inspire Germans and Prussians from the time of the Napoleonic Wars. As a young man he had gone to look at one of Jahn's gymnastic sessions and reported 'gymnastics, liberal nationalism, German nationalism, hatred of the French . . . for the most part unbelievable nonsense'.[77]

After the war he came under Thadden's influence and underwent a minor religious conversion. He placed his faith in the 'Holy Alliance' of European monarchs. The idea of the monarchy actively representing moral right appealed to Gerlach and his friends and it was not treated with the levity which greeted the mystical union elsewhere in Europe. He remained faithful to this idea; for him wars were only justifiable if they were Christian. The Crimean War was a Christian war. The wars against Austria and Denmark were not. The king played an important role in this

---

* The name of his estate, Trieglaff, derives ironically enough from a three-headed Wendish deity.

civitas dei; he was the father and protector of his people. It was an idea which appealed mightily to Frederick William who, despite the harshness he showed during the March days of 1848, indisputably loved and cherished his people.

The duties of the Prussian nobleman were predictably stern: possessions were only sanctified by the acceptance of duties, the simple ownership of land 'as a pleasure' was not. 'The communists are right about property without duty. In this sense we should not abandon the threatened rights of patronage, policing and the rule of law, because they are more duties than rights. . . . To simply preserve is a negative attitude: face forward to the dungheap, your back to the demands of the state. . . . What is noble is: your back to the dungheap, face forward to the enemy. But it is a form of nobility which does not exclusively belong to the many who here, possessing fine names, have bled on our battlefields over the centuries. It may also be acquired by those who have no such names. Indeed, it can be won by any citizen or peasant or any Prussian who loves his land. Let us not forget that it is the highest calling of the nobleman to ennoble the entire nation.'[78]

Gerlach remained true to his loathing for nationalism. If Germany was to be an empire it should be through the strengthening of Austria's position, not by Prussia running off with the imperial crown. He was underimpressed by Bismarck's wars which defied the treaty obligations of 1815 and which pursued a policy as illegitimate as that of Napoleon: 'Only truth, legality and loyalty afford a solid foundation for peace. These qualities are eternal and remain in eternity.'[79] The new Reich which came into being in 1871 remained doubtful in Gerlach's eyes: 'In all my outward relationships I have been nothing but a Prussian all my life; nonetheless I have to say that Prussia and Germany lie well below God's realm in my conception of things.'[80]

Gerlach may have seemed like a 'hopelessly backward thinking and reactionary' character to most of Bismarck's contemporaries,[81] but he was by no means alone in his lukewarm, if not antagonistic, attitude to the new empire. His views were shared by Bismarck's old friend, Hans Hugo von Kleist-Retzow, another Pomeranian

Junker with whom the later Chancellor had been inseparable in his youth, and whose step-niece, Johanna von Puttkamer, became Bismarck's bride.[82] Kleist-Retzow finally distanced himself from Bismarck over the war with Austria and especially over the indemnity demanded after the war of 1866. He was also fundamentally opposed to the *Kulturkampf*, not because he had any sympathy for the Catholics, but because he could only agree with Bishop Krementz that God's law was higher than man's.[83]

The 'old Prussians' and their resistance to the new Reich caused a split in the right. In the North German Federation of 1867, fifty-nine 'old Conservatives' sat apart from the sixty-seven 'free Conservatives' and eighteen Conservatives who formed Bismarck's supporters. On the other side of the chamber were the largely Hanoverian National Liberals and a few Socialists. With the *Kulturkampf*, the 'old Prussians' sided with the Catholic Centre Party. Not only were they concerned for the disappearance of Prussian values in the new state, they were appalled by Bismarck's vendetta against the diplomat Graf Harry Arnim-Suckow and his family. Even Bismarck's former newspaper, the conservative *Kreuzzeitung*, came out against him, leading the Chancellor to damn it in the Reichstag as a 'scandal sheet'.[84] In 1876, however, the elements of the Conservative Party re-formed and worked together to scrap the anti-Catholic *Kulturkampf* and promote paternalistic social policy.

In the 1880s the nature of Prussian conservatism underwent a major change. The old Paternalism was increasingly swept away by an aggressive nationalism. The economic situation in the east and the increasing competition from Russia and the United States on the grain markets led to a crisis, where the Junkers made demands for protection. It was on this issue that Wolfgang Kapp first entered the political scene in 1899.[85] The Junkers naturally dominated the Herrenhaus, or House of Lords, but they also loomed large in the eastern block in the Landtag. In 1900 Junkers represented eleven out of seventeen constituencies in East Prussia; ten out of fifteen in Posen; nine out of fourteen in Pomerania; six out of twenty in Brandenburg; and ten out of thirty-five in

Silesia.[86] This situation had naturally been facilitated by the three-class voting system still in force in Prussia. The franchise was scrapped under the Weimar constitution, when the old Prussian Conservative Party also disappeared. Its successor was the DNVP or Deutschnationale Volkspartei, founded by Joachim von Winter-feldt-Menkin, Graf Kuno Westarp and the former Vice-Chancel-lor, Karl Helfferich. Despite the DNVP's Prussian pedigree, after 1920 its increasingly racialist tone brought it support from all over Germany, notably Bavaria.

The infamous three-tier voting system had been the major obstacle to the Socialists gaining control in Wilhelmine times. Not surprising, then, that Otto Braun found the system 'infamous',[87] while his most recent biographer has called it 'absurdly compli-cated and monstrously unjust'.[88] All male Prussians over twenty-five years of age voted for the electoral college, who then voted in the deputies to the Landtag. The voters were divided into three categories according to the amount of tax they paid. Because there was a wide divergence of wealth from area to area, the results in the constituencies could be wildly different. In 1908, for example, the highest taxable bracket accounted for just four per cent of the adult male population. It therefore required only seven rich men to elect a *Wahlmann* or elector. In the middle bracket, a *Wahlmann* was chosen by twenty-six people, while the eighty-two per cent of the electorate who found themselves in the lowest taxable bracket needed 136 votes to produce one member of the electoral college. Added to this, work obligations often meant that members of the lowest tax group failed to vote. In 1908 only thirty per cent turned up at the polls. This explains why in that election the Socialists won 589,875 votes and only seven seats in the Landtag. The Conservatives polled a mere 380,830 in comparison, but their share of the seats was 152! For a long time the frustrated Socialists simply boycotted the Landtag and concentrated their attentions on the Reichstag, August Bebel referring to the 'Prussian mental-ity and Prussian electoral system as the mortal enemy of all democrats'.[89]

Naturally the Herrenhaus also received a fair dose of criticism from the left. Members were nominated partly by the Kaiser, as King of Prussia, and partly like the British House of Lords by hereditary right. The mayors of Prussia's main towns and cities also sat in the chamber. In an uncharacteristic outburst of sympathy for the detested Prussians, Konrad Adenauer once said that the Prussian Herrenhaus had a higher standard of debate than the *Bundestag* in Bonn, by virtue of its hand-picked membership.[90] This has also been the experience of countless British politicians put out to grass in the House of Lords. It is worth noting, too, that until 1918 and even 1945, the British suffrage, with its plural votes and university votes, was not much more democratic than the Prussian.

The 'Red Czar of Prussia', Otto Braun, was the most prominent Prussian Socialist of the Weimar years. Braun was born in Königsberg in 1872, the son of a cobbler who had fallen on hard times after his return from the Franco-Prussian War. His mother was the daughter of an agricultural worker from Wehlau, also in East Prussia. Throughout Braun's life the interests of his remote native region and those of Prussia as a whole were uppermost in his mind. With his great height and fine manners, Braun's ancestry was the cause of some speculation among his parliamentary colleagues: the Conservative politician Hermann Pünder thought that the nurses had mixed up the cradles when he was born: 'He should have been put in a count's cot.'[91] Braun left school at the age of fourteen and went to work in a lithographic studio. Two years later he joined the Socialists, then a rather middle-class body dominated by Kantian professors from the university and a group of Lutherans led by the Landtag deputy, Julius Rupp, the grandfather of the painter and printmaker Käthe Kollwitz. Rupp's Socialism had a strong religious stamp – 'the promised brotherhood of mankind' – which Rupp communicated not only to his son-in-law, Carl Schmidt, but also to his talented granddaughter.[92]

The population of Königsberg had swollen in the second half of the nineteenth century. The incidence of poverty was high and many members of the working classes were tempted by the left-wing parties. This was in strong contrast to the rest of agricultural East Prussia, which was a rural backwater dominated by huge Junker estates. The volatility of Königsberg was brought home to Miss Topham when she and the Kaiserin had to be rescued from a curious and increasingly hostile crowd when they strayed into the slums beside the railway station.[93]

History does not relate whether Braun was among the crowd of Socialists and 'Polish Jews' who heckled Her Majesty, but Braun was from early on an agitator for the cause and in 1893 he fulfilled his Conservative mother's prophecy and went to jail for ten days. He had by now swopped lithography for journalism and printed and edited his own sheet, the *Ostpreussische Landbote*. During those years he came into contact with the landowning Junkers for the first time as he stirred up the agricultural labourers and stood against a Graf Dohna for a working-class district of Königsberg, polling forty per cent of the vote. Braun was only defeated in the run-off.[94]

Braun's only son was killed in the Battle of the Mazurian Lakes. The First World War had a silver lining, however, in that it brought to an end the three-class suffrage, and the rule of the Kaiser and the Junkers. Braun had no desire to see the end of Prussia, as some of his less Borussophile colleagues were about to find out. Braun was to insist on Prussia's preservation to the end of his time as Minister-President in 1932, and in his own way he sought to develop, even expand, Prussia beyond its pre-1918 borders. He found little sympathy outside Prussia. The Weimar constitution, while retaining the former Prussian provinces together with the Landtag, imposed the *'clausulae antiborussicae'* on the upper chamber or Staatsrat: though Prussia was two-thirds of Germany, it was limited to two-fifths of the vote. This meant that Prussia had one vote in the Reichsrat per 1,412,000 of the population, where it took 127,000 Lübeckers and 98,000 inhabitants of Lippe.[95]

The main Socialist tenets of the Weimar constitution would have troubled Braun but little: the abolition of the Herrenhaus;

the scrapping of the three-class suffrage; the outlawing of noble titles; the secularisation of the state; not to mention the departure of the Hohenzollerns. A new problem now arose: the far left and the revolution. 'We really did not fight for decades against the dictatorship and brutal administration [*Säbelherrschaft*] of the Prussian Junkers to be burdened with the same sort of minority rule by the Spartakists and their independent allies [USPD].'[96] It was the old story of the limited revolution which allowed the new rulers to hang on to their creature comforts and to be able to hand them on to their heirs.

Braun also wished to preserve Prussia intact against the many non-Prussian voices who thought the time had come to create a unified Germany. His solution was to *expand* Prussia, to carry its message even further, to encompass the rest of Germany as yet unprussified. Braun had not reckoned with the Allies, who saw the Prussians as the instigators of the war, and intended to make the most of their opportunity to redraw its borders. Braun was firm in his opposition to Versailles. After the Nazi *Machtergreifung* someone asked him how it had been possible to seize power and destroy the Weimar state so easily. Braun replied, 'Moscow and Versailles.'[97]

Until the terms arrived, Braun, like the other Majority Socialists, had been fairly optimistic. Noske, for example, had reconciled himself to the loss of Alsace-Lorraine, minor territorial adjustments in Schleswig-Holstein in the areas where Danes were in a majority, or indeed in a few parts of the Prussian east, where the people were overwhelmingly Polish. He also foresaw indemnity payments to France and Belgium. What he had not envisaged was the cession of Memel and parts of East Prussia, the transformation of Danzig and parts of West Prussia into a 'free state' and the creation of the Polish Corridor.[98] Braun thought they would also lose the German colonies.[99]

Like the other Socialists (including the Independents) Braun was appalled when he heard the terms. 'It is simply mad!' he told a bourgeois deputy in Weimar. 'I can hardly believe it is so hot in Paris in May, for at a normal temperature this short-sighted, hate-

filled monstrosity could not be hatched. It almost appears that the cry which is passing through every nation at the moment, "No more war" is being suppressed by its very opposite: "War again soon." '[100]

Braun continued to speak against the treaty. In Lyck in the Mazurian Lakes, he called it 'the most shameless betrayal in the history of the world'; it was 'completely unacceptable and must never be signed.'[101] Later he modified that defiant stance. The Allies might force the Germans to sign, but the Germans would never abide by the terms: 'Better a terrible end than terror without end,' said Braun.[102]

Braun was aware of just how hard the treaty would hit the democratic state of Prussia, now shorn of those Junker warmongers who might have encouraged the Kaiser in his policy.* While Bavaria stood to lose a few square kilometres to the French-controlled Saar, Prussia lost a fifth of its territory, including thirty-five per cent of the state-owned domains, twenty-two per cent of the state forests and sixty-five to seventy per cent of its mines in Upper Silesia and the Saar. The last alone were worth 36 milliard gold marks. Prussia would have to find homes for the farmers whose land had been awarded to Poland: roughly a quarter of the pre-war figure. More, the Allies were demanding that two and a half million cows be rounded up and given in compensation.[103] To Eduard Bernstein, who had the gall to suggest that Poland might have an historic right to Memel, Upper Silesia and Mazuria, Braun exploded with fury: 'Rubbish!' He reminded Bernstein that if this was the case then he must recognise the German right to Alsace-Lorraine: 'It is nothing to do with questions of historical right, but with Wilson's solemnly sworn right to self-determination . . .'[104]

The Weimar Republic was to be eaten away from the left and the right. On 12 January 1920 there was an attempt to storm the Reichstag from the left which ended up with a shoot-out on the

* Not that Braun would have accepted that Prussia had been guilty of starting the war. It had been important for the Socialists to believe that the war had been fought in self-defence.

Marion Gräfin Dönhoff,
former editor of *Die Zeit*.

Prince Louis Ferdinand of Prussia,
the current pretender, photographed
in the 1930s.

Two views of Königsberg Cathedral: as it was, and as it is today.

The novelists Theodor Fontane and Gustav Freytag. The Neuruppin-born Fontane's novels charted the decline of Prussian virtue in the last years of the 19th century. The Silesian Freytag also warned Prussians of the consequences of Empire.

The Saxon general's son Heinrich von Treitschke, who saw the Prussian army as the marrow of German unity.

The Brunswick-born Oswald Spengler defined Prussian socialism in his influential work, *Preussentum und Sozialismus*.

The last President
of the Weimar
Republic: Paul von
Hindenburg
und von
Beneckendorff, the
hero of
Tannenberg.

Hermann Göring,
Prussia's last
Minister-President,
complete with his
pour le mérite, the
top Prussian
military decoration
he won as a First
World War air ace.

The trooping of the colours in Tempelhof.
The parade ground is now covered by Berlin's inner-city airport.

Changing the guard at Schinkel's Neue Wache on Unter den Linden.

The Garrison Church as it was.
Gaertner's painting of 1840.

The Garrison Church in 1959.
Despite the bombing of April 1945
it could have been restored
but was wantonly demolished
as late as 1968.

The Stadtschloss as it was. The ruins were demolished in 1960.

The romantic side of Potsdam before the bombing: the canals.

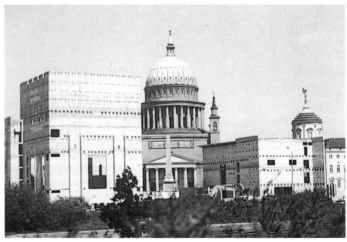

Potsdam soon after the fall of the DDR. The projected theatre building which obscured the view of Schinkel's Nikolaikirche has now been demolished.

Wilhelmine magnificence in Szczecin (the former Stettin).

The Prussian poor lived in *Mietskaserne* such as these to the north of the modern city centre.

The Kaiserhaus in Posnań (the former Posen). Completed in 1910 at a cost of six million RMs, it was described by Princess Marie Radziwiłł as 'a monstrosity, a pile of stones devoid of any semblance of architecture'. It is now the city's art centre.

A huge barracks building in Wrocław (Breslau) in 1992.

Magdeburg Cathedral as it was.

A rare survivor of fine architecture
in the city centre.

Halle: grandeur, and decline.

steps. Two months later it was the turn of the right and Wolfgang Kapp. The Kapp Putsch proved a humiliating experience for the Majority Socialist. In the Chancellery that morning he interpreted Seeckt's 'self-satisfied smile' as an indication that he was on the side of the *Putschisten*. It was only his wife who could convince him to flee to Dresden rather than submit to arrest by some 'rascal lieutenant with a unit of mutinous troops'.[105]

Braun thought he could sit things out at his home in Friedenau, in the south of Berlin, but as he left his official residence, which lay alongside the Ministry of Agriculture, he saw just such a 'rascal' with his troop advancing on the ministry. 'The officer greeted him politely and asked whether this was the entrance to the Prussian Ministry of Agriculture. Braun replied no less obligingly and told him that the door he required was a few metres further on . . .'[106] With this, Braun made rapid tracks in the opposite direction and the nearest railway station. He just had time to catch the next train to Dresden. Later he had to shave off his goatee beard and head for Stuttgart, while his Junker enemies prepared to take over Prussian agriculture: Braun was to retain a particular animus against the Pomeranian Hans-Jürgen von Dewitz and the East Prussian Freiherr von Wangenheim for their parts in the coup.

When the dust settled Braun became Prussian Minister-President and over the next dozen years the most stable element in the short and tragic history of the Weimar Republic. The gap, however, between Prussia and the Reich began to widen so that there were fewer and fewer contacts between the Prussian Ministry of State and the Reichs Chancellery on the opposite side of the Wilhelmstrasse. In the old Reich the Prussians had retained almost everything in their own portfolio with the exception of the navy and the post office. Under the Weimar constitution the Reich took over the army, the railways, the canals, the customs and a large part of Reich finance and social welfare. Justice, police, schools and local administration were the responsibilities of the individual state governments. Even despite the *clausulae antiborus-*

sicae Prussia retained enormous power and it was only with the greatest difficulty that the Reich could move against it.

Braun saw his job as defending Prussia against every move to break it down into more manageable units.[107] In this he was opposed by Erich Koch-Weser, who like the writer of the Weimar constitution Hugo Preuss, believed it was high time that Prussia be merged into Germany 'as Brandenburg had been amalgamated into Prussia'.[108] Koch-Weser pursued his goal with determination, but Braun was able to use the Reichsrat to good effect. He would agree to Prussia's dismantling only if Bavaria and Württemberg were also broken up. Naturally neither of the Catholic south German states was prepared to consent to this and Koch-Weser's scheme was checked. This was all Braun's work: both in 1919 and again before he took over the Minister-Presidency in January 1920, the Prussian government had been in agreement with the Reichs Ministry of the Interior that Prussia would be broken up.[109]

Braun defended his stance with an argument which harked back to the Treaty of Vienna: Prussia was necessary as a guarantee of Germany's borders. The Rhineland might easily fall to France, still anxious to acquire the left bank it had coveted since the French Revolution; Poland was as keen as ever to lay its hands on the eastern provinces. Braun had also to face strong separatist tendencies within the old Prussian provinces: the Rhineland, East Prussia, Hanover and Upper Silesia were all, for often very different reasons, anxious to rid themselves of Prussian government. Upper Silesia was the biggest trouble spot of the lot: an almost entirely Catholic province with a mixed German-Polish population ruled over exclusively by Prussian Protestants.

In October 1919 Upper Silesia had been detached from Lower Silesia in an attempt to deal with the problems arising from its different population structure. The Poles continued to woo the Upper Silesians, promising them autonomy within the Polish state. In July 1920 they granted Upper Silesia total autonomy (although they had yet to receive a square inch of Silesian territory). Given the unpopularity of the Prussian administration, Koch-Weser thought the best solution was to play the Polish game and offer Upper Silesia independence from Prussia. This would also have the advantage of showing the Prussians that times had changed.

The situation in Upper Silesia was further complicated by the actions of the Allies who had decided on a referendum. The results of the poll on 20 March 1921 gave 707,122 votes for Germany and 433,514 for Poland. On 20 October that same year the Allies decided to split the territory in two, awarding the richer, industrialised eastern part to Poland and the poorer, rural half to Germany. Many of the Poles in the east had settled there only because that was where the work was to be found. Braun was keener than ever that the remaining half would not be taken away from Prussia. On 22 March 1922 he made a fierce speech in Breslau to that effect. The real change in Upper Silesian attitudes, however, came only with the change to a gentler, more sensitive administration in the province, where Father Carl Ulitzka was campaigning for more recognition for the Catholics. In May the four *Landräte* were replaced by Catholic nominees of the Centre Party. Upper Silesia appeared satisfied: in September that year ninety-one per cent of the inhabitants of the Western part voted to remain Prussian and not to join the Reich as an autonomous province.[110]

This was Braun's moment of triumph: 'The Upper Silesian vote is a declaration in favour of the new republican and democratic Prussia.'[111] He felt vindicated in his view that what Germany wanted was not the scrapping of Prussia, but an expanded Prussia to act as a bond to hold Germany's disparate elements together. It was an argument in the purest Bismarckian tradition and Braun should be acknowledged as having done as much to keep Prussia going during Weimar as Hindenburg did for the Reich as a whole. One of Braun's most remarkable sides was his determination to pick up some of Germany's smallest territories and bring them under the Prussian umbrella. Waldeck-Pyrmont had fallen to Prussia in 1919. When changes in finance policy began to threaten the federal states of Thuringia, the two Mecklenburgs, Oldenburg, Anhalt, Lippe and Schaumburg-Lippe, Braun thought his moment had come. When the Finance Minister of Mecklenburg-Schwerin came to Braun for support, Braun asked him, 'When are you going to begin negotiating to join our state?'[112]

If some Germans were astounded by Braun's devotion to Prussia, others were baffled by the apparent bosom friendship between the new President, Field Marshal von Hindenburg, and the Königsberg printer. Braun later let it be known that there was little truth in the story that he and Hindenburg had become friendly. After Hindenburg's election in April 1925, Braun refused to fly the Prussian and German flags from Prussian ministry buildings, a gesture which even his closest supporters found unnecessarily petty. Hindenburg went out of his way to try to understand the position of Prussia's Socialist rulers, and with Braun himself he had a shared passion: shooting. At their first meeting Braun pointed out that the number of elk in East Prussia had doubled since the end of the war. This instigated a long discussion on the joys of elk-shooting. After Braun left the President's office, Hindenburg told an aide, 'Do you know, one can be very poorly informed about people sometimes? My friends in Hanover told me that Otto Braun was a fantastic troublemaker. Now I see that he is a completely reasonable man with whom one might discuss anything.'[113]

Myths grew up around their alleged friendship. The press reported long drinking sessions during which they exchanged hunting anecdotes. Braun was said to have deterred Hindenburg from resigning on his eightieth birthday. Unlike most republican politicans, Braun showed no fear of the Junker. Hindenburg was a colossal man standing 1.86 metres, but Braun was considerably taller, so that observers wondered which was the aristocrat and which the humble worker. In the Prussian state hunting reserve of Schorfheide to the east of Berlin, the two men shared the right to relax with a gun, but not together. Braun was quite categorical about this: Hindenburg was old and heavy on his feet, 'his hearing was poor and his sight was no longer good; but that was not important, he had old Prussian spunk, and that was the main thing.'[114]

Shared hunting interests could not keep such different men on good terms for ever and Hindenburg and Braun fell out over the latter's settlement policy in East Prussia. Heinrich Brüning also had problems with the President. He had great respect for him as a soldier, but disliked his political passivity and declined all invitations to the President's palace. As was well known, Hindenburg believed he was holding the nation in trust for the Hohenzollern restoration, an issue which left Brüning largely cold: 'I'm not disturbed by the idea of bringing back the monarchy,' he told the field marshal, 'but the things which would then have to be done in the realms of financial and social policy would be so unpopular that they could not help but sully the monarchy ... The restoration must come after the reforms.'[115]

As the economic situation worsened at the end of the decade, Braun also ceased to find common ground with the President. He reverted to tactless acts, such as scrapping the state subsidy to the Imperial Union Club. ('Prussia is ruled in an unbelievable way,' said Hindenburg. 'I can't imagine that my friend Braun would have gone along with this.'[116]) The final straw was Braun's banning of the Stahlhelm in Rhineland-Westphalia, an organisation of old soldiers with a strongly monarchist inclination. Hindenburg was an honorary member. Then there was Braun's *idée fixe*: the East Prussian estates.

Braun was frustrated that despite the revolution and Weimar the big estates were still there, with 1155 over 1000 hectares in the Grenzmark (the bits of Posen and West Prussia which had been granted to Germany after Versailles) and Pomerania alone. Braun thought that his effort to settle the land were being sabotaged by behind-the-scenes deals with prominent Junkers – Oldenburg-Januschau in particular.[117] He believed the Januschauer had coined the term 'Siedlungsbolschevismus' (settlement bolshevism) to describe the project currently being pursued both by Braun and the government commissioner for *Osthilfe*, Schlange-Schöningen. Once again Braun's intention was not to wreck East Prussia, far from it: he became 'sentimental'[118] at the mention of his native region, and felt that unless something were done, it would be swallowed up by Poland and Lithuania. He had not altered his position on the Corridor. In November 1930 he described it as a 'barb in the body of the German nation which stood in the way of true peace in Europe'.[119] The new settlements in East Prussia would strengthen the region and prevent the Poles from carrying out their plans to annex it.

Sadly for Braun, the stock market crash meant that he was now increasingly short on the necessary funds to see his project come to fruition. Brüning had had to take over responsibility for *Osthilfe*, and that with a heavy heart. There was also a bigger problem brewing as a direct result of the economic situation: the growing strength of the Nazi Party in the Prussian Landtag and the destruction of Braun's parliamentary majority.

Nazism had been slow to hit Prussia. Braun had early on dismissed it as a Bavarian phenomenon. As late as 1928 it was largely unknown in Prussia, where the right was represented by the traditionalist DNVP. Even in 1930, Braun's Minister for the Interior, Carl Severing, expressed the hope that Prussia might once again save Germany as it had done during the Wars of Liberation by defeating the Hitlerites. From 1928 Hitler had begun to turn his attentions to Prussia. On 16 November of that year he gave his first big speech in the Sportpalast in Berlin and in May 1929 he repeated the performance in Königsberg. At the time there were just six Nazi members of the Landtag.

Prussia took a long time to die. It had received a wound in 1871 which had robbed it of its strength; 1918 looked like being fatal, but Prussia had rallied under the unlikely figure of the 'Red Czar' Otto Braun; in 1932 came the '*Preussenschlag*' – the blow to Prussia – when the state was deprived of its representative government. After 1932 there were still Prussians, but Prussia itself ceased to have any influence on Germany's destiny.

The *Preussenschlag* was a dress rehearsal for Hitler's takeover just six months later. In both cases it is striking how few people were prepared to lift a finger to preserve a democratic body. It is not surprising that both the Nazis and the Communists should have difficulty concealing their joy at the destruction of Prussian government, but it was not only the extremists who participated to the tragic events of that July: Braun's Socialists were as tired and lethargic as their leader, worn out by the unequal task; the Centre Party did not even look into the question of strike action or calling out its paramilitary organisations. Instead it set its sights on the general election and left Prussia to die. For Adenauer in Cologne it was the time to settle an old score with Braun, who had put the dampeners on his attempts to lead a Rhineland separatist movement in the early 1920s. Adenauer was now President of the Prussian Staatsrat. It was a simple, sweet and very short-sighted revenge.[120]

The Centre Party remained strong in Prussia right up to the elections of 24 April 1932, effectively dominating in the Rhineland, Westphalia, Sigmaringen and Upper Silesia[121], and despite the turbulent relations between Prussia and the Reich, Braun's government remained one of Brüning's most important props.[122] Braun was exhausted. On 22 April he fell ill. Two days later came the fatal elections. Prussia was just the last in the series. Bavaria and Saxony had been deadlocked since the summer of 1930, with ungovernable majorities; Hessen and Hamburg in October 1931; and Württemberg in March 1932. The results in Berlin were no different: the left and centre parties dropped to 163 seats, while the Nazis rose to 162. To achieve a majority they needed to borrow only nine members of the DNVP. 'The bankruptcy of the parliamentary system was obvious.'[123]

Despite their inauspicious beginnings in Prussia the Nazis had gained in strength and popularity. Operating from his cramped 'opium den' in the Potsdamerstrasse, Goebbels had attracted converts through his newspaper *Der Angriff.* While Goebbels worked on the man in the street, Göring found converts among the upper classes. It was he who won over Auwi Hohenzollern. Together with the Communists the Nazis now began their campaign to disrupt the chamber and make the *Landtag* unworkable. On 25 May there was the famous '*Saalschlacht*' – a punch-up in the assembly. The Nazis declared it a victory and Goebbels was proud to note in his diary: 'Eight badly wounded in the different parties, this example will be a warning to them and should make them respect us.'[124] It was followed by a vote of no-confidence in Braun tabled by the Communists. On 30 May Brüning resigned, unable to obtain the special powers from Hindenburg which would allow him to govern by decree. It was now the turn of Franz von Papen and his so-called 'cabinet of gentlemen' composed in the main of reactionary noblemen.[125] Four days later Braun went on sick leave. He cleared his desk of papers and the walls of his office of antlers and, handing over to his deputy, Hirtseifer, retired to his house in Berlin-Zehlendorf.[126]

Braun's departure did not stop the trouble in the *Landtag*. The fights continued and debates were cancelled out by singing matches between the Communists and the Nazis; the *International* against the *Horst-Wessellied*. On 21 June, the Nazi Landtag leader, Hans Kerrl, demanded a Nazi Minister-President for Prussia. Pressure was put on the Prussian police to lift their ban on uniform parades. The Crown Prince appealed to Schleicher to ban the Communist Party. On 8 July, after a call from the future head of the Nazi 'People's Court' Roland Freisler, for a trial of the Berlin police chiefs (including Goebbels' chief bugbear, the despised Jew Bernhard Weiss), order broke down entirely. On this day 'the history of Prussia as a democratic state came to an end'.[127]

Demands were increasing from the right to wind up the Prussian *Landtag*. Papen went to Hindenburg at Neudeck and told him that there had been secret talks between the Communists and the Prussian government. This was not true. The only talks which had taken place had been between the head of the Prussian secret police, Rudolf Diels, and the Communists Kasper and Torgler. Hindenburg demanded proof.[128] Presumably Papen was able to make something of Diels' discussions which satisfied the President. On 18 July Hindenburg threatened to call off a state visit to the Rhineland if the ban on the Stahlhelm were not lifted. That same day the ex-Haketist, Alfred Hugenberg, demanded the replacement of the Prussian Minister-President by a commissar appointed by the President.

This is precisely what took place two days later. On 18 July Hirtsiefer and Severing had asked for a conference with Papen on the 20th. Papen's last talk with Hindenburg had taken place on 14 July, when the President had given him full powers to act as he wished. State Secretary Meissner foresaw the need to avoid a general strike of the sort which had played such an important role in bringing down the Kapp Putsch. When Hirtseifer and Severing arrived they were faced by Papen and the Minister of the Interior, Gayl. They were informed that due to the breakdown of order and security in Prussia, the government was suspended under Article 48, sections 1 and 2 of the Weimar constitution. Severing pointed out the illegality of this move. For Article 48 to be invoked there would have to be proof that the government had abused the law or the constitution. Severing refused to stand down, and told the ministers that they would have to arrest him. The leading ministers were sacked while Papen and Gayl gave way to Nazi demands and had the police chiefs arrested. They were subsequently released.[129] Later that day Papen spoke on the air-waves to justify his action. In Planck's press conference it was revealed that there had been an attempted *coup d'état* from the left.[130]

In the provinces the government sacked the Prussian officials who stood close to the Braun regime: out went the chiefs in Lower Silesia, Frankfurt/Oder, Liegnitz, Magdeburg, Königsberg, Merseburg; the Vice-President in Oppeln and the Police Presidents of Königsberg, Kiel, Cologne, Elbing, Oppeln and Magdeburg. The Nazis and the Communists were over the moon: it was a triumph. In the case of the latter, this short-sightedness was particularly poignant.

Behind the whole move stood the figure of the scheming *frondeur* and Staff Officer, Kurt von Schleicher; whispering to Papen and Gayl that they should not neglect to occupy police headquarters to prevent any resistance there. It was General Gerd von Rundstedt who carried out the security operation. The state of Prussia was now dead.

Subject Peoples

Victor Amadeus of Sardinia to his son, Charles Emmanuel: 'My son, you must consume the [Duchy of] Milan like an artichoke: leaf by leaf.'

Poland is an elected monarchy, at the death of its kings there are always troubles from factions. We must take advantage of this and gain by its neutrality, here a city, there another district, until the whole country has been consumed.

Frederick the Great, Testament
politique, quoted in Gaxotte ed.,
Frédéric II, 334.

When times were good, men chose to be Prussian; when the chips were down, Prussians defected *en masse*. Then there were those who had little choice in the matter: subject races in the east: Prusai, Wends, Poles, Lithuanians and Cassubians; the so-called *Beutepreussen* or 'booty Prussians' who had arrived with every extension of Prussian territory. In the west, too, Hanoverians, Hessians, Schleswigers, Holsteiners, Frankfurters, Saxons and Rhinelanders all fell to Prussia and all then had cause to regret the fact when the authorities in Berlin behaved with their habitual want of tact or consideration.

The Rhineland was Prussian from 1815, but the attitude of its liberal, Catholic population was not always so well disposed towards its governors. Konrad Adenauer's separatist tendencies after the First World War are well known. There is a story that the later Chancellor of the Bundesrepublik's father had been found, badly wounded, on the battlefield of Königgrätz with an Austrian standard in his hand. He was promoted lieutenant on the spot, but he declined the commission: his family were humble folk from Cologne, Adenauer *père* was engaged to be married and couldn't hope to raise the money to pay the 'caution', or payment to regimental funds required from all married Prussian officers.[1]

The hero's son became a member of the Prussian Herrenhaus when he was elected *Oberbürgermeister* or lord mayor of Cologne in 1917. Under the Weimar Republic Konrad Adenauer also played a significant role in the Prussian Staatsrat which succeeded the Herrenhaus in its functions. Adenauer never relished the prospect of travelling to Berlin. There is a story that as soon as the sleeper crossed the Elbe, he would pull down the blind and turn his head to the wall. *'Hier beginnt Asien!'* he said.*[2]

Travelling yet further into the 'core provinces' of Prussia, one Rhenish Reichstag deputy was deeply perplexed by the barrenness of the land after the crowded valleys of his fertile homeland. After hour upon hour of potato fields and pine forests he turned to his companion and asked, 'Where do these people who have been ruling us for so many years actually live?'[3] Stories attesting to the hatred of the 'civilised' west Germans for their 'barbaric' eastern rulers abound after 1866. There was an old joke in Frankfurt/ Main, that when you wanted to know where the city boundaries ended and Prussia began, all you had to do was to stick your fingers into the river: 'When it begins to stink, it is Prussia!'[4]

The Prussian army had behaved particularly badly in Frankfurt in 1866, but in general it would be impossible to make out that the Prussians behaved in their German provinces like an imperial power ruling over subject races.[5] Even in the east there were those who rarely raised their voices against Prussian rule. Despite all attempts to give them political motivation on the part of the Poles, the Cassubians of eastern Pomerania and West Prussia remained largely indifferent to them. Nor did this situation change much once the Poles had achieved dominion over the Cassubians: as Anna Koljaiczek puts it in Günter Grass's *Die Blechtrommel* (The Tin Drum), 'For you can't get rid of the Cassubians, they have to

---

* He borrowed the line from Metternich, who applied it – a little more realistically – to the Landstrasse to the east of Vienna's old city wall.

stay in there and stick out their little heads so that the others can clout them, because our lot isn't properly Polish and it isn't German enough either and if you're a Cassubian that's not good enough for the Germans or the Polacks.'[6]

With time the Cassubians would probably have been assimilated in much the same way as the Prusai in East Prussia. The Prusai were not the only non-German group in that distant Baltic territory: there were Mazurians and Lithuanians, too. Both had followed the Prussian path to Lutheranism, both continued to use their own languages in their own homes (Mazurian was a Polish-German *patois* largely unintelligible to either German or Pole). Both were generally loyal to Prussia and resisted attempts by the Poles and the Lithuanians to pull them over to their causes. The Lithuanians resisted rather less than the Mazurians, but then the Allies in Versailles were not offering the Mazurians anything more than the chance to become Polish. The Lithuanians, on the other hand, were to have their own state.

In some parts of eastern East Prussia and Mazuria, German, Lithuanian and Mazurian were spoken,[7] but the main Lithuanian enclaves were on the Memel River. In the 1830s, Memel had two main churches, one for its German population and the other for the Lithuanians,[8] and at the end of the century a Dr Gailagat represented Lithuanian interests in the *Landtag*. Perhaps because they were Protestants, the 30,000 Prussian Lithuanians showed little sign of being overjoyed when they were sent to join their Catholic cousins in 1919 as Memel was detached from East Prussia and awarded to the new Lithuanian sovereign state.[9]

Prussia's greatness had been achieved by colonisation, and the promise of further territorial acquisition was always considered a useful sop to the Prussian, and later German, people. Colonies, it was believed, could even forestall demands for reform of the archaic suffrage and spike the ever-growing success of the Socialists up and down the land. Had not Bismarck scuppered the power of the National Liberals by his successful wars and by effecting that German unification so dear to the men on the left?

Surely if the German army could bring back a large portfolio of new provinces there would be a period in which the noisy cries of the Socialists would be drowned by the chorus of patriotic devotion? This is what William II's advisors believed at the outbreak of the Great War and the diaries of his Chief of the Naval Cabinet, Müller, contain an unending litany of patriotic Prussians running to the Kaiser to suggest some new province which might become the jewel in the German crown.

In October 1915 we meet a German Balt called Silvio Broedrich who calls on the Kaiser to annex the Baltic territories of Russia.[10] In December it is the turn of Professor von Schultze-Gaevernitz who wishes to draw His Majesty's attention to Flanders (France was to get Wallonia).[11] In August 1916 a project was mooted to swap German Lorraine and northern Alsace for the industrial area of Briey to the north-west of Metz.[12] In April 1917, the war aims had become so grossly inflated that Müller thought them absurd: Courland and Lithuania, a large 'independent' Poland 'bound by military pact to Germany' but with cession of some territory to Germany. In return the Poles were to be offered East Galicia and half of Moldavia, while Austria was to be compensated with parts of Serbia and Romania. In the west Germany was to control Belgium and annex Liège and the coast (there was some talk of a ninety-nine year lease). Germany was to have Briey, too. The French would receive compensation in the shape of a chunk of southern Alsace, near the town of Belfort.[13]

Helfferich wasn't half as greedy: he thought a Polish buffer state and autonomy for Lithuania and Courland (with guarantees for the German populations) were enough. Moltke (the younger) was keen to award the Falkland Islands to Argentina after the war, presumably in retaliation for the German naval setback which occurred there in 1914. The Kaiser also wanted Malta, the Azores and Dakar.[14] Müller thought the Kaiser and his friends were living in cloud-cuckooland, but he was not opposed to all boundary changes and agreed with Gwinner of the Deutsche Bank that Poland should be returned to Russia but that Libau on the Courland coast should be retained. He also had his eyes on the

Belgian railway network and the Briey Basin. France was to be compensated in Alsace.[15]

Prussian and later German foreign policy was divided up between the 'easterners' and the 'westerners': those who thought policy should be based on an alliance with France or Britain and those who advocated closer ties with Russia. Prussia's interests were to secure her eastern borders, as these were always more likely to cause her trouble than her western ones before 1815. Frederick the Great was categorical about this: alliances were made on the basis of disabling the most dangerous foe. 'We are allied to Russia because she backs on to us in [East] Prussia and for as long as that arrangement lasts we have nothing to fear from the Swedes attacking us in Pomerania.' The situation could change, wrote Frederick, but Russia would always remain Prussia's best ally.[16]

The old Prussian friendship with Russia was to some extent based on proximity. As Frederick made clear, Prussia and Russia had a common border on the Memel River and to the east of East Prussia. Pastor Rehsener, whose cure was in Memel, was visited in the first quarter of the nineteenth century by a brother avid to see Russia. He 'went to the border on foot, but without a passport they wouldn't let him cross'. Checked in his desires, the young man picked up a pebble and threw it over the border post: 'He wanted to be able to say at least that he had thrown a stone into the Russian Empire.'[17] Many Germans – and not just German Balts – fought in the Russian army: Bismarcks, Mansteins and Schwerins, to name just three families, all played significant roles in the military history of both nations. Even in the First World War a large percentage of the Russian field commanders were of German stock.[18]

One famous name who fought with the Russian army was Carl von Clausewitz. Clausewitz was a classic easterner who saw a terrible danger for Prussia were Russia to liberalise its policy towards Poland. An independent Poland would be a natural ally of the French; a catastrophe which would end up with the two enemies of Prussia 'shaking hands at the Elbe'.[19] The great Moltke, was not as keen on Russia. The Russians, he wrote 'are unpleasant neighbours, they have absolutely nothing that one might desire of them after a victorious war. They don't have any money and we have no need of land.'[20] Poland, on the other hand, Moltke saw as a useful ally in a war against Russia. He nonetheless had reservations about the re-creation of the Polish state which would be 'the first great reversal of the European colonisation of the East'.[21] Moltke believed that Prussia had brought the Poles order and civilisation after the partitions.

Bismarck, too, was an easterner. Not only was the Russian alliance the cornerstone of his foreign policy, but he realised the advantage of such a pact in keeping down the rebellious tendencies of the Poles. The implications of the Prusso-Russo-Austrian alliance were not lost on the Poles themselves. In 1867 Władysław Czartóryski wrote: 'Prussia's might, underpinned by Moscow, falls on us as a double burden. Prussia ruling over a united Germany and with its hand stretched out to its Austrian brother would bind us with an iron fist, severing us from the west by an insurmountable wall.' Czartóryski goes on to say that in the security of its system of alliances, the three powers could then set about annihilating the Poles.[22]

Hans von Seeckt lived long enough to see a Polish state emerge after the First World War. Acutely anti-Polish, he saw the creation of an independent Poland as part of a French plot to eternalise the second front; 'continuing rape' he called it.[23] He directed particular venom at the Corridor created in 1919 to give Poland access to the sea, thereby cutting East Prussia off from the Reich. This, said Seeckt, had the effect of turning not just the two states 'but every single inhabitant' into mortal enemies. The aim was to create 'an unendurable situation', whereby the Poles would eventually pluck both Danzig and East Prussia like 'ripe fruit' from a tree. Seeckt pointed to the 'comedy' of Locarno, where significantly the borders of Germany had been guaranteed, but not those in the east. Seeckt was another easterner who saw in Russia 'the centre of world power and world destiny'. Not for nothing had this conservative Junker concluded a military deal with the Bolsheviks in the early years of Weimar.[24]

Most Prussians and Russians could see eye to eye with one another when it came to Poland. Neither had a great regard for the Poles. Even in 1945, when the Russians had defeated Hitler's armies and were busy shifting Poland to the west so that they might hang on to their booty from the Ribbentrop–Molotov Pact of 1939, Russians and Germans could enjoy a joke or two at the expense of the Poles. Magnus von Braun, like so many Junkers, spent some agonising months after the end of the war, waiting to find out whether his land was to become part of Germany or to be given to Poland. When he finally learned that Lower Silesia was to be occupied by Polish troops he despaired: they were even less disciplined than the Russians, he thought. When the Russian soldiers came up to the manor-house to confirm the report, Braun inadvertently dismissed the idea with a movement of his hand. 'The six or eight officers present fell about laughing and cheering.'[25]

The sad truth which both Prussians and Poles had to face up to was that if Prussia were to exist then Poland could not, and vice versa. As early as 1837, an anonymous journalist in the democratic journal *Polack* pointed out that Prussia, stripped of Silesia and its eastern provinces 'would be in no position to keep the Rhineland in order'.[26] Prussia reduced to just Brandeburg would be nothing more than a part of Germany. In 1848, the Polish nationalist Joachim Lelewel was at pains to prevent the Prussian parts of Poland being seen as part of a united Germany: their absorption would not just damage Poland, it would also weaken Germany.[27]

Germany as a nation state was quite a different matter from the colonial state of Prussia with its various subject peoples. As the process of unification speeded up in the 1860s the Poles began to worry. As the writer and journalist Maciej Wierzbinski pointed out in the middle of the Great War, 'The White Eagle will only rise out of the ruins of Prussia.' Germany would always be a danger as long as the fulcrum lay in Prussia and not further west.[28] During the plebiscites to determine the borders of the Polish state another journalist, Władysław Rabski, wrote, 'It's us or you ... without Silesia Germany cannot ... be dominated by Prussia. Without Silesia Poland will almost be a slave of Prussia; not a dam but a gateway to the east.'[29] Even in 1931 the battle was not over for M. Orzechowski: they needed to fight on for Oppeln, Danzig and East Prussia: 'No one in Poland has renounced these areas.'[30]*

Many Poles placed more faith in the Catholic, eastern-orientated, feudal Austria than they did in Prussia, and the Austrians tended to administer their Polish territories with a degree of liberalism unknown in either Russian or Prussian Poland. In 1933 the Polish Socialist Party thought that the promised *Anschluss* between the Reich and Austria would have the effect of weakening Prussian power by diluting the dominant Protestantism with a big dash of Catholicism.[31] The chief fear was of Russia, Poles liking to see themselves as the last bastion of civilisation before Europe degenerated into Asiatic Muscovy. The inferiority of Russia made Poles believe that there was a chance that Prussian attitudes towards them would change and that they would eventually begin to promote the idea of an independent Poland. To some extent this was the case when the Germans created a puppet Poland in the First World War.[32] Until quite late in the nineteenth century Poles believed that the Prussian sense of justice would lead them to liberate Poland and reject Russia. Bismarck was seen as the man who perverted Prussia away from the reasonable path – to some extent correctly.[33] In 1882 Bolesław Prus was still advocating the assumption of some of the Prussian virtues in the disputed territories: 'physical and intellectual power, thrift and solidarity'. Three years later his attitude had changed as a result of Bismarck's expulsion policy. The Prussian virtues were now 'falsehood, rapine, militarism and self-justification through success'.[34] Prus had witnessed the change in Prussian attitudes to the Poles. Formerly the negative approach had been confined to civil servants and schoolmasters who came into close contact with the Poles as a result of their work. By the 1880s it had spread to the whole of Prussian society.

* It is interesting that Orzechowski makes no mention of Lower Silesia and Pomerania.

II

The first to arrive were the Rugians, then came the Goths and the Gepidae, after them the Cassubians, from whom Oskar descended in a direct line. A little while later the Poles sent in Adalbert of Prague. He came bearing a cross and was axed to death by the Cassubians or the Prusai. That took place in a fishing village and the village was called Gyddanyzc. From Gyddanyzc people made Danczik, and then Danczig became Dantzig which was later written Danzig, and today Danzig is called Gdansk.[35]

Since the putative unification of the Germans . . . we don't know where the Germans end and the Prussians begin.[36]

In the eighteenth century Poland was still a huge empire ruling over its own large collection of subject peoples: Lithuanians, Little Russians, Ruthenians, Ukrainians, Moldavians, Czechs and Germans. Politically Poland was bankrupt, hindered by its individual, but fearfully weak, system of elected monarchy. The nobility or *szlachta* lived splendid lives, keeping up with the latest fashions to hit the nobilities of the west. The peasantry lived in abject misery.

There was never any love lost between the Poles and the Prussians, despite long centuries of neighbourhood. Silesia had fallen first to the Bohemians, then to the Austrians, and finally in the 1740s to the Prussians. Pomerania too had been overwhelmingly German since the early fifteenth century. In the seventeenth all question of Polish dominion had vanished as the territory was fought over by the Swedes and the Brandenburgers. By the mid-eighteenth the main areas of German colonisation had fallen to Prussia. There were however two last areas where there remained quantities of German farmer-peasants (known as *'Hauländer'* from their often Dutch origins) and noblemen. These were Great Poland (Wielkopolska), the future Grand Duchy of Posen and the Netze district; and West Prussia, where a good number of Junkers had clung on to their Germanity after the second Peace of Thorn. The main concentrations of Germans in West Prussia were in the towns and cities: Danzig, Thorn, Kulm, Marienburg, Marienwerder, and in the Ermland enclave in East Prussia, to the north of Allenstein and around the cathedral city of Frauenburg.

The *Hauländer* in the fields excited contempt from the Polish grandees, as did the incidence of Lutheranism in the German settled areas. Protestantism was known as 'the German faith'. 'A Pole is a lord, a German a vulgar fellow', 'the Devil spoke and dressed like a German',[37] 'uncouth', 'stingy', 'socially stiff', a 'vulgar preoccupation with money' were some of the accusations levelled at the Germans by members of the *szlachta*, revealing what were most likely business contacts with the merchants of the towns and cities who lost patience with the notorious ability of the Polish gentry to run up debts. In truth, however, the Junkers and the *szlachta* had their common points: they were both landed squires who had amassed land and a degree of independence while the monarchy was weak in the fourteenth and fifteenth centuries.[38]

Poland's chief German concern until the time of Frederick the Great was Saxony. Frederick's interests in the partitions were threefold: he wanted the areas of West Prussia and the Netze because he wanted a land bridge to East Prussia; he wanted control of the Weichsel River and Danzig, because he knew that all Polish trade was obliged to pass through the city and saw rich profits from the duties; he wanted more taxpayers and soldiers for his armies. Frederick had no great respect for the Poles. In 1771 he wrote to Voltaire to say that Poland would be carved up, and that it would be the fault of the 'stupidity of the Potockis, Krasińskis, Oginskis and that whole imbecile crowd whose names end in -ki'.[39]*

By the time the Poles became aware of Frederick's policy, it was already too late. From having been indifferent to Prussia in the past, the Polish attitude changed; the Polish historian Stan-

---

* In his poem, La Guerre des Confédérés (*Oeuvres*, vol. XIV, 1851, Berlin, 185–236) of 1771, Frederick describes the Poles as:
  La même encor [sic] qu'à la création,
  Brute, stupide et sans instruction,
  Staroste, juif, serf, palatin ivrogne,
  Tous végétaux qui vivaient sans vergogne.

isław Staszii described Prussia as an '[over]fed monster with a huge head', and Frederick as a duplicitous enemy with respect only for power and money. Naturally, the Jews were all Frederick's agents.[40]

The three partitions brought a good many Poles into the Prussias of Frederick the Great and Frederick William II; they also furnished the two kings with a yield of loyal Germans. In 1795, at the time of the Third Partition, the Germans outnumbered the Poles in the towns and cities of West Prussia, Great Poland and the Netze by 182,500 to 106,000. In West Prussia the figure was even greater in favour of the German-speaking population: 131,000 to 50,000. Only in Great Poland was the Catholic element greater: 35,000 to 28,000,[41] but some of the Catholics would have been Germans and a few of the Protestants Poles. Poles had hung on to most of the civic offices with the exception of the cities of Danzig, Elbing and Thorn. Danzig was very little Polish despite more than three centuries of paying homage to the Polish crown. There was scarcely a Polish houseowner and not a single Polish merchant. In Posen the merchants were chiefly Jews (307 out of 380), who outnumbered the Protestant population by three to two. In as far as Protestantism is an indication of race (it was not necessarily the case in Mazuria), Danzig was ninety per cent Protestant; Elbing, seventy per cent and Thorn fifty per cent.[42]

Later generations of Prussian administrators used language as a test rather than religion. In Marienwerder in south west Prussia in 1831, a survey showed that sixty-three per cent of the locality spoke German and thirty-seven per cent Polish. A similar poll taken in 1861 showed very similar results.[43] In Bromberg, where in the post-Vienna days the Prussians tolerated the existence of chiefly Polish *Landräte*, the Germans were the majority in five *Kreise*, but the Poles were indisputably in the majority across the board in both 1821 and 1838.[44]* By the mid-century the overwhelming majority of the population of Bromberg could speak

---

* In 1838 there were eleven Greek Orthodox in Bromberg; and in both 1821 and 1838, one Mennonite!

German, but despite the official figures, it is likely that the Polish element was still dominant, even in the city.[45] Despite this the Prussian authorities had behaved much like the British in Ireland, and had provided a Protestant pastor for every village.[46]

By the beginning of the Empire, Danzig's centre was ninety-nine per cent German; along with the cities and rural districts of Elbing and Marienburg. Dirschau was thirty per cent Polish and Preussisch Stargard as much as seventy-three per cent. The Cassubians dominated in Karthaus and Putzing.[47] Lastly it is worth stressing that the working-class population often travelled to where the lucrative work was to be found. Sometimes this made a nonsense of demographic surveys. To give one example, by the turn of the century there were between 30,000 and 45,000 Poles living within the administrative area of Düsseldorf. In three areas, Oberhausen, Alstaden and Hamborn, they represented more than twenty-five per cent of the population. There were 25,000 Mazurians in Essen at the same time who could not be induced to speak to their Polish neighbours.[48]

Until the often nefarious influence of social Darwinism crept into the equation, the attitude of Prussian administrators towards the Poles could best be described as impatient. The Poles were Catholics, liked to drink, were disorderly in dress and conduct and 'turbulent', to use a favourite word. The spendthrift, idle nature of the Polish grandees appalled the thrifty, sober-minded, middle-class Prussians who were sent out to run the *Landkreise* and *Regierungsbezirke* of the east. It was *not* considered a plum job. The similarities with the British administration in Ireland are striking.

True to his century, Frederick the Great thought the disagreeable side of his new Polish subjects could be educated out of them. While he believed that the best policy of all would be to rid West Prussia of its 'bad Polish stuff', he did not pursue a policy of expulsion. Instead he despatched schoolmasters in the hope of giving the Poles 'a Prussian character'.[49] The Poles were to be taught the nature of Prussian statecraft. German was introduced, but the Polish language (which Frederick had learned) was allowed to stand alongside. It was *Prussification* rather than Germanisation. There was no wide-ranging attempt to scrap the native culture as there was, say, in Bohemia after the Battle of the White Mountain.[50]

There were some exceptionally understanding administrators in the first half of the nineteenth century. The Kultusminister, Karl Friedrich Freiherr von Stein zum Altenstein, enacted a liberal policy which permitted Polish to be used in some faculties at the university and made no attempt to influence the religious practices of the Poles in the Grand Duchy of Posen (as Great Poland was now called). In 1822, Altenstein told officials in the Grand Duchy, 'Religion and mother tongue are the most sacred possessions of a nation. . . . The government which recognises, respects and protects them may be sure of winning the hearts of its subjects; but a government which shows itself indifferent to these, or even allows attacks on them, embitters and dishonours a nation and makes its members untrue and bad subjects. He who thought that it would contribute essentially to the cultural development of the Polish nation if it were Germanised, at least in speech, would find himself greatly in error.'[51] Altenstein believed that Polish should be used both in schools and before the courts, indeed even in the civil service itself.[52]

The government of Frederick William III insisted that there was no obstacle to Poles joining the civil service as long as they could speak German and knew the principles of Prussian law and administration[53]. The Polish revolution of 1830 put a stop to this process. *Oberpräsident* von Arnim called for an 'acceleration' of the process of teaching the Poles German and imbuing them with German culture in the wake of the revolt. In 1832, for the first time in the Grand Duchy, German was made the official language of communication within the administration. Naturally this led to increasing attacks in the Polish newspapers. 'The devil,' wrote one, 'the embodiment of evil, has from times immemorial, appeared in German costume, prefers to speak German and is variously called *niemczyk* [German].'[54]

The injustice in Arnim's case was that he very much approved the idea of building up the Grand Duchy of Posen to form the bulk of a buffer state between Prussia and Russia. In 1848, Arnim recognised that Polish cultural development in the Grand Duchy could not be repressed and advocated a joint German-Polish committee to find a solution. At the beginning the German population of the province were prepared to see a mixed regional assembly and administration as well as the introduction of Polish as an administrative language on a par with German. The first acts of violence, however, altered this view; Germans and Jews felt above all a need for protection from the Prussian army and administration.[55]

It was a sad reversal. In the early 1840s Frederick William IV had shown his desire to win the love of his subjects even in Posen. The liberalisation of the regime in the Grand Duchy had made it by far the most liberal part of Poland with a relatively free press and culture.[56] The eastern half of the Grand Duchy was still more than fifty per cent Polish (and twenty-five per cent Jewish), but the western end, especially the capital, Posen, was rapidly developing into a German provincial town. In the 1880s it was half German and a quarter Jewish. The Poles lived on the right bank of the Warthe by the cathedral, although their influence was apparent in the many Polish cultural institutions in the city centre, such as the Raczyński Library.[57] This German-Polish cohabitation was still evident during the Second World War when the art historian Udo von Alvensleben found a moment to explore its baroque treasures.[58]

The Grand Duchy still contained some enormous estates owned by families such as the Radziwiłłs, Czartoryskis, Sułkowskis, Raczyńskis and Działyńskis, some of which stretched well into the Grand Duchy of Warsaw. Members of the lesser Polish nobility found it in their hearts to co-operate with the Prussians: a General von Bogusławski became director of the Prussian Staff College. Fürst Anton Radziwiłł was after 1815 the Royal Prussian *Statthalter* in Posen. It was with his daughter Elisa that Prince William, the future King and Kaiser William I, fell in love, but was thwarted in his hopes of marriage by the stern dictates of Prussian household law.[59]

Much has also been made of the declaration by the Polish deputy Krzyanowski on 1 April 1871 on behalf of his Polish colleagues, to say that the Poles wanted to remain Prussian 'until God decides otherwise, we do not wish to be incorporated into the German Reich'.[60] The deputy was most certainly aware that being part of a German nation state was quite different from being a province of a 'synthetic' state like Prussia, and the chances of being able to secede or achieve autonomy were rather more distant than they had been before the creation of the Second Reich.

After the uprisings of 1830 and 1848 attitudes had changed. Prussian civil servants became increasingly wary of the Poles. A classic instance of this was that same Eduard Flottwell who had sat at the feet of Kraus in Königsberg. Flottwell was *Oberpräsident* of Posen from 1830 to 1841 and during that time developed an abiding hatred of Polish noblemen and priests. His dislike of Catholicism is all too clear: they were 'hypocrites', 'coarse', 'benighted', 'egotistical'; he also scorned the 'triumphal marches' of the Archbishop of Gnesen and Posen. It was at this time that Radziwiłł was dismissed as *Statthalter*, German was pushed in the schools and the courts and the remaining monasteries abolished and attached to the state-run *Gymnasiums*. Flottwell was also keen to get Germans to settle in the Grand Duchy. He laid his hands on some special state funds and used them to purchase bankrupt estates. His desire was to see a Junker element established in Posen.[61]

Flottwell was heavy-handed and tactless. In the provincial diets the Poles complained bitterly against his policies and more and more of them resigned from Prussian state service. It was Frederick William IV who put an end to Flottwell's reign: 'Your nationality is not to be undermined,' he told Count Edward Raczyński. In 1842 he promulgated the school ordinance which survived for another thirty years until a further spate of Pole-baiting came with Bismarck's *Kulturkampf*. A Catholic section was created in the Kultus Ministry in 1840 and chairs of Slavic

Literature and Philology established at the Universities of Berlin and Breslau. As the king put it, 'The French government has only succeeded in making good Frenchmen of the Alsatians by permitting them to remain German.'[62]

But the pendulum swung back again after the Revolution of 1848. The Poles were 'unteachable', they would never become good Prussians. It was therefore no concern of the administration if they disliked Prussian rule. The new attitude was summed up by the *Oberpräsident* von Puttkamer (himself from a family which had previously served the kings of Poland): '*Polentum* is and will remain an element hostile to the Prussian government, no matter what form in which it chooses to appear. To conciliate it is impossible. To extirpate it is inhumane (as well as impossible; at least it would take generations to do so). Therefore, nothing remains but to confine it energetically to the subordinate position it deserves.'[63]

Bismarck may have been born in the Mark, but at heart he was a Pomeranian like Puttkamer. There may be something to be said for the attitude that the Pomeranian Junkers felt increasingly threatened by the vigour of the Polish birthrate and the dwindling strength of the Junkers on the land.[64] Certainly Bismarck's attitude to the Polish question was particularly aggressive. After the 1863 uprising, he advocated a rapid Germanisation by suppressing the Polish element. At the end of his life he justified this approach in his memoirs, referring to the geographical layout of Prussia which would not allow for the sort of liberalism practised in the Polish provinces of Austria-Hungary. He saw a danger for East Prussia and Silesia and did his best to prevent the Russians from bringing up the question of an independent Poland. Keeping in with the Russians would make things easier on this score.[65]

As one historian has written, Bismarck's views on Poland were 'remarkable not for their originality but rather for the vehemence with which he expressed them. . . .'[66] On the other hand it cannot be denied that he accurately predicted the fate of those eastern provinces of Prussia after the creation of the Polish state in 1919 and even more so after 1945. If, wrote Bismarck, Poland were to revert to its 1772 borders 'the best sinews of Germany would be severed, millions of Germans would fall prey to Polish arbitrariness. Thus one would gain an uncertain ally, covetously awaiting any sort of trouble on Germany's part in order to tear away from it East Prussia, the Polish part of Silesia, the Polish regions of Pomerania. On the other hand one might wish to restore Poland in narrower limits, giving it only the decidedly Polish part of the Grand Duchy of Posen. In that event, only he who is completely ignorant of the Poles would doubt that they would be our sworn enemies so long as they had not conquered from us the mouth of the Vistula and, beyond that, every Polish-speaking village in West and East Prussia, Pomerania and Silesia. Only a German who allowed himself to be guided by tearful compassion and impractical theories would dream of establishing in the immediate neighbourhood of his own fatherland an implacable enemy always ready to externalise his feverish domestic turbulence in war and, in any serious complication we might find ourselves in, fall on us from the rear.'[67]

To resurrect Poland, thought Bismarck, would destroy three great powers, only to hand over the state to the Polish gentry, a crowd of people whose legitimacy was suspect even in the eyes of the Polish masses. The Poles were 'bitterly disappointed' by the settlement of 1871. Prussia, for them, was not a national state, rather a collection of territories put together by victory in war and wise dynastic ties. Germany, on the other hand, was every inch a nation state and the incorporation of Poland into Germany could only be seen as a setback. Before 1871 Russia was Poland's number one enemy. After 1871 it was Prussia and through Prussia, Germany.* Before 1870 the Poles had no negative feelings about Bavarians. After 1870 they learned to dislike them too.

Before 1870 Polish nationalism affected only a small part of the Polish population, chiefly the nobility and the intellectuals. After 1870 the lack of any decent alternative created by a German

---

* The attitude has survived. In Warsaw a Pole told the author that he would shoot a German first 'for pleasure' and a Russian afterwards 'for duty'.

nation pushed ever more of the population into active opposition: it was now the turn of the middle classes, the workers and the peasants.[68] The new German parties such as the National Liberals, were liberal and progressive only when it came to the Germans. This attitude was not extended to the Poles. Bismarck's furiously repressive policies – the *Kulturkampf* with its attack on the Catholic Church; the expulsions of 1885–1886 and the settlement laws; and the expropriations of Polish property under Chancellor Bülow – all had the effect of pushing the Poles further and further into resistance. All the Poles could hope for was a war between Prussia and Russia, which might end up by forcing one or other of the warring parties to create a Polish buffer state (this happened in the First World War). While Bismarck was Chancellor he was at pains to keep Russia allied to Germany. As soon as Kaiser William II came to the throne and assumed a degree of personal rule, he let the alliance drop.

III

July 1907. Hotel Metropol in Berlin.

Some gentlemen were singing the Polish national song '*Jeszcze Polska nie zginęła*' (Poland is not yet lost) without a trouble in the world. As I knew the gentlemen well, I went to their table and asked them as a joke, 'What would happen if you were to sing this song publicly in Warsaw?' 'We'd all be thrown into the Schlüsselburg (the prison), and then it would be Siberia,' said one of them. 'Or they'd hang us', was the opinion of another.[69]

It is without doubt true that the treatment of the Prussian Poles was worse under the Reich than it had ever been before 1870. Prussia was a *Rechtstaat* in which the law was supreme. In the period from 1870 to 1914 there were moments (at the time of the expulsions or the expropriations of Polish estates) when the rule of law was called into doubt. Nonetheless, the Poles could scarcely compare their treatment under the Prussians to the administration in the Grand Duchy of Warsaw where the slightest criticism was likely to land one in jail, if not result in banishment to Siberia.[70] To this day Poles will show you the former dividing line between Prussian and Russian Poland. On the Prussian side the houses are neat, brick, one-storey dwellings. In the Russian zone brick was banned before 1917 and the houses were made of wood. This had the advantage of allowing them to be burned down by the Czarist authorities in the event of civil unrest.[71]

Prussia was not a nation in the nineteenth-century sense of the word and Prussian conservatives always looked on nationalism with suspicion. When in 1807 one Justus Gruner proposed the systematic Germanisation of 'South Prussia' (the large slice of Mazovia which fell to Prussia under the Third Partition) the Prussian rulers 'recoiled from his prescriptions'.[72] On the other hand the Junkers knew that they had arrived in the east as a colonising force; and that Brandenburg-Prussia was created by just such a drive. For Kleist-Retzow this was a civilising mission which centuries before had absorbed the once Slavic Kleists and turned them into Germans: on 27 February 1886, he stood up in the Herrenhaus and declared, 'There is really no nation which is so able in colonisation as the Germans ... My family is a Slavic family, that it became German is something we owe to this colonisation.'[73] For this reason Kleist-Retzow opposed the creation of an independent Polish state as a retrogressive step 'countering history and divine providence'.[74]

Predictably enough, 'der Januschauer' was also against Polish demands for an independent state, and in favour of a progressive Germanisation of the Polish parts of Prussia. As he told Polish deputies to the Reichstag in 1908, 'Even after having been Prussian subjects for 136 years you still cling to the standpoint:

> Vous avez pu germaniser la plaine;
> mais notre coeur vous ne l'aurez jamais!*

If we cannot have your hearts, gentlemen, then we must have your land. ... The Prussian motto *suum quique* does not mean that the state simply ensures that everyone gets his share, no, the state also

---

* You have been able to Germanise the plain, but our hearts you will never have.

wants its own share. The state requires your recognition of the fact that the Hohenzollern house and the Prussian state are not ruling temporarily over the annexed Polish regions, but permanently. The secession of these regions may only take place when the crown itself is submerged in a sea of blood. . . . You Polish gentlemen,' added Oldenburg-Januschau encouragingly, 'you must not look backwards. The Polish Empire is behind you. Before you stands the state of Prussia which has yet to fill its mission to the world. . . .'[75]

A number of good Prussian principles had withered with the foundation of the Reich. The first of these was the hallowed virtue of toleration; although it should be said that Frederick William III had set something of a precedent here in his tussle with the Catholic Church. Bismarck's *Kulturkampf* was levelled at all Catholics in Germany and Prussia, but naturally it came down hard on the Poles who, like the Irish in the British Empire, saw their religion as an expression of their natural aspirations. The *Kulturkampf* put an end to the possibility of separate religious schools. Priests had to recognise the supremacy of the state over the Church. Those who did not, like Archbishop Ledóchowski of Gnesen-Posen, were imprisoned. In 1886 a German, Pinder, was appointed to the see, but proved a disappointment to Bismarck in that he not only showed his ability to speak fluent Polish, but he refused to advance German priests within the diocese. Under the May Laws the Catholic section of the Kultus Ministry was scrapped, Polish teaching in schools was confined to primary levels and German became the only permissible language in administration.[76]

The *Kulturkampf* was sanctified by laws, even if they went against some of the dearest principles of the Prussian state. The expulsions of Poles and Jews from Prussian Poland in 1883 were of doubtful legality. Around 32,000 were driven out in all, 'an action unprecedented in nineteenth-century Europe during a time of peace'.[77] It was a gesture which did not find favour with all Prussians by any means: the Silesian General Hans von Schweinitz thought it 'an imprudent and unnecessarily cruel measure'.[78] Bismarck's *Polenpolitik* had begun to smack of desperation. He was aware of the *Ostflucht* which was caused by German families selling off their unprofitable estates in the east and settling in the prosperous west. He must have been also conscious of the rising Polish birthrate; almost double that of the Germans.[79] It was in the 1880s that the National Liberals conceived the first plan to break up the eastern estates and settle them with German farmers.

In 1886, Bismarck's enemies succeeded in passing a vote of censure against him for the expulsions. The Chancellor reacted with renewed vigour against the Poles. This time his measures were directed against the nobles. A Royal Prussian Colonisation Commission was established with a fund of 100 million Reichsmarks to buy up Polish estates in Posen and West Prussia and parcel them out among German peasant farmers. Bismarck would have preferred to award the estates to poor Junkers, but the choice of the peasants was the price of his support from the west German National Liberals. Now he aimed to bring to an end 'the cancer-like spread of Polonisation'.[80]

Although so much of William II's foreign policy reversed the careful system of checks and balances erected by Bismarck, the Kaiser was no innovator when it came to his *Polenpolitik*. The language, however, was subtly different: Bismarck's *Kulturkampf* and his repressive policies towards the Poles had been aimed at strengthening the state and preventing the decline of the Junkers in the eastern provinces. The Kaiser was increasingly carried away by the claims of aggressive German nationalism of the sort being taught by Treitschke at Berlin University. He even conceived a plan to transform Prussia's Polish territories into a *Reichsland* or imperial province on the model of Alsace-Lorraine, finishing the Prussian connection for good.

The worst of German policy at the time was mitigated by Bismarck's successor, Chancellor Leo von Caprivi and a few fair-minded Posen *Oberpräsidenten*. Now that Russia was being pushed into the French camp, Caprivi realised that he might need Polish support in the event of war. He consequently liberalised education: 'A few hours a week of Polish instruction is a price worth paying to hold them on our side.'[81] Caprivi's policy paid off: the

Polish deputies came over to his side in the Reichstag, and the new Archbishop of Gnesen-Posen, Stablewski, spoke out against the Russians. In Posen itself Hugo Freiherr von Wilamowitz-Möllendorf tried to win the Poles round with benevolent administration. To his German critics he said, 'The ruthless struggle with and forcible suppression of everything Polish will not make Germans of the Poles.'[82]

Wilamowitz-Möllendorf's detractors were German nationalists of a new and more sinister breed who mixed a dash of racialism into the anti-Polish brew. Hitler's later coalition partner, the Hanoverian Alfred Hugenberg, arrived in Posen as an official of the Colonial Commission in 1894 and set up a branch of the Alldeutscher Verband or Pan German League. In April that year he began to print a newspaper called *Alldeutscher Blätter* which campaigned against Caprivi's more liberal *Polenpolitik*.[83] Another powerful opponent to Caprivi was the *Bund der Landwirte* or Union of Landowners with branches throughout Germany. Bismarck gave a considerable fillip to their campaign when he spoke against his successor at his estate at Varzin in Pomerania. From West Prussia and Posen came 2,000 people to hear the former Chancellor speak.

As far as the Poles were concerned, the most worrying organisation of the lot was the 'Hakata'. The word was coined from the first letters of the names of Ferdinand von Hansemann, a banker's son, Hermann Kennemann, described as a 'Junker of common origins', and a retired Prussian major called Heinrich von Teidemann. In 1894 they created the Verein zur Förderung des Deutschtums in den Ostmarken (Union for the Promotion of Germanism in the Eastern Provinces) or Ostmarkverein. Some have sought in the Hakata a sort of forerunner to Hitler's National Socialist movement as a racialist organisation of the extreme right. Its membership was largely confined to Posen and West Prussia; about 20,000 people: state officials, schoolmasters and Protestant clergymen. There were very few estate owners among the members.[84]

The Poles fought back. They set up their own organisations to ensure that Polish land never reached the market and was bought up by other Poles before the German colonists could get their hands on it. The Germans pursued their own plans to Germanise the towns. Theatres were built, the street names changed to German, German language newspapers proliferated. In Posen a new German administrative quarter rose up in the west of the city to house the inflated number of civil servants now stationed in the Grand Duchy. There the Kaiser built his massive neo-romanesque palace as an affirmation of Germany's intention to hang on to Posen, come what may.

Chancellor Hohenlohe had reverted to the tough line on the Poles, but the biggest Pole-baiter among the pre-war German Chancellors was Bülow. In 1887 he had written to Holstein to suggest that after a successful war against Russia, Prussia should recreate 'Congress Poland' and ship all its Poles into the new state. Even the virulently anti-Polish Bismarck thought that was going too far: 'One should not commit such eccentric thoughts to paper,' he wrote. His suppression of even Polish primary education led to the school strikes which broke out for the first time in 1900 and reached their peak in November 1906. When Archbishop Stablewski died, Bülow refused to license his successor, Likowski.

Meanwhile the Colonisation Committee was running into increasing difficulty in procuring land for settlers. As the Poles wouldn't sell they were obliged to buy from the many Germans who wanted to move west. This drove Hugenburg and his friends to the idea of calling for legislation to expropriate land from the Poles by forcing them to sell up. This policy was supported in the Reichstag by the National Liberals together with Hakata and the Pan Germans. The threat of expropriation began to make waves in the more liberal Austrian parts of Poland. The Austrian Ambassador, Count Ladislaus von Szögyényi, found Bülow's policy hard to credit: 'It is really unbelievable how openly his actions, and especially his disastrous *Polenpolitik*, are attacked in all circles, even among the high ranks of the military.'[85]

One means of giving the measure the semblance of legality was to make it applicable to both Polish and German estates, and simply fail to enact it in the latter case. The scheme was provoking a storm of protests in the foreign press and great concern among the less hot-headed members of the Kaiser's own entourage. Zedlitz-Trützschler expressed his reservations to the Germano-Polish Count Tschirschky: 'He quite agreed with me that every step the government was taking, especially by way of coercion, so far from having any good effect was absolutely dangerous, and largely resulted in the very opposite of what was intended.' Tschirschky concluded that the Germans were 'all the Emperor's victims: he is our cross'.[86]

Bethmann-Hollweg continued the policy with a degree of reluctance. As he told Graf Bogdan von Hutten-Czapski, 'It could only be in the government's interest to treat the moderate [Polish] circles in a not unfriendly manner . . .'[87] Bethmann resolved to make a minor gesture to maintain his support in the Reichstag and seize a rather smaller number of estates than had been previously decided. They were also to be those owned by 'harmless' Poles, who would be unlikely to cause trouble.[88] The job of enacting this policy fell to his Catholic Minister of Agriculture, Clemens von Schorlemer. After that the measure was quietly buried.

In August 1913 the Kaiser's expensive new palace was complete. On the 28th he held a banquet for 355 guests, thirty-six of whom were Poles. He made a speech in which he spoke of Posen's inhabitants 'regardless of their nationality and confession [being] drawn closely together through the bond of love for the homeland they share and through common loyalty to the King and Fatherland.'[89]

There were still one or two Poles who thought as Prussians. Some of these represented Polish constituencies in the *Reichstag* or the Prussian *Landtag*. Jósef Kościelski was deemed so pro-Prussian that his critics dubbed him 'the German Admiral'.[90] In June 1891 he told members of the *Landtag*, 'I do not think it should matter whether a Prussian prays to his God in German or Polish, whether he toasts his king in Polish or German. . . . Today there are only two parties: the state-supporting party of order and the state-destroying party of the revolution.' Kościelski believed that loyal Prussians could be made of the Poles providing they were treated with more consideration: 'The existence of Poles on the eastern borders is not what weakens Germany . . . rather, it is the attempt to Germanise them. Give that up and you will immediately gain in strength.'[91]

Such sentiments had become increasingly rare. Polish national demands had become uncompromising by the turn of the century. The Polish Socialists in the PPS (Polska Partia Socjalistyczna), set their hopes on a German Socialist victory. The politician and journalist Wilhelm Feldman believed Prussia was the chief enemy in Germany and that the country had been 'Prussified': 'The Prussian vampire [in 1871] began to suck the blood of the whole empire.' Militarism, chauvinism, 'modern' anti-semitism and colonialism were all, according to Feldman, attributes of Prussia which had been thrust upon the rest of Germany.[92]

The Polish Socialists were anti-Russian, which was not the case with Roman Dmowski's National Democrats. What they shared was their hatred of Prussia. Dmowski and Jan Ludwig Popławski insisted on the recreation of a 'Piast' empire for Poland with a path to the sea through East or West Prussia. Popławski advocated the emasculation of Prussia by the stripping away of all its eastern provinces. 'That way Prussia would lose a quarter of its population and would revert to the position and name of Brandenburg.'[93] Popławski proved prophetic. Piast ideas, mingled with anti-semitism and racialism in general, have proved a hardy perennial in Poland and they were behind Polish diplomatic initiatives in both the First World War and the Second. Dmowski did not think that Polish demands should stop at the 'historical' Polish borders. As all of Prussian land had been won from one or other form of Slavic race, then Prussia in its entirety might be seen as a colonial objective for a Greater Poland. Dmowski had to admit to a certain admiration for the Prussians. Were they not also largely Slavs? 'At any rate,' he wrote in 1903, 'let us not forget that Prussian society, though the very opposite of our *szlachta* type, is to a very great degree formed from the same racial material as our own; that today they are our hated enemies but at the same time the in many respects impressive Prussians are the descendants of common ancestors or the very least close relatives: the Elbian Slavs, the Pomeranians and so many Poles of the purest blood.'[94]

Something of the same aggressive, counter-colonial stance permeated the writings of the novelist Henryk Sienkiewicz, whose novel *Krzyżacy*, published in 1900, glorified the defeat of the Teutonic Knights. Since Frederick the Great's time, the Prussians had been characterised by their violence, crime, craftiness, disloyalty and lies. Bismarck was the personification of soulless power. Sienkiewicz believed that the appropriation of Prussian land was justified by the way the Prussians had behaved throughout history. It was merely paying them back with their own coin.[95]

Józef Piłsudski thought the Russians to be a greater danger to Poland than the Prussians. His was a wise waiting game: 'The Polish question will be solved to our advantage when Germany defeats Russia and is itself defeated by France.'[96] He advocated the acquisition of territory from both Russia and Prussia. Piłsudski was released from German fortress arrest on 9 November 1918 and allowed to travel to Warsaw. If the Germans thought this would defuse any problems they had on their eastern borders, they were mistaken. The very next day Piłsudski issued an ultimatum to the Germans. They were to evacuate Poland, leaving their trains and equipment behind them.[97]

In Warsaw the elected German soldiers' council made common cause with the Poles. The same was true in Posen. Berlin was now helpless to prevent the secession of the Grand Duchy, almost all the available soldiers had been transferred to the western front after the Treaty of Brest–Litovsk. The new German government was determined to hang on to the Grand Duchy but lacked the means to make it secure. Piłsudski's plan was bearing fruit. On Christmas Day 1918, the pianist turned politician, Ignacy Paderewski, entered Posen in the company of British officers. The German government issued a protest, but the soldiers' council was still in control of the garrison. They disarmed the officers and took the Polish side. More than a century of Prussian rule came to an end on 30 December when Interior Minister Ernst and Under Secretary Göhre gave in to Polish demands to evacuate the German garrison.

For Hindenburg the ministers' decision had been a sell-out. From the new German military HQ in Kolberg in Pomerania, a plan was drawn up to retake Posen. That offensive had just begun when Paderewski fled to Paris to gain support from Foch. Foch issued an order to the Germans to halt their advance and abide by the Polish demarcation lines. Foch's ultimatum came as a considerable blow to the already severely wounded German pride. In April 1919, General Haller's 100,000-strong Polish army was allowed to pass through Germany to reinforce Polish forces in the Grand Duchy.[98]

Few Prussians were ready to accept a revision of their borders in the east, even in areas such as the Grand Duchy and West Prussia where Poles were in an undeniable majority. Otto Braun was typical in this. He criticised the methods employed by the Hakata and similar organisations and expressed his sympathy for the national aspirations of the Polish people, but deplored their intentions towards his native province of East Prussia. Another bone of contention was the Corridor, and the fact that there had been no right to plebiscites in this area which had been designated Polish in order to give them access to the sea.[99]

By January 1919 there was considerable fear that the Poles would launch an attack in both West and East Prussia. On the 15th the *Oberpräsident* of West Prussia in Danzig issued orders to arm the people against Polish attack and create squads of home guards to protect the borders.[100] August Winnig, the former mason and Socialist politician, arrived from the Baltic states: 'I saw East Prussia threatened and I decided to travel [there] and then on to Berlin.'[101] The chief fear was that the Poles would try to seize Danzig while the German army was still in no condition to fight. In Allenstein the men had run amok and taken over the local newspaper. Another threat came from Soviet Russia as the Red

Army launched an attack on the Baltic States. The population of East Prussia saw the possibility that the Russians would not stop at the Memel if their offensive were successful.[102]

A further menace to East Prussia came from the new state of Lithuania. The Lithuanians lacked a decent port and their ambitions stretched to the whole north and western sides of East Prussia. Lithuanians, however, made up a scant 4.35 per cent of the East Prussian population. Only in the small town of Heydekrug were the Lithuanians in the majority, although forty-four per cent of the Memelers and twenty-two per cent of the Tilsiters were Lithuanian-speaking; in none of the other villages and towns in question did the Lithuanian population exceed ten per cent. Another nagging issue was the 30,000 or so Germans in Lithuania.[103]

The panic died down in East Prussia when it became clear that plebiscites would be held only to decide the nationality of certain areas of mixed population in Mazuria. These were also to be held in the Netze and West Prussia, where the people continued to be jittery until they had some indication of whether their village or town was to stay in the Reich or be awarded to Poland. In the end substantial parts of West Prussia went to Poland, including the old Ordensburgen of Kulm, Graudenz and Thorn as well as a chunk of the rural district of Marienwerder. As the towns and cities had generally possessed a majority of Germans, this presented the authorities with refugee problems. In the little village of Löbau, which was made Polish in the summer of 1919, homes had to be found for the population. Of the eighty-seven German inhabitants seventeen elected to go to Pomerania; thirty to the area east of the Vistula which remained in German hands; twenty-five to East Prussia; and fifteen to the now Polish towns of Kulm and Graudenz. The reason for choosing the towns was that, for the time being at least, the Germans believed they were safe in numbers there.[104]

Poland had also been required to sign a treaty to protect the minorities in the new state, Germans included, providing they had arrived before 1908. Particular stress was laid on the need to ensure the protection of the Jews. Delegates at the Versailles Conference had had reservations on this score.[105]

The plebiscites took place a year after the main areas had been detached, in July 1920. In the intervening time the Poles and Lithuanians conducted their own propaganda campaign in order to ensure that the maximum number of villages fell to them. Spurious figures were communicated to the Western Allies in order to justify claims, provoking panic in frontier towns such as Oletzko and Goldap where they imagined they would be handed over to the Poles without the chance to vote. This had been the case in Memel and Heydekrug, both of which had been given to Lithuania.[106] The plebiscites proved a disappointment to the new Polish state in many areas. In Allenstein in Mazuria, where many of the inhabitants were Polish-German 'autochthones', only 567 of a population of 14,500 voted for union with Poland.

Where the German population had sought refuge in the now Polish towns of West Prussia west of the Vistula and south of the Mazurian Lakes, the advance of the Red Army into Poland was observed with interest. In Soldau the Russian soldiers were greeted as liberators. When the town was retaken by the Polish army a few days later the soldiers plundered the houses of the Germans, who made up seventy-five per cent of the population. In the next few days 7,000 fled or were driven from their homes. One refugee reported, 'We escaped with nothing more than we were wearing.' No one had been permitted to take even personal effects with them. Later about two-thirds of the Soldauers returned home. It was a little foretaste of what would happen when history repeated itself in 1945.[107]

When it came down to it, neither side was happy with the results of the Versailles border revisions and the plebiscites. The Prussians were cross that the Allies had applied President Wilson's principle of national self-determination only when it suited their war aims; the Poles were unhappy that the new borders failed to make their state secure. Dmowski had pointed out as early as July 1917 that with the Germans still in Danzig and Königsberg, Poland was outflanked. The need for security would now dominate

Polish border policy until the country achieved something like the western boundaries it had hoped for in 1945.

Despite their continuing coveting of Prussia's eastern provinces, the Poles were remarkably slow to see the danger from Hitler. The old view that Catholic Austria acted as a useful check on Protestant Prussia must have influenced men like Piłsudski, who thought that Hitler's abolition of the federal structure of Germany, and with it Prussia's individual existence, was good news. The Poles were slow to delve into *Mein Kampf.* When they did, they saw in Hitler and the Hitlerites merely old wine in new bottles: they were Prussians with Prussian territorial ambitions. The Potsdam Day confirmed all this: the words 'German', 'Hitlerite' and 'Prussian' became interchangeable for Poles. In 1940, a Polish underground paper summed it up by saying, 'Sadly every German man and woman is a Prussian these days.'[108]

The equation of Nazism with Prussianism was to have its uses in foreign policy. In 1942 in London, Władysław Pałucki was already campaigning for a western border based on the Oder–Neisse Line, the extreme Piast position. Prussia for the Pole was still a living thing, the old enemy now wearing a brown shirt: 'Prussia . . . is a state without nationality, an accidental collection of people with no geographical borders, who have come together through robbery alone.'[109]

Pałucki's voice became a chorus. It was the voice of Dmowski, who had died in 1939, and sadly did not live to see his dream come true. By the end of the war, left and right were united in their war aims: they wanted the Germans driven out of the areas east of the Oder. Their position was doubtless influenced by the knowledge that Poland would be unlikely to win back those eastern parts of their country which the Russians had gained bloodlessly from Ribbentrop in August 1939. Some of the more extreme groups suggested that Berlin too should be Polish (it had, after all, like all of Germany east of the Elbe, been populated by Slavic Wends). It would be significant, after all: Berlin could be the 'showplace for Prussia's death'.[110]

Prussia was the old enemy. In 1943 one of Poland's war aims

had spoken of the need to detach the east Elbian provinces in their entirety and create a heavily supervised puppet state, while the 'innocent' German south could enjoy a degree of liberty. This was strangely prophetic. The east Elbian DDR was just such a state, watched over by Russia until its demise in 1989. That Prussia had been dead since before Hitler's arrival in power troubled the Polish diplomats not a jot.

The Decline of Tolerance

If the sovereign, motivated by misplaced zeal, decided to declare for one or other religion, the first thing we would see would be the formation of parties, arguments would become heated and little by little persecution would break out. Finally the persecuted religion would leave the country and thousands of subjects would enrich our neighbours with their numbers and industry. . . .

I shall not speak of religion. . . . It is however necessary [that the prince] observes the Reformed Church which is the one adopted by his ancestors, and that he knows enough theology to find the Catholic religion the most ridiculous of all.

> Frederick the Great, Testament
> politique, quoted in Gaxotte ed.,
> *Frédéric II*, 294, 362.

Religious toleration was one of Prussia's strongest cards. Its origins went back to the seventeenth century, to the Elector John Sigismund, the first German prince to tear up the principle *cuius regio eius religio* (the religion of the prince will be the religion of his subjects) which had been followed by German rulers since the religious wars of the sixteenth century. His action was provoked by his acquisition of the provinces of Cleves, Mark, Ravensberg and Ravenstein in 1614. That same year he signed the 'Blasphemy Edict' which forbade clergymen of any persuasion from attacking rival churches from the pulpit. The Elector himself became a Calvinist, while the people of Brandenburg were overwhelmingly Lutheran. Frederick the Great thought that his ancestor's change of faith was a cynical gesture to win the hearts of the Calvinists in Cleves,[1] but this is unlikely. John Sigismund seems to have been genuinely attached to the ideas of the Reformed Church.

The Blasphemy Edict was the first step; the second was the Edict of Potsdam promulgated by the Great Elector in 1685. This was a direct response to Louis XIV's decision to revoke the Edict of Nantes, thereby placing France's large Huguenot community outside the law. The Great Elector welcomed them all to his largely empty land. That same year 14,000 Frenchmen and women made their way to Brandenburg-Prussia. Six thousand of these settled in Berlin, where they made up a significant part of the population of what was still a small town. Just like the Huguenots who came to Britain and Ireland, they formed their own group, brought a knowledge of food and wine and opened inns and shops. In Berlin they founded the Collège Royale (the later Französisches Gymnasium).[2]

The Prussian Huguenots remained a closely knit group. Prussia's best-loved writer, Theodor Fontane, had no German blood. His grandfather had been drawing master to the children of Frederick William III and later Queen Louise's private secretary (the sculptor Gottfried Schadow remarked bitchily, 'He paints badly but he speaks French well'); his father, Louis Henri, a chemist, the profession briefly taken up by Theodor. Fontane's mother was the daughter of a silk merchant called Emilie Labry. The Fontanes came from Gascony, the Labrys from the Cevennes.[3] When Theodor came to marry in his turn, he too took a member of the French colony as his bride.

Until Frederick the Great set his sights on Silesia, most of the king's Catholic subjects were tucked away in the west. Up to a quarter of Frederick William I's soldiers were Catholics and, despite the king's own pietistic faith, he had chapels founded for them in Potsdam, Spandau and Berlin. Silesia brought Frederick the Great many more Catholics, especially in Upper Silesia, where the people were Catholic virtually to a man. Frederick was determined to make them welcome, as long as they showed some sign of wanting to become loyal Prussians. Those who didn't he drove out. There were areas of Silesia where Protestantism had made such progress that the priests preached to virtually empty churches, but the king would not allow these to be taken over by the Lutherans. In his Berlin 'Forum' he had Knobelsdorff and Boumann the Elder build the Catholic Church of Saint Hedwig. Everyone was to achieve salvation in his own way. In 1773 he welcomed to Prussia the Jesuits who had been banished from everywhere else, including Rome. In the same spirit he toyed with building a mosque in Berlin. Even Voltaire thought he was going too far: 'You accuse me of excessive tolerance. I am proud of this failing. Would that it were the only failing of which princes could be accused.'[4]

The Polish partitions swelled the ranks of Catholic Prussia yet further. The half-million subjects Frederick gained from the First Partition were mostly Germans, but they were also a majority of Catholics[5]; in West Prussia these were the responsibility of the Bishop of Ermland, whose see swung between Braunsberg and Heilsberg. In the nineteenth century the bishop came to rest in Frauenburg and a new see was created in Kulm when the Vatican set up a proper organisation for the Catholic Church in Prussia with the Bull 'De salute animarum' of 1821.[6]

The same period saw the beginnings of difficulties between the Prussian crown and its Catholic subjects. In May 1818, a Father Heubes in Benrath near Düsseldorf attacked the Lutheran Church from the pulpit, thereby violating the Blasphemy Edict. The *Oberpräsident* responded by imposing a ban on Heubes preaching.[7] In West Prussia increasingly anti-Catholic *Oberpräsidenten* such as Schön and Flottwell exacerbated the difficulties with the Church. Schön admitted that he would 'pray to the devil not to be a Catholic'. As long as the bishops remained loyal to Prussia, however, there was little direct conflict.[8]

Times changed. The atheism of Frederick the Great, the libertinism of his nephew Frederick William II, gave way to the simple homely devotion of Frederick William III and the pietism of Frederick William IV. In the immediate post-Waterloo years, many Prussian noblemen, above all those from Pomerania, went through a form of religious conversion. The leader of the 'movement', if it can be described as such, was Adolf von Thadden-Trieglaff. Thadden-Trieglaff brought together conferences of pastors on his estate. Pietist Junkers addressed one another as 'Bruder' or 'Brüderchen'. They took to visiting the peasantry and prisons, to encourage the inmates to see the light.[9]

Although the Pietists thought in terms of the purest Lutheran orthodoxy, they would have stopped short of promoting repressive measures against the Catholic Church. As Kleist-Retzow put it at the height of the *Kulturkampf*, 'It is not easy to act against the government which has gone a long way already. Probably the next Landtag will see the introduction of a bill against the [Catholic] Bishops. This fills me with horror. [Bishop] Krementz's line is of course correct, you must listen to God before the state, only this ruling of the Catholic Church obliging bishops to protect the dogma of infallibility cannot be identified with God's commandments as far as we are concerned. That is where the law comes in.'[10]

The Krementz case was to be the trial of strength for the new Reich. Now that a Prussian Chancellor controlled the whole of Germany he wanted to demonstrate that every German was subject to the state. His opponent was Pope Pius IX, who just six months before the creation of the German Reich had declared the doctrine of Papal Infallibility in the constitution of the First Vatican Council – *Pastor aeternus*.[11] The Pope had now set himself up above the king, the emperor and the state itself.

In fact church and state had been heading for trouble for some time: Frederick William III had been reduced to strong-arm tactics in his dispute with the Archbishop of Cologne over mixed marriages. The Archbishop, Freiherr von Droste-Vischering, had remained under house arrest until the king's death. At the heart of the problem seems to have been the king's desire to subdue his new Catholic subjects in the Rhineland and Westphalia. At the Würzburg Bishops' Conference of 1848, the Catholic bishops had called for an end to the state's interference in Church appointments, administration of funds and education. The Prussian state responded to this call for independence from its bishops by severely curtailing the guarantees of religious liberty which had been enshrined in the *Gesetzbuch* or legal code. From a thousand paragraphs it sank to just five articles.[12] There was still freedom of worship, but religion could not be used as an excuse to defy the demands of the state. The new code, however, was ambiguous when it came to appointments. This caused less grief in the

Catholic Rhineland than it did in Ermland and Kulm, as a result of the many Polish parish priests whom the state wished to control carefully. *Oberpräsident* Flottwell for one saw the Poles using religion as a cover for their national aspirations. One way to prevent this was to keep a close watch.

The Prussian hardliners had an unexpected ally in the 'Old Catholics', those who refused to accept what they saw as the innovations of the Vatican Council. In July 1870 they formed their own church and were denounced by the Pope. The chief centre for Old Catholicism was in Holland, but a small cell developed in Ermland and it was Bishop Krementz's attempt to put his diocese in order which led to the unleashing of Bismarck's *Kulturkampf*.

Krementz learned that a certain Professor Michelis at the Lyceum Hosanium in Braunsberg had gone over to Old Catholicism, and responded by forbidding him to teach. When the news of this ban reached the *Oberpräsident* of West Prussia, Horn, he had the order rescinded: Krementz had the right to prevent him from preaching, but as a professor, Michelis held his office from the king, and that could not be rescinded by the bishop.[13] Michelis appears to have known how to play the Protestant *Oberpräsident* by stressing the role of his own conscience. The official agreed therefore to take up the case with the Kultus Minister, Mühler. Mühler was unmoved by Horn's interpretation of the dispute as a disruption of public education. He saw it as an internal matter in which the state had no interest.

Krementz decided that his next course of action in his desire to impose orthodoxy on the school was to make all the teachers write down their interpretations of the Dogma. Another Old Catholic on the staff – Professor Menzel – went to Horn to protest. Horn assured Menzel that he had no need to write the exposition. The *Oberpräsident* was the 'curator' of the school, and he had the final say on what went on. Krementz responded by forbidding pupils to attend Menzel's classes. Krementz maintained that the state had no right 'to maintain a lapsed professor of theology in his office'.[14] The case dragged on till 1873 before the bishop was able to rid himself of both men.

Krementz's problems were just beginning. He had uncovered two more Old Catholics in the Seminary: Director Treibel and a religious teacher called Dr Wollmann. Krementz promptly removed their right to minister the sacrament and cancelled Wollmann's *missio canonica*. Mühler, however, refused to sanction their replacements. This brought Krementz in direct conflict with the minister. Krementz wrote to Mühler, pointing out the long history of Prussian toleration and directing his attention to the infringement of both the 1850 constitution and the *Gesetzbuch*. But for both Horn and Mühler the answer was simple: both the teachers were state servants, and as such only the state had the right to sanction their dismissal. Neither was looking for a fight, both aimed simply to uphold the law as they saw it. In February 1872 the new Kultus Minister, Falk, found a solution to the dispute. Pupils were allowed to attend the classes of another qualified teacher if they could not reconcile Treibel and Wollmann's lessons with their own orthodoxy, but both teachers remained on the staff. Now Krementz played what he mistakenly thought to be his trump card: he threatened to excommunicate both teachers. Writing to Falk, he set out his rights in canon law, and in his own reading of the Prussian constitution.

Falk was not impressed. Here was a Catholic bishop setting church ordinances above the constitution. He launched a 'frontal attack' against Krementz, pulling the Kaiser in on his side.[15] Krementz realised too late that he had done something foolish. He wrote back to both the Minister and the Kaiser, recalling his oath to the state. The Kaiser wanted more: an affirmation of the bishop's intention to obey the law in the future. The bishop, while asking for an audience with the Kaiser, was happy to recognise the state's authority in its own domains. It was at this moment that Bismarck entered the lists to fire the first shot of the *Kulturkampf* against the unfortunate Krementz. Bismarck wanted to make it clear that the state was supreme in *all* matters.*

---

* This attitude to the Church reached its high or low point in the Third Reich. Asked what his attitude was to the Führer, Dean Lichtenberg replied that he had 'only one Führer, Jesus Christ'. He died on the way to Dachau in 1943.[16]

On 20 December 1873, Bishop Philippus Krementz was found guilty on two counts before the Prussian courts. He had libelled the military commander of Insterburg, Gumbinnen, Friedland and Wehlau and the director of the workhouse in Tapiau, all in East Prussia. He was also found guilty of libelling Father Grunert, the Catholic padre to the garrison and to the Tapiau workhouse. Krementz was sentenced to a fine of 200 Thalers or, in the case of failure to pay, six weeks in prison. Grunert was another Old Catholic. In 1872, Krementz had excommunicated him and sacked him as a priest, but the military authorities had responded by offering the soldiers the choice between Grunert and an orthodox Catholic priest, Father Bluschy. In practice, however, the commanding officer of the garrison encouraged his soldiers to go to Grunert.

Krementz appealed and was acquitted of the charges in March 1875, although the workhouse continued to prefer the ministrations of Grunert until 1880 (more than half the inmates were Old Catholics). The next ball Krementz had to field was the law of 11 May 1873, the first of the famous anti-Catholic May Laws. The measure called into question the 1848 Prussian constitution by demanding German nationality for priests; an *Abitur* examination from a German *Gymnasium*; three years of theology at a German university or theological seminary recognised by the Kultus Ministry; and the passing of a state examination to prove the candidate's knowledge of history, philosophy and German literature. The purpose of the law was to switch the training of priests over from the Catholic seminaries to the state-run universities.[17] The law also threatened to close the remaining Catholic schools.

The Church dug in for a period of passive resistance while Bismarck's government rapidly promulgated a further six laws aimed at curtailing the power of the Catholics and ridding them of their power to make appointments unhindered by the *Oberpräsidenten*. The continued resistance up to 1877 led to Krementz incurring 20,000 Thalers in fines, approximately six times what he possessed in the church treasury. Falk toyed with the idea of replacing Krementz; the Archbishop of Gnesen-Posen was already languishing in jail and in March 1874 he had the Archbishop of Cologne arrested. In July it was the turn of the suffragan bishop of Gnesen-Posen; in August the Bishop of Paderborn. But much to everyone's surprise, Falk backed down. There was talk of court favouritism, and the suspicion that the humble tenant-farmer's son had a protector was reinforced when ten years later he was appointed to the Metropolitan see of Cologne. More likely is that Bismarck and Falk's policy had been essentially counter-productive: the way to make Catholics into good Germans was not to persecute their priests and bishops. It also led to shortages of teachers in former religious schools and nurses in the former religious hospitals. In 1880 the latter were tacitly accepted when the hospitals run by the Orders were exempted from the anti-clerical decrees.

The number of Catholics in Ermland was growing. In 1883 there were nearly twice as many as there had been forty years before, and they were dramatically short of priests. Many of the *Landräte* thought it wiser not to enact the more ferocious remedies of the *Kulturkampf*, which was just one more example of how the new Reich blew away the accepted principles which had guided the progressive Prussian state in its heyday.

II

> The Jews. We need this nation in our trade with Poland, but we must make sure that their numbers do not increase.[18]

Prussia was also the first German state to tolerate the Jews. Partly this was the result of Prussia's eastern orientation: Poland's towns, cities and even villages were quite often dominated by Jewish merchants and artisans; partly it was casued by Frederick the Great's self-conscious desire to play the role of the enlightened monarch. The Jews already made up 3,000 of the less than 100,000-strong population of Berlin when Frederick became king in 1740. When he invaded Silesia, he was careful to extend the protection Jews received within Brandenburg to his new province, the numbers of Jews in Silesia – and especially in its capital, Breslau – being far higher than in any city in Prussia.[19] Frederick also granted some Jewish merchants with licences to print money. One of them, Ephraim, built himself a lovely rococo palace with the proceeds which has miraculously survived the ravages of war in the centre of Berlin.*

It was to Berlin that Moses Mendelssohn made his way from Dessau to found the first of Berlin's great creative Jewish dynasties. His grandson, Felix Mendelssohn-Bartholdy, was to give the name international significance and establish Berlin in the front rank of world musical centres. At the end of the eighteenth century there was little anti-semitism in Berlin. Enlightened thinkers such as Christian Wilhelm Dohm and Johann Gottfried Herder saw it as a duty to 'improve' the Jews; giving them equal rights was all a part of this package.[20] In the first years of the last century, Jewish *salonières* such as Henriette Herz and Rahel Levin brought together the great names of Prussian society as well as the chief figures from the literary world. Their brief, sparkling existence was brought to an end by the defeat at Jena.[21] At more or less the same time the first work of modern anti-semitism, Grattenauer's *Wider die Juden* (Against the Jews), appeared and the short honeymoon was at an end. Those Jews who still moved in Gentile circles were called *Ausnahmejuden* or exceptional Jews. It is significant that when the first literary, nationalist bodies sprang up, like Achim von Arnim's *Christlich-Deutsche Tischgesellschaft*, it expressedly forbade the participation of Frenchmen, philistines, women and Jews.[22] Nor did any form of co-operation come back in the post-Waterloo years.[23]

The edict of 1812, which granted some if not all civic rights to the Prussian Jews, was only applicable to 'rump' Prussia: those areas remaining to Frederick William III after the draconian Treaty of Tilsit. Equality was granted to *all* Prussian Jews only in

---

* It has fared better than the synagogue in Breslau, which was still wrecked in August 1992. The synagogue in Berlin's Oranienburgstrasse was left in a ruinous state by the DDR. Since the reunification it has been restored to its former splendour.

1869, eleven years after Great Britain, three after Austria, two after Hungary and one year *before* Italy.[24] Most Prussian cities – especially as you travelled east – had a long history of association with the Jews, especially *Schutzjuden*, protected Jews, who had paid a fee for the privilege. In Königsberg there were Jews as early as 1680 and by 1747 their number had reached forty-seven families; in 1806 127 families. Two Königsberg families were later ennobled: the Friedländers (of whom there were already seventy-nine in 1812) and the Simsons.[25] Ennoblement was only possible for Jews who submitted to Christian baptism. To the north of Königsberg, in Memel, at the outside limit of the Prussian king's possessions, Pastor Rehsener made a little speciality of conversion. He claimed to have made 155 in his time as a pastor, some of them from as far away as Russian Armenia.[26] Rehsener reassures us that this was no 'hunt': the Jews paid calls on him and asked for instruction in the Christian faith; though he was not above luring them in: '*Judchen, komm doch ein wenig in meine Stube!* (Little Jew, come into my study for a bit!)' he said to one poor Jew he found quietly praying in a Memel pub.*

Widespread anti-semitism sprang up at the time of the foundation of the Reich. Princess Katharina Radziwiłł, who was by no means exempt from it, claimed in the 1880s there was 'no city in the whole world where the children of Israel were so excluded from society, or where society found more uses for their services'.[27] She found far less prejudice among the upper classes, who had turned progressively to the Jews for help in stock-market speculations. The most famous of these was Bismarck's banker, Gerson Bleichröder, 'one of the cleverest men of his day'.[28] As far as the anti-semitism of the middle classes was concerned, it was being whipped up by Pastor Adolf Stoecker, a Prussian from Halberstadt, a cathedral preacher and member of the Reichstag. Stoecker's 'Christian socialism', with its emphasis on paternalist policies towards the working classes and worship of the monarchy, found favour with the future Kaiser William II.

---

* The frequent use of the diminutive suffix 'chen' was a hallmark of East Prussian German.

Adolf Stoecker was different from Adolf Hitler. He insisted that his exploration of the Jewish 'problem' was 'without hatred or bitterness': 'We hate no one, we don't even hate the Jews; we acknowledge them as our fellow citizens and love them as the people of the Prophets and the Apostles, from whom our Saviour came forth; but for that reason we do not hold back from making people aware of the danger when Jewish newssheets offend our beliefs or when the Jewish spirit of mammon wrecks our nation.'[29] Treitschke also added his voice to the chorus of anti-semitism which hailed the new empire. Treitschke was a fairly tolerant man but he saw the new Germany threatened by immigration from the Russian east. He wanted the Jews to convert; his attacks were a natural reaction to 'German national feeling face to face with an alien element'.[30] The Jews 'should become German, and feel German in their heart of hearts'. While they failed to do so they were 'our misfortune'.[31]

Stoecker spoke of the 'unimaginable fury and mindless evilness' with which the Jewish press had fallen on him.[32] The German Jews stood accused of lack of patriotism; of 'uprooting the national feelings of the Germans'. For Rabbi Klein of Elbing, Stoecker was merely demonstrating his lack of Christian feeling in his attacks on the Jews.[33] The truth was that in Wilhelmine society the Jews had precious little chance to demonstrate their patriotism as so many careers were debarred to them. Some Prussians were aware that in closing the doors to the top jobs in the civil service, diplomacy and the army to the Jews, they were likely to lose talent to other nations where attitudes were more tolerant. One such was the Wilhelmine *Kultus Minister* and former *Oberpräsident* Graf Robert von Zedlitz-Trützschler, the father of the courtier and diarist: 'Not long ago Prince Bülow spoke to my father about Herr Goldschmidt-Rothschild,' wrote the younger Zedlitz-Trützschler, 'who has recently been admitted to the Diplomatic Service. "Now," he said, "we have got this delightful and hard-working young fellow in our Diplomatic Service. I have sent him to London, and he gets always the best of information. But in Germany he cannot get a commission in the Reserve." The Prince is quite right, it is a glaring case, but if it is suggested to our military chauvinists that a Jew may be an officer of the Reserve, they see red; and yet there have been many Jewish officers who fought with distinction before the enemy in time of war. But the most reactionary chauvinism has the word with us today.

'While he was still governor [*Oberpräsident*] of Hesse-Nassau, my father tried to use his influence to secure a commission in the Reserve for this same young Goldschmidt-Rothschild, as he was one of the last representatives of the house of Rothschild in Germany, and because he is a highly gifted, ambitious, well-educated and good-looking man of charming manners. The fact that he did not change his religion is only a proof of strength of character, both on his part and that of his family. To use this fact as an argument against his being gazetted, considering how many recently baptised Jews have become officers, is to put a premium on lack of conviction.

'My father is certainly a strong conservative, but in this Jewish question he cannot close his eyes to the fact that our policy with regard to it is not only narrow-minded and unjust, but demoralising. We are injuring ourselves by gradually forcing some of the best, most enterprising and wealthiest families out of the country and are courting danger by driving the Jews into opposition. It is surely obvious that, so long as the Jews can only hope for real improvement of their position from a moral or actual defeat of the government, if not of the country, then interest must, within limits, lie in our discomfiture. No sound conservative, it seems to me, who really desires the welfare of the state, can ignore such considerations as these, but I am astonished every day how seldom I find in anyone among my acquaintances the faintest inkling of them.'[34]

When the Jews were allowed into the army in the First World War they proved themselves determined fighters and patriots. Over 100,000 of them fought in the war, 80,000 of them at the front. They won 35,000 medals, 23,000 were promoted and 2,000 became officers. Over 12,000 were killed.[35] In the early days of the Third Reich, Nazi thugs often found to their chagrin that the men they had rounded up were bearers of the Iron Cross, first and second class.[36]

After the First World War, in the Weimar Republic, the Jews represented just 1.6 per cent of the Prussian population and 4.3 per cent of that in Berlin. About a quarter of these were non-assimilated Jews from Poland and Russia.[37] Many belonged to the cultural elite of the young republic, like the painter Max Liebermann and his cousin Walter Rathenau. There was no doubt about Rathenau's patriotism: he was a *Rittergutsbesitzer* or noble estate owner in the Mark, where his Schloss Freienwalde was close to the Chancellor Bethmann-Hollweg's on the Oder. Far from wishing to stab the war effort in the back, he thought Ludendorff's call for a truce premature.[38] Rathenau's attitude to his fellow Jews is almost reminiscent of Treitschke. In his book *Höre Israel!* (Listen Israel!) he described the Jews as an 'alien organism in [Germany's] body': 'The state made you citizens to bring you up as Germans. You have remained outsiders, but demand full equality? You speak of having carried out your duties, paid taxes and fought in the war. But there was more to fulfil here than duties, and that was trust . . . Yes, I am aware, there are individuals among you who are hurt and ashamed of being outsiders and half citizens in this country; those who from the oppressive atmosphere of the ghetto long for for German woods and mountain air. To you it is I speak.'[39] Rathenau's devotion to German culture makes his assassination by right-wing anti-semites in 1922 yet more poignant.

XII

The Prussian Soul under National Socialism

In the early days of the second Great War a dear old lady was perusing an illustrated weekly in the train, when suddenly she turned to a fellow passenger and said, 'I say, I *am* surprised to find that Göring is a Bavarian. I know such nice Bavarians. I was sure Göring was a Prussian.'

S. D. Stirk, *The Prussian Spirit, A Survey of German Literature and Politics, 1914–1940*, London, 1941, 202.

When the Second World War broke out in September 1939, most British people thought they were dealing with the animal they had last encountered in the trenches of 1914–1918: Prussia. Anthony Eden got the ball rolling. In a speech of 2 December 1939, he pointed out the 'close similarity and affinity between Prussianism and Hitlerism'. Ten days later J. B. Firth in the *Daily Telegraph* pronounced, 'The pike is in the pond and the pond will need a thorough netting before it is safe for decent fish.'[1] A small army of dons and donnish emigrés now went to work under the auspices of the Ministry of Information, penning anti-Prussian tracts for the edification of the general public who were anxious to see Hitler's war as a continuation of Prussian ambitions by other means.* Who could blame them? The territorial demands seemed much the same as those aired by the Kaiser and his staff officers in the Great War.[2] For the time being few people chose to look too carefully at the ideological issues so important to Hitler

---

* These tracts have a habit of turning up unannounced in second-hand book shops. One which the author found in a bookshop in Chambéry was Paul Winkler's, *Allemagne secrète* (Paris, 1946). This began life as *The Thousand Year Conspiracy: Secret Germany Behind the Mask* (New York, March 1943). An English edition appeared the next year. Winkler's thesis sees the whole of Prussian history, from the time of the Teutonic knights, as a conspiracy to invade Europe and rob its people of their liberty.

and the Nazis. Lord Vansittart even thrilled radio audiences with *Germans Past and Present,* a programme which charted the origins of German militarism all the way back to Roman times. Vansittart knew better in his more lucid moments, and in a light-hearted essay on the racialist creed of 'Vansittartism' in 1942, he went so far as to attribute a figure of twenty-five per cent for the 'good Germans', but admitted that he might have been over-generous, and that the figure could have been as low as ten per cent.[3]

Hitler had scotched any possible hopes of a Prussian revival as early as 30 January 1934, when the federal states of Germany were finally 'gleichgeschaltet' or brought into conformity with National Socialist thinking. The last vestiges of Bismarck's Reich were swept away and Germany became unified in a way that the reformers of the Weimar Republic had dreamed of, but as a result of the dogged resistance of Prussians such as Otto Braun, were never able to effect.[4] Hitler was nonetheless aware of the propaganda value of Prussianism. In the party and the Hitler Youth he extolled a revised edition of the Prussian virtues: store was set by the spirit of self-sacrifice, selflessness, hard work and cleanliness. One of the more light-hearted scenes in Leni Riefenstahl's *Triumph des Willens* involves a horde of happy Hitler-Jugend revelling in their morning wash.[5]*

Hitler also showed a tenacious faith in the myth of 'the miracle of the House of Hohenzollern': the withdrawal of the Czarist armies from the Seven Years War which allowed Brandenburg-Prussia not only to survive, but to come out of the war better off than when it had gone in. Above his desk in the Berlin Chancellery, Hitler kept a large portrait of Frederick the Great, whom he described as one of his great 'models'.[6] Much of the time he was goaded into worshipping the Prussian king by his propaganda chief, Joseph Goebbels, who was a great fan of Thomas Carlyle's biography of Frederick: 'What a [source of] strength and consolation in these bad times,' wrote Goebbels on 5 March 1945. A week later he gave Hitler a copy of the book, and directed the

---

* It comes as some relief in this astonishingly dull film.

Führer's attention to the episode in the hero's life when he relieved his brother, an earlier August Wilhelm of Prussia, of his command. This Goebbels hoped Hitler would do to his rival, Göring.[7] Goebbels' reading of Carlyle encouraged him to believe that Hitler would pull some trick out of his sleeve and save Germany at the last moment.[8] Magda Goebbels was less convinced. 'Frederick the Great had no children,' she told him, with a gesture towards their own six offspring all under thirteen.[9]

Goebbels had been born in Rheydt in the Catholic Rhineland in 1897, and his earliest connections with the Nazi Party were through its more Socialist, Strasserite wing: the same men who had proved such a boon to Fritz-Dietlof von der Schulenburg in his neo-Prussianism.[10] The Rhinelanders were *Beutepreussen*, and the young Joseph, in his youth as devoted a Catholic as Heinrich Himmler, scarcely thought as a Prussian. Joachim von Ribbentrop liked to see himself as a Prussian and had fought in a crack Prussian regiment during the Great War, but his entry into the Torgau Hussars had been effected by his stepmother, a von Prittwitz, the only Prussian member of the Ribbentrop family.[11]

Hermann Göring was actually a Prussian on his father's side at least: his mother was an Austrian Catholic. Although his childhood was spent in Franconia, he attended the *Kadettenanstalt* at Gross Lichterfelde before joining a Badenese regiment.[12] He proved himself better able than the other Nazi leaders to assimilate into top Berlin society and it was Göring who persuaded a number of Junkers and, indeed, Prince Auwi to join the party. His reward was the Minister-Presidency of Prussia, a mere sinecure after 1934, and just one of the many offices he filled before 1945. Göring collected ministerial portfolios with something of the same zeal as he amassed decorations. As far as he was concerned the chief advantage of being Minister-President of Prussia was that it gave him access to the former Hohenzollern game reserves only recently relinquished by the Socialist shooting enthusiast, Otto Braun.

Göring had the Kaiser's hunting lodge demolished to make way for a new house which was to be erected to the memory of his dead first wife, Karin. This prompted Braun, in exile in Switzerland, to a wry observation on the subject of Göring's lavish tastes: 'The hunting lodge at Hubertusstock is not extensive enough for my successor, though it sufficed for the Kaiser and was quite big enough for me and half the other Prussian ministers.'[13] Apart from holding sway over the vast Schorfheide and its furry and feathered inhabitants, the Minister-President's other spoils were the Berlin State Theatre, where his mistress and later second wife, Emmy Sonnemann, was tactfully called upon to perform in the spring of 1933,[14] and the State Opera in Unter den Linden. In his capacity as patron to the latter, he was able to keep Goebbels off Wilhelm Furtwängler's back for as long as it suited him.[15]

In all that he performed over the next twelve years, Hermann Göring showed a most un-Prussian taste for show, luxury and extravagance* which made him the butt of countless jokes. The art historian Udo von Alvensleben sniffed at his 'perfumed court train',[17] though that luxury item had a precedent in the Kaiser's day. On a journey to the Eifel Mountains, Alvensleben was astonished to discover a painting school run by a Professor Deiner where 'the best objects are always reserved for Göring; Karinhall is, says Deiner, the museum for the works of his school. A Gretchen-like pupil was drawing miniatures for a fairy-tale book which Edda Göring† was to get for Christmas. A court workshop for the Great Lord!'[18]

In January 1934 the Prussian Ministries disappeared, leaving Göring with just the police. The *Gleichschaltung* 'literally laid him out. He took to his bed.'[19] It was from this horizontal position that he spoke to Rudolf Diels, then head of the secret police or Gestapo. 'I've certainly mucked things up. How could I strengthen Prussia's position when Hitler wants to do the very same to the Reich? I cannot therefore give up the police. Never! Otherwise I'll

---

* Guderian observed Göring admiring an old master in an East Prussian *Schloss*: 'Magnificent!' Said the Reichsmarschal, 'I too am a man of the Renaissance. I adore splendour!'[16]
† Göring's daughter by Emmy Sonnemann.

become nothing but a puppet, a Minister President without a province.'[20] Before Göring was deprived of his power over Prussia, however, he was able to achieve something: he set up the Prussian Cultural Foundation, the *Stiftung Preussenhaus*, by the Potsdamer-platz which he endowed on 26 October 1933, In the turgid National Socialist language of the day, it is described as an institution which 'has been erected to look after the imperial idea on the basis of National Socialist ideology; as a visible sign of the realisation of the Prussian mission of a united Germany and as a lasting monument to its great past.'[21] The acknowledgement that Prussia might have been some sort of midwife to Germany and therefore to Nazism was not all that Göring was able to perform during his tenure of the Minister-Presidency. Just before Himmler made off with the policing functions of the state, Göring actually took the step of sending for trial some SA men who had overstepped the mark in their brutality towards prisoners at the 'wild' concentration camp at Bredow in the suburbs of Stettin. Göring responded to pressure and had them arraigned before the Provincial Criminal Court. Bredow Concentration Camp was closed on his authority. This rare act of compassion on the part of Hermann Göring was brought up by his defence counsel at Nuremberg.[22] He had little chance to repeat the gesture. Ten days after the trial, Himmler was safely in the saddle.

It would certainly be a mistake to exclude Prussia from all the responsibility for the Third Reich. As soldiers, and above all as generals, they played a more than prominent role. On the other hand, they did not aspire to the top jobs during the twelve years of Hitler's dictatorship. One source calculates that of the five hundred highest ranking Nazis, a paltry seventeen were Prussian – that is only 3.4 per cent. As Prussia made up two-thirds of the Reich in 1933, a properly adjusted figure for Prussian co-operation would be 328.[23] The Prussian Nazis rarely had their names in lights: the stars of the Prussian *Landtag* during the *Kampfzeit* were the now forgotten figures of Kerrl and Kube. The Silesian Kube was later discredited by his own party. Another

Silesian was Hitler's Secretary at the Reich Chancellery, Dr Hans Lammers, a hard-working – Nazi – civil servant. Both Admiral Dönitz and the Hitler Youth leader and later Gauleiter in Vienna, Baldur von Schirach were born Berliners; so was Leni Riefenstahl, the pro-Nazi film-maker. That other noted female Hitler fanatic, Hanna Reitsch, was from Silesia.[24]

Few of the notorious butchers were Prussians either. Dieter Wisliceny, Eichmann's right-hand man, was the son of a *Gutsbesitzer* in East Prussia, though his family was not even German in origin. More genuinely Prussian were the Silesian Kurt Daluege and the Pomeranian Junker Erich von dem Bach-Zelewski.

Kurt Daluege came from a minor civil service background and was brought up in Frankfurt/Oder where he excelled in sport as a result of his giant frame.[25] He volunteered for the army in 1916, but never quite made it to lieutenant. After the war he joined the nationalist Freikorps Rossbach and while a student at the Technische Hochschule in Berlin he founded the 'Frontbann', an organisation which he later merged with Röhm's SA.[26]

By 1926 he had mustered a force of 500 men, making the Berlin SA stronger than the party. He stage-managed the street fighting and the assaults on Communists in the Weimar years to a degree that it has been said of him that 'there was not one decisive bar brawl fought without Gausturmführer Daluege being there to direct it.'[27] In 1929 he switched from the SA to the SS, where he became one of Heinrich Himmler's chief rivals. His fellow Nazis liked to call his intelligence into question with the epithet 'Dummi-Dummi',[28] something borne out by Göring, who told Diels that Daluege was 'too stupid' to lead the Prussian police.[29] Göring nevertheless promoted him to Lieutenant-General of Police in 1933, and the Silesian pointed out that he was now the youngest general since Napoleon Bonaparte.[30] In the end the ambitions of this 'pseudo-Napoleon' were checked by Himmler when he took over the Prussian police and installed his Bavarian cronies in the top positions. Diels and his friends were 'rusticated' to the provinces[31] and Daluege had to make do with control of only the non-Prussian units. Here he set to work expelling the

suspected Marxists, liberals and Catholics.[32] Later he achieved
control of the *Reichs Ordnungspolizei*, or '*Orpos*' as they were
generally known: uniformed policemen whose job was to keep
order in the state. He was not an innovative Nazi. He played a
role in judging in the 'court martial' of 30 June–3 July 1934 which
executed a good many of his old friends from the SA.[33] During
the war his *Orpos* were used as *Einsatzgruppen* in the east: to
exterminate Jews, partisans and communists. In this role he
suggested they might also be used in France, but no one took him
up on it. After Heydrich's assassination, he stood in as Reichspro-
tektor in Bohemia, where he supervised the mass killings at
Lidice. He fell ill in 1943 and took no further part in the
slaughter. After his trial at Nuremberg he was extradited to
Czechoslovakia, where he was hanged.[34]

Erich von dem Bach-Zelewski represented another sort of Nazi:
the buccaneering type who was attracted by the chance of making
his name in war.* He was ruthless, though not wholly devoid of
human feelings. He was born in Lauenburg in eastern Pomerania
in 1899 and volunteered for the army at the age of fifteen. After
the war, he, like Daluege, joined a Freikorps before re-entering
the Reichswehr. When he left the army he fell on hard times and
ended up working as a taxi-driver until he inherited some land.
He joined the party in 1930 and moved into the SS soon
afterwards. He was convinced of Hitler's rectitude from the first.
Indicted on yet another count in 1961 he admitted to the court
that he was still 'an absolute Hitler man'.[35] He was a member of
Hitler's emasculated Reichstag until the end.[36]

Bach-Zelewski played a role in the 'Night of the Long Knives'
when he shot one of his rivals, the SS Cavalry leader, Anton
Freiherr von Hohberg und Buchwald, in the smoking room of his
family home.[37] At the beginning of the war, Himmler confided in
him his plan to kill 30 million Slavs. Bach-Zelewski was to play
his own part in this, but also in the extermination of Jews. In 1941
he reported 'filled with pride' that there were no more Jews in

* A sort of German 'Bulldog Drummond'.

Estonia. In Riga it is alleged that Bach-Zelewski killed 35,000 people.[38] Endless slaughter took a toll on his nerves and after a complete breakdown he had to be hospitalised. There he told the doctor, 'Thank God I'm through with it. Don't you know what's happening in Russia? The entire Jewish people ... is being exterminated there.' When he was released he asked Himmler to stop the killing. Himmler threatened him with a similar end if he didn't comply.[39]

Bach-Zelewski's name is chiefly associated with the brutal repression of the Warsaw Uprising in the summer of 1944. Although he was appointed to overall command of the operation, he didn't arrive until after the clamp down had begun under Oskar Dirlewanger and Mieceslaw Kaminski. The former was a sexual pervert from Württemberg with a doctorate in political science who had been released from prison by the Nazis; the latter was the leader of the Russian SS units in the German army.[40] Even Dirlewanger's command was only half German: the rest was made up of fierce Azerbaijanis. Himmler issued these two thugs with orders to kill every inhabitant of Warsaw and raze the city to the ground, which they would certainly have done given the chance. When Bach-Zelewski arrived, however, he counter-manded the orders and issued instructions that the killing of civilians would cease from that moment.[41]

Others had noticed that things had got out of hand in Warsaw. Guderian was shocked and went to Hitler with a request to remove both Dirlewanger and Kaminski. Bach-Zelewski also put pressure on Himmler through Eva Braun's brother-in-law, the jockey Hermann Fegelein. Bach-Zelewski was given authority to remove Kaminski and had him quietly shot. He covered his tracks by making it look like an accident so as not to alarm the Russian soldiers under Kaminski's command.[42] This delicate operation earned him high praise from Hitler, who said Bach-Zelewski was 'one of the cleverest of men'.[43] With the chief butchers out of the way, Bach-Zelewski continued the operations in a purely military fashion. When a Polish prisoner reproached him for German

savagery, coming from the race which had bred Goethe and
Schiller, Bach-Zelewski replied, 'This is war.'[44]

There was nonetheless a 'spirit of chivalry about the surrender
of General Bór-Komorowski'.[45] A photograph shows the two men
shaking hands and the Polish soldiers were allowed to go into
captivity with their personal effects. Both the Polish general and
his staff survived the war. At Nuremberg Bach-Zelewski, who
turned 'queen's evidence' at the trial, even received praise from
the Polish commander. Later he claimed to have been the person
who slipped Göring the poison for his suicide. He got away with a
short sentence, but his crimes had a habit of catching up with him
and leading to fresh indictments: first for his part in the Röhm
killings and later for his activities with the *Einsatzgruppen*. He
nonetheless contrived to stay alive until 1972, when he died in a
Munich hospital.[46]

II

Alter Fritze, steig' hernieder*
und regier' die Preussen wieder.
Lass – in diesen schweren Zeiten –
Lieber Adolf Hitler reiten.

> Placard attached to the equestrian
> statue of Frederick the Great in Unter
> den Linden after a heavy bombing raid
> in 1943.[47]

If the Prussians were not noted for butchery, for the most part
they were no heroes either. They distinguished themselves in the
field, as they had always done, but their opposition to the
increasingly brutal policies of Hitler's regime was only piecemeal.
Hitler had been careful to rein in the working classes through his
internal security network; many of the regime's most potent

---

* Old Fritz get down off your high horse;
Put Prussia on the winning side.
In these hard times one might just force
Adolf Hitler to take a ride.

opponents were away fighting a war for Germany's survival which left them neither time nor opportunity to act against the Nazis. Only a comparatively tiny number of Prussians – or Germans – enjoyed the privilege of being in the right place at the right time; or indeed, of knowing the right people to talk to.

Typical of the attitudes of the Junkers in Prussia was the art historian, Udo von Alvensleben, who was recalled to the colours in 1939 at the age of forty-two. In the Great War he had served as 'young officer and troop leader'. The Second World War caught him in the throes of conflicting emotions, 'torn away from fruitful work, and faced with the prospect that, whether we get victory or defeat, more probably [the latter], both will prove unfortunate.'[48] Like a good many of his class, Alvensleben retained the Pietistic Lutheranism of his ancestors. As the war continued the atheistic nature of the regime began ever more to show its hand. In April 1941 he attended the funeral of a General Hube in Berlin and noted the short, godless memorial delivered by Guderian. It brought back memories of Manfred von Richthofen's* burial in the last war and the 'deeply moving funeral service' which had taken place in the *Gnadenkirche*.[49]

A few days of leave in his manor-house at Wittenmoor in the Altmark gave Alvensleben the chance to scan the death announcements in the newspapers, with their great toll of 'relatives, friends and acquaintances': 'A nation which lives in religious and legal anarchy, cannot rule others, at least, not without recourse to violence. . . . We're heading for chaos. Everything which is coming will be undertaken with signs of lunacy. Perhaps we need the catastrophe, else it will be impossible to heal this great madness.'[50]

On 15 February 1943, Alvensleben paid a call on the dying Hammerstein-Equord, the former Chief of the General Staff. Hammerstein's pessimistic view of Germany's moral dilemma accorded well with Alvensleben's: 'A nation which has lost all feeling for right and wrong or good and evil; which commits such

---

* The air ace, popularly known as the 'Red Baron' who was shot down over France in 1918.

crimes, deserves to be exterminated. . . . I am ashamed to have belonged to an army that has witnessed and authorised all [these] crimes . . .'[51] Less than a month later, Alvensleben had a talk with Ulrich von Hassell, the former Ambassador to Rome, a Brandenburger who was at that time one of the leading lights of the conservative opposition around Colonel General Beck and Carl Goerdeler. Alvensleben revealed his unwillingness to accept the full package proposed by the resistance, that it was necessary to take all measures to bring down the regime which had committed such atrocities. Hassell evidently spoke frankly about the state of the opposition: 'He sees countless people and describes the situation in sarcastic terms. From my point of view we cannot mentally attack the front from the rear, and as the position lies, we can have only one thought: defend ourselves to the utmost; even if the consequences of victory – which can hardly be expected – can only be conceived with horror. The necessary cleansing from within must proceed from ourselves.'[52]

It is not enough to observe that Hassell died on a Nazi gibbet, while Alvensleben died in his bed at the age of sixty-five: Hassell had – to his great credit – taken an extreme position and very few of his fellow Junkers, with their ancient military tradition and subservience to the state, were prepared to follow him. Alvensleben had no desire to conceal what he had heard and witnessed as a staff officer travelling throughout occupied Europe. In Italy at the end of August 1943, he wrote, 'We must describe the inferno of our days with a thousand tongues. The horrible perspectives, the intellectual chaos, the misleading of the masses, the crimes of nations, the belittling of mankind; and in contrast, the uplifting of our hearts, achievement and sacrifice.'[53]

Alvensleben grew cautious after 20 July 1944, and resisted the chance to comment on the objectives of those men – some of them close friends – who were executed in its wake. 'There is a head-in-the-sand mentality reigning in the army where the mass favours either exaggerated optimism or defeatism. In the times of aristocratic order this was quite different, what we find today is plebeian rather than German. . . . The thought of this war going on and what happens when it finishes tortures me. The atrocity propaganda put out by our enemies in the First World War which we rightly angrily rejected, has proved prophetic of the monstrosities of this war. We must now seek to heal, to save, to repair the damage, to build anew. . . . How I love this sad old continent, how I hate the forces which are wrecking it.'[54]

If Alvensleben refused to commit himself to resistance, others accepted the need to plan Germany's future after the war, but believed the elimination of the man and his minions lay outside their capacities. One of these was Helmuth James Graf von Moltke, the great-nephew of the famous field marshal whose victories unified the disparate strands of Germany. On at least three occasions, the Moltke country house Kreisau (a present from a grateful nation after 1871) was the scene for round-table talks which brought together incisive minds from all over Germany to discuss rebuilding at the end of the war. Kreisau, both in its Silesian grand synods and in the smaller talks in Berlin and elsewhere, was a sort of think-tank; but despite Moltke and the names of some of its major participants, the Kreisau Circle was far from Prussian in its thinking. Not only did it foresee the need to break up the clumsy bulk of Prussia as it had existed within the Reich, it also planned to play down the whole notion of sovereign states in a future Europe. The Kreisauers saw the abandonment of sovereign states specifically in the light of the border problems which caused friction between Germany and Poland.

Moltke was a man of shrewd judgement. He had an instinctive dislike for the Nazis which he expressed in what was often an overbearing tone of aristocratic disdain. In a long letter to his English friend, Lionel Curtis, which he sent from Stockholm in March 1943, Moltke made an estimate of the numbers of prisoners then held in concentration camps, the number of them who had already been disposed of, and the number who had been released from this form of internment: 'And those who are killing people in occupied countries are to a great extent the same people who have killed or imprisoned Germans, unless they are drawn from other countries, especially from Latvia. By the way, most of the brutal SD-men, murderers, etc., have been drawn either from Austria or from the Sudetenland, the minority are toughs from the smaller Germany, and probably quite a minute minority only from Prussia.'[55]

Moltke possibly felt he had to make the point in the face of British propaganda, which continued to focus on Prussian infamy. Moltke was rare in having precise knowledge of the camps through his position as legal advisor to the German High Command, whose brief was to investigate breaches of international law. Not even all the émigrés were happy to go along with the British stance: in Oxford the academic Gerhard Leibholz (who was married to Dietrich Bonhoeffer's sister, Sabine) wrote 'Concerning the thesis that there is a necessity to crush "Prussianism", the following facts should be of interest. The leading National Socialists and ideologues are not Prussians (Hitler, Hess, Darré, the Baltic author Rosenberg), the Frenchman Gobineau, the Englishman [Houston Stewart] Chamberlain. The National Socialist movement originated in Austria and South Germany and absolutely not in Prussia. What's more the confessing Church derives its strongest support from the old Prussian provinces. Finally, the most Prussian social elements were those who approved of the bond between throne and altar. Only those who would not see this bond as a representation of Christian life would contend that the strength which is even today present within the armed forces is in many ways based on close contacts with the Catholic and Confessing Churches and maintains its opposition to the regime.'[56]

Moltke was at pains to tell Curtis that the fight against Nazism was not confined to any particular class: 'If there is anything you can say about classes it is this: broadly speaking, the middle classes are Nazi or at least most highly afflicted by one form of totalitarianism or another, and the lower ranks of the Prussian nobility as far as it still possesses land are least afflicted, are in fact practically immune from any kind of totalitarianism. The nobility of the higher ranks from dukes upwards and the nobility of the South and West of Germany are much more afflicted by this disease and the urbanised nobility is really part of the middle classes. These middle classes tend, where they are anti-Nazi, to be philo-Bolshevist, philo-Russian, etc. They feel uncertain of themselves and hope for the great new strength that shall come from the East.'[57]

Moltke represented the young, radical wing of the resistance which wished to usher in a wholly different Germany at the end of the war. Carl Goerdeler he saw as a stuffy, old-style German bourgeois politician: 'Kerenski,' he hissed at him, in the course of one of the joint meetings between the older men and the Kreisauers.[58] Goerdeler was born in Schneidemühl in Posen in 1884, the son of Julius Goerdeler, a typical Prussian official who later became a member of the *Landtag*. Julius's granddaughter has described his colours as 'black and white'[59] (the colours of the Prussian flag). Like many Prussians, his loyalty to the Reich came second.

Carl Goerdeler took the usual path into the bureaucracy ending up before the Great War as a civil servant in Solingen near Düsseldorf. After serving in the war, he came back distraught at Germany's defeat. He took leave of the town hall in Solingen and travelled to East Prussia to organise the resistance to Allied revisions in West Prussia. If Goerdeler was a 'passionate nationalist',[60] he was also a sensible and popular administrator. He became assistant mayor in Königsberg, and in 1930, *Oberbürgermeister* of Leipzig. He was Brüning's choice as successor in 1932. Hindenburg chose Papen instead. Goerdeler worked with the Nazis at first, but with the progressive introduction of their totalitarian style, he fell out with them. The final straw occurred when they took the opportunity presented by his absence in Scandinavia to remove the statue of the Jewish composer Mendelssohn from its place outside the Leipzig Gewandhaus. When Goerdeler returned to Germany he resigned.[61]

Throughout the last years of peace, Goerdeler was an indefatigable representative of the 'other' Germany. He travelled all over Europe and held talks with officials in order to put the views of the German opposition and enlist their support. Many in Britain were struck by his apparently 'Nationalist' aims: he wanted to see the elimination of the Corridor, and thought the ideal solution for Poland would be a return to the old Polish-Lithuanian state, which would have afforded them the necessary access to the sea.[62] After the war started he believed that Germany should be allowed to hang on to some of the land it had won through force.

Goerdeler was the opposition's first choice as a future leader of a non-Nazi Germany, with Colonel General Beck as the 'regent' or president. Neither man was successful at organising the coup necessary to remove Hitler from the scene. By 1944, Stauffenberg had brought a new dynamism into the German resistance, and many of the younger men and Socialists were ready to push Goerdeler aside.

Orders to arrest Goerdeler were issued even before 20 July, and the former mayor fled, making his way to the east. The Nazis slapped a one-million RM reward on his head. He was spotted and given away as he went to Marienwerder in West Prussia for a last look at his parents' graves.[63] Goerdeler's life did not end there, however. From August 1944 until February 1945 he was set to work writing endless memoranda on the structure of a future, non-Nazi Germany. He was not alone in this work; the former Prussian Finance Minister, Johannes Popitz, was also given pens and paper and asked to put down his thoughts on reforming the administration. Behind this curious move was Otto Ohlendorf, one of the Nazi 'intellectuals' who, having considerable doubts as to the survival of the regime, endeavoured to keep these two leading politicians alive for the use of a future Germany. The memoranda were to be like the stories of Scheherazade, a delaying tactic to stave off execution. At the beginning of 1945, Ohlendorf requested a further six months for Popitz to write his projects. The hard-liners lost patience, however and both men were hanged just two months before the regime collapsed.[64]

Both Goerdeler and Popitz wanted to see a Hohenzollern resoration if the right Hohenzollern could be found. For many the first choice was the Crown Prince's second son, Louis Ferdinand, who had had a varied life in the United States where he had worked at Ford's in Detroit and knew the American President and his wife. Louis Ferdinand's elder brother, Prince William, married a member of the minor German nobility, Dorothea von Salviati, thereby falling foul of Hohenzollern household law, and being obliged to relinquish his claims to the throne. Louis Ferdinand's first brush with National Socialism occurred when he returned to Berlin from Detroit to do his doctorate and went out to the Sportpalast to witness Hitler speaking on *Preussentum und National-sozialismus*. After the speech a friend said, 'I suppose we are going to hear a lot more from this man who looks like Charlie Chaplin and speaks like a Viennese concierge.'[65]

After Hitler came to power, his friend Putzi Hanfstaegel arranged a meeting between Louis Ferdinand and the Führer at the Chancellery. Hitler was slightly better dressed than usual, noted Louis Ferdinand, but he observed a speck of blood on the Austrian's collar: 'His behaviour was polite and easy going in an Austrian way . . . he spoke with a rather hoarse Austrian accent, to which he tried somewhat unsuccessfully to lend a degree of North German or Prussian harshness. . . . At the beginning he was modest and almost shy. . . . He addressed me simply as "Prince". I thought I'd have a go at testing his vanity and awarded him the title of "Your Excellency". From that moment onwards he called me "Your Royal Highness". In this more relaxed vein, the talk turned to cars, and Hitler delivered a forty-minute monologue on the subject.'[66]

During the war, Louis Ferdinand worked in the legal department of Lufthansa, where he was a colleague of Dietrich Bonhoeffer's brother Klaus and Otto John. Through these two men, the prince was introduced to the younger circle of the resistance, who took to him. The older men still preferred the Crown Prince as a candidate. Louis Ferdinand met the Kreisauer foreign policy expert, Adam von Trott zu Solz, himself the son of a former Prussian Kultus Minister, in a *Weinstube* and after a few drinks, Trott 'expressed himself positively as to his character'. At that stage the younger men still countenanced a restoration, but as the war wore on, only John and Popitz were left to champion Louis Ferdinand.[67] In 1943, Louis Ferdinand made the unwise move of telling his father about the negotiations: the Crown Prince shouted in English, 'Hands Off!' Then in German, 'Don't you get involved at all.'[68] If anyone was to become Kaiser, it was to be the Crown Prince.

Like his father, Louis Ferdinand came under suspicion after 20 July 1944 and was subjected to a seven-hour interrogation at the Gestapo's Prinz Albrechtstrasse headquarters. Although any number of the men with whom he had held talks had also been arrested and even tortured, it is to their credit that none of them seems to have incriminated the Hohenzollern prince. After his release, Louis Ferdinand took refuge at Gut Cadinen in East Prussia. He was there when the Russian offensive looked set to cut off the Vistula in January 1945. Louis Ferdinand crossed the frozen Haff on a sledge. He was one of the last to succeed: half an hour later the Russians shelled the ice. Louis Ferdinand's escape recalled the exploits of an earlier Hohenzollern, the Great Elector '. . . who like me, had to cross the Haff on a sledge in deepest winter; however, that was as a victor, not as a refugee.'[69]

If one had to select just one of the early Nazis who drove the Junkers into opposition Walther Darré would be the ideal choice. His books *Das Bauerntum als Lebensquell* (The Peasantry as the Source of Life) and *Neuadel aus Blut und Boden* (New Nobility from Blood and Soil) both attacked the nobility as a moribund institution and advocated its replacement by a new nobility culled from the peasantry. Like Heinrich Himmler, Darré used his experience as a small farmer and breeder and applied it to mankind. If animals had their studbooks, why not humans?[70] Darré, in his search for historical allies, had come across an interesting quotation from Treitschke: 'The Prussian nobility as a class has for three centuries only brought about misfortune.'[71] The Almanach de Gotha was, says Darré 'a roll call of asses'. 'What Germany really needs is a true nobility in the old German sense; a return to the crusading nobility of the Middle Ages.'[72]

This was the sort of language which was calculated to annoy principled Prussian conservatives like Ewald von Kleist-Schmenzin. Kleist-Schmenzin had first noticed Hitler at the time of the beer-hall Putsch, and written him off as a 'buffoon'.[73] He nonetheless sat down and read *Mein Kampf* and Alfred Rosenberg's *Mythus des 20 Jahrhunderts* when they came out. Hitler's racialism offended against his religious beliefs. As a Pomeranian nobleman he was hardly philo-semitic, but he disliked the idea of anti-semitism as a political card: 'an imported product from Vienna' he called it.[74] Kleist-Schmenzin's Pietistic faith had to face up to an increasing inhumanity towards man. It was precisely this which gave rise to the *Pfarrernotbund* (the Pastors' Emergency League) in 1933, when the 6,000 clergymen in the Prussian east signed a petition to protect the Church from political interference.[75]

Not only was the racial content of both books disturbing, Kleist-Schmenzin also feared Rosenberg's desire to fight a war with Russia: 'Kleist remained enough of a Prussian to perceive instinctively the danger of a German Soviet war.'[76] Even more than by the lunacy of an aggressive war, he was appalled by Hitler's deep contempt for history: 'Only a fool could believe you could write off the experiences of centuries.' The time of the racial migrations was over. Kleist-Schmenzin was horrified enough by what he had read to want to question the author further. In 1932 he had an interview with Hitler in Göring's Berlin flat. Kleist-Schmenzin sat in the only armchair, while Hitler had to make do with a hard seat. Hitler spouted one of his endless monologues. It was indeed true, everything which Kleist-Schmenzin had read in *Mein Kampf*. That same year, the Pomeranian nobleman wrote a small pamphlet, *Nationalsozialismus – eine Gefahr* (National Socialism – A Danger), which went through two editions, attacking Hitler's views on race, Socialism, religion and government and the erection of the party over the state. 'This madness must be destroyed,' wrote Kleist-Schmenzin, it is 'a danger for the nation and an enemy of selfless patriotic ideas.'[77]

Hindenburg was casting around for a replacement for Brüning. His eyes fell briefly on his friend Oskar von den Osten-Warnitz,

Kleist-Schmenzin's father-in-law. Kleist-Schmenzin, whose views were deeply divided from those of Osten-Warnitz, asked if he might serve as his Minister of the Interior. Hindenburg chose Papen instead of Osten-Warnitz, and Kleist-Schmenzin never had the chance to put his anti-Nazi policies into action.[78]

When Hitler came to power the following January, Kleist-Schmenzin wrote an open letter to Hugenberg, announcing his withdrawal from the DNVP on the grounds of the party's coalition with Hitler and the NSDAP. Not long after Kleist-Schmenzin received his first calls from local Nazi thugs. He suffered his first bout of imprisonment in April that year when he tried to prevent the Nazis from flying a swastika from the tower of the local church. He was out before the Night of the Long Knives when there was a predictable attempt to murder him.[79]

Kleist-Schmenzin spent the years leading up to the outbreak of war doing what he could to bring about Hitler's fall. To this end he even travelled to England and secured a promise of support from Winston Churchill. After 20 July 1944 it was a foregone conclusion that the Junker would be arrested. The Gestapo were at his door the following morning, having surrounded the manor-house with their men. Kleist-Schmenzin thought for a while about taking a gun to the policemen: at least he'd be able to take one of them with him. In the end he gave himself up peacefully. He was not tried until 3 February the following year, when he appeared in the dock alongside Fabian von Schlabrendorff. The President of the Court, Roland Freisler, summoned Kleist-Schmenzin and read out the charges against him. He was accused of high treason, did he have anything to say in his defence? '*Jawohl*, I have been committing high treason consistently and with all the means at my disposal since 30 January 1933. I have never made any bones about my fight against Hitler and National Socialism. I hold this fight as ordained by God, and God alone will be my judge.'[80]

Freisler was reduced to silence: a rare occurrence. He interrupted the hearing and called Schlabrendorff, but before he could proceed with the case there was an air-raid warning. As the raid looked serious, the prisoners were re-manacled and the court went down to the cellar. The court-house received a direct hit and the pressure from above dislodged a heavy beam from the cellar roof. It fell to the ground, hitting Freisler and smashing his skull.[81]

Kleist-Schmenzin might have derived some small consolation from the death of one of the foulest hanging judges in modern history, but his reprieve was short. On 23 February he was back in court before President Lämmle. The case dragged on until 15 March before Kleist-Schmenzin was finally condemned to death. On 9 April 1945, not two weeks before the Russians entered Berlin, Kleist-Schmenzin was led from his cell in Berlin-Plötzensee to the execution chamber. On the way he passed Hermann Freiherr von Luninck, who noted Kleist-Schmenzin's relaxed attitude and radiant eyes – '*Wiedersehen, Luninck,*' he shouted across to his friend. Even the Nazi judge who read out the sentence before Kleist-Schmenzin lay down on the guillotine, had to admit, 'He went to his death like a hero.'[82]

Schmenzin had long since fallen to the Red Army, who murdered any members of the family they found there. Later the Poles killed Kleist-Schmenzin's mother. As Kleist-Schmenzin's biographer has written, even before the blade fell on the Junker's neck, 'the world for which Ewald von Kleist had fought and suffered, no longer existed.'[83]

III

Now they are destroying my Prussia.

> Ewald von Kleist-Schmenzin in the
> Berlin Casino Club, 30 January 1933.

The Second World War was a war after all, and most Prussians believed that going to war was part of their duty to the state. Some of the obvious objectives in this war would not have troubled their consciences too much. Few Prussians or Germans approved of the eastern borders as they had been laid down by Versailles. With the Polish campaign of the Six Weeks War, Hitler was to remedy all that, and that could only make him more popular.

The same sense of duty, the same spirit of sacrifice. The destruction of the old families was even more terrible than in the Great War. Most of them died as officers, some as high-ranking officers, serving the National Socialist state. It was not the state of *suum quique*; they were not to get their share. This time they were only there to die for Hitler.

It is the acquiescence of the field marshals and the commanding generals which has shocked us most in the post-war years: that such men were prepared to allow such atrocious things to go on behind their lines, if not actually participate in the crimes.

When the war broke out, Henning von Tresckow was Ia (or GSO I) to an infantry division in the east. Like many of his background, he had mixed emotions about the war: yes, he wanted to see the revision of the borders so that Danzig and East Prussia were no longer isolated from the Reich, but no, he did not wish to see Hitler vindicated. A third problem also arose: strategically he saw no good coming from the destruction of Poland, a useful buffer state between Germany and Soviet Russia. The atrocities he witnessed in Poland stiffened his resolve to bring about the downfall of Hitler and his regime. His method, then and later in the war, was to try to bring round the generals with whom he came into contact as a staff officer. He had no more success with his uncle, General, later Field Marshal, von Bock than he did with either Rundstedt or Manstein. But this did not deter him from trying.

After the fall of France, Tresckow was promoted lieutenant-colonel. The speed of France's defeat had come as a shock to Tresckow, as it had to many Germans. That year in Paris, he told Luise von Benda, later the wife of General Jodl, that if Churchill succeeded in bringing America into the war, the only part of Germany left to them would be the old Electorate of Brandenburg, and Tresckow himself would command the royal bodyguard.[84]

In June 1941 Tresckow took over the position as Chief of Staff to Army Group Centre in preparation for the invasion of Russia.

It was a depressing prospect for a soldier and a staff officer; he believed that the army had not an eighth of the equipment it required for the task. Army Group 'C', on the other hand, became the new centre of his resistance operations. Here he gathered around him the circle of friends which he culled largely from IR 9 in Potsdam: Fabian von Schlabrendorff became his ordnance officer and closest confidant in his conspiratorial activities; then there was Major von Gersdorff, from another distinguished Prussian family, whose job it was to look after enemy intelligence. The other members of his staff were Heinrich Graf Lehndorff, Major Hans Graf von Hardenberg and Berndt von Kleist. The special task allotted to Lehndorff and Hardenberg was to work on Bock; they were his ordnance officers.[85]

Bock was windy. He proved tractable when it came to crimes against humanity and refused to put through the order to shoot snipers and partisans, but he would not join the opposition. As Bock's nephew, Tresckow enjoyed considerable licence to criticise his commanding officer. When Bock told Gersdorff to fly to Berlin on his behalf to protest against the order, Tresckow said it was useless for a mere major to do such a thing: 'You must fly to Hitler, along with Leeb and Manstein.' Bock wouldn't be bullied by his nephew. He told Gersdorff to go, and if Hitler's adjutant wouldn't see him, he was to take the complaint to the army's commander-in-chief, Brauchitsch. 'Gentlemen,' said Tresckow, 'you have all heard. Field Marshal von Bock has protested.'[86]

Hitler backed down that time. On 24 May Brauchitsch rescinded the order to the extent that it was now no longer the concern of the army. This left the business of dealing with irregulars to the SD's *Einsatzgruppen*. With the army they may have found some mercy. Now they found none. On 6 June the famous Commissar Order was issued: all Russian political commissars were to be shot on capture. Tresckow told his officers that the order would not be carried out within Bock's command: 'As long as I am Ia to Army Group C no commissar will be shot. A Russian who gives himself up is taken into captivity and he saves his life. Every soldier knows this.'[87]

New trials came with the discovery of the butchery at Borissow. It was revealed that 7,000 civilians had been massacred under the noses of the Army Group. Tresckow went to his uncle. 'This must never happen again. We *must* take action. We rule Russia by force of arms. If we behave without circumspection then we will set a precedent.' Bock made a feeble protest, but the SD *Sondercommando* was nonetheless withdrawn from his field of operations. There were no further atrocities committed in this sector of the Russian front. The commandant in Borissow took his own life.[88]

By the middle of October 1941, Tresckow could no longer see the chance of victory and said as much to Bock. Bock asked him for an alternative plan.

'There is only one solution: we must assassinate Hitler.'

'I won't hear such things, it is high treason. I won't have the Führer insulted.'

'But that that is not just my point of view, it is my conviction.'

'That is monstrous. If you don't go from this room, I will.'

As Tresckow showed no signs of moving, Bock stormed out of the meeting.[89] Tresckow wanted nothing less. When Carl Goerdeler approached him with the idea of imprisoning Hitler, he told him that only a dead Hitler could allow Germany to recover. When it was suggested that he might wear a bullet-proof vest, Tresckow replied that he would shoot him in the neck or the head, nor did he fear losing his own life in the attempt.[90] Eventually the prospect of using explosives suggested itself to him. Although this seemed less gentlemanly it was a better and more efficient method: 'We mustn't shilly-shally; ridding the world from the greatest criminal of all time is worth the deaths of a few innocent people.'[91]

The killing of Hitler had become an article of faith. The tyrant had 'broken his oath a thousand times' Tresckow told Margarethe von Oven. Hitler was 'the root of all evil . . . in the world. Without the death of the dictator there could be no new beginning. That was why there had to be an assassination.'

The circle was growing. Tresckow won over Alexander Stahlberg, Manstein's ordnance officer, with the special intention of having him work on the field marshal. Two of Tresckow's fiercest allies were the brothers Philipp and Georg von Boeselager. In March 1943 the group got its first opportunity to prove itself when Hitler visited the Army Group headquarters. All Boeselager's officers were prepared to act, but Tresckow made the mistake of telling Field Marshal von Kluge. 'For God's sake you will do nothing today!' Kluge told them. It was then that they had the idea of putting the explosive in the cognac bottles and detonating them in Hitler's plane. Even so, the chances of killing Hitler on 13 March 1943 were not as good as they had foreseen. He was surrounded by faithful SS guards and the only opportunity which presented itself was in the conference room. But this would have meant killing not only Hitler, but also Kluge and the staff chiefs.[92]

When Tresckow went on leave that spring he informed his wife Erika of the plot. She was the daughter of the former Prussian Minister of War and Chief of the General Staff Erich von Falkenhayn: 'Do you also wish to stick your head in the sand like an ostrich? It is going to be better for you in the long run if you know the reality. I want my wife to be with me in this. Certainly, later people of what they like to call our class will throw the first stones. . . . I cannot understand how there can be people who call themselves Christians today, who are not at the same time furious opponents of this regime. A truly convinced Christian *can* only be a convinced opponent.'[93]

While Tresckow was away on leave in Potsdam that spring he had the chance to attend the confirmation of his two sons in the Garrison Church. The whole family were present, with countless relations travelling up for the occasion. Tresckow used the opportunity to give as good a definition of the Prussian mission as ever penned. Addressing his two sons he said, 'You must never forget that you were born on Prussian soil and that your minds have been formed in Prusso-German thought. Today you are being confirmed in old Prussia's holiest place. [The combination of the two] involves a great responsibility in itself, the responsibility of truthfulness, of inner and outward discipline, for the fulfilment of duty to the final degree. But one should never speak of

Prussianism without making it clear that it does *not* end here. It is so often misunderstood. The concept of freedom can never be removed from true Prussianism. True Prussianism is the synthesis of bond and liberty, between natural subordination and a ruling class which wholly understands the needs [of its subordinates], between pride in yourself and understanding for others, between rigour and compassion. Without this association of ideas there runs a danger of decline into soulless soldiery and narrow-minded self-opinion. Only in this synthesis does Prussia's German and European mission lie, only there do we find "the Prussian dream".'*[94]

It had taken Fritz-Dietlof von der Schulenburg a long time to shake off the last drops of Nazi ideology which clung to his radical philosophy. When the moment came he slipped out of the civil service and into the army. This had a considerable advantage for members of the opposition: the army was still Seeckt's creation, an apolitical body, and the price of silence in 1934 was that it was to remain so until 20 July 1944. No one needed to be a member of the Nazi Party as long as they were serving in the armed forces.[95] In 1938, Schulenburg had done his preliminary training as a reserve officer in Potsdam. Not for nothing had he chosen IR 9, or 'Graf 9', as it was called from the large numbers of aristocrats serving in its officer corps.[96] IR 9 was also the core of the army's resistance to National Socialism: nineteen officers and former officers of IR 9 were implicated in 20 July 1944.[97]

Schulenburg set about working on the younger officers of the regiment. Many complained that they were bound by their oath of allegiance to Hitler. Schulenburg did his best to counter their fears: 'The oath to this criminal was meaningless anyway,' he told Hans Karl Fritzsche. By April 1943 he was becoming notorious for his attempts to win soldiers over to the opposition, and the story reached the ears of the Gestapo. That month he was briefly taken into custody, although the fact that he had been, until

* Neither child survived.

recently, Vice President of the Berlin Police, seems to have cut some ice. Perhaps they also took into consideration his position as a Nazi *alte Kampfer*.[98] Schulenburg did not stop at speaking to officers in the army. He was prepared to bring over members of the SS too. He told two SS generals that Hitler had to be assassinated and seems to have been equally frank with Werner Best, the head SS man in Denmark.[99]

Schulenburg approached everything with the same fierce determination. He had been a passionate Nazi, now he was a passionate opponent. There was not one branch of the resistance in which he didn't play some small role, running this way and that between the *Honoratioren* of the older generation and the Kreisauers of the younger one, between the military and the trades unions, between the SS and the army, between the Conservative monarchists and the old Socialists. He took enormous risks: it seems likely that he used the Esplanade Hotel in Berlin as a place to duplicate documents, including the sermons of the Roman Catholic Bishop of Westphalia, Graf Galen, who had spoken in the pulpit against the Nazi persecution of the Church and the extermination of the mentally ill.[100]

His circle was vast and, as often as not, very Prussian: those for whom the 'chimes of Potsdam rang in their hearts'. In East Prussia he prepared the ground for a group of people to take over power after the Putsch: among others Marion Gräfin Dönhoff, Heinrich Graf Lehndorff and Heinrich Graf zu Dohna* were to play their roles. In Potsdam he had recruited a number of committed young officers: Lieutenant Hans-Ewald von Kleist, the son of Ewald von Kleist-Schmenzin, Second Lieutenant Georg Sigismund von Oppen and Ludwig Freiherr von Hammerstein-Equord, the son of the former Chief of Staff, were just three of them. Hammerstein remembers his meetings with Schulenburg. They took place every month at the Casino, or officers' club in Potsdam. He recalls the fervour with which Schulenburg spoke of the need to kill Hitler.

'Are you ready?' he asked.

* Dohna was to be the head man in East Prussia.[101]

'I am ready right now!' Hammerstein had replied. With Oppen and Kleist, Hammerstein was to blow Hitler up in the course of a parade to model new Wehrmacht uniforms. At the last moment the parade was called off. Kleist's and Oppen's names were the only ones Hammerstein ever knew. He recalls one other episode involving Schulenburg at this time. He had gone to see his cousin, the Finance Minister and former Rhodes Scholar Lutz Graf Schwerin von Krosigk, and revealed the entire plot to him. Krosigk could not believe his ears and simply stared at Schulenburg. Schulenburg had come away from the meeting seething with rage. 'We'll have him hanged!' he had said. After the war Hammerstein was not slow to see the irony of that statement. Krosigk died in his bed.[102]*

After returning to the Russian front, Tresckow resumed his activities and his attempt to win over the field marshals. Another fruitless attempt was made to interest Manstein – 'Prussian field marshals do not mutiny'. With Kluge, however, the officers had more luck. Gersdorff and Tresckow explained to him their feeling that Germany could not be saved unless Hitler was killed. Kluge listened patiently and finally opened his arms: '*Kinder*, I'm with you!' He shook their hands. Tresckow was sceptical at once, and rightly so. Kluge proved indecisive on the day, thereby preventing the fall of the western front in Normandy which might have ended the war in the west ten months earlier. 'But, Field Marshal, now you mustn't go back on it.'[103]

It is impossible to say now whether the 20 July plot would have worked more smoothly had Tresckow been in Berlin, rather than Stauffenberg. Stauffenberg had the obvious disadvantage of his injuries. He had lost a hand and retained just two fingers on the other, a situation which did not make it easy for him to prime explosives. When he was interrupted on the day, half the charge had to be abandoned and thrown away. It seems certain that no one would have survived had the full load of explosives gone off

---

* Krosigk was also closely related to another plotter, Graf von Schwerin-Schwanenfeld. He made no attempt to intercede on either man's behalf, although to the Gestapo he expressed concern for Schwanenfeld's family.

in the bunker. But it was Stauffenberg and not Tresckow who, by virtue of becoming Chief of Staff to General Fromm, had access to the Führer's conferences. Stauffenberg was also the man who brought motivation to the plot in Berlin, where it was crumbling with indecision and moral dilemma. While the different groups stood around waiting for the Putsch to go ahead, Goerdeler and Beck did little to speed up the vital blow which would set the Walküre orders in motion.

Tresckow and Stauffenberg had nothing but respect for one another. They had met in 1941 in Borissow. Tresckow, the Prussian soldier, admired the south German's energy, musical skill and love of literature; Stauffenberg had the clarity and relentless determination of Tresckow's military thinking. In the run-up to the great day, however, Tresckow was impotent; stuck out on the Eastern Front preparing for the great Russian offensive which would destroy his Army Group just one week after the failure of the attempt on Hitler's life.

Schulenburg was in the thick of things in Berlin, attending the last-minute conferences. On 18 July he and his family left for Trebbow in Mecklenburg. It was his wife's birthday on the 20th. The next day he returned to Berlin. He told his wife there was a fifty-fifty chance of success. The next day he arrived in the Bendlerstrasse Military Headquarters some time after Stauffenberg had flown in from Rastenburg. Schulenburg already knew that the blast had failed to kill the tyrant. He had detailed his young officer friends to be on hand that afternoon. In the hall of the building he ran into Fritzsche and told him 'it was all over, as Hitler was obviously still alive.' 'We must go on in spite of this, drink the cup down to the lees. We must sacrifice ourselves. People will understand us later.' He drew Fritzsche into a neighbouring office and there they sat down on a camp bed. He proceeded to shred the papers in his briefcase. Then he told the other man it was his wife's birthday. He brought a fresh sausage out of his case which his wife had sent him that morning. Together they ate it. Then he went up to Stauffenberg.[104]

At one o'clock the following morning, Tresckow heard Hitler's speech on the wireless in which he announced his survival of the blast and his determination to deal with the conspirators; he resolved to shoot himself. He knew that he would be tortured and he thought they might get names out of him. When his friend Schlabrendorff tried to get him to wait, he refused: 'When someone loses a gamble like this, one must suffer the consequences.' Tresckow faced his end with astonishing bravery: running into Captain Eberhard von Breitenbach, Tresckow said he was sorry that Breitenbach could not witness his death. 'I don't wish to give our enemies the satisfaction of taking me alive.' He told the captain of his plan to drive out to no man's land and to stage an attack by partisans. '*Aufwiedersehen* till we meet again in a better world.'[105]

When he reached the 28th Jäger Division's lines, Tresckow called Schlabrendorff for news. There was nothing to give him any cause to go back on his decision. He travelled out to no man's land with a Major Kuhn. When they reached the woods, he sent Kuhn back for a map. Kuhn heard shots and the sound of a grenade going off and threw himself to the ground. When he went back to Tresckow he found him dead. Half his face had been blown off by the grenade.[106]

Schulenburg had been apprehended in the Bendlerblock. He was tried before the People's Court. His concluding words have come down to us: 'We undertook this deed to save Germany from untold misery. I am quite aware that I shall be hanged as a result, but I do not regret what I have done and I hope that another will find a more auspicious moment to finish the job.'[107]

XIII

The End

OBITUARY

After a brief illness and in great pain, having undergone a number
of amputations from the head and from other parts of his body; our
deeply beloved great-grandfather, anxious defender and dear quartermaster the *Prussian State* passed away from the nervous shock he
received on May 7 1945, at the age of 285 [sic] years. Members of
the family: Wilhelmina Era, stepdaughter; Germania, née Brandenburg, wife; the Spirit of Potsdam, ward; Baron Barras Militarism,
comrade in arms; Prussian Bureaucrat, private secretary; Baron
Junker, administrator of his many estates ...

> *Odra* (Polish newspaper), June 1947.
> Quoted in Andreas Lawaty, *Das Ende*
> *Preussen in polnischer Sicht*, 199.

'I was just thinking,' he said, 'how extraordinary it all is. My life is
extraordinary. Doesn't the Party badge on my lapel disturb you?'

'I know who you are,' she replied.

'It's not a disguise, you know, *gnädige Frau*. It is the truth. I am a
German, a real Johann Müller. Do you understand that?'

'I understand,' she answered quietly. 'There are all sorts of
Germans. Everyone knows that, please ...'

'Everybody knows that now, but when the war starts up again,
when this whole shambles takes on a new dimension, the Poles will
forget that there are all sorts of Germans. Who will I be then? What
will happen to me?'

> Andrzej Szczypiorski, *Pócżatek*
> (translated into German as *Die schöne*
> *Frau Seidenman* by Klaus Staemmler),
> Zürich, 1988, 140.

The state had perished. Its people lived on through war, their
values eroded by the dictates of their totalitarian rulers. The land
would go next, those endless plains of sand, filled with deep pine
forests and secret lakes, which Junker and peasant had tilled and

farmed since the arrival of the first Germans in the High Middle Ages.

First came the bombs which destroyed the cities in the west. From the end of November 1943 to the capitulation in May 1945, the British and the Americans destroyed nineteen buildings in twenty in the capital Berlin. Few if any cities were spared the treatment: on 14 April 1945 most of the centre of Potsdam was smashed to smithereens; Magdeburg was almost totally obliterated on 16 January of the same year; medieval Halberstadt lost eighty per cent of its buildings on 8 April, when the Americans destroyed the city; only a thin strip of crumbling half-timbered houses attests to Nordhausen's picturesque pre-war state; the centre of Stettin went in another massive Allied air-raid, leaving only the villas and long, straight streets of *Mietshäuser* to testify to the fact that this was once part of Prussia.[1]

The Russian advance shattered the peace which had reigned in the east. Shelling rather than bombs destroyed Danzig, Marienburg, Allenstein, Breslau and Frankfurt/Oder. Often the retreating Germans played a part in the destruction of historic Prussia. In Küstrin, for example, they blew up the sixteenth-century fortress where Frederick the Great had seen his friend Katte executed. As often as not the manor-houses in the east were pillaged by the SS before the Russians and the Poles had a chance to scavenge for what was left.

Silesia, Pomerania, West and East Prussia had all had a quiet war until the end of 1944. The towns and cities had been filled with evacuees and it was possible for a primary school teacher like Marianne Günther to live her 'quiet days in Gertlauken' doing little more than baking biscuits and going for bicycle rides. The war came home to the East Prussians in the summer of 1944, when the entire centre of Königsberg was destroyed by the British. Then came Nemmersdorf. On 21 October 1944, the Russian Army entered East Prussia and German territory for the first time. They stayed just one night before they retreated. In that night they killed seventy-two women and one man. Most of the women had been raped (including one aged eighty-four); some of the victims had been crucified.

Babies had their heads smashed in. The luckiest had got away with a simple bullet in the back of the skull.[2] Encouraged by the blood-curdling invective of journalists such as Ilya Ehrenburg, the Red Army was making it quite clear that they were not going to forget similarly bestial acts which had taken place in Russia.

The German Army held the Russians back until 17 January 1945, then they broke through in the east and advanced on Insterburg. The civilian population of East Prussia who had been hanging around wondering what to do were finally given permission to leave for the west. Almost simultaneously the first Russian units arrived in the area of Elbing, thereby cutting off the escape route. For most people the only solution was to try to make it over the frozen Haff. One of these was the journalist Marion Gräfin Dönhoff, who had been looking after the family estate of Friedrichstein. She was one of the lucky ones who crossed the ice before the Russians began shelling.

She had been travelling for two weeks when she arrived at Varzin, the estate Bismarck had bought with the cash voted him after the victories of 1866. Outside the *Gutshaus*, Gräfin Dönhoff saw two huge harvest wagons piled high with boxes. This was the Bismarck Archive, waiting to be transported to safety in the other Bismarck estate, Friedrichsruh. Inside the house, Gräfin Dönhoff found the Iron Chancellor's daughter-in-law, Gräfin Sybille Bismarck, 'a small, frail, highly amusing woman of great age . . .' who had been married to Otto von Bismarck's youngest son, Bill. Gräfin Bismarck proved such good company that, despite the growing danger from the Red Army, Marion Dönhoff did not leave the house for two whole days.

Gräfin Bismarck was not intending to leave at all. Convinced that she would not survive the journey, she had had a grave dug in the garden, knowing that when the time came, no one would have time to bury her properly. In the meantime she continued to play the *grande dame*: 'The old servant, who had no desire to leave either, continued to serve at table. There was one splendid red wine after another – vintages which one would never have imagined [drinking] in one's wildest dreams. No reference was ever made to what was going on outside and to what was still in store. She told lively ... stories about her father-in-law, of the Kaiser's court and of the time when her husband ... was *Oberpräsident* of East Prussia.

'The time finally came to say goodbye and ride on. I turned round as we were half way to the garden gate for a last look. She stood, lost in thought, under the porch waving still with her tiny handkerchief. I think she was even smiling, but I couldn't see for certain.'[3] It is presumed that Gräfin Sybille von Bismarck committed suicide before the arrival of the Russians.[4]

Königsberg was declared a 'fortress' to be held to the last. In this miserable position, bombarded night and day, it clung to life for three months. The Russians entered the city on the night of 8 April.[5] Various desperate attempts had been made to escape. Trains had run down the enemy lines laden with civilians and returned with their load, unable to chance a breakthrough. An estimated half million Germans succeeded in escaping across the frozen Haff, though thousands perished when the Russians began to bomb the ice.[6] Up to 25,000 of those who tried to escape on the hospital ships which left from Pillau met a similarly gruesome end. Although they were clearly marked, the Russians sank no fewer than twelve of these between January and March. The sinking of the *Goya* with 7,000 refugees on board, was the greatest single loss of life in the history of navigation, far greater than the *Titanic* or the *Lusitania*.[7]

On 25 March, the first Russian shells fell on Danzig. The medieval core was still burning from an air-raid on 24 March.[8] 'The Häkergasse, Langgasse, Breitgasse, Grosse and Kleine Wollwerbegasse were burning, the Tobiasgasse, Hundegasse, the Altstadt and Vorstadt ditches were burning, the city walls were burning and the Long Bridge. The Krantor was made of wood and burned particularly well.'[9] Sometime during the pounding of the city 'the man from Bavaria', Albert Forster, left Danzig to its fate.[10] He was prudent enough to take a submarine rather than trust his fate to a surface vessel.[11] On 30 March the Poles had hoisted their flag over the ruins of the town hall.

For those who for one reason or another had not managed to run, life now took an even greater turn for the worse. One of the most moving accounts of the torments of the human soul ever written is Hans Graf von Lehndorff's *East Prussian Diary*, which charts his time in the east from January 1945 until May 1947. Lehndorff was a doctor, a cousin of the Steinort Lehndorffs. He was also a profoundly religious man. Just before 20 July 1944, his cousin Heinrich had come to see him in Insterburg to ask him if he would help after the assassination. Lehndorff had searched the scriptures for the authority to act against a tyrant. In the Epistle to the Romans he had found the instruction: 'Let every soul be subject unto the higher powers . . .' Lehndorff asked whether one must put up with everything: 'Must one go on idly watching a madman dragging a nation to its destruction?' From the Apostle Paul he learned: 'The choice lay simply between guilt and guilt.'[12]

After the failure of the assassination attempt Lehndorff heard of his cousin's fate. As the owner of an estate, Heinrich Lehndorff-Steinort had been released from the army and now lived in one part of the old house, while the 'Second Bismarck', Joachim von Ribbentrop lived in another to be close to the Führer's East Prussian headquarters in Rastenburg nearby. On 20 July he had put on his uniform in preparation for taking over the military command in Königsberg. When nothing came of his long wait in Königsberg, he drove back to Steinort. The Gestapo were there the following morning, but somehow he managed to escape through an open window and dodge the police dogs by running into the lakes. Having eluded the Gestapo he changed his mind, worried what the SD men would do to his family. He gave himself up.

That was not the end of Heinrich Lehndorff's story, however. He managed to achieve something unique in the bloody aftermath of the bomb plot: he escaped from a black maria in the streets of Berlin and was able to travel as far as Mecklenburg. The Gestapo, however had removed his shoe-laces, and after four days on the run, his feet were so swollen that he needed to recuperate. Sadly he knocked on the wrong door. The forester was a local official and turned him over to the authorities. He was hanged on 4 September.[13]

Hans Lehndorff had occasion to remember his cousin's fate after 9 April 1945. At first he carried on working in the hospital, although the conditions became progressively less and less bearable. His assistant 'Doktora' was raped while she was operating on a patient. Later she took her own life. The surgeon himself was swept up at random with some other Königsbergers and led into captivity. '*Gitlair kapoot!*' (Hitler's had it!) yelled the Russian soldiers as they passed him on the road. 'Hats off, thought I, if it's taken all *this* to bring *that* about!'[14] That night the women were led off one by one to the call of '*Davai suda!*' Later the Russians learned a German version of the call which was to strike terror into women on the eastern side of Germany for a generation: '*Frau komm!*'

That there was complete approval for this policy among Russian High Command comes from no less an authority than Alexander Solzhenitsyn, then a captain in the artillery: 'All of us knew very well that if the girls were German they could be raped and then shot . . .'[15] A Russian major put it like this: 'Any of our chaps had simply to say "Frau komm", and she knew what was expected of her. . . . Let's face it. For nearly four years, the Red Army had been sex-starved . . . but the looting and raping in a big way did not start until our soldiers got into Germany. Our fellows were so sex-starved that they often raped old women of 60, or 70, or even 80 – much to these grandmothers' surprise, if not delight. But it was a nasty business, and the record of Kazakhs and the other Asiatic troops was particularly bad.'[16]

Hans Lehndorff escaped from his guards and spent a few nights on the run near the old Prussian coastal resort of Rauschen. In the distance they could hear the battle raging for the port of Pillau. The Russians caught up with him again and for the next few weeks he lay, critically ill, in a newly built Russian prison camp. Here the inmates died in their hundreds. Once again, Lehndorff's medical knowledge kept him alive and sane. Lacking doctors to the degree they did, the Russians always stopped short of killing him. He escaped from the Russians a second time and made for the Masurian Lakes around Grasnitz. He wanted to find out what had happened to his mother and family. His mother was the daughter of Elard von Oldenburg-Januschau, a woman with a considerable amount of courage who had recently spent some time in Gestapo detention.

At Ponarien he was able to glean some news from an old family retainer. His brother-in-law's mother had been shot; his aunt, released from Gestapo prison with her daughter, had disappeared; the daughter had been carried off. He resolved to travel on, in search of his aunt, Frau von Stein. He found her living in the old gardener's cottage of the manor, eking out a miserable existence working for the Russians, as so many of the female Junkers did at that time: looking after the livestock and warding off the occasional drunken nocturnal visits from soldiers.[17]

Lehndorff stayed on in Grasnitz for some time, working as a doctor and holding religious services, but he was anxious to learn the fate of his mother and brother who had been in Januschau at the beginning of 1945. Lehndorff reached Januschau on 21 January 1946. The estate, once the pride of the old fox, Olden-burg-Januschau, where plots were laid to bring down the Weimar Republic and establish a German dictatorship, was now the property of the Russians. The Januschauer could be grateful for one thing: he had died three years before the outbreak of war. The courtyard had been closed off with a wooden gate and a portrait of Stalin fixed above it. The manor-house itself had come through the war unscathed. Lehndorff was introduced to the Commandant who was strutting round the courtyard dressed in nothing but a fur coat and a pair of boots. The Russian agreed to allow the surgeon to stay on and tend the sick.

That evening Lehndorff finally learned the details of his mother and brother's fate. They had left for the West with a party of Germans the year before in an attempt to cross the Nogat at Marienburg. When they learned that the position was hopeless they stopped at a small manor-house to wait for the Russians. When the Russians came, Lehndorff's brother was badly injured by a Russian with a knife. When the Russians found out who he was, they took him out and shot him and his mother with him. A further sixteen people had been shot or burned alive. Lehndorff was relieved to hear the news: 'For ever since I had heard that they hadn't escaped from West Prussia, the thought of their possible fate had haunted me at every step.'[18]

Arson, rape and murder dominated life in the old Prussian provinces in the first weeks of the occupation. Most of the able-bodied men and a few of the women were driven off to Russia, along with the livestock and anything valuable which had survived the conflagrations in the *Herrenhäuser*. Before the deportation of the final 100,000 East Prussians to East Germany in November 1948; the surviving population of Königsberg had been reduced to eating their dead. Of the 110,000 Königsbergers who surrendered, only 25,000 survived the three-and-a-half years of Russian occupation. Few of those deported to Russia returned, none of the livestock and, as for the works of art, the Germans are still waiting.

Left behind in the villages were the women, old men and children. There are a good many stories testifying to the strength and bravery of these Prussian women in adversity,[19] and a few more which show how well the children adapted to the new situation.[20] They had all witnessed much: spectacular acts of barbarism such as the hacking off of the arms and legs of an old Herr von Livonius-Grumbkow who was then tossed mercilessly to his pigs to be consumed.[21] Those who survived those days and made it to the West are reluctant to speak of their experiences to this day; and one can understand why.

Cut off from information from the West, the survivors relied first on the Russians and then on the Poles for news. When the hopelessness of the situation dawned on those who remained on the land, they generally opted for the chance to join one of the transports to the West. The Russians and Poles were not giving them the choice anyhow. Ravaged by epidemics and riddled with venereal disease contracted from the Russian soldiers, the expelled Prussians were a sorry sight arriving in cattle trucks and railway wagons at the new Polish-German border. What little they had been able to carry with them, what little they had been able to salvage from the attacks of the soldiers, was torn from their hands either by gangs of licensed brigands along the way or by the Polish authorities at the borders.[22] What they found on the other side of the Oder was only marginally better: Brandenburg, like Saxony, Thuringia and Mecklenburg, had become the Russian zone.

In Brandenburg the great houses so carefully inventoried by Theodor Fontane were looted and in many cases burned to the ground. To be a Junker became a crime punishable by imprisonment or death; in many cases the two punishments were the same. As soon as Sachsenhausen Concentration Camp was emptied of the prisoners lodged in it by the Nazis, for example, the Russians promptly refilled it with a new collection of Germans: Nazis, certainly, but not just: Conservatives, Junkers and anyone who looked as if they might prove a problem to the new regime. Many of these died. In the last few years, since reunification, the mass graves of these German victims of Stalin have been unearthed. In Frankfurt/Oder, the Russians ran another concentration camp where there were frequent executions.[23] It was there that Hermine, the Kaiser's pro-Nazi second wife, died.

The important art collections from the National Gallery downwards travelled east. Those which have not made their way into private collections over the past fifty-odd years are still there.[24] Art, however, was only a small part of what left the Russian zone: the entire industrial basis was dismantled, loaded up and shifted to Russia. When the work was finished they even pulled up fifty percent of the railway lines, a loss which dictates the chronic slowness of east German trains to this day. The big estates in the Brandenburg Mark were obviously broken up and turned over to the Soviet *kolkhoz* system of collective farming. It was a fine excuse to frighten away the few brave landowners who had remained behind. In one case the scholarly Junker Hans Hasso von Veltheim-Ostrau had to witness a drunken mob rip up the ancient trees in his park, break open the family vault and hang the skeletons of his ancestors from the branches. He took the hint and retreated behind the Elbe.[25]

In the 'Recovered Territories' the Poles set to work giving Polish names to the old German towns. Some of these had them already, others did not. In Danzig a name had to be found for every street (an identical situation must have existed in the other large cities: Stettin and Breslau, for example). Gdańsk, at least, was a variant of the old Polish name of the place, when it was a fishing village, but finding suitably pithy translations for the medieval German street names proved a thankless task. Moreover, they were having trouble with the Russians, who were just as anxious to remove the industrial base in Poland's former German lands as they were in Brandenburg.[26]

The Russians were not going to give back the part of Poland they won from Ribbentrop. As the Germans moved out the Polish population of those eastern territories across the Bug moved in. One man remembers visiting Goldap in East Prussia in the early 1950s. It was a ghost town. The neat little houses were still furnished; the light bulbs still in their sockets. Poles from Lithuania did not move in till a few years later. Breslau, now Wrocław, was to receive the population of the city of Lvov. All Lvov's institutions from the university to the churches had to find new homes in the shattered remnants of the Prussian Silesian capital.[27] The new inhabitants of Gdańsk and Pomerania were drawn from Wilno (Vilnius) and Bromber (Bydgoszcz).[28]

The scale of the complementary operation – shifting the Germans out of Poland – was enormous. It is estimated that some nine million German inhabitants of the former Prussian territories of Poland, Russia and the Russian zone of Germany went west before 1949. Between 1949 and 1963 a further 2,718,661 Germans were expelled from Poland, Czechoslovakia and Hungary. The number of deaths which occurred during this peacetime operation is given as 1,225,000 for the Prussian provinces alone, and this does not include any prisoners of war or any of the men who were forced to work in Russia: there were around 218,000 of these rounded up from the villages at the end of the war. The Russians had learned a few tricks from the Germans, including the abduction of thirty-four exceptionally bright children from a school in Pomerania. They were whisked off to Russia and never seen again.[29]

Despite expulsions at a rate of 5,000 a day, the Poles took a long time to Polonise the former Prussian east. The Mazurian Autochthones packed their bags and left for Germany some twenty years after the end of the war. Poland used the remaining Germans as a bargaining counter with the Bundesrepublik. Papers were withheld from those who wanted to go until the West Germans agreed to loans or foreign policy concessions. Even after the last batch left for Germany in the early '80s, there were still pockets of Germans in Poland, notably half a million Upper Silesian German Catholics around the town of Opole (Oppeln). The Polish government did not formally admit to the presence of these former Prussian subjects until the Polish-German Treaty of Friendship in June 1991.*[30]

Despite the anxiety expressed in the German press, Frederick the Great's burial on 17 August 1991 went off peacefully. There was no demonstration by the skinheads who threatened to descend on Potsdam and use the occasion to chant pro-Nazi slogans, get drunk and get into a few good brawls. About a thousand people protested peacefully against the king's return and, having made their gesture, went home to bed.

The coffin arrived from the west at the station at Wildpark to the east of Potsdam. It was brought to Sanssouci and then paraded through the streets of the town while a crowd of 60,000 looked

---

* Even in West and East Prussia there is the odd survival. On a train from Gdańsk (Danzig) to Malbork (Marienburg), the author was approached by a German who had secretly returned to his home in 1949. He said that Olsztyn (Allenstein) was as much as twenty per cent German. The verger in the Protestant church in Olsztyn denied this. He put the figure in the town as 300. There may be more in the surrounding countryside. There are currently ten Germans living in Kaliningrad (Königsberg), where they are tolerated by the Russian authorities, and have set up their own Lutheran church in the old Kreuzkirche in the city.

on. Many carried flowers to honour the dead king. Kurt Geisler of the *Berliner Morgenpost* even discovered a Bavarian in full rig standing enjoying the ceremony. The Bavarian appeared much put out when the local journalist asked him what he was doing there.[31]

After King Frederick William was installed in the Hohenzollern vault in the Friedenskirche, a party was held at the Neues Palais, where the Minister-President of Brandenburg, Manfred Stolpe, and the historian Christian Graf von Krockow analysed the significance of Frederick's return to Brandenburg and Potsdam. One assumes they had dinner.

Frederick the Great stipulated that he wanted to be buried at midnight. Perhaps that was a little late for Chancellor Kohl and the seven members of the Hohenzollern family. The burial began at 11.30 p.m. True to the king's wishes, it was a private affair. A few hundred spectators lined the road Zur historischen Mühle which runs along the back of Sanssouci. Rather more policemen held them in check. There was not a skinhead or neo-Nazi in sight.

The presence of the Bundeswehr, who had led the procession that afternoon, had been reduced to a small musical band at the graveside. As the coffin was lowered into its final resting place, the reedy voices of the Hohenzollerns, along with that of Chancellor Kohl, broke into the Leuthen Chorale: 'Nun danket alle Gott!' My neighbour, a British army officer, joined in. He had learned the song, he said, at his public school. There was nothing more to see. We headed back to the car and went home.

The fuss, it seemed, had all been for nothing. The skinheads and neo-Nazis were unlikely to have known who Frederick the Great was, and had they known more about the Philosopher of Sanssouci, they would have found him a far less exciting idol than Adolf Hitler. The amazing truth was that Prussia had gone to its grave even before that great monarch who had first brought its name into the drawing rooms and parlours of Europe and the New World had found eternal peace.

Notes

Introduction: Dead Bodies

1) Rudolf Augstein, Preussens Friedrich und die Folgen, *Der Spiegel*, 33, 1991, 40–47.
2) James Stern, *The Hidden Damage*, London 1990, 222.
3) Ibid., 241.
4) Werner Knopp, *Preussens Wege, Preussens Spuren: Gedanken über einen Versunkenen Staat*, Düsseldorf 1981, 72.
5) Gottfried Neidhart, Schweigen als Pflicht. Warum Konrad Adenauer die Stalin-Note vom 10. März 1952 nicht ausloten liess, *Die Zeit*, 6 March 1992. Marion Gräfin Dönhoff, Von der Schwäche starker Politik. Das Streben nach überlegenheit gefährdet die Chance aus der Geschichte zu lernen, in *Weit ist der Weg nach Osten*, Munich 1988, 305–313.
6) Axel Schützsack, *Der preussische Traum: Der Hohenzollernstaat im Spannungsfeld von Gehorsam, Pflicht und Freiheit*, Moers 1981/1982, 24.
7) Reprinted in Sebastian Haffner, *Preussen ohne Legende*, 3rd edition, Hamburg 1982, 508–509.
8) Conversation with Sir Frank Roberts, London 24 April 1992.
9) Golo Mann, Das Ende Preussens, in O. Busch & W. Neugebauer, *Moderne preussische Geschichte, 1648–1947, Eine Anthologie*, Berlin & New York, 1981, I, 260.
10) Ruth Andreas-Friedrich, *Schauplatz Berlin*, Nachwort von Jörg Drews, 2nd edition, Kassel 1985, 167.
11) George Clare, *Berlin Days, 1946–1947*, London 1989, 42. Also Andreas-Friedrich, *Schauplatz Berlin*, 111–112.
12) Marion Gräfin Dönhoff, Die Flammenzeichen rauchen. Der Aufstand vom 17. Juni, in *Weit ist der Weg nach Osten*.
13) Gustav Seeber, Preussen seit 1789 in der Geschichtsschreibung der DDR, in *Preussen in der deutschen*

Geschichte nach 1789, ed. Gustav Seeber & Karl-Heinz Hoack,
Berlin (East) 1983, 13–14.

14) Knopp, *Preussens Wege*, 73; Seeber & Hoack, *Preussen*, 28;
Schützsack, *Der preussische Traum*, 31; Christian Graf von
Krockow, *Warnung vor Preussen*, Berlin 1981, 11.

15) Reinhard Rürup, *Topography of Terror, Gestapo, SS and
Reichssicherheitshauptamt on the 'Prinz-Albrecht-Terrain'. A
Documentation*, trans. Werner Angress, Berlin 1989, 16.

16) Schützsack, *Der preussische Traum*, 33; *Preussen: Versuch einer
Bilanz*, Ausstellung Berlin 1981 (exhibition catalogue),
herausgegeben von Gottfried Korff, text von Winfried Ranke,
Reinbek, 1981.

17) Ibid.

18) Bodo Scheurig, *Henning von Tresckow, Eine Biographie*,
Oldenburg & Hamburg, 1973, 35.

Chapter I: An Empire Built on Sand

1) Walter Görlitz, *Die Junker: Adel und Bauer im deutschen Osten*,
Glücksberg/Ostsee 1956, 2.

2) Haffner, *Preussen*, 39.

3) Georg Dehio, *Handbuch der deutschen Kunstdenkmäler*, Berlin/
DDR, Potsdam, Munich, Berlin 1983, 141.

4) H. W. Koch, *A History of Prussia*, London & New York 1978,
24.

5) Ibid. and Görlitz, *Junker*, 2–3.

6) Erzbishopf Norbert und die Prämonstratenser in der Mark, in
Theodor Fontane, Aufsätze, in *Wanderungen dürch die Mark
Brandenburg*, 3rd edition, Munich & Vienna 1991, Vol. III,
552–544. Donald Attwater, *The Penguin Dictionary of Saints*,
Harmondsworth 1965, 256–257.

7) Christopher Duffy, *Frederick the Great, A Military Life*, London
1985, 1; Görlitz, *Junker*, 6.

8) Fontane, Aufsätze in *Wanderungen*, III, 471–494.

9) Theodor Fontane, *Meine Kinderjahre*, in *Fontanes Werke in fünf
Bänden*, Aufbau Verlag, Berlin & Weimar 1986, 97.

10) Görlitz, *Junker*, 6.

11) James W. Gerard, *My Four Years in Germany*, London, 1917,
29

12) Michael Burleigh and Wolfgang Wippermann, *The Racial State: Germany 1933–1945*, Cambridge 1991, 131–135.
13) Görlitz, *Junker*, 2–3.
14) Koch, *History*, 24.
15) William II, *My Ancestors*, trans. W. W. Zambra, London 1929, 4–5.
16) Ibid., 7–8.
17) Koch, *History*, 28.
18) William II, *Ancestors*, 7; Haffner, *Preussen*, 60.
19) *Die Prusai*. Die Ureinwohner Ostpreussens. Geschichte und Frühgeschichte. Austellung Offenbach am Main, 17.10.1992–14.11.1992 (catalogue), 4. Also Norman Davies, *Heart of Europe: A Short History of Poland*, Oxford and New York 1984, 318.
20) Haffner, *Preussen*, 49.
21) *Die Prusai*, 6.
22) Koch, *Prussia*, 8.
23) Davies, *Heart of Europe*, 288.
24) Heinrich von Treitschke, *Das deutsche Ordensland Preussen*, ed. W. S. Lyon, London 1893, 3.
25) Ibid., 8.
26) Ibid., 13.
27) Ibid., 12; *Die Prusai*, 9.
28) Ibid.
29) Treitschke, *Ordensland*, 20.
30) Carl Tighe, *Gdańsk: National Identity in the Polish-German Borderlands*, London 1990, 13.
31) Koch, *History*, 14.
32) Treitschke, *Ordensland*, 31.
33) Tighe, *Gdańsk*, 23–24.
34) *Die Prusai*, 4; Kurt Forstreuter, *Wirkungen des Preussenlandes*, Cologne/Berlin 1981, 281.
35) Frederick the Great, *Mémoires pour servir à l'histoire de la maison de Brandenbourg*. In *Oeuvres historiques choisies de Frédéric le Grand*, tome premier, Leipzig 1875, 26.
36) Ibid., 38–39.
37) Koch, *History*, 45.
38) Ibid., 48.
39) Haffner, *Preussen*, 63.
40) Frederick the Great, *Mémoires*, 80.

41) Ibid., 81–82. See the letter of Frederick of Homburg to his wife printed in Theodor Fontane, *Die Grafschaft Ruppin* in *Wanderungen*, Vol. I, 413–414.

42) Koch, *History*, 62.

43) Frederick the Great, *Mémoires*, 90.

44) Ibid., 110.

45) Duffy, *Frederick the Great*, 6.

46) The original letter referring to the kidnap is in the Geheimes Staatsarchiv in Berlin: Brandenburg-Preussisch Hausarchiv. (B.P.H.) Rep. 47 Nr. 366 dated 15 September 1732. The height of the *Lange Kerls* is complicated by the Prussian foot, which was equivalent to 1.03 British feet. A good height was considered to be 5.10. See Willard R. Fann, Foreigners in the Prussian Army 1713–56, Some Statistical and Interpretative Problems, in *Central European History* 1992.

47) Knopp, *Preussens Wege*, 13.

48) Fann, Foreigners, in *CEH*.

49) The account is taken from Fontane, *Wanderungen*, I, 843.

50) Ibid., I, 852–853.

51) Ibid.

52) Walther Hubatsch, *Frederick the Great: Absolutism and Administration*, trans. Patrick Doran, 2nd edition, London 1975, 25.

53) Frederick the Great, *Mémoires*, 144.

54) Koch, *History*, 110.

55) Wolfgang Venohr, *Fridericus Rex: Friedrich der Grosse – Porträt einer Doppelnatur*, Bergisch Gladbach, Jubilee edition, 1988, 112.

56) Ibid.

57) Christian Graf von Krockow, *Friedrich der Grosse, Ein Lebensbild*, Bergisch Gladbach, 1987, 61.

58) Dehio, *Handbuch*, 347–348.

59) Haffner, *Preussen*, 83–84.

60) Fontane, *Das Oderland*, in *Wanderungen*, I, 574.

61) Ibid.

62) Frederick the Great, Testament politique in Pierre Gaxotte ed., *Frédéric II roi de Prusse*, in Le Memorial des siècles établi par Gérard Walter, Paris 1967, 331.

63) Koch, *History*, 127.

64) Wilhelmine, margravine de Bayreuth to Voltaire, 27 December 1757, B. P. H. Rep. 46 Nr. 77.

65) F. L. Carsten, Preussen und England, in *Preussen und das Ausland*, herausgegeben von Otto Busch, Berlin 1982, 29–30.

66) Wilhelmine, margravine de Bayreuth, to Voltaire.

67) Voltaire, *Candide*, 1759, ed. O. R. Taylor, Oxford 1942, Chapter III, 5. Voltaire, *Dictionnaire philosophique*, Paris Garnier Frères, 1967, 228–232.

68) Haffner, *Preussen*, 147.

69) Krockow, *Friedrich der Grosse*, 120–121.

70) Ibid., 124.

71) Frederick the Great, *History of the Seven Years War*, quoted in Hubatsch, *Frederick*, 101.

72) Ibid., 182.

73) Quoted in Hubatsch, *Frederick*, 184.

74) Frederick the Great, *Mémoires de la guerre de 1778*, Potsdam 20 juin 1779. MS in B.P.H. Rep. 47 Nr. 293.

75) Koch, *History*, 139.

76) (Mirabeau), *Histoire sécrète de la cour de Berlin, ou correspondance d'un voyageur françois depuis le 5 juillet 1786 jusq'au 19 janvier 1787*. Ouvrage posthume (sic). Tome premier, Paris 1789, 95.

77) Ibid, Tome II, Rotterdam 1789, 136.

78) Gottfried Blumenstein, Mozarts grosse Streichquartette, sleeve notes to Mozart, the *Late String Quartets*: 'Haydn', 'Prussian'. Alban Berg Quartet. Teldec 1976. Blumenstein is not well served by his English translator who has rendered Friedrich Wilhelm II as Frederick II.

79) Lovis Corinth, Berlin nach dem Krieg, in Irmgard Wirth, *Berliner Maler: Menzel, Liebermann, Slevogt, Corinth in Briefen, Vorträgen und Notizen*, 2nd edition, Berlin 1986, 287.

80) Quoted, Koch, *History*, 143.

81) Fabian von Schlabrendorff, *Offiziere gegen Hitler*, Zurich, 1946.

82) Schützsack, *Der preussische Traum*, 68.

83) Ibid., 52–53.

84) Davies, *Heart of Europe*, 308. Tighe, *Gdańsk*, 38; Norman Davies, *God's Playground, A History of Poland*, Volume II, *1795 to the Present*, Oxford, 1981, 114. Haffner, *Preussen*, 177.

85) Ibid., 203.

86) Albrecht von dem Bussche, *Heinrich Alexander von Arnim: Liberalismus, Polenfrage und deutsche Einheit. Das 19 Jahr-*

hundert im Spiegel einer Biographie des preussischen Staatsmannes,
Osnabrück 1986, 35.

87) Quoted Haffner, *Preussen*, 214.

88) Gaxotte, *Frédéric II*, 330.

89) Haffner, *Preussen*, 218.

90) Ibid., 219.

91) Harald von Koenigswald, *Pflicht und Glaube: Bildnis eines
preussischen Lebens* (F. A. L. von der Marwitz), Leipzig, n.d., 8.

92) Walther Hubatsch, *Die Stein-Hardenbergschen Reformen*,
Darmstadt 1977, 1–2.

93) Haffner, *Preussen*, 241.

94) Rehsener, op. cit. 36.

95) See Adalbert Bezzenberger, *Ostpreussen in der Franzosenzeit:
Seine Verluste und Opfer an Gut und Blut*, Königsberg 1913;
Willy Quandt, Hans-Joachim Bahr eds. *Am Ostseestrand von
Pommern bis Memel: Leben und Wirken des Pfarrers Carl Gottlieb
Rehsener. 1790–1862 Von Ihm selbst erzählt*, Köln und Berlin
1976, 36.

96) Michael Howard, *The Franco-Prussian War*, London 1961,
251; see also Chapter IV, n12.

97) Wolfgang Büttner, S'ist Lützow's wild verwegene Jagd, in *Die
Zeit*, 16 July 1993.

98) Friedrich Wilhelm III, *Memorandum*, April 1809. B.P.H. Rep.
49 Nr. 93.

99) Koch, *History*, 196.

100) Ibid.

101) Haffner, *Preussen*, 270.

102) Ibid., 300.

103) Ibid., 307.

104) Frank-Lothar Kroll, Politische Romantik und romantische
Politik bei Friedrich Wilhelm IV, in Otto Busch, ed., *Friedrich
Wilhelm IV in seiner Zeit*. Beitrag eines Colloqiums,
historischen Kommission zu Berlin. Berlin 1987, 94; Hans-
Joachim Schoeps, *Das andere Preussen: konservative Gestalten
und Probleme im Zeitalter Friedrich Wilhelm IV*, 5th edition,
Berlin 1981, 9.

105) Robert Hellman, *The Red Room and White Beer*: The 'Free'
Hegelian Radicals in the 1840s. Washington D.C. 1990, 66.
The sketch is printed on 67.

106) Ilse Kleberger, *Eine Gabe ist einer Aufgabe: Käthe Kollwitz*, Berlin 1980, 56–64.

107) Theodor Fontane, *Der achtzehnte März*, in *Werke*, 268–269.

108) Haffner, *Preussen*, 318. Von dem Bussche, *Arnim*, 35.

109) Horst Conrad & Bernd Haunfelder, mit einem Vorwort von Lothar Gall, *Preussische Parlementarier, ein Photoalbum 1859–1867*, Düsseldorf 1986, 12.

110) Haffner, *Preussen*, 326.

111) Ibid.

112) Quoted in Franz Herre, *Kaiser Wilhelm I, der letzte Preusse*, Cologne 1981, 406.

113) Koch, *History*, 249.

114) Schützsack, *Der preussische Traum*, 64.

115) Knopp, *Preussens Wege*, 24.

116) Haffner, *Preussen*, 386.

117) Extracts from the Crown Prince's diary. B.P.H. 52 Nr. 14. 12/1, 10/1.

118) Herre, *Kaiser Wilhelm I*, 408–409.

119) Ibid.

120) Ibid., 412.

121) Ibid., 414.

122) Quoted in Hellmut Diwald, Kein Requiem für Preussen, in Hellmut Diwald ed., *Im Zeichen des Adlers: Porträts berühmter Preussen*, Bergisch Gladbach 1981, 6.

Chapter II: The Last King of Prussia

1) Michael Balfour, *The Kaiser and His Times*, London, 1964, 73.

2) Letter from Geheimer Med Rat Professor Dr August Martin, B.P.H. Rep. 53 Nr. 18–19.

3) *Imperator et Rex, William II of Germany*, by the author of 'The Martyrdom of an Empress', London and New York, 1904, 11–12.

4) Letter from Professor Dr Martin, ibid., Nr. 19.

5) Ibid.

6) Ibid.

7) Conversation with my friend, the paediatrician Dr Fiona Clarke, London, 31 December 1992. Dr Clarke maintained that had the child presented its shoulder injuries would have

been limited to the arm. Birth by caesarian section would have made no difference in a case of cerebral palsy.

8) Frederick the Great, Testament politique, in Gaxotte, *Frédéric II*, 356.

9) Ibid., 363. Koch, *History*, 136.

10) Balfour, *The Kaiser*, 80.

11) Count Robert Zedlitz-Trützschler, *Twelve Years at the Imperial German Court*, trans. Alfred Kalisch, London, 1924, 82.

12) Ibid., 84.

13) Ibid., Introduction, x.

14) Balfour, *The Kaiser*, 112.

15) Ibid., 118.

16) Ibid.

17) Ibid., 230, quoting from Lord Newton, *Lord Lansdowne, A Biography*, 197.

18) Herzogin Viktoria Luise (von Braunschweig), *Ein Leben als Tochter des Kaisers*, Göttingen-Hannover, 1965, 36.

19) Ibid.

20) Balfour, *The Kaiser*, 231.

21) Viktoria Luise, *Ein Leben*, 36.

22) Walter Görlitz ed., *The Kaiser and His Court, The Diaries, Note Books and Letters of Admiral Georg Alexander von Müller, Chief of the Naval Cabinet, 1914–1918*, with a foreword by Sven von Müller, trans. Mervyn Savill, London, 1961, 264, 30 April 1917.

23) John C. G. Röhl, *Kaiser, Hof und Staat: Wilhelm II und die deutsche Politik*, Munich, 1987, 29–32.

24) Ibid., 32.

25) Norman Rich, *Friedrich von Holstein, Politics and Diplomacy in the Era of Bismarck and William II*, Cambridge, 1965, Vol. II, 445.

26) Zedlitz-Trützschler, *Twelve Years*, 54.

27) Ibid., Introduction, xv.

28) Röhl, *Kaiser*, 21.

29) Görlitz ed., *Müller*, 17.

30) Ibid., 173.

31) John C. G. Röhl, The Emperor's New Clothes: A Character Sketch of Kaiser Wilhelm II, in John C. G. Röhl and Nicolaus Sombart eds, *Kaiser Wilhelm II, New Interpretations, The Corfu Papers*, Cambridge, 1982, 53.

32) Rich, *Holstein*, II, 491.
33) Zedlitz-Trützschler, *Twelve Years*, 90.
34) Röhl, *Kaiser*, 105.
35) Zedlitz-Trützschler, *Twelve Years*, 90.
36) Ibid., 174.
37) Röhl, *Kaiser*, 21–22.
38) Görlitz, *Müller*, 337.
39) Röhl, *Kaiser*, 22.
40) Rich, *Holstein*, II, 560.
41) 'Comte Paul Vasili' (Princess Katharina Radziwiłł), *La Société de Berlin, augmenté de lettres inédites*, twelfth edition, Paris, 1884, 15, 37. I am grateful to Philip Mansel for providing me with a copy of this book.
42) Röhl, *Kaiser*, 25–26, which reprints Röhl's essay in Röhl and Sombart eds., *New Interpretations*, 42–45.
43) Röhl, *Kaiser*, 27.
44) Zedlitz-Trützschler, *Twelve Years*, 102.
45) Röhl in Röhl & Sombart, *New Interpretations*, 43.
46) Quoted in Friedrich Wilhelm Prinz von Preussen, *Das Haus Hohenzollern 1918–1945. Mit 61 Seiten Dokumente in Faksimile.* Munich, 1985, 49.
47) Sigurd von Ilsemann, *Der Kaiser in Holland, Aufzeichnungen des letzten Flugeladjutanten Kaiser Wilhelms II*, herausgegeben von Harald von Koenigswald, Vol. I, Amerongen und Doorn, Munich, 1967, 218.
48) John Wheeler Bennett, *Knaves, Fools and Heroes*, London, 1974, 179.
49) Röhl, *Kaiser*, 24.
50) James W. Gerard, *My Four Years in Germany*, London, New York, Toronto, 1917, 38.
51) Zedlitz-Trütschler, *Twelve Years*, 218–219.
52) Miss [Anne] Topham, *Memories of the Kaiser's Court*, London, 1914, trans. into French as *Souvenirs de la Cour du Kaiser*, Paris, n.d., 190–191.
53) Balfour, *Kaiser*, 82. This may well have happened as late as December 1909. See Marie Radziwiłł in Fox ed., 109.
54) Zedlitz-Trütschler, *Twelve Years*, 277.
55) Ibid., 98.
56) Röhl, *Kaiser*, 20.
57) Zedlitz-Trützschler, *Twelve Years*, 62.

58) Görlitz, *Müller*, 26–27.

59) Rich, *Holstein*, II, 812; Evelyn Princess Blücher, *An English Wife in Berlin*, 7th edition, London, 1920, 46. See also Wilhelm Voigt, *Wie ich Hauptmann von Köpenick wurde, Mein Lebensbild*, mit einem Vorwort von Hans Hyan, Leipzig and Berlin, n.d., 147.

60) Gerard, *My Four Years*, 179.

61) Görlitz, *Müller*, 359.

62) Peter Berglar, *Walther Rathenau Ein Leben zwischen Philosophie und Politik*, Graz, Vienna and Cologne, 1987, 194–195.

63) See Harry F. Young, *Maximilian Harden, Censor Germaniae. The Critic from Bismarck to the Rise of Nazism*, The Hague, 1959, 89–113.

64) Isabel Hull, Kaiser Wilhelm II and the 'Liebenberg Circle', in Röhl and Sombart eds., *New Interpretations*, 194–196.

65) Rich, *Holstein*, II, 487.

66) Ibid., 487–488.

67) Ibid.

68) Zedlitz-Trützschler, *Twelve Years*, 104.

69) Ibid., 119.

70) Ibid., 148–149.

71) Görlitz, *Müller*, 274.

72) Rich, *Holstein*, II, 531.

73) Frederick the Great, Testament politique, in Gaxotte, *Frédéric II*, 356.

74) Balfour, *The Kaiser*, 152.

75) Zedlitz-Trützschler, *Twelve Years*, 148.

76) Ibid., 159.

77) Röhl, *Kaiser*, 103.

78) Görlitz, *Müller*, 345.

79) Ibid.

80) Ibid., Introduction, xxi.

81) Zedlitz-Trützschler, *Twelve Years*, 28.

82) Rich, *Holstein*, II, 765.

83) Zedlitz-Trützschler, *Twelve Years*, 88–89.

84) Ibid., 93.

85) Görlitz, *Müller*, 81.

86) Balfour, *The Kaiser*, 289–293; Viktoria Luise, *Ein Leben*, 55–57; Hugh David's recent biography of the journalist's son, *Stephen Spender, A Portrait with Background*, London, 1992, is

silent about Harold Spender's role in this international
incident, but that is not the only gap in the book.

87) Rich, *Holstein*, II, 820.
88) Zedlitz-Trützschler, *Twelve Years*, 226.
89) Balfour, *The Kaiser*, 125. Viktoria Luise, *Ein Leben*, 49, tries
vainly to refute the accusation that her father was a *reise-Kaiser*.
90) Gerard, *My Four Years*, II.
91) Miss Topham, *Souvenirs*, 112–113.
92) Röhl, *Kaiser*, 81–85. Cyril Spencer Fox ed., *This Was
Germany: An Observer at the Court of Berlin*, letters of Princess
Marie Radziwiłł to General di Robillant, 1908–15, London,
1937, 12, 26, 28–9.
93) Hedda Adlon, *Hotel Adlon*, Munich, 1955, 10.
94) Balfour, *The Kaiser*, 153–154.
95) Preussen, *Haus Hohenzollern*, 27–28.
96) Ibid., 40–41.
97) Ibid.
98) Franz Mehring, *Historische Aufsätze zur preussisch-deutschen
Geschichte*, Berlin, 1946. Introductory essay by Fred Oelssner, x.
99) *Kaiserlicher Kunstbesitz aus dem holländischen Exil Haus Doorn*,
Berlin 1991 (exhibition catalogue), 13.
100) Zedlitz-Trützschler, *Twelve Years*, xvi.
101) Miss Topham, *Souvenirs*, 83–84.
102) Zedlitz-Trützschler, *Twelve Years*, 137–138.
103) B.P.H. Rep. 53 Nr. 418. Zedlitz-Trützschler, *Twelve Years*,
42.
104) Balfour, *The Kaiser*, 161.
105) Zedlitz-Trützschler, *Twelve Years*, 41.
106) Miss Topham, *Souvenirs*, 74; Balfour, *The Kaiser*, 161–162;
Ilsemann, *Kaiser in Holland*, II, 279.
107) Quoted in Wirth, op. cit., 246.
108) B.P.H. Rep. 54 Nr. 136.
109) B.P.H. Rep. 53 Nr. 242 is one example of many.
110) Conversation with Ludwig Freiherr von Hammerstein-
Equord, Berlin-Dahlem, 28 June 1991.
111) Viktoria Luise, *Ein Leben*, 245.
112) Preussen, *Haus Hohenzollern*, 59.
113) Ibid., 113.
114) Ilsemann, *Kaiser in Holland*, II, 153.

115) Ibid., 153; Preussen, *Haus Hohenzollern*, 60.
116) David Irving, *Göring, A Biography*, London, 1989, 99.
117) Preussen, *Haus Hohenzollern*, 63.
118) Irving, *Göring*, 99.
119) Ilsemann, *Kaiser in Holland*, II, 153, 158, 171, 179.
120) Viktoria Luise, *Ein Leben*, 267.
121) Ilsemann, *Kaiser in Holland*, II, 192, Preussen, *Haus Hohenzollern*, 65.
122) Viktoria Luise, *Ein Leben*, 267.
123) Ilsemann, *Kaiser in Holland*, II, 192–194.
124) Ibid.
125) Ibid.
126) Ibid., 193, 195.
127) Ibid.
128) Viktoria Luise, *Ein Leben*, 266–267.
129) Preussen, *Haus Hohenzollern*, 198.
130) Ibid., 200.
131) Ibid.
132) Ibid., 90–91.
133) Ilsemann, *Kaiser in Holland*, II, 192.
134) Preussen, *Haus Hohenzollern*, 91.
135) Ilsemann, *Kaiser in Holland*, II, 190–191.
136) Preussen, *Haus Hohenzollern*, 95.
137) Ibid., 93–94.
138) See the lives of the Kaiser by Tyler Whittle, *William II*, London, 1977, and Virginia Cowles, *The Kaiser*, London, 1963.
139) Preussen, *Haus Hohenzollern*, 239.
140) Viktoria Luise, *Ein Leben*, 267.
141) Preussen, *Haus Hohenzollern*, 93–94.
142) B.P.H. Rep. 54 Nr. 136.
143) Ibid.
144) See, for example, Detlev J. K. Peukert, *Die Weimarer Republik*, Frankfurt/Main, 1987, 259, A. J. Nicholls, *Weimar and the Rise of Hitler*, third edition, London, 1991, 138.
145) Ilsemann, *Kaiser in Holland*, II, 204–206.
146) B.P.H. Rep. 53 Nr. 168/1.
147) Ibid.
148) Ibid.
149) B.P.H. Rep. 54 Nr. 37.

150) In reality Hitler was living in a dosshouse painting postcards of Viennese monuments which another ex-tramp hawked through the coffee houses. See Alan Bullock, *Hitler, A Study in Tyranny*, Harmondsworth, 1962, 32–33, and *Hitler and Stalin, Parallel Lives*, London, 1991, 19.
151) According to the Prinz von Preussen, *Haus Hohenzollern*, 109, the Kaiser gave up on the idea of the Nazis reviving the monarchy after 17 September 1932.
152) Ibid.
153) Ibid.
154) Ibid., 112 from Ilsemann, *Kaiser in Holland*, II, 222.
155) Hans Rothfels, *The German Opposition to Hitler*, London, 1970, 50–51.
156) Ilsemann, *Kaiser in Holland*, II, 272.
157) Ibid., II, 287.
158) Preussen, *Haus Hohenzollern*, 208, 214.
159) Heinrich Brüning, *Memoiren 1918–1934*, Stuttgart, 1970, 145.
160) Preussen, *Haus Hohenzollern*, 55.
161) B.P.H. Rep. 53 Nr. 167/2.
162) Ibid.
163) Ibid.
164) Preussen, *Haus Hohenzollern*, 140.
165) B.P.H. Rep. 53 Nr. 167/1.
166) Ibid.
167) Ibid.
168) Ibid.
169) B.P.H. Rep. 53 Nr. 167/3.
170) Ibid.
171) Ibid.
172) Ibid.
173) B.P.H. Rep. 53 Nr. 167/4.
174) B.P.H. Rep. 53 Nr. 167/6.
175) Ibid.
176) Ibid.
177) *Hitler's Table Talk*, quoted Preussen, *Haus Hohenzollern*, 258.
178) B.P.H. Rep. 53 Nr. 167/6.
179) Ilsemann, *Kaiser in Holland*, II, 165.
180) Gerard, *My Four Years*, 42.
181) Viktoria Luise, *Ein Leben*, 20.
182) Ibid., 267–268.

183) Ilsemann, *Kaiser in Holland*, II, 16–17.
184) Ibid., 134.
185) Ibid., 146.
186) Ibid., 155.
187) Ibid., 183.
188) Preussen, *Haus Hohenzollern*, 174.
189) Ilsemann, *Kaiser in Holland*, II, 232.
190) Ibid., 249.
191) Ibid., 264.
192) Preussen, *Haus Hohenzollern*, 179.
193) Ilsemann, *Kaiser in Holland*, II, 280.
194) Preussen, *Haus Hohenzollern*, 220.
195) Ilsemann, *Kaiser in Holland*, II, 280.
196) Ibid., 313.
197) Ibid.
198) Preussen, *Haus Hohenzollern*, 146–147.
199) *Kaiserlicher Kunstbesitz*, 10.
200) Ilsemann, *Kaiser in Holland*, II, 345.
201) Ibid.

Chapter III: Prussian Virtues and Vices

1) Knopp, *Preussens Wege*, 91. A possible exception is Gerd Heinrich's *Geschichte Preussens, Staat und Dynastie*, which catalogues the main virtues. See 22–26.
2) Magnus Freiherr von Braun, *Von Ostpreussen bis Texas: Erlebnisse und zeitgeschichtliche Betrachtungen eines Ostdeutschen*, 2nd edition, Stollhamm, 1955, 44.
3) Görlitz, *Die Junker*, 2–3.
4) Ibid., 23.
5) Bodo Scheurig, *Ewald von Kleist-Schmenzin: Ein Konservativer gegen Hitler*, Oldenburg and Hamburg, 1968, 15–16.
6) Schützsack, *Der preussische Traum*, 13.
7) Gustav Freytag, *The Crown Prince and the German Imperial Crown: Reminiscences*, 7th edition, trans. George Duncan, London, 1890, 22–23.
8) Ibid., 23.
9) Ibid., 24.
10) Theodor Fontane, *Effi Briest*, 1894–1895, in *Werke*, Vol. IV, 35.

11) Schützsack, *Der preussische Traum*, 48.
12) Ibid.
13) Ibid., 81.
14) Herre, *Kaiser Willhelm*, 399.
15) Elard von Oldenburg-Januschau, *Errinerungen*, Leipzig, 1936, 20.
16) Marion Gräfin Dönhoff, *Kindheit in Ostpreussen*, Berlin 1988, 46. The same story is to be found in Marion Gräfin Dönhoff, *Namen die keiner mehr nennt: Ostpreussen – Menschen und Geschichte*, 1962, paperback edition, Düsseldorf/Cologne, 1964, 130.
17) Ursula von Kardorff, *Diary of a Nightmare: Berlin 1942–1945*, trans. Ewan Butler, London, 1965, 94.
18) Ibid., 61.
19) Ibid., 97.
20) A. J. P. Taylor, *Bismarck, The Man and the Statesman*, London, 1955, 135.
21) Miss Topham, *Souvenirs*, 23.
22) Theodor Fontane, *Schach von Wuthenow: Erzählung aus der Zeit des Regiments Gensdarmes*, 1882, in *Werke*, Vol. II, 92.
23) Magnus von Braun, *Von Ostpreussen bis Texas*, 29.
24) Miss Topham, *Souvenirs*, 213.
25) Ibid., 235.
26) Udo von Alvensleben, *Besuche vor dem Untergang: Adelsitze zwischen Altmark und Masuren*. Tagebuchaufzeichnungen zusammengestellt und herausgegeben von Harald von Koenigswald, Frankfurt/Main, Berlin, Vienna, 1978, 221.
27) Ibid., 41.
28) Ibid., 44–45.
29) Ibid.
30) Dönhoff, *Kindheit*, 71.
31) Ibid., 208.
32) Emil von Lessel, *Böhmen, Frankreich, China, 1866–1901: Errinerungen eines preussischen Offiziers*. Eingeleitet, erläutet und herausgegeben von Walther Hubatsch, Cologne and Berlin, 1981, 144–145.
33) Ibid., 129.
34) Miss Topham, *Souvenirs*, 200–201.
35) Zedlitz-Trützschler, *Twelve Years*, 11.
36) Görlitz, *Die Junker*, 62.

37) Lessel, *Böhmen, Frankreich, China*, 141.

38) Rehsener, op. cit., 109.

39) Rich, *Holstein*, I, 167–168.

40) Miss Topham, *Souvenirs*, 28.

41) Ibid.

42) Freytag, *Crown Prince*, 30.

43) Gustav Freytag, The New and Old Imperial Ceremonial, from *Im neuen Reich*, 1871, reprinted in ibid., 120–121.

44) Corinth, *Selbstbiographie*, in Irmgard Wirth, 246.

45) B. P. H. Rep. 53 Nr. 418.

46) Sigurd von Ilsemann, *Der Kaiser in Holland, Aufzeichnungen des letzten Flügeladjutanten Kaiser Wilhelms II*, herausgegeben von Harald von Koenigswald, Vol. II, *Monarchie und Nationalsozialismus 1924–1941*, Munich, 1968, 278.

47) Scheurig, *Tresckow*, 122–123.

48) Brian Bond, Brauchitsch, in *Hitler's Generals*, ed. Corelli Barnett, London, 1989. Paperback edition 1990, 77.

49) Walter Görlitz, Blomberg, in ibid., 136–137.

50) Conversation with Ludwig von Hammerstein.

51) Lessel, *Böhmen, Frankreich, China*, 60–61.

52) B.P.H. Rep. 47, Nr. 228. *Exposé du gouvernement prussien, des principes sur lequels il roule, avec quelques reflexions politiques.* Écrit de la main du roi Frédéric II. MS 1776.

53) B.P.H. Rep. 47, Nr. 245.

54) Scheurig, *Kleist-Schmenzin*, 16.

55) Scheurig, *Tresckow*, 12.

56) Görlitz, *Die Junker*, 154.

57) Ibid., 214.

58) Ibid., 255.

59) Theodor Fontane, *Der Stechlin*, Berlin, 1897, in *Werke*, Vol. V, 12.

60) Fontane, *Irrungen, Wirrungen*, Berlin, 1887, in *Werke*, 35–36.

61) Rehsener, op. cit., 94–97.

62) Zedlitz-Trützschler, *Twelve Years*, 221.

63) Röhl, *Kaiser*, 87, 104–105.

64) Miss Topham, *Souvenirs*, 40.

65) Ibid., 42.

66) Ibid., 35.

67) Röhl, *Kaiser*, 112.

68) Zedlitz-Trützschler, *Twelve Years*, 36.

69) Ibid., 49.
70) Udo von Alvensleben, *Lauter Abschiede: Tagebuch im Kriege*, herausgegeben von Harald von Koenigswald, Frankfurt/Main, Berlin, 1972, 270.
71) Zedlitz-Trützschler, *Twelve Years*, 165.
72) Ibid., 80–81.
73) Otto Braun, *Von Weimar zu Hitler*, 2nd edition, Hildesheim, 1979, 368.
74) Görlitz, *Die Junker*, 92.
75) Scheurig, *Tresckow*, 150–151.
76) Zedlitz-Trützschler, *Twelve Years*, 34.
77) Rich, *Holstein*, Vol. I, 259 and 303. See also Gordon A. Craig, *The Politics of the Prussian Army 1640–1945*, Oxford, 1955. Paperback edition 1964, 282, n. 5.
78) Zedlitz-Trützschler, *Twelve Years*, 28–29.
79) Ibid., 88.
80) Otto Braun, *Von Weimer*, 203.
81) Magnus von Braun, *Von Ostpreussen bis Texas*, 47.
82) Brüning, *Memoiren*, 64.
83) Schützsack, *Der preussische Traum*, 22.
84) Ibid., 52.
85) Frederick the Great, Testament politique, in Gaxotte ed., *Frédéric II*, 304.
86) This story exists in many versions. I have taken that given by Theodor Fontane in *Das Oderbruch* in *Wanderungen*, Vol. I, 760–762. Fontane had clearly visited the family at Friedersdorf and seen the famous tombstone. In other versions Marwitz returns to the colours and becomes a general. Compare Duffy, *Frederick*, 334; Görlitz, *Die Junker*, 110; and *Preussen: Versuch einer Bilanz*, 1981, 595.
87) Fontane; see previous note.
88) Görlitz, *Die Junker*, 110.
89) Ibid., 254.
90) Conversation with Ludwig von Hammerstein.
91) Ibid. Alfred M. de Zayas, *Die Wehrmacht-Untersuchungstelle: Deutsche Ermittlungen über alliierte Völkerrechts, Verletzungen im Zweiten Weltkrieg*, 4th edition, Munich, 1984, 308–9. For Göring and Graf Sponeck, see Irving, *Göring*, 350–351.
92) Martin Middlebrook, Paulus, in Barnett ed., *Hitler's Generals*, 370.

93) Conversation with Ludwig von Hammerstein, who heard it from Beck himself. Beck was a friend of his father's, Colonel General Kurt Freiherr von Hammerstein-Equord.

94) Robert O'Neill, Fritsch, Beck and the Führer, in Barnett ed., *Hitler's Generals*, 36. The passage has been quoted many times. O'Neill's source is Wolfgang Foerster, *Ein General kämpft gegen den Krieg*, Munich, 1949, 21.

95) Bodo Scheurig, 'Preussischer Tradition und Ver fall', in *Die Zeit*, 16 July 1993.

96) Christian von Krockow, *The Hour of the Women*, trans. Krishna Winston, London, 1992, 28.

97) Berglar, *Rathenau*, 41.

98) Carl Zuckmayer, *Der Hauptmann von Köpenick, ein deutsches Märchen in drei Akten*, 1931, Fischer Verlag edition, Frankfurt/Main 1990, 109.

99) Brüning, *Memoiren*, 63.

100) Schützsack, *Der preussische Traum*, 187.

101) Zuckmayer, *Hauptmann von Köpenick*, 87.

102) Schlabrendorff, *Offiziere*, 28.

103) Scheurig, *Tresckow*, 44.

104) Ibid., 102.

105) Fontane, *Der Stechlin*, 191.

106) Claus Guske, *Das politische Denken des Generals von Seeckt*, in Historische Studien Heft 422, Lubeck and Hamburg, 1971, 146.

107) Generaloberst Hans von Seeckt, *Moltke: Ein Vorbild*, Berlin, 1931, 28.

Chapter IV: The Parade Ground

1) Hans Gehre, *Der Hauptmann von Köpenick, Interpretationen und Materialien didaktisch-methodische Hinweise*, Hollfeld, 1983, 15.

2) Voigt, *Wie ich . . .*, 9.

3) Ibid., 101–102.

4) Ibid., 103–104.

5) Ibid., 109.

6) Ibid., 119.

7) Ibid., 123.

8) Gehre, *Interpretationen*, 16.

9) Ibid., 16–17, 23.

10) Craig, *Prussian Army*, 237. See also Bernt Engelmann, *In Hitler's Germany*, London, 1988, for the adventures of the Jewish Erich Elkan who survived the Second World War by passing himself off as a uniformed Major von 'Elken'.

11) Zuckmayer, *Hauptmann von Köpenick*, Act I, Scene 7, 50. See also Craig, *Prussian Army*, 237.

12) Michael Howard, *The Franco-Prussian War, The German Invasion of France 1870–1871*, New York, 1961, reprinted 1990, 350.

13) Herre, *Kaiser Wilhelm I*, 415.

14) Lessel, *Böhmen, Frankreich, China*, 25.

15) Craig, *Prussian Army*, 240.

16) Hubatsch, *Frederick the Great*, 205–206.

17) Schützsack, *Der preussische Traum*, 80.

18) Ibid., 83.

19) Gerard, *My Four Years*, 46–56.

20) Gustav Lehmann, *Trophäen des preussischen Heeres, in der königlichen Hof und Garnisonkirche zu Potsdam*, Berlin, 1898. This is a loving record of all the captured standards in the church.

21) See, for example, Magnus von Braun, *Von Ostpreussen bis Texas*, 44.

22) Craig, *Prussian Army*, 21.

23) Ibid., 235

24) Görlitz, *Die Junker*, 312–313, 401–406. Craig, *Prussian Army*, 362 n2.

25) Guske, *Seeckt*, 8.

26) Ibid.

27) Magnus von Braun, *Von Ostpreussen bis Texas*, 45–46.

28) Ibid.

29) Ibid.; Görlitz, *Die Junker*, 351; Marion Gräfin Dönhoff, *Kindheit*, 67–68.

30) Scheurig, *Tresckow*, 28–29.

31) Ibid.

32) Ibid., 30.

33) Ibid., 32–33.

34) Zedlitz-Trützschler, *Twelve Years*, 11.

35) Craig, *Prussian Army*, 319.

36) Oldenburg-Januschau, *Errinerungen*, 126, 135, 174.

37) Ibid., 184.

38) Ibid., 207.

39) Craig, *Prussian Army*, 216.

40) Ibid., 233.

41) Scheurig, *Tresckow*, 16. Jacques Benoist-Méchin, *Histoire de l'armée allemande*, 2 vols, Paris, 1984, I, 624–625.

42) Brüning, *Memoiren*, 577.

43) Magnus von Braun, *Von Ostpreussen bis Texas*, 228.

44) Heinrich von Treitschke, *The Organisation of the Army, being @ 23* of his '*Politik*' (lecture on Politics), trans. Adam L. Gowans, London & Glasgow, 1914, 7.

45) Freytag, *The Crown Prince*, 13.

46) Howard, *Franco-Prussian War*, 60 n3, 113, 229.

47) Freytag, *The Crown Prince*, 165.

48) Howard, *Franco-Prussian War*, 3, 77.

49) Ibid. 5–6, 96 n1, 217.

50) Freytag, *The Crown Prince*, 44–45.

51) Howard, *The Franco-Prussian War*, 66.

52) Lessel, *Böhmen, Frankreich, China*, 27.

53) Ibid., 30, 34.

54) Ibid., 28.

55) Fontane, *Die Grafschaft Ruppin*, in *Wanderungen*, 481–483.

56) Lessel, *Böhmen, Frankreich, China*, 92.

57) Peter Padfield, *Himmler, Reichsführer SS*, London, 1990, 32–33.

58) Knopp, *Preussens Wege*, 60.

59) Görlitz, *Die Junker*, 162–163, lists foreigners in the army; Frederick the Great was partial to Italians with doubtful proof of noble birth.

60) Fontane, *Der Stechlin*, 22–23.

61) Görlitz, *Die Junker*, 312–313.

62) Waldemar Erfurth, *Die Geschichte des deutschen Generalstabes 1918–1945*, second edition, Göttingen, Berlin, Frankfurt, 1960, 11.

63) Ibid.

64) Ibid., 41–42.

65) Ibid.

66) Ibid., 42–43, n55.

67) Benoist-Méchin, *Histoire*, I, 226 n2.

68) Ibid., 264–266.

69) Craig, *Prussian Army*, 365.

70) Friedrich Karl von Plehwe, *Reichskanzler Kurt von Schleicher, Weimars letzte Chance gegen Hitler*, Esslingen, 1983, 35.
71) Erfurth, *Geschichte*, 44–45. Benoist-Méchin, *Histoire*, I, 266. Both quote from General Groener, *Lebenserrinerungen*, 501.
72) Erfurth, *Geschichte*, 45.
73) Benoist-Méchin, *Histoire*, I, 266–267.
74) Ibid.
75) Ibid., 268.
76) Ibid., 269.
77) Erfurth, *Geschichte*, 46.
78) Ibid., 47.
79) Ibid., 48.
80) Ibid., 30.
81) Seeckt, *Moltke*, 33.
82) Ibid., 33–34.
83) Craig, *Prussian Army*, 397–399.
84) Ibid.
85) Erfurth, *Geschichte*, 92.
86) Ibid., 74.
87) Ibid., 76. Plehwe, *Schleicher*, 45.
88) Ibid., 46. Erfurth, *Geschichte*, 80.
89) This story generally has Hammerstein imprisoning his father-in-law, but Lüttwitz escaped imprisonment. My source is a paper on Kurt Freiherr von Hammerstein-Equord written by his son, Ludwig Freiherr von Hammerstein-Equord, and given to me by the author. Sadly the document is neither titled nor dated.
90) Hermann Rauschning, *Hitler Speaks, A Series of Political Conversations with Adolf Hitler on his Real Aims*, London, 1939, 154–156.
91) Craig, *Prussian Army*, 482.
92) Ian Kershaw, *The Hitler Myth, Image and Reality in the Third Reich*, Oxford, 1989, 54–55.
93) Craig, *Prussian Army*, 471.
94) Henning Köhler, *Das Ende Preussens in französischer Sicht*, mit einem Geleitwort von Otto Busch, Berlin, New York, 1982, 83–86.
95) Ibid.
96) Ibid.
97) Quoted in S. D. Stirk, *The Prussian Spirit, A Survey of German*

Literature and Politics, 1914–1940, London, 1941, 20.
Chesterton's collection *The End of an Armistice*, 1940, seems to
be very rare indeed. There is no copy in the British Library.

98) Plehwe, *Schleicher*, 226.

99) Craig, *Prussian Army*, 465. Hammerstein document, see n89
supra.

100) Craig, *Prussian Army*, 469 and Hammerstein doc., see n89
supra.

101) Hammerstein doc., see n89 supra.

102) Craig, *Prussian Army*, 476.

103) Benoist-Méchin, *Histoire*, I, 739.

104) Craig, *Prussian Army*, 480.

105) Erfurth, *Geschichte*, 129.

106) Ibid.

107) Görlitz, Blomberg, in Barnett ed., *Hitler's Generals*, 135–137.

108) Klaus-Jürgen Müller, *Armee und nationalsozialistisches Regime
1933–1940*, Stuttgart, 1969, 255–258. Irving, *Göring*,
194–201. Irving has obtained new information from the
Blomberg family.

109) Alvensleben, *Lauter Abschiede*, 17.

110) Heinz Guderian, *Panzer Leader*, forword by B. H. Liddell
Hart, trans. Constantine Fitzgibbon, tenth edition, London,
1970, 431, 439, 442.

111) Alvensleben, *Lauter Abschiede*, 183.

112) Frederick the Great to Maria-Antonia of Saxony, quoted in
Duffy, *A Military Life*, 298.

113) *Exposé du gouvernement prussien*, B.P.H. Rep. 47 Nr. 228.

114) Jonathan Steinberg, *Yesterday's Deterrent, Tirpitz and the Birth
of the German Battle Fleet*, London, 1965, 28.

115) Ibid., 33.

116) Ibid., 35.

117) Ibid., 33–34.

118) Ibid., 39. Also Görlitz, *Müller*, xx.

119) Steinberg, *Yesterday's Deterrent*, 39.

120) Ibid., 41.

121) Zedlitz-Trützschler, *Twelve Years*, 87.

122) Steinberg, *Yesterday's Deterrent*, 61.

123) Balfour, *The Kaiser*, 124–125.

124) Steinberg, *Yesterday's Deterrent*. The design is shown flanking
page 81.

125) Ibid., 18.
126) Ibid., 21.
127) Ibid., 36.

Chapter V: Carmine Stripes

1) Friedrich von Bernhardi, *Deutschland und der nächste Krieg*, Stuttgart & Berlin, 1912, 2, 7. The English edition is entitled *Germany and the Next War*, London, 1912, translated by Allen H. Powles. The cover is decorated with a nice, black Prussian eagle.
2) Bernhardi, *Deutschland und der nächste Krieg*, 9.
3) Ibid., 12.
4) Ibid., 124.
5) Ibid., 89–124 passim.
6) Ibid., 74.
7) Ibid.
8) Walter Görlitz, *The German General Staff, Its History and Structure, 1657–1945*, with a preface by Cyril Falls, London, 1953, 95.
9) Treitschke, *The Organisation of the Army*, 6. Adolf Hausrath, The Life of Treitschke, in *Treitschke, His Life and Works*, London 1914, 48.
10) Michael Howard, 'Preussen in der europäischen Geschichte' in *Preussen, seiner Wirkung auf die deutsche Geschichte*, Vorlesungen von Karl Dietrich Erdmann et al, Stuttgart, 1985.
11) Treitschke, *Army*, 12–13.
12) Princess Blücher, *An English Woman*, 75. H. R. Berndorff, *General zwischen Ost und West*, Hamburg, 1953, 15.
13) Knopp, *Preussens Wege*, 18.
14) Christian von Massenbach, *Eine biographische Skizze seiner Schicksale, Unschuldigungen, und Verteidigungsgründe*, 1817, 14.
15) Ibid., 24.
16) Görlitz, *General Staff*, 20–23.
17) Seeckt, *Moltke*, 80.
18) Görlitz, *General Staff*, 20–23.
19) Ibid.
20) Hansgeorg Model, *Der deutsche Generalstabsoffizier. Seine Auswahl und Ausbildung in Reichswehr, Wehrmacht und Bundeswehr*, Frankfurt/Main, 1968, 11–12.

21) Massenbach, *Biographische Skizze*, 129.
22) Görlitz, *General Staff*, 30–36.
23) Ibid., vi.
24) Görlitz, *Die Junker*, 167.
25) Görlitz, *General Staff*, 30–36.
26) Ibid., 15–20, 23–27.
27) Ibid.
28) Guderian, *Panzer Leader*, 455.
29) Görlitz, *General Staff*, 39.
30) Ibid., 40.
31) Carl von Clausewitz, *Vom Kriege*, sixteenth edition, mit historisch-kritischer Würdigung von Werner Hahlweg, Bonn, 1952, 107.
32) Ibid., 108.
33) Ibid., 201.
34) Ibid., 89–90.
35) Werner Hahlweg in ibid., 28.
36) Ibid.
37) Ibid., 42.
38) Clausewitz, *Vom Kriege*, 97.
39) Ibid., 91–92.
40) Seeckt, *Moltke*, 25–26.
41) Ibid., 175.
42) Görlitz, *General Staff*, 69–77.
43) Seeckt, *Moltke*, 37–38.
44) Ibid., 62.
45) Ibid.
46) Görlitz, *General Staff*, 71.
47) Ibid., 73.
48) Ibid., 75.
49) 'Vasili', *La Société de Berlin*, 131.
50) Seeckt, *Moltke*, 183.
51) Ibid., 114.
52) Howard, *Franco-Prussian War*, 192–193.
53) Ibid., 83, 84, 85, 89, 99, 149.
54) Ibid., 129, 300–301, 412.
55) Ibid., 356 n4.
56) Ibid., 436.
57) Ibid., 443.
58) Seeckt, *Moltke*, 114.

59) Görlitz, *General Staff*, 122.
60) Ibid.
61) Ibid., 126.
62) Lessel, *Böhmen, Frankreich, China*, 164–165.
63) Ibid.
64) Görlitz, *General Staff*, 128.
65) Ibid., 129.
66) Ibid., 134.
67) Ibid., 138.
68) Ibid., 142.
69) Quoted in Berndorff, *General zwischen Ost und West*, 16.
70) Görlitz, *General Staff*, 166.
71) Guderian, *Panzer Leader*, 455.
72) Ibid.
73) Volker Ullrich, . . . höchste Zeit, dass der Kanzler verschwindet, in *Die Zeit*, 10 July 1992.
74) Guderian, *Panzer Leader*, 463–465.
75) Ibid. Introduction by B. H. Liddell Hart, 12.
76) Ibid.
77) Ibid.
78) Guderian, *Panzer Leader*, 20.
79) Ibid., 22.
80) Ibid., 24.
81) Ibid., 29.
82) Ibid., 32.
83) Ibid., 458.
84) Ibid., 32–33. For Beck's political thought, see Wilhelm Ritter von Schramm ed., *Gemeinschaftsdokumente für den Frieden, 1941–1944*, Munich, 1965.
85) Seeckt, *Moltke*, 20.
86) Cyril Falls, Introduction to Görlitz, *General Staff*, v–x.
87) Görlitz, *General Staff*, 12–13.
88) Howard, *Franco-Prussian War*, 62. Görlitz, *General Staff*, 140.
89) Berndorff, *General zwischen Ost und West*, 17.
90) Model, *Der deutsche Generalstabsoffizier*, 14.
91) Ibid., 15.
92) Lessel, *Böhmen, Frankreich, China*, 415.
93) *Étude comparative sur le récrutement et l'organisation du corps d'officiers en Prusse et en France* par un officier d'État major, Paris, 1871, 6–11.

94) Ibid., 17–18.
95) Ibid., 22.
96) Model, *Der deutsche Generalstabsoffizier*, 16–18.
97) Ibid., 17–18.
98) Ibid., 19.
99) Ibid., 22.
100) Ibid., 22–23.
101) Ibid., 23.
102) Ibid., 25.
103) Ibid., 30.
104) Ibid., 38, 53–54.
105) Ibid., 58.
106) Scheurig, *Tresckow*, 50–51.
107) Ibid., 52.
108) Ibid.
109) Ibid., 56.
110) Model, *Der deutsche Generalstabsoffizier*, 70–71.
111) Ibid., 135–139.
112) Quoted in Guske, *Seeckt*, 11.
113) Quoted in Plehwe, *Schleicher*, 16.
114) Guske, *Seeckt*, 7–8.
115) Berndorff, *General zwischen Ost und West*, 13. Plehwe,
     Schleicher, 14–15.
116) Berndorff, *General zwischen Ost und West*, 12.
117) Ibid., 13.
118) Plehwe, *Schleicher*, 15.
119) Guske, *Seeckt*, 13.
120) Ibid., 14.
121) Ibid.
122) Berndorff, *General zwischen Ost und West*, 17.
123) Plehwe, *Schleicher*, 17.
124) Ibid., 18.
125) Ibid., 19.
126) Guske, *Seeckt*, 9.
127) Ibid., 10.
128) Ibid., 14.
129) Ibid., 19.
130) Ibid.
131) Ibid., 29.
132) Ibid., 19.

133) Ibid., 31.
134) Ibid., 38.
135) Ibid., 39.
136) Ibid., 61.
137) Ibid., 22.
138) Ibid., 50.
139) Ibid., 55.
140) Ibid., 73.
141) Ibid., 89.
142) Ibid., 11.
143) Ibid., 16.
144) Ibid.
145) Ibid., 19.
146) Ibid., 15.
147) Ibid., 147.
148) Ibid., 165.
149) Berndorff, *General zwischen Ost und West*, 37.
150) Ibid., 83.
151) Ibid., 84. Plehwe, *Schleicher*, 54. For the political role played by Horcher's restaurant in the Third Reich, see my article, 'Grand Restaurant with a Past' in the *Financial Times*, 30 January 1993.
152) Plehwe, *Schleicher*, 54.
153) Guske, *Seeckt*, 120.
154) Ibid., 148.
155) Ibid., 158.
156) Craig, *Prussian Army*, 379 and n2.
157) Guske, *Seeckt*, 191.
158) Ibid., 200.
159) Ibid., 201.
160) Craig, *Prussian Army*, 393–394; and see 394 n1.
161) Ibid., 395.
162) Erfurth, *Geschichte*, 97.
163) Plehwe, *Schleicher*, 63–64.
164) Berndorff, *General zwischen Ost und West*, 85.
165) Ibid., 90.
166) Craig, *Prussian Army*, 417, 420. Erfurth, *Geschichte*, 115. Guske, *Seeckt*, 232.
167) Erfurth, *Geschichte*, 115.

168) Plehwe, *Schleicher*, 102–103. Craig, *Prussian Army*, 421.
     Erfurth, *Geschichte*, 119–122.
169) Axel Schild, *Militärdiktatur mit Massenbasis, Die Querfront-
     konzeption der Reichswehrführung um General von Schleicher am
     Ende der Weimarer Republik*, Frankfurt & New York, 1981,
     45–46.

Chapter VI: Pink Prussia

 1) See Nicolaus Sombart in Röhl and Sombart eds., *New
    Interpretations*, 290, 299.
 2) Hans von Tresckow, *Von Fürsten und andere Sterblichen:
    Errinerungen eines Kriminalkommissars*, Berlin, 1922, 107.
 3) Ibid., 109.
 4) Ibid., 112.
 5) Ibid., 111.
 6) Ibid., 111–112.
 7) Ibid., 113.
 8) Ibid., 115. Rich, *Holstein*, II, 775.
 9) Tresckow, *Von Fürsten*, 115–116.
10) Ibid., 118–119.
11) Ibid.
12) Ibid., 141–142.
13) Ibid., 142–143.
14) Ibid., 120.
15) Ibid., 144.
16) Ibid., 120–121.
17) Ibid., 123.
18) Ibid., 124–125.
19) Ibid.
20) Ibid., 126–127.
21) Ibid., 128.
22) Ibid., 129.
23) Ibid.
24) Robert Graf von Zedlitz-Trützschler, *Zwölf Jahre am deutschen
    Kaiserhof*, Berlin and Leipzig, 1924, 171–172. Discussion of
    the various scandals around the Kaiser's court was omitted
    from the English text of Zedlitz's book.
25) Hull, Kaiser and 'Liebenberg Circle', in Röhl & Sombart eds.,
    New Interpretations, 203.

26) Röhl, *Kaiser, Hof und Staat*, 36–38.
27) Ibid., 41.
28) Hans Wilhelm Burmeister, *Prince Philipp Eulenburg-Hertefeld 1847–1921. His Influence on Kaiser Wilhelm II and his Role in German Government 1888–1902*, Wiesbaden, 1981, 31.
29) Young, *Harden*, 113.
30) Hull, Kaiser and 'Liebenberg Circle', in Röhl & Sombart eds., *New Interpretations*, 194–196.
31) Ibid., 196.
32) Zedlitz-Trützschler, *Zwölf Jahre*, 171.
33) For an account of the Wilde trial see Richard Ellmann, *Oscar Wilde*, London, 1987, 414–450.
34) Tresckow, *Von Fürsten*, 138.
35) Hull, Kaiser and 'Liebenberg Circle', in Röhl & Sombart eds., *New Interpretations*, 197.
36) Röhl, *Kaiser, Hof und Staat*, 68.
37) Hull, Kaiser and 'Liebenberg Circle', in Röhl & Sombart eds., *New Interpretations*, 197.
38) Ibid., 199.
39) Ibid., 197.
40) Röhl, *Kaiser, Hof und Staat*, 64–65.
41) Ibid.
42) Hull, Kaiser and 'Liebenberg Circle', in Röhl & Sombart eds., *New Interpretations*, 200.
43) Tresckow, *Von Fürsten*, 169, 181.
44) Zedlitz-Trütschler, *Twelve Years*, 252–253.
45) Röhl, *Kaiser, Hof und Staat*, 27.
46) Ibid., 26–27.
47) Sombart, in Röhl & Sombart eds. *New Interpretations*, 308.
48) Young, *Harden*, 89. Rich, *Holstein*, II, 769.
49) Young, *Harden*, 96.
50) Rich, *Holstein*, II, 769.
51) Ibid.
52) Ibid., II, 770.
53) Tresckow, *Von Fürsten*, 138.
54) Johannes Haller, *Aus dem Leben des Fürsten Philipp zu Eulenburg-Hertefeld*, Berlin & Leipzig, 1926, 344.
55) Rich, *Holstein*, II, 771–772.
56) Ibid., II, 777. Young, *Harden*, 97.
57) Ibid., 98. Balfour, *The Kaiser*, 275.

58) Rich, *Holstein*, II, 778. Zedlitz-Trützschler, *Zwölf Jahre*, 161.
59) Tresckow, *Von Fürsten*, 164.
60) Ibid.
61) Ibid., 165.
62) Ibid., 166–167.
63) Zedlitz-Trützschler, *Twelve Years*, 184–185.
64) Zedlitz-Trützschler, *Zwölf Jahre*, 161.
65) Tresckow, *Von Fürsten*, 168–169. Rich, *Holstein*, II, 778.
66) Tresckow, *Von Fürsten*, 169–172.
67) Ibid., 180–181.
68) Young, *Harden*, 4.
69) Tresckow, *Von Fürsten*, 183.
70) Ibid.
71) Rich, *Holstein*, II, 761–763, 776.
72) Ibid., II, 758.
73) Ibid., II, 767. Young, *Harden*, 113.
74) Rich, *Holstein*, II, 766.
75) Zedlitz-Trützschler, *Zwölf Jahre*, 160.
76) Rich, *Holstein*, II, 771.
77) Tresckow, *Von Fürsten*, 185.
78) Ibid., 191.
79) Ibid., 199.
80) Ibid., 142–143. Marie Radziwiłł, 12–16 July 1908, in Fox ed., 36.
81) Rich, *Holstein*, II, 779–781.
82) Ibid., II, 782–788.
83) Young, *Harden*, 104.
84) Ibid., 107.
85) Rich, *Holstein*, II, 782–788.
86) Ibid., II, 788–799.
87) Young, *Harden*, 102–103.
88) Ibid., 110. Haller, *Aus dem Leben*, 338.
89) Rich, *Holstein*, II, 789–790.
90) Eulenburg's diaries are printed in Haller, *Aus dem Leben*, 418.
91) Ibid., 420.
92) Ibid., 419.
93) Young, *Harden*, 110.
94) Haller, *Aus dem Leben*, 336. Tresckow, *Von Fürsten*, 152–153.
95) Tresckow, *Von Fürsten*, 152–153.
96) Ibid., 153–154.

97) Ibid., 155.

98) Hull, Kaiser and 'Liebenberg Circle', in Röhl & Sombart eds., *New Interpretations*, 201.

99) Tresckow, *Von Fürsten*, 155–159.

100) Haller, *Aus dem Leben*, 418–430, passim.

101) Tresckow, *Von Fürsten*, 201–202. Marie Radziwiłł, 4 July 1908, in Fox ed., 33.

102) Ibid., 204.

103) Ibid., 204–205.

104) Ibid., 207.

105) Ibid., 207–208.

106) Balfour, *The Kaiser*, 276. Rich, *Holstein*, II, 795.

Chapter VII: The Junkers and the Court

1) Görlitz, *Die Junker*, 24–26.

2) Ibid., 6–7.

3) G. K. Kypke, *Geschichte des Geschlechts von Kleist*, 1878. Görlitz, *Die Junker*, 11.

4) Ibid.

5) Ibid., 15–16.

6) Ibid. 101–104. In the works of Theodor Fontane, Silesians are always characterised by their lofty titles and immense wealth.

7) Görlitz, *Die Junker*, 104.

8) Ibid., 42. Gräfin Dönhoff, *Kindheit*, 179–180.

9) Görlitz, *Die Junker*, 20.

10) Magnus von Braun, *Von Ostpreussen bis Texas*, 39.

11) Görlitz, *Die Junker*, 90.

12) Oldenburg-Januschau, *Errinerungen*, 6–8.

13) Lawrence J. Baack, *Christian Bernstorff and Prussia, Diplomacy and Reform Conservatism 1818–1832*, New Brunswick, New Jersey, 1980, 1.

14) Reinhard Doerries, 'Count Albrecht von Bernstorff (1890–1945), the Man and the Diplomat'. Lecture delivered at the German Historical Institute, London, 3 December 1992.

15) See Gregory W. Pedlow, *The Survival of the Hessian Nobility, 1770–1870*, Princeton, 1988.

16) Schützsack, *Der preussische Traum*, 82.

17) Ibid., 81.

18) von dem Bussche, *Arnim*, 282. Pedlow, *Survival*, 26 n31. Görlitz, *Die Junker*, 55.
19) Tresckow, *Von Fürsten*, 173.
20) Röhl, *Kaiser, Hof und Staat*, 110.
21) Görlitz, *Die Junker*, 59–60.
22) Gräfin Dönhoff, *Kindheit*, 18.
23) Oldenburg-Januschau, *Errinerungen*, 10.
24) Görlitz, *Die Junker*, 203–204.
25) Ibid., 269.
26) Oldenburg-Januschau, *Errinerungen*, 8.
27) Görlitz, *Die Junker*, 277.
28) Gräfin Dönhoff, *Kindheit*, 150.
29) Magnus von Braun, *Von Ostpreussen bis Texas*, 226–227.
30) Alvensleben/Koenigswald, *Besuche vor dem Untergang*, 37.
31) Görlitz, *Die Junker*, 333.
32) Oldenburg-Januschau, *Errinerungen*, 212.
33) Görlitz, *Die Junker*, 333.
34) Ibid., 334.
35) Ibid., 335.
36) Gräfin Dönhoff, *Kindheit*, 49–50.
37) Heinrich Brüning, *Memoiren*, 243.
38) Ibid.
39) Hans Schlange-Schoeningen (sic), *The Morning After*, translated by Edward Fitzgerald, London, 1948, 62–63.
40) Ibid., 62.
41) Ibid., 69.
42) Ibid., 80.
43) Brüning, *Memoiren*, 385.
44) Magnus von Braun, *Von Ostpreussen bis Texas*, 205.
45) Görlitz, *Die Junker*, 366. Oldenburg-Januschau, *Errinerungen*, 222.
46) Ibid., 218.
47) Ibid.
48) Ibid.
49) Hagen Schultze, *Otto Braun, oder Preussens demokratische Sendung. Eine Biographie*, Frankfurt/Main, Berlin, Vienna, 1977, 680.
50) Gräfin Dönhoff, *Kindheit*, 51–52.
51) Magnus von Braun, *Von Ostpreussen bis Texas*, 218.
52) Schultze, *Braun*, 677–687, passim.

53) Magnus von Braun, *Von Ostpreussen bis Texas*, 219.
54) Ibid., 220.
55) Schlange-Schoeningen, *Morning After*, 84–85, 87.
56) Görlitz, *Die Junker*, 370.
57) Gräfin Dönhoff, *Namen die keiner mehr nennt*, 64. Also *Kindheit*, 70–73,
58) Gerard, *My Four Years*, 6.
59) Fontane, *Die Grafschaft Ruppin*, in *Wanderungen*, I, 306.
60) 'Vasili', *La Société de Berlin*, 42.
61) Ibid., 43.
62) Ibid., 177.
63) Evidence from the display cabinets at Schloss Wernigerode itself. When I visited the *Schloss* on 5 June 1991 it was still a museum of 'feudalism' designed to edify the socialist school-children of the DDR.
64) 'Vasili', *La Société de Berlin*, 172.
65) (Johann Friedel), *Briefe über die Galanterien von Berlin, auf einer Reise gesammelt von einem österreichischen Offizier, 1782*. New edition Berlin, 1987. There is little evidence that Friedel ever visited Berlin.
66) Zedlitz-Trützschler, *Twelve Years*, 23–25. For Schloss Albrechtsberg, see Volker Helas, *Villenarchitektur, Villa Architecture in Dresden*, herausgegeben von Peter Gössel und Gabriele Leuthäuser, Cologne, 1991, 68–77.
67) Zedlitz-Trützschler, *Twelve Years*, 220.
68) Ibid., 221.
69) Miss Topham, *Souvenirs*, 105.
70) Gerard, *My Four Years*, 6–8.
71) Ibid., 9–10. Marie Radziwiłł, 19 February 1909, in Fox ed., 72.
72) Gerard, *My Four Years*, 40.
73) Ibid.
74) Ibid., 37. Miss Topham, *Souvenirs*, 161–162.
75) Gerard, *My Four Years*, 68.
76) See Fontane, *Havelland*, in *Wanderungen*, II, 178–179.
77) Miss Topham, *Souvenirs*, 98. There is a recipe for carp cooked in beer in Maria von Treskow, *Berliner Kochbuch. Aus alten Familienrezepten*, Weingarten 1987, 62; also A. A. Löwenthal 'Des Kaisers Karpfenreich', in *Gesammelte Schriften*, Tübingen and Stuttgart. Vol. VI, 225–227.

78) 'Vasili', *La Société de Berlin*, 139.
79) Röhl, *Kaiser, Hof und Staat*, 92.
80) Ibid., II.
81) Zedlitz-Trützschler, *Twelve Years*, 122–123.
82) Ibid., 133–134.
83) von dem Bussche, *Arnim*, 5.
84) Haller, *Aus dem Leben*, 423.
85) Görlitz, *Müller*, 203.
86) Berndorff, *General zwischen Ost und West*, 46–47.

Chapter VIII: School and University

1) Wolfgang Menge, *Alltag in Preussen: Ein Bericht aus dem 18. Jahrhundert*, Beltz, Weinheim & Basel, 1991, 122–144.
2) Rehsener, *Am Ostseestrand*, 27.
3) Albrecht von dem Bussche, *Die Ritterakademie zu Brandenburg*, Frankfurt/Main, Bern, New York, Paris, 1989, 41, 51, 100–101. I am grateful to Professor Knud Caesar for directing me to this source.
4) Knopp, *Preussens Wege*, 22.
5) von dem Bussche, *Ritterakademie*, 52, 102.
6) von dem Bussche, *Arnim*, 207 n27.
7) Michael Sauer, Die Entwicklung des Graudenzer allgemeinbildenden Schulwesens im 19. Jahrhundert in *Beiträge zur Geschichte Westpreussens*, No. II, Münster, 1989, 119–123.
8) Horst Mies, *Die preussische Verwaltung des Regierungsbezirks Marienwerder 1830–1870*, Cologne, Bonn, 1972, 160.
9) Ibid.
10) Irene Berger, *Die preussische Verwaltung des Regierungsbezirks Bromberg, 1815–1847*, Cologne & Berlin, 1966, 143.
11) Ibid., 10.
12) Klaus Helmut Rehfeld, *Die preussische Verwaltung des Regierungsbezirks Bromberg, 1848–1871*, Cologne & Berlin, 1968, 29.
13) Liselotte Kunigk-Helbing, Volkstumspolitik im südlichen Ermland während der Zwischenkriegszeit in *Zeitschrift für die Geschichte und Altertumskunde Ermlands*, Band 46, 1991, 83–86.
14) Ibid., 87.

15) Lothar Gall, *Bismarck, I The White Revolutionary*, 5. Ernst
Engelberg, *Bismarck: Urpreusse und Reichsgründer*, Berlin 1986,
95.
16) Ibid.
17) Ibid., 96.
18) Heinrich, *Preussen*, 181, 184–6. von dem Bussche,
Ritterakademie, 272.
19) Miss Topham, *Souvenirs*, 122–124.
20) One executed alumnus was Albrecht von Hagen, 1904–1944.
21) von dem Bussche, *Ritterakademie*, 35.
22) Ibid., 43, 46.
23) Ibid., 65, 107–110.
24) Ibid., 112, 207–211. Elard von Oldenburg-Januschau,
Errinerungen, 17.
25) von dem Bussche, *Ritterakademie*, 18, 117.
26) Ibid., 120–123.
27) Ibid., 124–135.
28) Ibid.
29) Ibid., 55–57.
30) Ibid., 72–75, 172.
31) Ibid.
32) Ibid., 86, 249.
33) Ibid., 167–168, 207, 223.
34) Ibid., 263. Görlitz, *General Staff*, 4.
35) Tresckow, *Von Fürsten*, 46–47.
36) A. von Crousaz, *Geschichte des königlich preussischen Kadetten-
Corps, nach seiner Entstehung, seinem Entwicklungsgange und
seinen Resultaten*, Berlin, 1857, 5–6.
37) Ibid. 16.
38) Ibid., 18.
39) von dem Bussche, *Ritterakademie*, 271.
40) *Étude comparative*, 12–13.
41) Lessel, *Böhmen, Frankreich, China*, 18.
42) Ibid.
43) Ibid., 19.
44) Ibid.
45) Ibid.
46) Ibid.
47) Ibid., 21.
48) Ibid.

49) Ibid.
50) Ibid.
51) Ibid.
52) Ibid.
53) Guderian, *Panzer Leader*, 16.
54) Miss Topham, *Souvenirs*, 140.
55) Viktoria Luise, *Ein Leben*, 18. Miss Topham, *Souvenirs*, 140–147.
56) Viktoria Luise, *Ein Leben*, 19.
57) Görlitz, *Die Junker*, 303–305.
58) Magnus von Braun, *Von Ostpreussen bis Texas*, 35.
59) von dem Bussche, *Ritterakademie*, 52.
60) Walter Gerschler, *Das preussische Oberpräsidium der Provinz Jülich–Kleve–Berg in Köln 1816–1822*, Cologne & Berlin, 1968, 92–94.
61) von dem Bussche, *Arnim*, 32.
62) Engelberg, *Bismarck: Urpreusse*, 115.
63) Ibid., 117.
64) Heinz Ohff, *Joseph Freiherr von Eichendorff*, Berlin, 1983, 37–38.
65) Ibid., 42–43.
66) Hans-Jürgen Belke, *Die preussische Regierung zu Königsberg 1808–1850*, Cologne & Berlin, 1975, 14–15.
67) Rehsener, *Am Ostseestrand*, 50.
68) Ibid., 56.
69) Ibid.
70) Ibid., 61.
71) Tresckow, *Von Fürsten*, 39.
72) Ibid., 40.

Chapter IX: Civil and Political

1) Schützsack, *Der preussische Traum*, 105–107, 148.
2) Röhl, *Kaiser, Hof und Staat*, 141.
3) Ibid., 142.
4) Ibid., 145.
5) Ibid.
6) Rich, *Holstein*, II, 491.
7) Röhl, *Kaiser, Hof und Staat*, 147–148.
8) Rich, *Holstein*, II, 501.

9) Röhl, *Kaiser, Hof und Staat*, 149.
10) Ibid., 146.
11) Rich, *Holstein*, II, 687.
12) Ibid., II, 839.
13) Ibid., II, 835.
14) Röhl, *Kaiser, Hof und Staat*, 153.
15) Görlitz, *Die Junker*, 301.
16) Röhl, *Kaiser, Hof und Staat*, 156.
17) Klaus Schwabe ed., *Die preussischen Oberpräsidenten, 1815–1945*, Büdinger Forschungen zur Sozialgeschichte, Boppard am Rhein, 1985, 9.
18) Georg Christoph von Unruh, Der preussische Oberpräsident-Entstehung, Stellung und Wandel eines Staatsamtes, in Ibid., 26–27.
19) Rüdiger Schütz, Die preussischen Oberpräsidenten von 1815– bis 1866, in Ibid., 37.
20) Von Unruh in Ibid., 30.
21) Röhl, *Kaiser, Hof und Staat*, 156–157.
22) Gerard, *My Four Years*, 74.
23) Görlitz, *Müller*, 173.
24) Brüning, *Memoiren*, 62.
25) Rudolf Klatt, *Ostpreussen unter dem Reichskommissariat*, mit ein Geleitwort von Magnus Freiherr von Braun-Neucken, Heidelberg, 1958, 186.
26) Ibid., 187 n8.
27) Brüning, *Memoiren*, 62.
28) Klatt, *Ostpreussen*, 193.
29) Ibid.
30) Brüning, *Memoiren*, 64.
31) Schultze, *Braun*, 229.
32) Braun, *Von Weimar zu Hitler*, 21.
33) Ibid., 38.
34) Ibid., 39.
35) Ibid., 43.
36) Ibid., 44.
37) Ibid., 48.
38) Schultze, *Braun*, 230.
39) Ibid.
40) Ibid.

41) Oswald Spengler, *Preussentum und Sozialismus*, Munich, 1920, 11.
42) Ibid., 1–2.
43) Ibid., 15.
44) Ibid., 29.
45) Ibid., 32.
46) Ibid., 38.
47) Ibid., 37.
48) Ibid., 39.
49) Ibid., 40.
50) Ibid., 42.
51) Ibid., 46.
52) Ibid., 60.
53) Ibid., 90.
54) Schützsack, *Der preussische Traum*, 17.
55) Ulrich Heinemann, *Ein konservativer Rebell: Fritz-Dietlof Graf von der Schulenburg und der 20. Juli*, Berlin, 1990, 1.
56) Gottfried von Nostitz, quoted in Giles MacDonogh, *A Good German, Adam von Trott zu Solz*, London, 1989, 286.
57) Heinemann, *Schulenburg*, 3.
58) Ibid., 6.
59) Ibid., 4.
60) Ibid., 12.
61) Ibid., 10.
62) Ibid., 14.
63) Ibid.
64) Ibid., 17.
65) Ibid., 22–23.
66) Letter to Charlotte Kotelmann, 22 October 1932. Quoted in ibid., 181.
67) Ibid., 24.
68) Ibid.
69) Letter to Charlotte Kotelmann, 6 November 1932, quoted in ibid., 183.
70) Ibid., 26.
71) Ibid., 27.
72) Ibid., 34–35.
73) Ibid., 35–36.
74) 'Vasili', *La Société de Berlin*, 34–35.
75) Görlitz, *Die Junker*, 348.

76) Schoeps, *Das andere Preussen*, 1.

77) Ibid., 5.
78) Ibid., 38–39.
79) Ibid., 1.
80) Ibid., 44.
81) Ibid., 2.
82) Hermann von Petersdorff ed., *Bismarcks Briefwechsel mit Kleist-Retzow.*, n.d., 5.
83) Hermann von Petersdorff, *Kleist-Retzow, ein Lebensbild*, Stuttgart & Berlin, 1907, 413.
84) Görlitz, *Die Junker*, 266–267.
85) Ibid., 300.
86) Ibid., 296.
87) Braun, *Von Weimar zu Hitler*, 24.
88) Schultze, *Braun*, 157.
89) Ibid., 158, 225.
90) Gräfin Dönhoff, *Kindheit*, 35, quoting Golo Mann, *Das Ende Preussens*.
91) Schultze, *Braun*, 250.
92) Ibid., 39–41.
93) Miss Topham, *Souvenirs*, 241–244.
94) Schultze, *Braun*, 82–91.
95) Herbert Hömig, *Das preussische Zentrum in der Weimarer Republik*, Mainz, 1979, 306–311.
96) Schultze, *Braun*, 239.
97) Braun, *Von Weimar zu Hitler*, 5.
98) Gustav Noske, *Von Kiel bis Kapp, zur Geschichte der deutschen Revolution*, Berlin, 1920, 148–149.
99) Schultze, *Braun*, 257.
100) Braun, *Von Weimar zu Hitler*, 69.
101) Schultze, *Braun*, 257.
102) Ibid., 258.
103) Ibid.
104) Ibid., 259.
105) Ibid., 290.
106) Ibid., 291.
107) Ibid., 313–317.
108) Ibid., 317.
109) Ibid., 318.
110) Ibid., 412–414. Braun, *Von Weimar zu Hitler*, 117.

111) Schultze, *Braun*, 414.
112) Ibid., 600.
113) Ibid., 488–489.
114) Ibid., Braun, *Von Weimar zu Hitler*, 172–173.
115) Brüning, *Memoiren*, 145, 453.
116) Schultze, *Braun*, 492.
117) Braun, *Von Weimar zu Hitler*, 390.
118) Schultze, *Braun*, 674.
119) Ibid., 676.
120) Ibid., 395–396.
121) Hömig, *preussische Zentrum*, 306–311.
122) Karl Dietrich Bracher, *Die Auflösung der Weimarer Republik. Eine Studie zum Problem des Machtverfalls in der Demokratie*, fifth edition Düsseldorf, 1978, 441.
123) Schultze, *Braun*, 725–728.
124) Ibid., 729.
125) Magnus von Braun, *Ostpreussen bis Texas*, 208.
126) Schultze, *Braun*, 733.
127) Bracher, *Auflösung*, 506.
128) Ibid., 507.
129) Ibid., 511–514.
130) Rudolf Morsey, *Zur Geschichte des Preussenschlags am 20 Juli 1932* in *Vierteljahrbuch für Zeitgeschichte*, 4e Heft, 430–439.

Chapter X: Subject Peoples

1) Schütsack, *Der preussische Traum*, 38.
2) Graf von Krockow, *Warnüng*, 10.
3) Knopp, *Preussens Wege*, 44.
4) Stirk, *The Prussian Spirit*, 22.
5) Carsten, Preussen und England, in Otto Busch ed., *Preussen und das Ausland*, 40.
6) Günter Grass, *Die Blechtrommel*, Luchterhand ed., Frankfurt/Main 1974, 512.
7) Rolf Engels, *Die preussische Verwaltung von Kammer und Regierung Gumbinnen, 1724–1870*, Cologne & Berlin, 1974, 9.
8) Rehsener, *Am Ostseestrand*, 140.
9) Reinhard Hauf, *Die preussische Verwaltung des Regierungsbezirks Königsberg 1871–1920*, Cologne & Berlin, 1980, 18, 146.
10) Görlitz, *Müller*, 95.

11) Ibid., 123–124.

12) Ibid., 197.

13) Ibid., 261.

14) Ibid., 266–270.

15) Ibid., 308.

16) Frederick the Great, Exposé, B.P.H. Rep. 47 Nr. 228.

17) Rehsener, *Am Ostseestrand*, 98.

18) Görlitz, *Die Junker*, 122.

19) William W. Hagen, *Germans, Poles and Jews, The Nationality Conflict in the Prussian East, 1772–1914.* Chicago & London, 1980, 86–87.

20) Seeckt, *Moltke*, 120.

21) Ibid., 56–57, 114.

22) Andreas Lawaty, *Das Ende Preussens in polnischer Sicht. Zur Kontinuität negativer Wirkungen der preussischen Geschichte auf die deutsch-polnischen Beziehungen*, Berlin & New York, 1986, 33.

23) Hans von Seeckt, *Deutschland zwischen West und Ost*, Hamburg, 1933, 30.

24) Ibid., 31–32, 38.

25) Magnus von Braun, *Von Ostpreussen bis Texas*, 314–316.

26) Lawaty, *Das Ende Preussens in polnischer Sicht*, 23 n15.

27) Ibid., 25.

28) Ibid., 74.

29) Ibid., 75.

30) Ibid., 76–77.

31) Ibid., 16, 30, 79.

32) Ibid., 29, 47–51, 63–64.

33) Ibid., 63.

34) Ibid.

35) Grass, *Die Blechtrommel*, 487.

36) Stefan Buszczynski, quoted in Lawaty, *Das Ende Preussens*, 42.

37) Hagen, *Germans, Poles and Jews*, 25–31.

38) Ibid., 31.

39) Ibid., 36.

40) Quoted in Hanna Labrenz, *Das Bild Preussens in der polnischen Geschichtsschreibung*, Rheinfelden, 1986, 36–37.

41) Hagen, *Germans, Poles and Jews*, 14–15, 16–17.

42) Ibid.

43) Mies, *Marienwerder*, 15–17.

44) Berger, *Bromberg*, 143–145.
45) Rehfeld, *Bromberg*, 27.
46) Rehsener, *Am Ostseestrand*, 98.
47) Albrecht Wien, *Die preussische Verwaltung Regierungsbezirks Danzig 1870–1920*, Cologne & Berlin, 1973, 17–18.
48) Gisbert Knopp, *Die preussische Verwaltung des Regierungsbezirks Düsseldorf in den Jahre 1899–1919*, Cologne & Berlin, 1974, 119–120, 128.
49) Hagen, *Germans, Poles and Jews*, 41–43.
50) Ibid., 44.
51) Ibid., 82.
52) Ibid.
53) Von dem Bussche, *Arnim*, 207.
54) Berger, *Bromberg*, 165.
55) Ibid., 166.
56) Von dem Bussche, *Arnim*, 208–213.
57) Hagen, *Germans, Poles and Jews*, 91.
58) Alvensleben, *Lauter Abschiede*, 37.
59) Görlitz, *Die Junker*, 223. For Hohenzollern Household Law, see the letter to his grandson, Prince William, B.P.H. Rep. 53 Nr. 32. Also there is a discussion of this in Preussen, *Das Haus Hohenzollern*, 27–30.
60) Schützsack, *Der preussische Traum*, 43.
61) Hagen, *Germans, Poles and Jews*, 87–90.
62) Ibid., 91–92.
63) Ibid., 121
64) See Tighe, *Gdańsk*, 65–83, passim.
65) Lech Trzeciakowski, Preussische Polenpolitik im Zeitalter der Aufstände (1830–1864) in Klaus Zernack ed., *Polen und die polnische Frage in der Geschichte der Hohenzollern Monarchie 1701–1871*, mit einem Geleitwort von Otto Busch, Berlin, 1982, 96.
66) Hagen, *Germans, Poles and Jews*, 123.
67) Ibid.
68) Lawaty, *Das Ende Preussens in polnischer Sicht*, 23.
69) Hans von Tresckow, *Von Fürsten und andere Sterblichen, Errinerungen eines Kriminalkommissars*, Berlin, 1992, 192–3.
70) Ibid., 63.
71) Conversation with and demonstration by Professor Bohdan

Kacprzyński in the course of a journey from Warsaw to Ostrołęka, 19 May 1992.

72) Hagen, *Germans, Poles and Jews*, 76–77.

73) Petersdorff, *Kleist-Retzow*, 3.

74) Ibid., 353.

75) Oldenburg-Januschau, *Errinerungen*, 93–94.

76) Hagen, *Germans, Poles and Jews*, 128–131.

77) Ibid., 132.

78) Ibid.

79) Ibid., 133.

80) Ibid.,135.

81) Ibid., 170.

82) Ibid., 172.

83) Ibid.

84) Ibid., 174.

85) Ibid., 188.

86) Zedlitz-Trützschler, *Twelve Years*, 168–169, 172.

87) Hagen, *Germans, Poles and Jews*, 196.

88) Ibid., 200–201.

89) Ibid., 203.

90) Davies, *God's Playground*, 137.

91) Hagen, *Germans, Poles and Jews*, 226.

92) Lawaty, *Das Ende Preussens in polnischer Sicht*, 53–54.

93) Ibid., 56–57.

94) Ibid., 60.

95) Ibid., 66–68. Davies, *God's Playground*, 136.

96) Lawaty, *Das Ende Preussens in polnischer Sicht*, 54, 68–79.

97) Erfurth, *Geschichte*, 33–34.

98) Ibid., 35–36.

99) Braun, *Weimar zu Hitler*, 337.

100) Akten des königlichen Landratsamtes des Kreises Löbau Wpr. zu Neumark Wpr. XIV, A 200/41, OPI 499, 15 January 1919.

101) Klatt, *Ostpreussen*, 59.

102) Ibid., 89.

103) Ibid., 108.

104) Akten Löbau, XIV, A 200/41, IA Nr 6717C.

105) See John Maynard Keynes, *The Economic Consequences of the Peace*, London, 1919. Article 93 of the Versailles Treaty.

106) Klatt, *Ostpreussen*, 249.

107) Ibid., 242–243.

108) Lawaty, *Das Ende Preussens in polnischer Sicht*, 91.
109) Ibid., 93.
110) Ibid., 100.

Chapter XI: The Decline of Tolerance

1) Pierre Paul Sagave, Preussen und Frankreich, in Otto Busch ed., *Preussen und das Ausland*, 62.
2) Ibid., 66. The final figure for Huguenot immigrants would be nearer to 20,000.
3) Fontane, *Meine Kinderjahre*, in *Werke*, 74–75, 79–80, 83–84.
4) Heinrich, *Preussen*, 182. Hubatsch, *Frederick the Great*, 194.
5) Mies, *Marienwerder*, 164.
6) Ibid.
7) Gerschler, *Jülich–Kleve–Berg*, 173.
8) Mies, *Marienwerder*, 164.
9) Schoeps, *Das andere Preussen*, 5–6.
10) Petersdorff, *Kleist-Retzow*, 413.
11) J. N. D. Kelly, *The Oxford Dictionary of Popes*, Oxford, 1986, 309–311.
12) Thomas Stamm-Kuhlmann, *Königin Preussens grosser Zeit: Friedrich Wilhelm III, der Melanckoliker auf dem Thron*, Berlin, 1992, 538–9, 544–5. Günter Dettmer, *Die Ost- und Westpreussischen Verwaltungsbehörder im Kulturkampf*, Heidelberg, 1958, herausgegeben von Walter Hubatsch, 14–15.
13) Ibid., 25–26.
14) Ibid., 28.
15) Ibid., 34.
16) See Helmuth James von Moltke, *Letters to Freya: A Witness against Hitler*, edited and translated by Beate Ruhm von Oppen, London, 1991, 184–185.
17) Dettmer, *Kultwkampf*, 43–44.
18) Frederick the Great, Testament Politique, in Gaxotte ed., *Frédéric II*, 294.
19) Hubatsch, *Frederick the Great*, 3, 79, 116.
20) Hannah Arendt, *Rahel Varnhagen, Lebensgeschichte einer deutschen Jüdin aus der Romantik*, eighth edition, Munich, 1990, 19.
21) Ibid., 86.

22) Ibid., 118–120.

23) Ibid., 170.

24) Bildarchiv Preussischer Kulturbesitz, *Juden in Preussen, Ein Kapitel deutscher Geschichte*, second edition, 1981, 167.

25) Stefan Hartmann, Das Generalverzeichnis der Königsberger Juden vom 24 März 1812 als Familien und Sozialgeschichtliche Quelle, 35–42 in *Preussenland*, 29/1991, No. 3, 36, 40.

26) Rehsener, *Am Ostseestrand*, 7, 113.

27) 'Vasili', *La Société de Berlin*, 153.

28) Ibid., 156.

29) Adolf Stoecker, *Das moderne Judenthum in Deutschland, besonders in Berlin. Zwei Reden in der christlich-socialien* [sic] *Arbeiter partei*, Berlin, 1880, 2, 15.

30) Karl Fischer, *Heinrich von Treitschke, und sein Wort über unser Judenthum. Ein Wort zur Verstandigung*, Leipzig, 1880, 5. Hausrath, *Treitschke*, 98–9, 113–15.

31) Ibid., 34.

32) Stoecker, *Das moderne Judenthum*, 2.

33) Gottlieb Klein, *Zur 'Judenfrage' unsere Anforderungen an des Christenthum des Herrn Stöcker* (sic), Zurich, 1880, 7, 8, 12.

34) Zedlitz-Trützchler, *Twelve Years*, 217–218.

35) *Juden in Preussen*, 352.

36) Ruth Andreas-Friedrich, *Berlin Underground 1938–1945*, New York, 1947.

37) *Juden in Preussen*, 342.

38) Berglar, *Rathenau*, 51.

39) Ibid., 249.

Chapter XII: The Prussian Soul under National Socialism

1) Stirk, *Prussian Spirit*, 17–18.

2) The classic book on the subject is Fritz Fischer's *Griff nach der Weltmacht*, of 1961. For the continuity of Germany's war aims in the Second World War, see Karl Hildebrandt, *Foreign Policy of the Third Reich*, London, 1970 and Andreas Hillgruber, *Germany and the Two World Wars*, London, 1981.

3) Lord Vansittart, 'Vansittartism' in *The Nineteenth Century*, Vol. CXXXI, May 1942, 203–208. I am grateful to the explorer

James Barclay for sending me this article by his step-grandfather.

4) Sabine Höner, *Der nationalsozialistische Zugriff auf Preussen. Preussischer Staat – und nationalsozialistische Machteroberungs stategie 1928–34*, Bochum, 1984, 492.

5) Jürgen Mirow, *Das alte Preussen im deutschen Geschichtsbild seit der Reichsgründung*, Berlin, 1981, 199.

6) Joseph Goebbels, *Tagebücher 1945, Die letzten Aufzeichnungen*, Hamburg, 1977, 195–196.

7) Ibid., 327, 344.

8) Ibid., 370.

9) Ibid., 55.

10) Roger Manvell and Heinrich Fraenkel, *Doctor Goebbels*, London, 1959, 6, 60–65.

11) Michael Bloch, *Ribbentrop*, London, 1992, 4, 8.

12) Irving, *Göring*, 25–32.

13) Emmy Goering (sic), *My Life with Goering*, London, 1972, 20. Braun, *Weimar zu Hitler*, 67.

14) Emmy Goering, *My Life*, 24–25.

15) See my article 'Conduct Unbecoming' in *Opera Now*, April 1991, 6–11.

16) Guderian, *Panzer Leader*, 444.

17) Alvensleben, *Lauter Abschiede*, 119.

18) Ibid., 19.

19) Rudolf Diels, *Lucifer ante portas*, Stuttgart, 1950, 92.

20) Ibid.

21) Geheimes Staatsarchiv, S. 403.

22) Robert Thévoz, Hans Branig, Cecile Löwenthal-Hensel, *Die Geheime Staatspolizei in den preussischen Ostprovinzen, 1934–1936. Pommern 1934–1935 im Spiegel von Gestapo Lageberichten und Sachakten*, 2 vols, Cologne & Berlin, 1974, I, 33–34.

23) Graf Krockow, *Preussen*, 8.

24) Robert Wistrich, *Wer war wer im Dritten Reich*, Munich, 1983, passim.

25) Shlomo Aronson, *Reinhard Heydrich und die Frühgeschichte von Gestapo und SD*, Stuttgart, 1971, 50.

26) Ibid., 51.

27) Ibid., Heinz Höhne, *The Order of the Death's Head. The Story of Hitler's SS*, trans. Richard Barry, London, 1969, 61.

28) Ibid.
29) Diels, *Lucifer*, 92.
30) Höhne, *Death's Head*, 77.
31) Robert Lewis Koehl, *The Black Corps. The Structure and Power Struggles of the Nazi SS*, Wisconsin, 1983, 94.
32) Ibid., 121.
33) Ibid., 100.
34) Wistrich, *Wer war wer.*
35) J. K. Zawodny, *Nothing but Honour, The Story of the Warsaw Uprising 1944*, London, 1978, 54.
36) Wistrich, *Wer war wer.*
37) Höhne, *Death's Head*, 121.
38) Wistrich, *Wer war wer.*
39) Ibid., 363.
40) Günther Deschner, *Warsaw Uprising*, London, 1972, 59.
41) Ibid., 79.
42) Ibid. Zawodny, *Warsaw Uprising*, 56.
43) Höhne, *Death's Head*, 545.
44) Zawodny, *Warsaw Uprising*, 193.
45) Deschner, *Warsaw Uprising*, 149–151.
46) Zawodny, *Warsaw Uprising*, 54. Wistrich, *Wer war wer.*
47) Quoted in Venohr, *Fridericus Rex.*
48) Alvensleben, *Lauter Abschiede*, 15.
49) Ibid., 164.
50) Ibid., 209.
51) Ibid., 257.
52) Ibid., 260.
53) Ibid., 313.
54) Ibid., 410.
55) Moltke, *Letters*, 288.
56) Gerhard Leibholz, Die Deutschlandpolitik Englands im zweiten Weltkrieg und der Widerstand, in Bruno Heck ed., *Widerstand, Kirche, Staat: Eugen Gerstenmaier zum 70 Geburtstag*, Frankfurt & Vienna, 1976. Quoted in MacDonogh, *A Good German*, 238.
57) Moltke, *Letters*, 289.
58) Eugen Gerstenmaier, *Streit und Friede hat seine Zeit, Ein Lebensbericht*, Frankfurt, Berlin, Vienna, 1981. Quoted in MacDonogh, *A Good German*, 243.
59) Marianne Meyer-Krahmer, *Carl Goerdeler und sein Weg in den*

Widerstand. Eine Reise in die Welt meines Vaters, Freiburg im Breisgau, 1989, 22.

60) Ibid., 30.
61) Ibid., 92–93.
62) Ibid., 111.
63) Ibid., 25.
64) Geheimes Staatsarchiv Rep. 335 (IMT) Fall 9, 283, testimony of Dr Jur Erhard Häding.
65) Preussen, *Haus Hohenzollern*, 61–62.
66) Ibid., 67.
67) Letter from Helmut Conrad to Clarita von Trott. Quoted in MacDonogh, *A Good German*, 219.
68) Preussen, *Haus Hohenzollern*, 269.
69) Viktoria Luise, *Ein Leben*, 354.
70) R. Walther Darré, *Neuadel aus Blut und Boden*, Munich, 1938, 144–145.
71) Ibid., 12.
72) Ibid., 39.
73) Scheurig, *Kleist-Schmenzin*, 89.
74) Ibid., 91–93.
75) Eberhard Bethge, *Dietrich Bonhoeffer, Theologe, Christ, Zeitgenosse*, Munich, 1967, 363–365.
76) Scheurig, *Kleist-Schmenzin*, 93.
77) Ibid., 95.
78) Ibid., 109–110.
79) Ibid., 135.
80) Ibid., 189–196.
81) Ibid., 196.
82) Ibid., 199.
83) Ibid.
84) Scheurig, *Tresckow*, 88–89.
85) Ibid., 98–99.
86) Ibid., 102.
87) Ibid., 110–111.
88) Ibid., 111.
89) Ibid., 117.
90) Ibid., 125–126.
91) Ibid., 128.
92) Ibid., 138.
93) Ibid., 146–147.

94) Ibid., 147.
95) Conversation with Peter Bielenberg, Tullow, Co. Carlow, 8 July 1989.
96) Heinemann, *Schulenburg*, 69–70.
97) Ibid.
98) Ibid., 148–149.
99) Ibid., 158.
100) Ibid.
101) See Moltke, *Letters*, 333.
102) Heinemann, *Schulenburg*, 162–163. Conversation with Ludwig von Hammerstein, 28 June 1991.
103) Scheurig, *Tresckow*, 151–152.
104) Heinemann, *Schulenburg*, 168–169.
105) Scheurig, *Tresckow*, 190–192.
106) Ibid., 192–193.
107) Heinemann, *Schulenburg*, 172.

Chapter XIII: The End

1) Information from my visits to the towns and cities in question, 1991–1992.
2) Ulla Lachauer, Nemmersdorf, 21. Oktober 1944: Die Vertreibungsverbrechen – Gedanken über das Sprechen und Schweigen und ein Gespräch darüber, in *Die Zeit*, 23 October 1992. Marianne Peyinghaus, *Stille Jahre in Gertlauken Errinerungen an Ostpreussen*, Berlin, 1985.
3) Gräfin Dönhoff, *Namen*, 29–30.
4) Görlitz, *Die Junker*, 414.
5) Hans Graf von Lehndorff, *Ostpreussisches Tagebuch, Aufzeichnungen eines Arztes aus den Jahren 1945–1947*, Munich, 1961, 65–66.
6) Bundesministerium für Vertriebene, *Die Vertreibung der Deutschen Bevölkerung aus den Gebieten östlich der Oder–Neisse*, Bonn, 1953. 1/1 41E gives 450,000 for the Haff and 200,000 for the Nehrung. Alfred M. de Zayas, *Nemesis at Potsdam: the Anglo-Americans and the Expulsion of the Germans*, 2nd edition, London, 1979, 75. Tighe, *Gdańsk*, 184.
7) Ibid., 188–189.
8) Ibid., 192–193.
9) Grass, *Die Blechtrommel*, 479–480.

10) Ibid., 135.
11) Tighe, *Gdańsk*, 194.
12) Lehndorff, *Tagebuch*, 93.
13) Gräfin Dönhoff, *Namen*, 65–67.
14) Lehndorff, *Tagebuch*, 85.
15) De Zayas, *Nemesis*, 68., Tighe, *Gdańsk*, 199.
16) Ibid. Peter Gosztony, *Der Kampf um Berlin 1945 in Augenzeugenberichten*, Düsseldorf, 1970, 58. Bundesministerium für Vertriebene, 1/1 61E, also stresses the role performed by Asiatic troops.
17) Lehndorff, *Tagebuch*, 193–194.
18) Ibid., 227.
19) Stalin ordino: deportateli tutti, la Prussia dev'essere Sovietica, *Corriere della Sera* 25 May 1993; Zum Schluss Schokolade, *Der Spiegel*, 28 June 1993.
20) See Krockow, *Hour of the Women*.
21) See Käthe von Normann, *Ein Tagebuch aus Pommern*, Munich, 1987.
22) The scene is described by Krockow, *Hour of the Women*, 83. Görlitz, *Die Junker*, 414.
23) There are too many accounts of this to cast any doubt on the fact that it occurred as a matter of course. See, for example, Lehndorff, Normann, Krockow. There is a well-evoked description of it in Grass's *Die Blechtrommel*.
24) Wo früher das Fallbeil tötete, in *Der Tagesspiegel*, 24 August 1992.
25) Robin Gedye, The Fortunes of War, in *Sunday Telegraph*, 13 November 1991. Günter Wermusch, Das Geheimnis des kleinen Bunkerbergs, in *Die Zeit*, 6 March 1992. Peter Sager, Letzte Geiseln des Krieges, *Zeitmagazin*, 20 November 1992.
26) Alvensleben/Koenigswald, *Besuche*, 141–148.
27) Tighe, *Gdańsk*, 206–207.
28) Author's visits to Wroclaw, 9, 10, 11, 12 August 1992.
29) Tighe, *Gdańsk*, 211.
30) Ibid., 216–217. De Zayas, *Nemesis*, XXV, Bundesministerium der Vertriebene, 1/1 83E.
31) Helga Hirsch, Vieles geklärt, Die Unterstützung der deutschen Minderheit muss auch den Polen zugute kommen, in *Die Zeit*, 7 June 1991.
32) *Berliner Morgenpost*, 18 August 1991.

Index

officer corps (army): composition, 142–5, 152–4, 161; and Kapp Putsch, 158; training and education, 186–9; and Nazi indoctrination, 192
Ohlendorf, Otto, 364
Olbricht, General Friedrich, 192
Old Catholics, 341, 343
Oldenburg-Januschau family, 235, 239
Oldenburg-Januschau, Elard von: military career, 146; defends Prussian Guards, 153; Seeckt on, 198; as East Prussian archetype, 241–2; and Kapp, 242; and Hindenburg, 244, 246; and East Prussian relief, 245–6, 301; education, 260; opposes Braun's estates policy, 301; opposes Polish independence, 324–5; death, 385
Oliva (Oliwa), 20
Olmütz Punctuation (1850), 55–6, 62
Olsztyn *see* Allenstein
Oppen, Hedemann von, 209
Oppersdorff-Oberglogau, Graf Hans von, 243
Orders and decorations, 152–4
'Orpos' (Reichs Ordnungspolizei), 356
Orzechowski, M., 313
Oskar, Prince: joins Stahlhelm, 91; and Nazis, 92; education, 261
Osnabrücker Tageblatt, 105
Osten-Warnitz, Oskar von der, 367–8
Osterna, Peppo von, 20
Ostflucht (flight from the east), 240, 325
Osthilfe (East-Relief), 245, 301–2
Ostpreussische Landbote (newspaper), 294
Ottokar, King of Bohemia, 20
Oven, Margarethe von, 372
Owen, Wilfred, 6

pacifism, 170
Paderewski, Ignacy, 331–2
Palucki, Wladyslaw, 335
Pan German League (Alldeutscher Verband), 327–8
Pan German movement, 182, 185
Panse, Wolf-Dieter, 10
Papal Infallibility, 340
Papen, Franz von, 92, 95–6, 148, 163–4, 304–5, 363, 368
Paris: siege and bombardment of (1870), 114, 178
Pastors' Emergency League *see* Pfarrernotbund
Paulus, Field Marshal Friedrich, 133, 190
Perbrandt family, 234
Perponcher, Graf, 249
Persius, Ludwig, 52
Peter III, Emperor of Russia, 38
Petersen, Axel, 221
Pfarrernotbund (Pastors' Emergency League), 367
Pfuel family, 232
Piast empire (Poland), 330, 335
Pieck, Wilhelm, 8
Pietism, 51, 339, 359, 367
Pilsudski, Józef, 331, 335
Pirch family, 232
Pius IX, Pope, 340
Plamann Institute, Berlin, 258

Planck, Erwin, 305
Pless, Fürst Hans Heinrich von, 243
Plessen, General Hans von, 81, 219
Plön (school), 267
Podewils family, 232
Podeyn ('Baronin von Schönhausen'): Berlin homosexual bath house, 209, 221
Polack (journal), 312
Poland: post-1945 compensation, 6; conflict with Prusai, 19; and Teutonic Knights, 21–2; George William of Prussia pays homage to, 23; overlordship of Prussia ended (1657), 26; Frederick the Great acquires parts of, 39; Prussian territorial accessions in, 42–3; post-1919 territorial claims and acquisitions, 154–5, 243, 298–9, 302, 309, 332; 1919 conflict with Russia, 155, 334; Seeckt's disdain for, 201–2, 311; noble families in, 234; attracts German noble families, 243; and school education, 256–8, 328; and Cassubians, 307–8; and Prussian alliances, 310–11; and Bismarck's eastern policy, 311, 321–3, 325–6; German and Russian view of, 311–12; position between wars, 311–13; German farmer-peasants (*Hauländer*) in, 314–15; political system, 314; relations with Prussia, 314–24, 330; religion, 316–17; three partitions, 316, 324, 339; characteristics and culture, 317–19; as independent state, 321, 324–5, 331–4; 1871 settlement, 322; nationalism in, 322–3, 330; Russian rule in, 323–4; 1883 expulsions from Prussian part, 325–6; birthrate, 326; expropriation and reallocation of estates, 326–9; and German nationalism, 327–30; and protection of minorities, 333–4; boundaries, 334–5; and Hitler threat, 335; Goerdeler's proposals for, 364; Hitler invades and occupies, 370; 1945 'Recovered Territories', 388–9; German post-1945 migration to west from, 388; 1991 Treaty of Friendship with Germany, 389
Polish Corridor, 295, 302, 311, 332, 364
Polish language: teaching of, 256–7, 325; status, 316, 318–19
Popitz, Johannes, 364, 366
Poplawski, Jan Ludwig, 330
Posen (*now* Poznań): Wilhelm II builds new palace in, 127, 328–9; culture and demography, 319; German administrative quarter, 328
Posen, Grand Duchy of: under Frederick William IV, 53, 319; houses burned, 242; Germans in, 314, 320; religion in, 318–19; as buffer state, 319; Bismarck on, 322; and Polish independence, 331–2
Potsdam: bombed (1945) and rebuilt, 2, 380; buildings and monuments destroyed by DDR, 9; Garnisonkirche, 9, 11, 110, 142, 161–2; as Prussian centre, 10; improved and beautified, 34, 52; Neues Palais, 126; homosexuality in, 208; court at, 251–2
Potsdam Day (*Tag von Potsdam*, 21 March 1933), 97, 161, 335
Potsdam, Edict of (1685), 25, 337

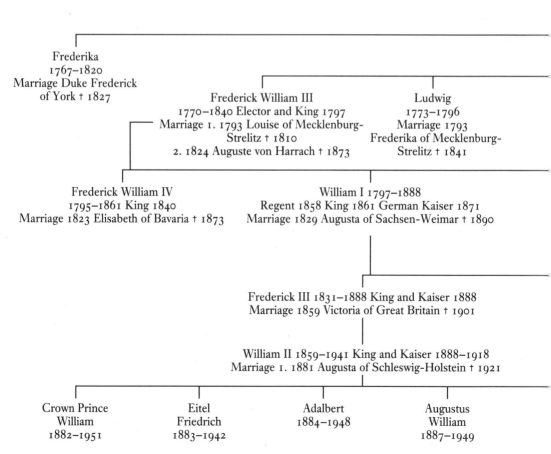

Louise 1680–1705
Marriage 1700 Landgrave Frederick I
of Hesse-Cassel † 1751

Williamina
1709–1758
Marriage 1731
Margrave
Frederick of Bayreuth
† 1763

Frederick II
the Great 1712–1786
Elector and King 1740
Marriage 1733
Elisabeth of
Brunswick-Wolfenbüttel
† 1797

Frederika Louise
1714–1784
Marriage 1729
Margrave
Charles of
Ansbach † 1757

Philippa Charlotte
1716–1801
Marriage 1733
Duke Charles of
Brunswick-Wolfenbüttel
† 1780

Frederika
1767–1820
Marriage Duke Frederick
of York † 1827

Frederick William III
1770–1840 Elector and King 1797
Marriage 1. 1793 Louise of Mecklenburg-
Strelitz † 1810
2. 1824 Auguste von Harrach † 1873

Ludwig
1773–1796
Marriage 1793
Frederika of Mecklenburg-
Strelitz † 1841

Frederick William IV
1795–1861 King 1840
Marriage 1823 Elisabeth of Bavaria † 1873

William I 1797–1888
Regent 1858 King 1861 German Kaiser 1871
Marriage 1829 Augusta of Sachsen-Weimar † 1890

Frederick III 1831–1888 King and Kaiser 1888
Marriage 1859 Victoria of Great Britain † 1901

William II 1859–1941 King and Kaiser 1888–1918
Marriage 1. 1881 Augusta of Schleswig-Holstein † 1921

Crown Prince
William
1882–1951

Eitel
Friedrich
1883–1942

Adalbert
1884–1948

Augustus
William
1887–1949